Table of Contents

Contents

Personality and Socialization

Personality and Socialization

DAVID R. HEISE

THE UNIVERSITY OF NORTH CAROLINA AT CHAPEL HILL

RAND McNALLY & COMPANY • Chicago

To my own independent variables, Mom, Elsa, and Stephen

Preface

All of the articles in this book are concerned with the ways social experiences affect personality and character. But thousands of other articles also deal with this topic, so why did I choose just these?

A great deal of selection was accomplished through two criteria: recency and the use of procedures that provide a high level of confidence in the conclusions. I considered very few older publications assuming that almost always a fairly recent study could be found—one published within the last decade-and-a-half—that would incorporate and extend prior work. I employed the second criterion—adequacy of procedures—so that this book would provide the reader with a solid foundation for understanding the relations between the individual and society. This second criterion implied an emphasis wherever possible on objective measurements, on large and representative samples of individuals, on sophisticated methods of data gathering and data analysis, and, in the case of review articles, on cautious extraction of regularities from diverse individual studies. I know that this criterion eliminated many stimulating articles that were only exploratory in intent; but it also had the effect of assembling the most unyielding facts about socialization and personality development.[1]

1. Robert C. Hanson, "Evidence and Procedure Characteristics of 'Reliable' Propositions in Social Science," *American Journal of Sociology,* 63 (1958), 357–370.

Preface

These two criteria still left hundreds of articles that might have been included in the book. From these, I selected articles focused on outstanding traditions of research, articles dealing with issues of special social consequence, and articles that might reveal unexpected regularities when fitted together in a book of this kind. Where there were several articles on a single topic, I tried to pick the one that was most comprehensive and readable. Even with the additional criteria, I produced a reader twice as long as this one. I chose the most relevant, the most conclusive, the most seminal articles. I apologize to those authors who so kindly provided reprinting permissions but whose works are not reprinted.

This compilation serves as a sourcebook in that it presents some of the major theses of many prominent social scientists. However, scholars should consult the original articles before making exact citations to text or tables since nearly every article has been edited in the interests of space and readability. Typically one will find additional text and tables in the original source, as well as additional information on the significance of tests.

David R. Heise

1

Some Aspects of Personality Relevant to the Study of Socialization

David R. Heise

Personality refers to the recurring patterns in the way a person perceives, thinks, and acts. No single chapter could summarize the major currents of thought on this topic. The presentation here is only an attempt to outline some available understandings concerning personality and character by using a perspective that seems relevant to studying the growth of human individuality in social contexts. Psychological differences are divided into three domains, depending on whether they are predominately a function of neurophysiological variations, environmental exposures, or a person's unique history in constructing understandings and solving problems. A few of the important types of variation within each of these domains are noted.

Traits—The Neurophysiological Base

All people share certain neurologically based capacities (to speak, to plan, to emote, etc.), and these are not matters of personality but of human nature. On the other hand, some neurological variations do seem to dispose people toward different activities or different styles of activity. While little is really known about the relation between specific neurological processes and aspects of personality, it is still

Written especially for this volume.

desirable to try to identify traits with a significant neurophysiological basis, because the implication is that understanding such traits requires giving attention to population genetics and to biological ecology, as well as to processes of socialization and social control.

Traits are tentatively classified as neurophysiological when they are known to be genetically determined to a large degree and when their impacts are observable under a wide variety of circumstances. Some characteristics having these two features will be found below.

Heritability and ubiquity certainly do not imply that a trait develops *entirely* as a function of neurophysiological factors. In fact, every known psychological trait develops to some degree as a function of environmental influences or personal constructions. The aim here is not to obscure this fact, but to identify traits that are subject to a good deal of biological determination as well as to other kinds of influences.

Intelligence

An intelligent person is able to re-view familiar facts from different perspectives and to adapt old understandings to new circumstances (Jensen, 1969, pp. 10–11). Tests designed to measure this capacity usually consist of problems calling for reconceptualization of something familiar or for processing available information in novel ways. Scores are assigned in terms of a person's speed and accuracy in completing such problems. Intelligence is a contributing factor in performances on a great variety of tasks and activities, even those meant to measure less cognitive aspects of personality (Hundleby, Pawlik, and Cattell, 1965, p. 14). And, of course, intelligence can operate with respect to innumerable different kinds of information.

While it is possible to speak of general, overall intelligence, it should be realized that a particular person can be more intelligent with respect to some kinds of materials than others. Some major subclassifications of intelligence are: (1) verbal: the ability to manipulate word symbols and semantic meanings; (2) numerical: facility with numbers and quantitative relationships; (3) spatial: the ability to hold visual images in mind and transform them; (4) reasoning: the capacity to grasp rules and their interrelationships. These four types of intelligence are the ones most frequently measured, but many additional types have been proposed. Indeed Guilford has theorized that 120 distinguishable kinds of intelligence should exist even though present tests are not nearly precise enough to discriminate all these types (Guilford, 1972).

A few points about intelligence testing are worth noting. Proper testing requires full cooperation and alertness on the part of the testee, but this is not always attained. Furthermore, since intelligence relates to the manipulation of available information, intelligence tests may be confounded by what a person has already learned in his or her cultural context. "Culture-free" tests are meant to reduce this problem by calling for manipulation only of information that everyone shares, but there is no way of guaranteeing that this goal is attained with respect to every individual. Finally, since there are different classifications of mental ability, it sometimes is misleading to construct a single score that inevitably weights some abilities more than others.

Intelligence is subject to an unusual amount of genetic determination. Certainly more than half of the observable variation is genetic in origin, and Jensen (1969) estimated the heritability to be about 80 percent. A heritability of zero indicates that a trait is determined entirely by environmental factors; a heritability of 100 indicates that environment plays no part at all and that all of the variations are due to differences in genes.

Introversion—Extroversion

The public notion of introversion-extroversion stresses differences in sociability, but that is just one aspect of a larger pattern. Both research and theory (Eysenck, 1961) suggest that besides avoiding the high levels of stimulation involved in social gatherings, introverts as compared to extroverts more readily develop conditioned reactions and are more socialized in the sense of displaying more guilt, more persistence, and more reliability. Introverts react more to stress, repress their problems less, and respond less to sedative drugs than do extroverts. Maladjusted introverts are likely to suffer from anxiety or depression whereas maladjusted extroverts are more inclined toward hysteria or antisocial behavior.

The basic variations are believed to arise out of differences in how much the brain inhibits perceptions and sensations (Eysenck, 1961). For extroverts, sensations and experiences evidently are more muted, and so extroverts are less inclined to avoid intense stimulation than introverts, perhaps even seeking it as a kind of stimulation hunger.

Introverts, because of excessive sensitivity to sensation, are inclined to avoid intense stimulation and prolonged excitement.

The heritability of introversion-extroversion appears to be more than 50 percent (Vandenberg, 1967; Jinks and Fulker, 1970).

Emotionality

People differ in the degree to which they are overcome by feelings, especially the negative emotions like anxiety, guilt, and shame. One possible explanation is that emotionally labile persons have less developed neural mechanisms for controlling pain and discomfort (Berlyne, 1971, pp. 82–86). Whatever the neurological base, more emotional persons manifest their propensity in a variety of ways. They are more often annoyed, fearful, or embarrassed in social situations; they tend to deprecate themselves and have little self-confidence; they tend to be reclusive, but when in social situations they are submissive to the immediate authority and social standards; and they more often make extreme statements letting their feelings get in the way of logic and organization (Hundleby, Pawlik, and Cattell, 1965, pp. 224–225; Eysenck, 1961). Such characteristics are at the core of neuroticism, though emotionality alone does not necessarily imply self-defeating behavior patterns; high emotionality also is a frequent feature in other behavior disorders like criminality (sociopathy). Heritability of emotionality is around 50 percent (Jinks and Fulker, 1970).

Meaning Disturbances

Imagine sitting at a table with a snake for a centerpiece in a room where the walls are tissue paper, in a crowd of pirates moving rapidly in incomprehensible patterns. A cafeteria might be experienced something like this by a schizophrenic, a person who has somehow lost the capacity to participate in ordinary cultural understandings and consequently develops bizarre delusions and behaviors in seeking some sort of psychic contact with objects and with other human beings (Wallace, 1970, p. 217). Extreme psychotics live in such worlds almost constantly, their brains no longer capable of producing comprehensive orderings. However, nearly all of us occasionally experience similar states briefly when, because of stress, inexperience, or in a foreign and unfamiliar situation, we are incapable of constructing sensible meanings. Schizophrenia can involve a variety of thought disorders such as delusions of guilt and unworthiness, impaired logic and memory, hallucinations, and vivid beliefs that one is being talked about or otherwise acted on. Behaviorally, a schizophrenic might attempt suicide, be inexplicably aggressive, display emotions that seem out of place in the immediate situation (laughing, crying, flight, etc.) or manufacture strange postures, grimaces, and immobilities. No one of these symptoms alone necessarily indicates schizophrenia, but a cluster of them usually does (Eysenck, 1961).

Schizophrenia is called a functional psychosis, which means that it supposedly is caused by problems of experience rather than by a specific neurological pathology. Increasingly, a more complex view seems warranted: schizophrenic decay seems to be actuated by environmental problems, but different persons have varying biochemical dispositions for this kind of psychic deterioration (Wallace, 1970, pp. 216–217). In fact, a substantial degree of heritability for the disposition now is established (Rosenthal, 1970, p. 132).

Schizophrenia is not the only form of psychosis, but it is a common form, and its occurrence is related to social factors (e.g., see Kohn's analysis in Chapter 26 of this book). Another common form is the manic-depressive syndrome, characterized by a state of despair and worthlessness, or by a state of exaggerated enthusiasm and bold aggressiveness, or by a swinging back and forth between these two states. Few social correlates have been found for the manic-depressive syndrome, so even though it does constitute a pathological kind of "individuality," the syndrome does not appear often in the literature relating personality and social life.

Other Traits

Intelligence, introversion-extroversion, emotionality, and schizoid tendencies are the essential constituents of the biochemically influenced domain of personality. Other traits that might seem to belong here either are known to have low heritabilities, or have not been studied enough to determine heritabilities, or do not seem to show the situational ubiquity that justifies treating them as basic aspects of personality.

It is of particular interest to note some aspects of personality with heritabilities so low that it is plausible to consider them mainly as a

5

function of environmental experiences or of personal constructions. Attitudes and interests are in this class, even though low genotypic correlations have been found for a few specific attitudes and interests, as religiosity (Thompson, 1968). Dominance or social assertiveness seems to have some minor relations with genotypic variations but mostly as a function of other factors. Criminality (sociopathy) has no significant constitutional base (Rosenthal, 1970, pp. 223–229), contrary to some opinions.

Environmental Interactions

The second major domain of personality is defined by relations between people and their environment. The body as a servomechanism and the voice as a medium of communication routinely serve to modify the physical and social world, by translating an individual's plans and intentions into reality. At the same time the environment, incorporated through the sensory organs, evokes subjective understandings and affective reactions. Since humans display few instinctual patterns, most ways of acting and responding toward specific social or physical objects are learned, and consequently they vary a good deal with the individual's unique history of experiences. Because a culture's social ecology affects the presence and absence of objects, the frequency of different experiences, and the kinds of verbalizations one hears, this same domain of personality is also one in which sociocultural regularities are very noticeable.

Needs and Interests

Satisfactions arise from events that link individuals to specific objects or persons, as in eating or sexual intercourse, or from more autistic events, like masturbation or elimination, or sometimes from events that are only witnessed, like dramatizations and concerts. The one rule that comprehends the variety of origins seems to be that people experience pleasure when their anticipations almost, but not quite perfectly, are confirmed in reality (Berlyne, 1971, pp. 86–94).

Concern here is less with the general nature of satisfactions than with the differences among people in seeking and experiencing pleasure. There are two fundamental kinds of variation. People prefer different modes of stimulation for obtaining pleasure and within any mode people vary again because they find their pleasures in different objects.

Research has documented the fact that people display different degrees of attraction for sexual action (Gebhard, 1971), aggression (Berkowitz, 1962, pp. 256–300), achieving (McClelland et al., 1953), aesthetic understanding (Berlyne, 1971, pp. 264–265), and so on. Some part of a person's personality no doubt can be communicated by a profile showing how much he or she is inclined to use each of these modes of stimulation as a source of pleasure and satisfaction. In fact, a prevailing exercise in the history of personality theory has been to try to define a list of the "basic" modes of receiving satisfaction as a plan for assessing the strength of individual "instincts" or "needs." The efforts have foundered, not because it is considered uninformative to talk about preferred modes of pleasure, but because the lists repeatedly have grown unwieldy in size. In fact, it seems that any action can be developed into a mode of receiving pleasure (Allport, 1961, p. 229) and it is barely stretching the point to say that practically any verb specifies the basis of a possible "need."

One approach to condensing the analysis of needs and interests is to try to discover whether preferences tend to occur in concert, the idea being that there may be only one or a few basic dimensions of variation, although one's position on a basic dimension is expressed in many specific ways. The most popular hypothesis proposes a basic dimension that has the pleasures of mastery and self-control at one end, with the pleasures of sensuality at the other end. In one form or another this hypothesis has been highly favored by social scientists studying whole cultures (Benedict, 1934; Sorokin, 1962; Gouldner and Peterson, 1962). While this may be a valuable idea about the organization of cultural norms, and while it does seem to provide an organizing principle for individual attitudes and values (see "authoritarian personality" under attitudes below), the idea seems to have little validity as a theory applying to needs and motivations. Time and again, studies of individual needs and interests have revealed a multitude of different kinds of variation, with no single overriding dimension being evident (Tyler, 1965, pp. 198–202).

Another approach to simplification is to focus only on those preferences that have some special value for distinguishing among people in terms of life styles. For example, it might be argued that everyone engages in so much eating and elimination behavior that whatever the differences among people, they are mere nuances of little interest; or, that since intellectual interests are so rare in a general population, most people cannot be discriminated on this basis, and so the "need" is largely irrelevant for a general personality theory. In fact, research in the last few decades has concentrated on relatively few needs, like desire to achieve and desire to affiliate with others (Atkinson, 1958), and specific vocational interests (Tyler, 1965) that have high variability in middle-class populations within agrarian and industrialized societies. Valuable as such work has been, it should not obscure the fact that people are really multifaceted in their preferences for various kinds of action and events, and focusing on one or another interest involves a certain degree of personal or cultural bias. In fact, even the "small" variations in attraction to eating are indicative of personality differences (Schachter, 1971); Freud believed interest in elimination events are a factor in personality development; and even preferences for abstract thinking may be more important than they seem, in that they do perhaps have significance for life styles in highly industrialized populations (see Kohn, 1969; and Kohn and Schooler, Chapter 12 in this volume).

As if it were not awesome enough to have to allow that nearly any form of action can become the basis of a "need," it is necessary to go further and observe that needs can usually be attached to a variety of objects, and these attachments or cathexes also constitute a significant aspect of personality. Idiosyncracies exist in tastes for different foods, and the same kind of idiosyncracies exist in tastes for sexual objects (Gebhard, 1971). While the first fact may strike us as mundane and the second as bizarre, both represent the same principle, and the principle can be applied again and again. People seek to achieve with respect to different goals, to relax with different kinds of people, and differ in the selection of topics they find most interesting to think about. So each different need or mode of satisfaction has not only an intensity but also a directionality in the sense of a preferred object or goal.

Experiences with particular acts and objects may or may not lead to associated interests, needs, and cathexes, but it is safe to say that a particular interest, need, or cathexis will not develop without experience with the correlated act or object. Thus one source of the motivational differences among people must be due to differences in what they have *not* experienced, and individual histories can be important in this sense. Moreover, differences among people from different cultures and subcultures may be largely attributed to this factor since groups differ in the acts and objects they make available to their members.

Cognitions

People do not perceive and understand their world in a completely objective way; rather, they construct their realities as they go along, partly on the basis of energy emanations from the physical world, always selecting from a multitude of possible impressions in order to register events that are most understandable in terms of familiar categories and attitudes (Bruner, 1958). Since emotions and behavior follow from definitions of the situation, they, too, are indirectly a function of the categories and attitudes carried over from past learning and used in present constructions. This kind of theorizing is what has led social psychologists to their immense interest in individuals' cognitions and attitudes.

Most cognitions and attitudes correspond a good deal with intrinsic properties of physical reality. People everywhere distinguish between laughter and thunder and generally the feeling is that laughter is fairly pleasant while thunder is somewhat fearful (Osgood, 1964). Different cultures tend to transform or distort such basic categories and attitudes in one way or another, as, for example, in the modern technological understanding of thunder compared to ancient religious interpretations. A culture also may add what seem to be useful concepts, along with associated attitudes, even though there is little or no perceptual manifestation of the category, as in the case of "leprechauns" or "atoms." So in an indirect way, many of a person's understandings and attitudes toward events are a function of the intrinsic nature of reality and, in addition, to the cumulated interpretations embedded in the culture the person has learned.

Each person, though, has a unique history of experience both with reality and with his or her culture that lends an individual twist to personal understandings. Especially in complex civilizations, far more cognitive categories and knowledge exist than can be assimilated by any one person, so a person's unique career in learning segments of the culture contribute to his or her individuality in understanding the world. It is in this sense that one's profile of knowledge is actually an aspect of personality. Of course, more is involved than knowledge within a formal discipline or profession. People acquire immense amounts of cultural knowledge about everyday life, and here, as in the more formal fields, there are variations due to how much knowledge has been assimilated as well as to choices between alternative theories presented by different "schools of influence," like social classes (Heise and Roberts, 1970).

Very likely, most individuals develop a certain amount of completely unique knowledge in addition to assimilating their cultures, and this, too, contributes to their individuality by influencing their understanding and response to events. For most people, the amount of unique knowledge probably is relatively small compared to culturally assimilated knowledge, but little is known about this.

Attitudes

Attitudes, or dispositions to feel about things in a certain way, most often are assimilated along with cognitive categories and knowledge, and so they, too, tend to reflect both the intrinsic qualities of things and a culture's idiosyncratic distortions. But attitudes are more subject to unique disturbances as individuals experience their personal series of private pleasures and traumas and as they apply their own private configuration of knowledge, linking particular objects to valued or feared events. No doubt many of these variations in attitude are almost random and show little regularity from one person to another. But one general pattern of variation has been identified—authoritarianism—and it represents an important dimension of attitudinal differences in many studies of personality.

While there are no doubt many subtle personality factors that distinguish a demagogue and his followers from more democratic persons, research has focused predominantly on attitudinal variations that express and serve certain fears and resentments (Brown, 1965, Chapter 10). Research has led to the insight that a great many attitudinal variations are indeed correlated and they do seem to be partly produced by differences on a single, more fundamental dimension. At one (oversimplified) extreme are persons who attribute profound significance to religion and to loyalty to both family and country. These persons invest intense value in the individual's responsibility to support and obey rules; they despise sources of weakness and decay whether these amount to sensual self-indulgence, the sapping of moral strength by an over-indulgent government, or the demoralizing influence of an unaccountable stranger, out-group, or communication medium. The emotions invested in God, country, and family are so intense, that almost any threat to these is seen as catastrophic; and so life is in almost a constant state of moral crisis. At the other extreme are those who elevate the individual to supreme importance. Valuing individuals in general as opposed to just the self possibly distinguishes sub-types here. In any case, religion, country, family all are seen as services to the individual rather than as values requiring subordination of self. The gravest danger lies less in weakness than in the forces that would constrain or destroy the individual's fulfillment, whether through sensual self-indulgence, personal achievement, or appreciation of alien ways and customs.

Presenting just these two extremes of authoritarianism should not imply that all the distinct opinions are highly correlated or that no in-between, mixed state exists. In fact, some persons may be individualistically (or democratically) oriented on some issues and have a subordination (authoritarian) view on others. And, too, a person could combine the two perspectives, believing in both individualism and subordination, each up to a point.

Self-Concept

Of all the many topics a person may learn and feel about, "self" is the most significant. This is not merely because the self is a universal "discipline." The important thing is that the conceptions and attitudes one has toward the self are a component in the definition of every personal situation and are most ubiquitous factors in a person's emotions and actions. The simple notion that people try to maintain their selves and improve their position with respect to private ideals is a potent explanation of people's actions in most situations.

The self is subject to numerous classifications, each representing a distinct social identity or status. Sex identities are fundamental; added on are family identities, ethnic and nationality identities, occupational identities, conceptions of personal appearance, and so on (Kuhn, 1960). The prominent identity can easily change as a person moves between situations—from, say, a work setting to the home—making salient one role rather than another. The prominent identity in a situation can also be provoked by the views of immediate others, as when a physician is reacted to as a male or female rather than as a doctor.

The self-identity that is immediately salient in a situation is one factor in conjuring up certain definitions of the situation, as when a physician sees the stranger in his office as a person seeking treatment. Because knowledge is held about the routines associated with different identities, the salient identity also provides a basic program of action, as when a physician questions a person about bodily complaints. And the salient identity sets a particular self-attitude that controls the person as an actor in the sense that is meant by a term like "professional demeanor."

It is probably misleading to talk about *the* self-concept, because, in general, the self-concept comprises all the ascribed and achieved private and social identities that a person has, while in specific circumstances the self-concept amounts to a particular composite of the identities that are salient to that situation. The general self-concept really amounts to all the knowledge that one has gained about the self, while the definition of a situational self-concept varies with the circumstances. At either level, though, self-concepts constitute an important part of personality, and are peculiarly interesting because of their high degree of social determination. Society largely determines what identities any individual will have. Knowledge about these identities is largely cultural and learned, and in particular situations one's salient identities can depend as much on the views of others as on one's own preferences.

Dominance

One important difference among individuals in the way they relate to their environments is in their levels of dominance and assertiveness. Some individuals initiate acts and vocalizations in a situation while others seem reserved, passive, or detached. Even though persons in a group readily assess one another's assertiveness as a unitary trait (Borgatta, 1964), it seems likely that assertiveness in a particular situation is a function of several psychological factors—a person's preferred level of control, the difference between the person's preferred level and the level experienced in the situation, and the person's impression of the importance of the people and objects around him. Assertiveness and dominating behavior in a group demands that a person prefer a relatively high level of control, that he feels a discrepancy between the preferred level of control and that actually attained, and that available persons or objects are important enough to be "worth" acting on. Absence of any of these factors could produce low assertiveness. A person accustomed to a low level of power can maintain that state passively, so initiative is not needed, especially when a dominating person is around to take care of problems that arise. A person whose preferred and actual power match also has little cause for initiating acts except as a response to others or to situational disturbances; in particular, a secure leader may emit few assertiveness or dominance displays. Finally, a person confronted with tasks or people deemed unimportant is likely to show little initiative, except perhaps in a playful way; in particular, a person striving to develop a deeper, more powerful, or more important self is likely to relate passively with that considered unimportant, as no sense of mastery can be built up in dealing with insignificant things.

It follows that assertiveness-dominance is largely a function of self-attitudes and attitudes toward others. Assertive-dominant behavior, therefore, can vary a good deal across situations, even though some people may be more sensitive to power discrepancies and more initiating generally. Furthermore, assertiveness-dominance would seem to be just one corner of a quadrille which includes alienation, contented weakness, and secure powerfulness.

Modes of Analysis and Construction

The final domain of personality involves differences among people in their creative, constructive processes, in the ways they relate idea to idea to form larger wholes, perceptually and with respect to social and moral interpretations of events. This domain is not studied as much as others; therefore only two types of variations will be discussed.

At the perceptual level, people differ in their propensities to analyze units apart from their surrounding setting (field independence) as opposed to incorporating objects and their backgrounds into interdependent wholes (field dependence). Witkin (Chapter 19 in this volume) describes this trait in detail and discusses many of its sociocultural correlates. This characteristic also has been studied by Cattell (Trait U. I. 19; Hundleby, Pawlik, and Cattell, 1965), who suggests that the field independent person is not only analytic and accurate at the perceptual level but also is likely to display logicalness, unusual ability to concentrate, independence from social pressures, and a complacent aloofness from others. Thus, this perceptual style seems to have broad implications for the way people construct their realities and relate to others around them. The trait appears to be determined about half by genes (Hundleby, Pawlik, and Cattell, 1965, p. 199), and might well have been treated as a neurophysiological factor were it not for its special relevance to reality construction and ego processes.

A different perspective on reality construction is provided by notions of cognitive and moral stages in development (Piaget, 1932; Loevinger and Wessler, 1970; Kohlberg and Kramer, Chapter 18 of this volume). Three major stages are usually postulated. During the first, a person tends to organize interests, feelings, and actions predominantly around his or her own person, and activty is devoted largely to indulging and protecting the self. During the second stage, the preeminent focus shifts to concern with ways of acting and outward appearances, and thoughts and action come to be largely dedicated to maintaining and expressing rules and conventions. At the third level, there is heightened concern with feelings, and meditations as well as actions reflect a dominant altruistic concern for others' welfare and their freedom to act out their independent natures. Each of these three stages may be divided into two sub-stages: (1) a period when the person enthusiastically orients to the focus of the stage as an intrinsic source of satisfaction and fulfillment, and (2) a later period when the focus of the stage is seen to exist within a larger network of constraints that need to be considered and manipulated in order to achieve fulfillment.

Thus, at first, a person narcissistically relates to the self as the basic source of fulfillment and satisfaction. Movement into a higher stage occurs when the narcissism becomes less compulsive, more methodical, and more subject to defensive responses as the person realizes that the state of self is affected by regulations. As social and environmental control of the self is further recognized the person searches for a more comprehensive mode of fulfillment, and ultimately becomes dedicated to rituals, rules, and conventions as mysterious, even mystic, wellsprings of meaning and significance. Later, the man-made nature of routines is recognized, and as some of its intrinsic mystery is lost, they are employed more instrumentally, with more attention devoted to the social development and maintenance of desirable rules. Insight into the human origins of convention ultimately leads to attaching preeminent significance to humans themselves, so in the final stages, uncompromised mystery, depth, and significance are found in other people, and the person becomes dedicated to knowing, loving, nurturing, and understanding others in all their uniqueness. Finally, one also recognizes the inevitability of human tragedy and comedy, and that disappointments must sometimes grow out of devotion to others. An important feature of stage theory is that prior stages are not abandoned in moving to higher levels but rather are incorporated within a larger framework. Thus, in the final stage, a person presumably attempts to integrate narcissism, sensitivity to social convention, altruism, and awareness of exterior forces into a single, unified philosophy.

What a person sees, thinks, feels, and does is determined a good deal by the adoption of these stages, since each stage provides a kind of paradigm for constructing interpretations of events and for developing expectations and plans. Thus, some differences among people can be most economically comprehended by understanding that they employ different modes of organizing experience—narcissistic, conventional, and altruistic, with further distinctions between simple zealousness and more complicated reflectiveness. Later stages do tend to be associated with older age (Loevinger and Wessler, 1970, pp. 50–51), but crises may lead to regressions (e.g., see Kohlberg and Kramer, Chapter 18 in this volume).

Interrelations

No doubt there is interaction between genetic endowment, environmental experience, and a person's constructive paradigms. Traits like intelligence, introversion-extroversion, and emotionality lead to selection of experiences which might also affect responses to experiences, thereby influencing the development of particular interests, attitudes, and the self-concept. Such traits might also correlate with the development of particular insights about the world, thereby contributing to or suppressing ego maturation. Similarly, moving to a new ego stage might sensitize a person to new experiences that create or modify attitudes, interests, and the self-concept; and ego changes might also release basic abilities and dispositions that were not expressed before. In turn, the action system can produce circumstances like increased or decreased stress that might modify the effective levels of intelligence, introversion, emotionality, etc., or that could lead to acceleration or regression in ego development.

Just acknowledging these interactions, without delving into the details (which are mostly unknown in any case), highlights how individuality is a very intricate function of genetic, experiential, and creative processes. All of these bases should be fully appreciated as one turns to the rest of this book, concentrated as it is on a single source of personality development—the social environment in which a person grows and lives.

References

Allport, Gordon W. *Pattern and Growth in Personality*. New York: Holt, Rinehart, 1961.

Atkinson, John W., ed. *Motives in Fantasy, Action, and Society*. Princeton: Van Nostrand, 1958.

Benedict, Ruth F. *Patterns of Culture*. Boston: Houghton Mifflin, 1934.

Berkowitz, Leonard. *Aggression: A Social Psychological Analysis*. New York: McGraw-Hill, 1962.

Berlyne, D. E. *Aesthetics and Psychobiology*. New York: Appleton-Century, 1971.

Borgatta, Edgar F. "The Structure of Personality Characteristics," *Behavioral Science*, 9 (1964), 8–17.

Brown, Roger. *Social Psychology*. New York: Free Press, 1965.

Bruner, Jerome. "Social Psychology and Perception," in E. E. Maccoby, T. N. Newcomb, and E. L. Hartley, eds., *Readings in Social Psychology*. New York: Holt, Rinehart, 1958, 85–94.

Eysenck, H. J. "Classification and the Problem of Diagnosis," in H. J. Eysenck, ed., *Handbook of Abnormal Psychology*. New York: Basic Books, 1961, 1–31.

Gebhard, Paul H. "Human Sexual Behavior: A Summary Statement," in D. S. Marshall and R. C. Suggs, eds., *Human Sexual Behavior: Variations in the Ethnographic Spectrum*. New York: Basic Books, 1971, 206–217.

Gouldner, Alvin W., and Richard A. Peterson. *Notes on Technology and the Moral Order*. Indianapolis: Bobbs-Merrill, 1962.

Guilford, J. P. "Thurstone's Primary Mental Abilities and Structure-of-Intellect Abilities," *Psychological Bulletin,* 77 (1972), 129–143.

Heise, David R., and Essie P. M. Roberts. "The Development of Role Knowledge," *Genetic Psychology Monographs,* 82 (1970), 83–115.

Hundleby, John D., Kurt Pawlik, and Raymond B. Cattell. *Personality Factors in Objective Test Devices.* San Diego: Robert R. Knapp, 1965.

Jensen, A. R. "How Much Can We Boost IQ and Scholastic Achievement," *Environment, Heredity, and Intelligence,* reprint series no. 2. Cambridge: Harvard Educational Review, 1969, 1–123.

Jinks, J. L., and D. W. Fulker. "Comparison of the Biometrical Genetical, MAVA, and Classical Approaches to the Analysis of Human Behavior," *Psychological Bulletin,* 73 (1970), 311–349.

Kohn, Melvin L. *Class and Conformity: A Study in Values.* Homewood, Ill.: Dorsey Press, 1969.

Kuhn, Manford H. "Self-Attitudes by Age, Sex, and Professional Training," *Sociological Inquiry,* 1960, 39–55.

Loevinger, Jane, and Ruth Wessler. *Measuring Ego Development,* vols. 1 and 2. San Francisco: Jossey-Bass, 1970.

McClelland, D. C., J. W. Atkinson, R. A. Clark, and E. L. Lowell. *The Achievement Motive.* New York: Appleton-Century, 1953.

Osgood, Charles E. "Semantic Differential Technique in the Comparative Study of Cultures," *American Anthropologist,* 66 (1964), 171–200.

Piaget, J. *The Moral Judgement of the Child.* London: Kegan Paul, 1932.

Rosenthal, David. *Genetic Theory and Abnormal Behavior.* New York: McGraw-Hill, 1970.

Schachter, Stanley. "Some Extraordinary Facts about Obese Humans and Rats," *American Psychologist,* 26 (1971), 129–144.

Sorokin, P. A. *Social and Cultural Dynamics,* vols. 1-4. New York: Bedminster Press, 1962.

Thompson, W. R. "Genetics and Personality," in E. Norbeck, D. Price-Williams, and W. McCord, eds., *The Study of Personality: An Interdisciplinary Appraisal.* New York: Holt, Rinehart, 1968, 161–174.

Tyler, Leona E. *The Psychology of Human Differences.* New York: Appleton-Century, 1965.

Vandenberg, Steven G. "Hereditary Factors in Normal Personality Traits (as Measured by Inventories)," *Recent Advances in Biological Psychiatry,* 9 (1967), 65–104.

Wallace, Anthony F. C. *Culture and Personality,* 2nd ed. New York: Random House, 1970.

Part I
The Family

Parental influence is a major force on development of the child, beginning early and lasting for years. Besides providing the child with a genotype, parents dominate childhood in terms of the frequency and exclusiveness of parent-child interactions and in terms of the parents' high power to enforce their own wills. The first two selections in this section summarize much of what is known about parental impact. The other two articles, Chapters 4 and 5, focus on how the overall structure of the family, and the child's position within that structure, can contribute to developing personality and character.

A number of other chapters should be consulted to extend understanding of family effects. Maternal and paternal deprivations (Chapters 21 and 22) are conditions occurring when typical family patterns are not maintained, and the effects of these conditions provide insight into what is provided to a child in a normal family life. Fried, in Chapter 24, discusses some additional aspects of family disorganization. Chapter 20 deals with the psychological development of boys in societies where father-absence is the norm rather than the exception. Chapter 9 deals with the family from the standpoint of husband and wife. A section of Chapter 19 reviews research findings relating maternal behavior and the development of field independence in children. Value orientations involved in child rearing, and their correlates with nationality and social class, are topics in Chapters 12 and 17.

The first two chapters in this section report some differences in the psychological development of males and females. Additional differences between the sexes are reported in Chapter 19 (concerning field independence) and Chapter 8 (concerning patterns of intimacy).

The two dimensions of love and control, used in Chapter 3 to type parent-child relationships, are elaborated further by Kemper in an effort to comprehend emotional relationships in adulthood (Chapter 10). The same basic relational system also seems implicit in the topology of correctional institutions given in Chapter 15.

2

Report on Personality Consistency and Change from the Fels Longitudinal Study

Howard A. Moss and Jerome Kagan

The idea that early experiences influence adult personality is widely accepted, and inferential evidence can be obtained easily by asking people with different personalities about their early life. However, more direct evidence and a real understanding of the process has awaited studies in which people were observed as children and then years later assessed as adult personalities. This chapter presents the results of one such study, and the evidence indicates that early relationships with the mother are indeed instrumental in personality formation. However, the processes involved can be subtle and the outcomes unexpected. For example, one of the discoveries reported below is that even males and females who start with similar personalities and experiences as children can end up differently as adults because of cultural pressures involved in sex roles.

Two major assumptions of developmental theory are that selected adult response patterns are established at an early age, and that maternal treatment during the initial years of life is a significant determinant of personality development. Until recently most of the existing evidence for the stability of behavior and of the enduring influence of early maternal actions came from individual case histories, personal documents, retrospective reports and various informal, qualitative observations. Now, however, the recent completion of long-term longitudinal programs has provided direct objective evidence of these phenomena (Bayley and Schaefer, in press; Schaefer and Bayley, 1960, 1963; Kagan and Moss, 1960a, 1962; Moss and Kagen, 1961). The present paper summarizes some of the major findings derived from an analysis of the longitudinal data collected by the Fels Research Institute.

Method

Subjects and Procedure

The subjects were 36 males and 35 females from the Fels Research Institute's longitudinal population. They were enrolled in the project at birth, during the years 1929 to 1939. At the time of a recent

Abridged from Howard A. Moss and Jerome Kagan, "Report on Personality Consistency and Change from the Fels Longitudinal Study, in *Vita Humana,* 7 (1964), 127–138. Reprinted by permission of the publisher, S. Karger AG Basel/New York, and the authors.

adult assessment they were 20 to 29 years of age. These subjects were predominantly middle class and came from a variety of vocational backgrounds.

This study consisted mainly of correlations between variables based on the childhood information on the subjects and comparable variables assessing their adult behavior. The childhood data included: (a) longitudinal observations of the child's behavior during the first 14 years of life in a variety of settings and (b) annual Stanford-Binet Intelligence Test Scores. The adult data came from a five-hour interview.

One of the authors studied reports based on direct observation of each child between birth and 14 years of age and rated that child for a comprehensive list of variables. A seven-point scale was used in making each rating. The reports used to determine the child ratings were based on: (a) semi-annual home observations of the child interacting with the mother and siblings; (b) semi-annual observations of the child in the Fels Experimental Nursery School and Day Camp settings; (c) interviews with the child; (d) observations of the child in the classroom; and (e) interviews with the mother. These reports were prepared by psychologists and other professional workers from the Fels staff. The material for each subject was divided into four age periods: 0–3; 3–6; 6–10; and 10–14. The rater first read all the information for each subject for the age 0–3 and made those ratings for which he had adequate information. Following a period of interpolated work he studied each subject's material for age 3–6 and again made his ratings. This procedure was repeated for periods 6–10 and 10–14. Approximately 6 months intervened between evaluation of the data for any one subject for each age period. The rater felt that the time interval and the large number of intervening ratings was sufficient to minimize memory of ratings for one period when making ratings for subsequent periods.

Most of the childhood variables dealt with the areas of achievement, passivity and dependency, aggressive behavior and maternal treatment of the child. These variables were selected because of their theoretical significance and the fact that consistently good information was collected concerning them over the years of longitudinal data collection. Similar dimensions were emphasized and evaluated by the other author from the adult interview material. Better than 80 percent of the child and adult ratings yielded interrater reliability coefficients of 0.70 or higher. The author who rated the childhood variables had no knowledge of the adult material and the author who made the adult ratings had no knowledge of the childhood material. In this way complete independence was maintained for the two sets of ratings.

The results of this study have been reported in detail elsewhere (Kagan and Moss, 1962), so we will limit ourselves to highlighting some of the major findings and considering their general significance. *The popular conception that many adult behaviors are established during the childhood years was verified.* Childhood ratings for aggression, passive-dependency, and achievement behaviors were significantly correlated with analogous behaviors from the adult assessment. However, these response classes showed differential stability for the sexes and this patterning of correlations is of additional theoretical significance. The basic hypothesis used for explaining these sex differences is that a behavior will show long-term stability if that behavior is congruent with the cultural definition of the sex role of the individual. . . .

Childhood aggression, beginning for the age period 3 to 6, shows continuity with similar adult behavior for males but not for females. This relationship becomes most pronounced for the ratings made at the 10 to 14 age period. Conversely, childhood passive-dependent behaviors are associated with adult dependency for females but not for males. Again the magnitude of these correlations is greatest for the oldest childhood period. On the other hand, childhood achievement behaviors are predictive of similar adult activities for both males and females. The continuity with adult achievement behavior occurs as early as the preschool years for females and is well established for both sexes by the early school years.

This pattern of correlations provides compelling evidence for the importance of cultural forces in determining the stability of various response systems. Aggression is culturally defined as appropriate sex-role behavior for males but not for females, and passive-dependent behavior is regarded as acceptable for females but not for males. The culture, through parents, peers, and the mass media, acts to modify the stability of response systems in accordance with the current definition for appropriate sex-role behavior. This would account for aggression showing long-term stability only for males, and passive-dependent behavior being stable just for females. Achievement behavior is approved of for both sexes so that once a response system is established in this area, it tends to be maintained.

Maternal Behavior

As we previously indicated, the longitudinal material was also used for evaluating mothers' treatment of their children. For each age period, mothers were rated for hostility, protection, acceleration, and restrictiveness toward their children. The stability of maternal behavior over the first 10 years was determined, and also each maternal variable was correlated with the sons' and daughters' behavior for the childhood and adult years. Abridged definitions of the maternal variables are as follows:

Maternal hostility: This variable assessed maternal criticism of the child and hostile statements, acts and expressions of dissatisfaction with the child.

Maternal protection: This variable assessed the degree to which the mother showed nurturant, solicitous behavior toward her child and encouraged the child's dependency on her.

Maternal acceleration: This variable assessed the degree to which the mother showed excessive concern for her child's cognitive and motor development and her tendency to place excessive expectations on this level of achievement.

Maternal restrictiveness: This variable assessed the mother's attempts to force the child to adhere to her standards, her rigidity in her child-rearing practices, and her lack of tolerance for idiosyncratic behavior in the child.

Maternal acceleration and protection were moderately stable for boys but not for girls; whereas restrictiveness and hostility were more stable for girls than for boys. . . . Restrictiveness, in particular, showed remarkably high stability for girls over the first ten years. The differential stability in maternal practices toward boys and girls reflects how the sex of the child modifies the mother's behavior. Furthermore, this differential stability of maternal treatment ties in with the fact that certain maternal behaviors are selectively predictive of boys' behaviors and others selectively predictive for girls. . . . Protection, which was stable only for boys, correlated with the boys' IQ but not the girls', and conversely, restriction which was stable only for girls was negatively associated with just the girls' IQ scores.

The mothers' ratings for 0–3, 3–6 and 6–10 were correlated with their sons' and daughters' ratings for concurrent and subsequent age periods, including the adult interview material. . . . *An important fact . . . is that maternal treatment for the 0–3 age period was generally a better predictor of the child and adult ratings than maternal treatment assessed later in the child's life.* In most instances the early maternal ratings were more predictive of behavior when the child was older than were the concurrent maternal ratings. For example, . . . maternal protection of boys at 0–3 was more predictive of passivity at 6–10 than the comparable maternal behavior rated at 6–10; . . . the protection ratings for 0–3 were considerably more predictive of achievement in boys at 6–10 and 10–14 than the maternal ratings at the older age periods; and . . . early protection was again more highly associated with the 6–10 and 10–14 ratings on conformity behavior than with the more contemporary maternal ratings. These selected correlational patterns illustrate the greater (or clearer) influence of early maternal treatment. However, an overall inspection of these results reveals that most of the correlations presented exhibit this phenomenon.

. . . Maternal protection for 0–3 was correlated with boys' IQ at all ages, dipping below statistical significance only at the adult level; whereas protection for 3–6 and 6–10 was completely unrelated to IQ for boys. Thus, the apparent significance of early maternal treatment . . . is buttressed by . . . findings involving objective test results. Maternal restriction, on the other hand, did not show this pattern.

In a number of instances early maternal treatment is correlated only with the child's behavior when the child is considerably older than the time of the maternal assessment. Many of these relationships first become manifest when the child reaches adult status. We have labeled this relation between early maternal actions and the child's adolescent and adult behaviors a "sleeper effect." Protection of daughters during 0–3 . . . was an excellent predictor of withdrawal in adult women ($r = 0.52$; $p < 0.01$) whereas protection of daughters during ages 3–6 and 6–10 showed negligible relationships to this adult variable. Hostility toward daughters during the first three years of life predicted a reluctance to withdraw from stress during the adult years. Another example of this "sleeper effect" involved intellectual mastery. . . . A protective and non-hostile attitude during the first 3 years of life predicted, for men only, involvement in intellectual mastery for the later child and adult years. It is interesting to note that maternal protection and hostility during the first 3 years had just the opposite effect on future intellectual interests among girls. . . . Protection during the first 3 years first becomes predictive of conformity in boys and girls when they are somewhat older.

A plausible explanation for the "sleeper effect" is that a given maternal treatment during infancy may be the initiation of a chain of developmental events leading to a specific behavior when the child is older. For example, protectiveness during the early years could influence the child to become more dependent on solicitous and affectionate behavior from his mother and other adults. As he gets older he may be required to conform to adult standards in order to continue receiving this type of adult attention. This could account for the delayed association between early protection and the later conformity behavior.

These results suggest a basic developmental hypothesis: that during the early (formative) years, the influence of the mother's treatment on the child's behavior is maximal. In addition, the maternal behaviors during the early years of life may be more reflective of her basic attitudes and values toward her child than her later behavior toward him. The reason for this may be that as the child gets older he becomes more capable of evoking specific maternal reactions because of his growing uniqueness as a stimulus.

A mother typically establishes expectations of what her child should be like; the standards to which his behavior should conform. The greater the discrepancy between her expectations and her evaluation of the child, the greater the likelihood that she will modify her behavior and exert pressure on the child in an attempt to direct him toward behavior that is more congruent with her expectations.

During infancy the child's personality is relatively ambiguous and the discrepancy between her standards and what she perceives in the child is necessarily small. The mother sees the child as she would like to see him, and he is an object primarily to be acted upon. The form and content of many maternal behaviors toward an infant, as compared with maternal behavior toward a 10-year-old, are not so contaminated by the effect of the child's behavior on the mother. To illustrate, a mother's concern with the intellectual achievement of her two-year-old is more likely an index of her basic needs than her degree of concern with the performance of her 10-year-old who might be failing in school. Some mothers change their expectations and values as the child develops, and the mother's lack of concern with the school achievement of her 10-year-old daughter who is failing could be a recently acquired defensive maneuver to protect the mother from disappointment. Similarly, encouragement of independence, a critical attitude, or overprotection toward the 10-year-old may be newly developed reactions to a child's excessive dependence, emerging rebelliousness, or fragile defenses respectively. Excessive permissiveness or protection toward a three-year-old is more likely a reflection of more fundamental attitudes. Thus, the high correlation we obtained between maternal hostility or protection during the first three years and adult behavior in women could be due to the fact that these practices during the first three years, in comparison to similar practices at 10, provide a more sensitive index of the mother's basic attitudes toward her child and hence of her more lasting effect on the child's developing behavior.

The main findings discussed in this paper concern the differential stability of child and maternal behavior as a function of the sex-role of the child, and the long-term influence of early maternal treatment with the special case of the "sleeper effect." These results could only have been obtained from a longitudinal design and help elucidate the specific contribution of this type of research for confirming and generating hypotheses concerning human development.

References

Bayley, Nancy, and E. S. Schaefer. "Correlations of maternal and child behaviors with the development of mental abilities: data from the Berkeley growth study," *Soc. Res. Child Development Monographs,* in press.

Kagan, J., and H. A. Moss. *Birth to Maturity: A Study in Psychological Development.* New York: Wiley, 1962. "The stability of passive and dependent behavior from childhood through adulthood," *Child Development,* 31 (1960), 577–591 (a).

Moss, H. A., and J. Kagan. "The stability of achievement and recognition seeking behavior from childhood to adulthood," *J. Abnormal Soc. Psychol.,* 62 (1961), 543–552.

Schaefer, E. S., and Nancy Bayley. "Consistency of maternal behavior from infancy to preadolescence," *J. Abnormal Soc. Psychol.,* 61 (1960), 1–6. "Maternal behavior, child behavior and their intercorrelations from infancy through adolescence," *Soc. Res. Child Development Monographs,* 28 (1963).

3
Consequences of Different Kinds of Parental Discipline
Wesley C. Becker

A great deal of research on parent-child relationships has been carried out, but all too often results have seemed to conflict. While nearly all researchers have found that loving parents produce more adjusted children than hostile parents, studies disagree concerning the kind of personality that loving parents produce or the kind of personality that hostile parents produce. Studies also have conflicted in defining the consequences of strict versus permissive discipline; for example, sometimes strict discipline has been seen to produce neurotic children and at other times obedient, well-behaved children have been identified as a consequence. In this chapter, Becker provides an overall framework to accommodate this variety of studies. The degree of love and the degree of control exercised in a parent-child relationship are seen to interact, and the different combinations have qualitatively different outcomes. The chapter helps to clarify a politically volatile area. It would seem that when conservatives call for more obedience and liberals call for more permissiveness, they both assume the existence of loving parent-child relationships; and when obedience or permissiveness is condemned, it is condemned because of the kind of person it produces when parent-child relationships are hostile.

The "Gross Anatomy" of Parent Behavior

To develop a reasoned understanding of the research on discipline, it is . . . important to realize that discipline is but a part of the interaction that occurs between parent and child. The line between discipline and other aspects of parent behavior which influence the child (particularly affectional relations) is difficult to determine from the naturalistic research literature. However, by studying the ways in which various aspects of parent behavior relate to each other, we

Reprinted from Wesley C. Becker, "Consequences of Different Kinds of Parental Discipline," *Review of Child Development Research,* vol. 1, edited by Martin L. Hoffman and Lois Hoffman (New York: Russell Sage Foundation, 1964), 169–208. Reprinted by permission of Basic Books, Inc., and the author. Footnote has been numbered.

The author wishes to express his gratitude to Barbara Anderson for her diligent assistance in obtaining references and preparing the manuscript; to Gordon Paul, Leigh Triandis, and especially Martin Hoffman for their helpful comments on the manuscript; and to the National Institute of Mental Health, whose support of our research on parents and children (Grant M-4881) made this undertaking possible.

stand a better chance of gaining some perspective on the problem and are in a better position to know when certain findings may be confounded by the effects of other variables. In recent years, a number of investigators have used a method of analyzing correlations, called factor analysis, in an attempt to simplify the conceptualization of relations between various parent behaviors. Factor analysis is a tool which can help to determine a minimum number of orthogonal dimensions necessary to account for the empirical correlations among variables. (Orthogonal dimensions are dimensions which are uncorrelated with each other, or, in the language of plane geometry, perpendicular to each other.) For example, in Figure 1, rather than thinking in terms of 14 different aspects of maternal behavior, factor analysis would suggest that it might be more reasonable to think of two dimensions of maternal behavior—Love versus Hostility and Control versus Autonomy. *Within this framework,* a democratic mother would be one who is both loving and autonomy granting, while a protective mother is loving and controlling. A considerable economy in conceptualization can thus be achieved.

The model presented in Figure 1 was developed by Schaefer (1959, 1961) to summarize a number of studies which suggest that most of the concepts developed over the past two decades to describe types of parents can be reduced to a combination of two main dimensional concepts. It is important to realize that these factor concepts, while derived from empirical analysis, are *not necessarily* of any greater scientific value than the typological concepts which preceded them. They certainly are not any more *real.* Like any other construct created in the mind of man, they are created to help achieve a better understanding of the phenomena under study, and if they achieve this goal, can be considered useful.

In recent years, several studies have correlated a wide range of variables pertaining to discipline as well as other aspects of parent behavior (Baldwin, Kalhorn, and Breese, 1945; Becker et al., 1959; Becker et al., 1962; Roff, 1949; Sears et al., 1957; Takala, Nummenmaa, and Kauranne, 1960). During the past year, this author has attempted to tie these studies together through a series of factor analyses. The results of this work suggest that it may be important to consider at least three general dimensions in looking at parent behavior. Figure 2 provides a graphic representation of the three-dimensional model generated from the series of factor analyses. This

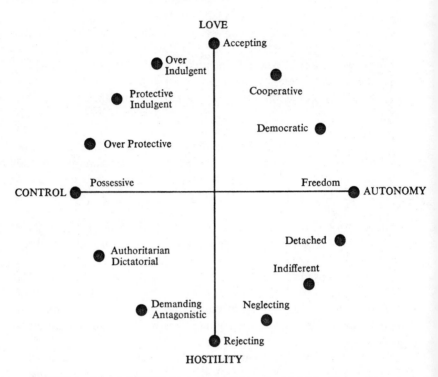

FIGURE 1. Schaefer's (1959) Hypothetical Circumplex Model for Maternal Behavior.[1]

alternative model differs from Schaefer's in that we have subdivided his control versus autonomy dimension into restrictiveness versus permissiveness and anxious-emotional involvement versus calm-detachment. The warmth versus hostility dimension is defined at the warm end by variables of the following sort: accepting, affectionate, approving, understanding, child-centered, frequent use of explanations, positive response to dependency behavior, high use of reasons in discipline, high use of praise in discipline, low use of physical punishment, and

1. Reprinted from the *Journal of Abnormal and Social Psychology,* 59 (1959), 226–235, by permission of the American Psychological Association and the author, Earl S. Schaefer.

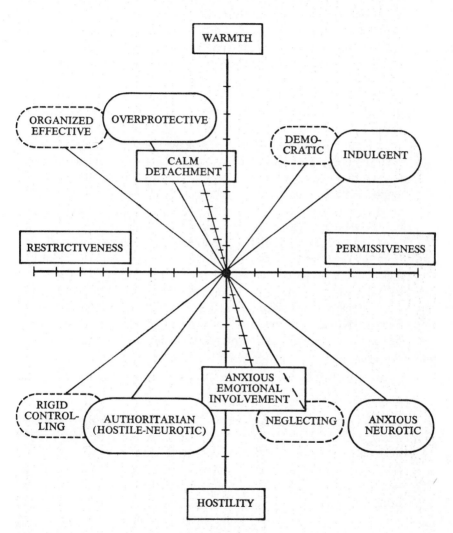

FIGURE 2. Becker's Hypothetical Model for Parental Behavior.

(for mothers) low criticism of husband. The hostility end of the dimension would be defined by the opposite characteristics. The restrictiveness versus permissiveness dimension is defined at the restrictive end by: many restrictions and strict enforcement of demands in the areas of sex play, modesty behavior, table manners, toilet training, neatness, orderliness, care of household furniture, noise, obedience, aggression to sibs, aggression to peers, and aggression to parents. Anxious emotional involvement versus calm-detachment is defined at the anxious end by: high emotionality in relation to child, babying, protectiveness, and solicitousness for the child's welfare.

In Figure 2 we have attempted to show how the various concepts referring to types of parents fit into the model and point to the need for the third dimension to encompass important distinctions. For example, both the democratic parent and the indulgent parent (by definition) are high on the dimensions of warmth and permissiveness, but the indulgent parent is high on emotional involvement while the democratic parent tends to be low on this dimension (calm-detached). Both the organized-effective parent and the overprotective parent are high on warmth and restrictiveness, but the overprotective parent again shows more emotional involvement than the organized-effective parent. The argument can be thus carried around the model, showing how the typical concepts for types of parents can be thought of as being defined by various combinations of three dimensions of parent behavior.

Relevance for Discipline Research

In addition to providing a conceptual framework which may be useful in integrating research, the results of these factor analytic studies carry more direct implications for research on discipline. A point of major significance is the fact that the nature of the affectional relations between parent and child is correlated with the use of certain kinds of discipline. In particular, the use of praise and reasons has been repeatedly found associated with warmth variables, and the use of physical punishment with hostility variables (Bandura and Walters, 1959; Becker et al., 1962; Sears et al., 1957; Unger, 1960, 1962). This point is of significance, since (a) there is a considerable body of research where use of praise, reasons, and physical punishment has played an important role in the definition of types of discipline without considering the possibility that the results could also be attributed to correlated differences in affectional relations, and (b) other findings suggest both kinds of variables—discipline and affectional relations—have similar consequences for child behavior. Thus it is necessary to exercise great care in trying to disentangle special effects of type of discipline, per se. We will document these points more carefully in the following section.

The examination of the more global relations among child rearing variables also leads to a conclusion that there is a general dimension of restrictiveness versus permissiveness in dealing with children which is relatively independent of affectional relations. By independent, we mean that *on the average* restrictive (or permissive) parents are neither predominantly hostile nor warm, but can show all degrees of warmth and hostility. In addition to pointing to a possibly important dimension to examine for consequences in the child, the fact that this dimension is independent of warmth versus hostility makes it theoretically possible to average out the effects of affectional relations in examining the effects of restrictiveness versus permissiveness. Actually, as we interpret the research, some of the more interesting implications occur when the effects of restrictiveness versus permissiveness are examined in a hostile or warm context, rather than independently of either. Because of the absence of direct research relating emotional-involvement versus calm-detachment to disciplinary practices, this dimension is not elaborated later in this paper.

Love-Oriented and Power-Assertive Techniques

Since 1938 there have been a large number of investigations of the consequences of discipline, which, for convenience, will be considered under the general classification of love-oriented versus power-assertive techniques. Definitions of types of discipline have varied considerably, as have the populations studied and consequent child behaviors. Love-oriented techniques have generally included positive methods, such as use of praise and reasoning; and negative methods which threaten the love relation to the parent, such as isolating the child from the parent, showing disappointment, and withdrawing love. As will be seen, some results suggest that it may be important in considering the effects on children to separate love-oriented discipline into positive and negative methods. Power-assertive techniques most typically have included physical punishment, but in some cases have been extended to include yelling, shouting, forceful commands, and verbal threats. The consequent variables in the child have focused primarily on the inhibition and expression of aggression by the child, the child's reaction to transgressions, and the child's resistance to temptation. In an overly simplified way, the research in this area may be summarized as suggesting that approaches to discipline which focus on using the love relationship with the child to shape his behavior are more likely to be correlated with internalized reactions to transgression (feelings of guilt, self-responsibility, confession) and with nonaggressive or cooperative social relations. On the other hand, power-asserting techniques in controlling the child are more likely to correlate with externalized reactions to transgression (fear of punishment, projected hostility), and with non-cooperative, aggressive behaviors. The effect of type of discipline on resistance to temptation has produced highly conflicting findings.

In trying to understand the implications for child rearing of this complex body of literature, we will first look in some detail at the findings concerning aggression in the child. In these studies of aggression, the antecedent parent variables have centered largely on power-assertive techniques, although the positive love-oriented methods (praise, reasons) are also frequently involved in defining low power-assertion. It is important throughout this section for the reader to keep in mind possible variations in definitions for the parent variables from study to study.

Aggression

As part of a rather extensive study of nursery school children, Sears, Whiting, Nowlis, and Sears (1953) examined the consequences of punitiveness of mother for aggressive behavior. Punitiveness was defined largely by the degree of physical pain or discomfort generated by the mother when the child acted in an aggressive or asocial manner. Physical punishment is the key variable defining the punitive end of the scale, and use of reasons is central to the definition of the non-punitive end of the scale. Contrary to the investigators' expectations that punishment for aggression would act to inhibit its expression, the findings were as follows. For boys, there was a positive relation between punitiveness and overt aggression in school. For girls, the relationship was curvilinear. Girls of both high and low punitive mothers showed less aggression in school than girls of moderately punitive mothers. Using 30 of these same subjects a year later and the same ratings of maternal punitiveness, Hollenberg and Sperry (1951) found a direct *positive relation* between maternal punitiveness and aggression in doll play for both boys and girls. This suggests that high maternal punitiveness had actually produced as strong an aggressive reaction in girls as in boys, but that for some reason, its expression was inhibited in the schoolroom situation.

Becker and his colleagues (1962) reproduced almost exactly the findings relating punitiveness of mother to teacher's ratings of aggression in children. Boys' school aggression was directly related to mothers' use of physical punishment (and low use of reasoning), while girls' aggression showed the curvilinear relation. However, *home* ratings of aggression (averaged parent ratings) showed direct positive relations to mothers' punitiveness for both boys and girls. Similar relations to home ratings are reported by Eron, Banta, Walder, and Laulicht (1961) and by Sears and associates (1957). If high punitiveness is producing the inhibition of aggression for girls at school, one would have expected even more evidence of inhibition of aggression in the presence of the punitive agent. This apparently was not the case. Further perplexing effects were found when Becker et al. (1962) examined the relationship of fathers' punitiveness to child aggression. For girls, positive linear relations are found at school and home; while for boys, more aggression is found when father is either high or low in punitiveness. Closer examination of the data suggested that the perplexing results might be a product of the failure to consider the frustrating effects of *both parents*. When hostility and punitiveness for both parents were summated, approximately linear relations to child aggression were found for both boys and girls at home, and boys at school. For girls at school, as the summated index increased, aggression increased but quickly reached an asymptote; it is as if sex-role appropriateness set a limit on the expression of aggression for girls outside of the home. (See Kagan and Moss, 1962.) In general, these results suggest a positive relation between parental power-assertion and child aggression, although the aggressive effects are not apparent in all situations and the effect of type of discipline has not been untangled from other sources of frustration.

Hoffman (1960) provides further evidence on the relation between a punitive approach to discipline and child aggression. Parents' reports of a full day's interaction with their nursery school child were coded for evidence of *initial unqualified power-assertion* and *reactive unqualified power-assertion*. The first variable reflects the frequency with which the initial attempts to control the child consist of direct commands, threats, material deprivations, and physical force (without explanation), and the second variable reflects the frequency with which the same procedures are used when first attempts to gain compliance fail. Strong relations were found between mothers' (but not fathers') reactive power-assertion and the child's hostility toward other children, power-assertion to other children, resistance to influence by other children, and resistance to influence by teacher. Hoffman speculates that the failure to find consistent relations between initial power-assertion and child aggression may be due to the fact that the parents' power-assertion has more lasting effects when used in situations of heightened conflict and involvement, that is, when the child fails to comply to the initial influence procedure.

Beverly Allinsmith (1960) extended the generality of findings of this sort to a group of junior high school boys. Six story beginnings were used where a loved or feared older person was unfair or was unintentionally a source of frustration. The responses to story beginnings were classified according to the directness of the aggression expressed. When physical punishment was the predominant form of discipline by mother, the boys were more likely to express aggression directly. When psychological discipline (appeals to pride and guilt, expressions of disappointment, shaming) predominated, aggression was likely to be expressed indirectly (or not at all). These relations held for both middle-class and working-class samples, even though psychological discipline was more likely to be used by middle-class mothers and physical punishment by working-class mothers. Using peer judgments, it was also found that boys who received physical punishment were more likely to respond to frustrations from their teachers by getting mad or talking back.

A cross-cultural study by Lambert, Triandis, and Wolf (1959) also supports a relationship between the use of power-assertive techniques and aggression. Where more pain-generating punishment is used in child rearing, the gods were perceived primarily as aggressive rather than benevolent. The perceptions of the gods in this study are assumed to be a projective manifestation of emotional attitudes generated by the child-rearing practices.

The aforementioned studies, while containing some unresolved complexities, suggest that one "consequence" of a punitive approach to discipline is aggression. In trying to understand the meaning of this relationship, we are faced with difficulties. First, a series of studies (too numerous to list) provide rather overwhelming evidence that hostile parents have aggressive children. Earlier we noted that hostile parents also tend to use more physical punishment and less reasoning and praise. We are faced with a situation where certain techniques of discipline and certain emotional attitudes of the parent tend to occur jointly and have similar consequences for the child. Thus we do not know for sure that the obtained relation between physical punishment and aggression is primarily a result of the kind of discipline used, a joint effect of hostility and type of punishment, or primarily an effect of the parents' hostility. If we could find enough warm parents who relied primarily on physical punishment, or enough hostile parents who were not physically punitive, it might be possible to disentangle such effects. The only direct evidence on this question is not very conclusive. Sears and associates (1957) used partial correlations to show that maternal coldness and physical punishment contributed about equally to aggression in the child. There is a need for research to give this question closer consideration.

Given the empirical association between physical punishment (separately or in combination with hostility) and child aggression, how might this relation be accounted for? Three hypotheses stand out in the literature. The first has already been mentioned and assumes that physical punishment is frustrating and thus instigates anger. The second notes that the physically punitive parent is setting a model of aggressive behavior for the child, which in effect sanctions aggression as well as showing the child how to be aggressive. The third postulates a direct reinforcement of aggression behavior by hostile-punitive parents.

Direct evidence for the first hypothesis has not been collected, even though it is the leading hypothesis to account for the relation between power-assertive methods and aggression in the child. The authors of

Frustration and Aggression (Dollard et al., 1939, p. 40) were the first to formulate explicitly such a relationship on the basis of observational evidence. They would put it this way: the punishment of acts of direct aggression serves as additional frustration which instigates aggression against the punishing agent. It is easy to understand why research with children has not attempted to test this proposition through direct experimental manipulation. At present, the correlational evidence presented in this section provides the strongest support for this hypothesis.

The possible importance of modeling effects has been carefully explored in a series of laboratory experiments by Bandura (1962). The models provided the child have been demonstrated to be very potent in shaping the child's behavior. For example, in one study (Bandura, Ross, and Ross, 1961), a group of nursery school children was exposed to aggressive adult models, while another group was exposed to subdued and nonaggressive models. A control group was not exposed to any model. The children were then mildly frustrated and tested for the amount of imitative (behavior like that of the model) and nonimitative aggressive behavior in a new setting with the model absent. The children who had been exposed to an aggressive model displayed significantly more aggression than the control group, while those exposed to a passive model displayed significantly less aggression than the control group. The children in the aggressive-model condition also showed, with a high frequency, the specific kinds of aggressive responses used by the model. These responses occurred very rarely in the other groups. The tenability of the modeling hypothesis is strengthened by findings such as these, but these studies do not tell just how important modeling is in the real life situation. Some naturalistic studies are a little more helpful on this point. McCord, McCord, and Zola (1959) found that boys with deviant parental models were more likely to participate in criminal activities. This effect of models was over and above that contributed by the hostility or warmth of the parent-child interaction. In a subsequent study of aggression (McCord, McCord, and Howard, 1961), it was found that parental deviance (aggression, escapism, or an eccentric role in the family) correlated with aggression in boys, but an aggressive model by itself did not. They suggest that the absence of a model of inner control was common in the background of aggressive children. The findings by Hoffman (1960) discussed previously also point to a modeling effect. Children with power-assertive mothers were more likely to use power-assertive techniques in attempting to influence other children. In general, the importance of modeling in mediating aggression in children has been quite well supported by the evidence.

The possibility of a direct reward of aggression by power-assertive parents has not been clearly established. In a study of aggressive and withdrawn boys, Bandura (1960) found that mothers of the aggressive boys, while quite punitive when aggression was expressed toward them, were more permissive than mothers of inhibited boys when the aggression was expressed toward peers or siblings. The findings for fathers of aggressive boys, however, indicated that they were more punitive for aggression toward parents, as well as *less* permissive of aggression to peers. In our own work (Becker et al., 1962), we have found that when mother is high in use of physical punishment, she is also likely to insist that her children fight for their rights with other children. As will be seen in the section on permissiveness, it is clear that implicit or direct reward for aggression increases its expression. However, the evidence is not clear in demonstrating that this hypothesis can account for the positive relation between power-assertive methods and child aggression.

Power-assertive discipline and the inhibition of aggression. Laboratory studies of the effects of punishment on animals have rather consistently shown that punishment will inhibit a strongly motivated behavior by arousing anxiety (Skinner, 1938; Estes, 1944). There is some evidence to suggest that inhibition also takes place in the naturalistic setting as a consequence of the consistent use of punitive techniques over a period of time. In a follow-up of his kindergarten study, R. R. Sears (1961) found that early punishment by mother, which at the age of five was positively associated with aggression in the home, lost this association with open aggression by age twelve and tended to relate to inhibited or deflected forms of aggression (prosocial aggression, for example, "When a person has broken a rule, he should be punished for it," and self-aggression). In a similar vein, McCord and associates (1959) found the lowest crime rates to occur where both parents were consistently punitive during the early years. Assuming low crime rates among these boys to imply that they tended to be less aggressive and more inhibited, these results support Sears in suggesting that given enough time or consistency of application, power-assertive approaches to discipline do appear capable of promoting inhibition of aggressive behavior.

Reactions to Transgressions

Several studies have produced suggestive relations between love-oriented disciplines and signs of guilt, or acceptance of self-responsibility in reaction to transgressions. In a cross-cultural study, Whiting and Child (1953) rated the prevalence of use of love-oriented techniques of discipline (use of praise, isolation, withdrawal of love) in a variety of different cultures. They then evaluated the degree to which responsibility for cause of illness was attributed to the individual's own behavior, in order to obtain a projective index of level of guilt for each culture. Higher guilt scores were found for cultures where love-oriented techniques predominated. W. Allinsmith (1960) provides evidence that middle-class mothers of junior high boys who used predominantly psychological punishment (appeals to pride and guilt, expressions of disappointment, shaming), in contrast to physical punishment, had boys who manifested greater guilt on a story completion test. The relationship was not found to hold for lower-class families. In a later study with middle-class college students (Allinsmith and Greening, 1955), it was found that male students who reported greater use of psychological discipline by their parents were found to have higher guilt-over-aggression scores on a story completion test than subjects whose parents used physical punishment. The female subjects in their sample showed only a slight relationship in the same direction. The authors point out that this difference may be due to the fact that the story situation was more appropriate for boys. Similar results were obtained in Heinicke's (1953) study of five-year-old boys. His measure of guilt was based on the boys' responses to interview questions dealing with problems of right and wrong, and how they would react when they had done something wrong. Frequent use of praise and infrequent use of physical punishment and isolation related to high guilt. Expression of affection toward the child also was positively related to guilt reactions in the child.

Aronfreed (1961) examined post-transgression behavior in terms of whether it was motivated by internal or external forces. Using incomplete stories in which the central figure commits an aggressive act, the responses of a group of sixth-grade children were coded in terms of whether the central figure sought to correct the situation, accepted responsibility for his action, and did not focus on external punishment; or whether the focus was on externally motivated actions and punitive consequences. Techniques of discipline were classified into *induction* and *sensitization* categories on the basis of parent interviews. Induction techniques are those which are capable of arousing unpleasant-feeling reactions in the child about his misbehavior, independently of external threat, and which encourage the child to accept responsibility for his actions. Some examples are insisting on restitution or apology, asking why he did that, explaining to the child why it was wrong, or not punishing if the child shows recognition that he has done wrong. Sensitization techniques are those aimed only at inhibiting the child's unacceptable behavior by focusing on the painful consequences. Physical punishment, yelling, shouting, and so on, would be included here. The high similarity to the love-oriented versus power-assertive groupings is apparent. As expected, use of induction techniques was positively related to internally motivated, self-corrective actions, while use of sensitization techniques was related to externally motivated actions and punitive consequences.

A highly similar result was obtained by Hoffman and Saltzstein (1960). Children's moral judgments about violations were classified as expressing an internalized standard or merely the fear of detection and punishment. The boys who tended to have internalized standards reported that their mothers were less likely to use force, threat of force, deprivation, or direct commands (power-assertive techniques) in disciplining them, and that mothers were more likely to stress how the child's misbehavior hurt the parent. Mothers of internalizers were also reported to be more affectionate. Internalization in girls was related only to use of rational appeals by father, and the absence of threats by the mother to have father discipline them. Internalized subjects of both sexes gave more guilt responses in a story completion test.

Two studies suggest that the negative love-oriented disciplines (withdrawal of love, expressions of disappointment, and the like) relate to signs of conscience only when mother has a warm relation with the child. Using their full sample, Sears and associates (1957) found no correlation between withdrawal of love and conscience. However, when only warm mothers were considered, use of withdrawal of love related positively to signs of conscience. Similar results were reported by LeVine (1961). Withdrawal of love was positively associated with remorse after transgression only when warm mothers were considered. It might also be noted that in the study by Allinsmith reported earlier, his definition of psychological discipline involved primarily negative love-oriented methods (appeals to pride and guilt, expressions of disappointment, shaming). His finding that psychological discipline related to guilt only for middle-class mothers might possibly be attributed to a frequently obtained difference in warmth between the middle-class and working-class families. The fact that negative love-oriented techniques seem to be effective primarily where there is love to lose makes good sense.

It is of interest that LeVine also found use of reasoning to be the best predictor of confession and remorse after transgression. Sears and associates (1957) also found use of reasons and praise (the positive love-oriented techniques as we have classified them) to be the best predictors of signs of conscience (along with low physical punishment). In addition, Burton, Maccoby, and Allinsmith (1961) fully replicated these findings, as well as the relationship between warmth and signs of conscience. There is a strong suspicion from the patterning of the evidence, that the positive love-oriented techniques (praise, reasons) which are highly correlated with warmth variables, need to be considered separately from the negative love-oriented methods (withdrawal of love, isolation, expressions of disappointment). The latter relate to guilt indices primarily when there is love to lose.

Unger (1960, 1962) made an attempt to disentangle the effects of warmth versus hostility and type of discipline with respect to guilt-after-transgression. He related a projective measure of guilt-after-transgression to psychological (praise, reasons) versus physical punishment and to the warmth versus hostility of each parent. Evaluations of parent behavior were obtained from the questionnaire responses of sixth-grade children. The effects of type of discipline were examined separately for parents high and low in warmth. The warmth of each parent was found to have the *major* influence on guilt scores, but type of discipline showed significant effects (in the expected direction) for mothers low in warmth and fathers high in warmth. Also, the trend for mothers high in warmth was in the expected direction. Type of discipline had no effect for fathers low in warmth. LeVine (1961) provides additional evidence for an effect of reasoning, independent of warmth. When the mothers in her study were divided into warm and cold groups, the relationship of reasoning to confession and remorse remained for each group.

In summary, these various studies suggest that internalized reactions to transgression in the form of guilt or acceptance of self-responsibility for misdeed are more likely to occur when the parent is warm and uses techniques of discipline which utilize the love relations to the parent for their effects. The use of praise and reasoning appears to have the most predictable effects across studies, while love-with-drawing methods seem effective primarily when the parent is high in warmth.

A number of hypotheses have been proposed to help account for the empirical relations. The importance of anxiety over displeasing the parent has been stressed by many investigators since Freud originally emphasized it (1933). The fact that love-withdrawing methods seem to be more effective when there is more love to lose adds some support to this notion. However, research to date has not pinned down this variable in a way to demonstrate its explicit role. A modeling effect has also been hypothesized as being important. The parent using love-oriented discipline provides a model of self-restraint in dealing with the child. But whether the parent also provides a model of self-criticism after misdeed has not been demonstrated, though it is not unlikely. The frequent concurrence of use of reasons by the parent and internalized reactions to transgressions by the child suggests two further possibilities. First, the parent who talks and reasons with the child about his misbehavior is more likely to provide the child with a clear understanding of what he did wrong, so that the anxiety about misbehavior is connected to the right cues. Secondly, as Aronfreed has suggested, explanations and reasons provide the child with internal resources for evaluation of his own behavior; that is, the child gains explicit training in making moral judgments.

Both Aronfreed and Hill have taken a closer look at the differences in learning conditions likely to be present when love-oriented or power-assertive techniques are used. Hill (1960) proposed that the love relation itself may not be the critical factor, but rather the reinforcement by the parent of explicit reactions from the child. Love-oriented discipline is likely to continue until the child makes some symbolic renunciation of his wrong-doing. Thus self-admission and verbal recognition of wrong-doing may be reinforced by regaining parental approval and ending the punishment. Physical punishment is more likely to occur all at once and be over, and what the child does toward the end of preventing future occurrences is not related to the ending of punishment. LeVine (1961) has taken a preliminary step toward testing Hill's hypothesis. Mothers completed a questionnaire concerning the degree to which their children tended to confess and show remorse after transgression (and the degree to which the children resisted temptation). They also described their techniques of discipline, with care being taken to have them describe the conditions leading to the ending of punishment. The mothers who continued discipline (regardless of its nature) until the child verbalized that he was sorry were more likely to have children who confessed wrong-doing and expressed remorse.

Aronfreed (1963; Aronfreed, Cutick, and Fagan, 1963) has developed another theoretical model to account for the learning of self-criticism in response to transgression. Hill assumed that confession of wrong-doing and expressions of remorse were learned because they were reinforced by escape from punishment. Aronfreed postulates that the criticizing responses from the parent are adopted by the child if the *parents'* responses (rather than the child's) are associated with the termination of anxiety induced by transgression and punishment. Thus the parents' responses become cues that punishment is over, and the child, after a transgression, can reduce his own anxiety about punishment by reproducing these cues. Self-criticism is, then, reproducing the parent criticism which signals the end of the anxiety. The paradigm is a general one to account for the learning of responses generally classified as identification with the aggressor. "After a child has had some experience with a transgression, punishment itself may come to serve as a cue signifying the termination of anxiety that accompanies its anticipation" (Aronfreed, 1963). Aronfreed suggests that the occasionally obtained associations of love-oriented discipline with signs of conscience may be due to the intertwining of withdrawal of love with a high degree of cognitive structuring (reasons) and certain properties of the timing, rather than being a special effect of withdrawing love.

Resistance to Temptation

The consequences of love-oriented and power-assertive classifications of discipline have also been explored in a series of studies of resistance to temptation. In contrast to the previous group of studies, the question focuses on what the subject does under pressure to violate his standards rather than on his reactions after transgression. Also, in contrast to the previous section, the results of various studies show greater inconsistencies.

MacKinnon (1938) initiated research on this question with an experimental study of cheating by college males. The subjects were asked to solve 20 problems, each on a separate page. For some of the problems they could look at the solutions in a book on the table, but were prohibited from looking at others. Without their knowing it, the subjects were observed through a one-way screen. MacKinnon found that those who cheated reported that their fathers used predominantly physically aggressive forms of punishment rather than love-oriented techniques (parental indications that they were not worthy of love, fall short of parents' ideals). Consistent with the results discussed earlier, MacKinnon also noted that violators tended to vent their anger outwardly during the frustrations of the test, while nonviolators tended to blame themselves. Also, nonviolators indicated that they would feel badly if they had violated a prohibition, while violators indicated that they would not.

Findings partially consistent with these were obtained by Allinsmith in the study cited earlier. Two story-beginnings were used where the central figures had not yet transgressed, but were tempted to do so. Resistance to temptation was assessed by whether or not the hero transgressed in the completed story. While his measure of psychological and physical discipline did not relate to resistance to temptation, the use of explained requests (reasons) rather than arbitrary demands did.

Several more recent studies have adapted the experimental paradigm used by MacKinnon for use with younger children (Burton et al., 1961; Grinder, 1962; Sears, Rau, and Alpert, 1960). The test for resistance to temptation involved placing the child in a game situation where he was tempted to violate the rules to win a prize. A one-way screen was used to observe the child's behavior during the game. The trend of the findings in the Sears and Grinder studies was for resistance to temptation to relate to love-oriented (praise, reasoning, withdrawal of love) rather than physical forms of control. Burton and associates found just the opposite direction of effects; that is, higher resistance to temptation tended to be associated with use of physical punishment and scolding. In the study discussed previously, LeVine (1961) obtained findings consistent with Burton's. Higher resistance to temptation was positively associated with use of physical punishment and deprivation of reward, and negatively associated with use of reasoning.

In his recent review of research on moral development, Hoffman (1963) considered in detail some of the possible reasons for the inconsistent results in this area. Experimental temptation situations attempt to set a desire for a certain reward against a competing sanction against cheating. To measure accurately the strength of resistance to temptation one must be sure that subjects are equated in their desire for the prize. No attempts were made in these studies to control for this desire. Also, since the tasks used usually involved competition with a standard of excellence, it would be important to control for the children's achievement strivings.

Another source of difficulty may be with the theory itself. Studies of resistance to temptation have started with the expectation that the child-rearing antecedents would be similar to those obtained for guilt, since one is assumed to resist temptation in order to avoid strong guilt. As Hoffman points out, this assumption can be questioned not only by the lack of consistent empirical evidence for common parental antecedents, but also because indices of guilt and resistance to temptation have not been consistently found to be correlated with each other. MacKinnon (1938), Grinder (1962), Sears and associates (1960), and Grinder and McMichael (1963) reported a low positive relation between resistance to temptation and guilt; W. Allinsmith (1960) and Maccoby (1959) reported no relation; while Burton and associates (1961) and LeVine (1961) reported a negative relation. It seems quite possible, particularly for the young child, that the presence of guilt reactions to transgression do not necessarily imply that the child will resist temptations in order to avoid guilt. The possible reasons for this are largely speculative. Hoffman (1963) suggests that the child may lack the cognitive apparatus to discriminate relevant cues and anticipate consequences, or the child may be aware of consequences and lack the necessary controls. Those who approach the problem from a learning theory point of view have suggested that the learning of guilt in response to transgression and the learning of controls in the face of temptation involve separate problems. A guilt response to transgression is more likely to occur when the punishment follows the transgression, whereas punishment at the onset of the deviant act is more likely to tie anxiety to the preparatory responses themselves and thus serve to inhibit the deviant act. Burton, Maccoby, and Allinsmith attempted to test this hypothesis by asking the mothers in their study the following question: "Suppose you wanted him to learn not to play with something—like the TV set or matches. If you saw that he was tempted to touch it, would you stop him before he touched it or wait to see if he really played with it and *then* correct him?" (1961), p. 703). The results were contrary to the hypothesis. Allowing the child to "touch" the object and then stopping him was significally related to resistance to temptation. The authors suspect that their results may be deceptive. They suggest that the notion of "wait till he actually plays with it" reflected the mother's waiting to be sure what the child was up to before punishing, and that in fact, their mothers did not let the child go very far with the act. Thus "wait till he actually plays with it" may have actually been punishment at the onset of the deviant act. This example serves to illustrate further some of the methodological difficulties in reaching firm conclusions in this area.

Probably the most coherent generalization we can draw from the studies of resistance to temptation is that how one reacts to misdeed is not necessarily related to whether one will resist temptation in the first place.

Summary: Love-Oriented and Power-Assertive Techniques

Power-assertive techniques of discipline tend to be used by hostile parents, and in this context, tend to promote aggression in young children, resistance to authority, power assertion to other children, and externalized reactions to transgression (fear of punishment, projected hostility). There is suggestive evidence that, in time, consistent use of power-assertive techniques leads to an inhibition of overt aggression, but the hostility generated is still detectable in the form of prosocial-aggression and self-aggression. The aggression-inducing effects of power-assertive techniques are assumed to be mediated by the following mechanisms: (a) occurring in a hostile context, power-assertion is more likely to serve as a further frustration of the child and lead to a counter-aggressive anger reaction; (b) the model of aggressive behavior set by the parent shows the child how to be aggressive as well as implicitly sanctioning it; and (c) there is also some evidence to suggest that hostile-punitive parents actually directly reinforce or encourage aggressive behaviors to others.

Love-oriented techniques of discipline tend to be used by warm parents and in this context tend to promote acceptance of self-responsibility, guilt, and related internalized reactions to transgression. Their effectiveness in promoting these behaviors are probably due to four characteristics of the parents' behavior: (a) warmth, which makes the parent important to the child and obviates the need for more severe forms of discipline to gain compliance; (b) the providing of a model of controlled behavior; (c) the providing of verbal cues (reasons) which facilitate understanding of what is expected and aid the child's development of an anticipation of consequences; and (d) certain aspects of the timing of punishment termination.

While a number of studies have attempted to relate love-oriented and power-assertive techniques to the child's ability to resist temptation, the results at present do not suggest any consistent generalizations.

Restrictive and Permissive Approaches to Discipline

The degree to which parents place demands and restrictions on the child in a broad grouping of task areas, and insist on compliance to these demands and restrictions, has been found in recent statistical analyses to form a global dimension useful in describing parent-role behavior. In the study by Sears and associates (1957), a permissiveness versus restrictiveness factor was found which included both level of restrictions and the degree of strictness in enforcing them in the areas of sex play, modesty, table manners, toilet training, neatness, orderliness, care of household furniture, noise, obedience, aggression to sibs, aggression to peers, and aggression to parents. Becker and associates (1962) replicated this factor almost exactly for mothers and for fathers of five-year-olds. The statistical evidence implies that there is a strong tendency for parents who are strict or restrictive in one area to be so in other areas of child rearing. Thus it is reasonable to conceptualize a global dimension of restrictiveness versus permissiveness and consider its possible consequences for the child. This global dimension might be thought of as reflecting the degree of control exerted over the child without specifying the way in which such control is achieved. Yet the statistical evidence also implies that there is considerable room for individual parents to be more restrictive or permissive in some areas than in others. That is, the correlations among the various child-rearing areas are not so high as to preclude some differentiation in the degree of restrictiveness or permissiveness of individual parents in their treatment of, for example, sexual behavior versus aggressive behavior, or aggression to parents versus aggression to peers. It is quite likely that a more careful examination of such differential effects will be undertaken in the near future.

A major difficulty in integrating the present research literature in this area is the wide variety of definitions which have been used. Only a few studies have used definitions which even approach the one discussed above. Generally, studies which have classified parents as dominant or submissive have used definitions which are good approximations to restrictiveness and permissiveness. A number of other terms also have some relevance for the question at hand. For example, indulgence can be thought of as a combination of permissiveness, warmth, and emotional involvement (see Figure 2); overprotectiveness as a combination of restrictiveness, warmth, and emotional involvement. Differences between indulgent and overprotective parents would presumably reflect the effects of restrictiveness versus permissiveness in a warm, emotional context. Similarly, the laxity of the neglecting parent who fails to supervise the child can be thought of as a variety of permissiveness combined with a detached hostility (rejection), and the behavior of the authoritarian parent can be considered a combination of restrictiveness, hostility, and emotional involvement. Surprisingly, when simple semantic assumptions of this sort are made, a fairly consistent picture of the consequences of restrictiveness versus permissiveness emerges.

The organization of this section is as follows. First, a few studies will be examined where the warmth or hostility of the parent is probably not seriously contributing to the results. These studies will serve to give an overview of some of the general trends. After this, the research will be grouped to bring out certain interactions of restrictiveness and permissiveness with warmth and hostility.

General Implications

Generally, the results support the common-sense supposition that restrictive discipline fosters inhibited behaviors, and permissive discipline more uninhibited behaviors. For example, in an early study in the area, Symonds (1939) compared children with dominating parents with those whose parents were submissive. Dominance was defined as the use of much control, restrictiveness, strictness, severe punishment, criticism, or excessive planning for the child's needs (overprotectiveness). Submission was defined as giving the child a great deal of freedom, acceding to the child's demands, indulging the child, being permissive, deserting and neglecting the child, and/or showing lax and inconsistent discipline. Children of dominating parents were better socialized and more courteous, obedient, neat, generous, and polite. They were also more sensitive, self-conscious, shy, and retiring. Children of submissive (permissive) parents were more disobedient, irresponsible, disorderly in the classroom, lacking in sustained attention, lacking in regular work habits, and more forward and expressive.

In her study of nursery school children, Radke (1946) provides support for the findings that children with restrictive parents (defined in terms of the amount of freedom available to the child) show inhibited (passive, non-rivalrous) and socially withdrawing (unpopular) behaviors. R. R. Sears (1961), on the other hand, provides data to support the relation between permissiveness and overtly aggressive behavior. His permissiveness factor (defined earlier), based on ratings of mother when the child was five, was positively correlated with anti-social aggression in boys at both age five and at age twelve, but not in girls. As Kagan and Moss (1962) have suggested, the sex-role sanctions against the expression of aggression in girls makes the prediction of consistent effects in the aggression area for girls a much more difficult task.

Probably one of the most significant contributions to our understanding in this area in recent years comes from the Fels longitudinal study (Kagan and Moss, 1962). It is the only available study that considers the effects of age of the child in relation to the mother's restrictiveness, and systematically explores the consequences for the child over a thirty-year period. Restrictiveness of mother was defined as the degree to which mother attempted to force the child, through punishment and threat, to adhere to her standards, and the degree to which deviations from standards were punished. Mother's restrictiveness was evaluated from all the available home observation and interview material, and averaged ratings were determined for three age periods (birth to three, three to six, and six to ten). The children were rated on a wide variety of behaviors for the same time periods, and for age ten to fourteen and as adults (by interview).

For mothers of girls, there was a high degree of consistency in restrictiveness between age periods. This consistency, as well as sex-typing goals, may account for the broader range of significant effects in girls. For boys, mothers' early restrictiveness was not related to later restrictiveness, but consistency was present after the early period (birth to three). For both boys and girls, later restrictiveness was more highly associated with maternal hostility. Restrictiveness during the first three years appeared to have lasting inhibiting effects on both boys and girls. Restricted children were more conforming, less aggressive, less dominant and competitive with peers, more dependent on adults, and showed less mastery behavior. It is of interest that in adulthood, girls who were restricted in the early years remained dependent on parents as permitted by sex-typing mores, but restricted boys did not.

Examination of the effects of maternal restrictiveness assessed when the child is between three and six years of age revealed some interesting variations in effects. For boys, fearful and dependent behaviors were present from age three to ten, but a shift occurred at adolescence to more competitive and aggressive behaviors. In adulthood, the tendency not to criticize parents remained, but was accompanied by an anger indicator (retaliation to frustration or attack). It would appear that restrictiveness at ages three to six is more likely to generate aggression, but the aggression is manifested in socially approved forms (competitiveness, indirect aggression to peers, and justifiable retaliation). These trends became clearer for boys when mothers' restrictiveness was considered for the six-to-ten-year period. At this time, both dependency behavior and aggression toward mother and peers related to restrictiveness. During adolescence, recognition seeking, fear of peer rejection, and dominance of peers all suggest an attempt to gain peer acceptance and rebellion from mothers' control. The adult indicators confirmed the presence of suppressed hostility in measures of the readiness to retaliate and ease of anger arousal.

For girls, a change appeared in the correlates of restrictiveness at the three-to-six period. The girls under the most restrictions were aggressive and not withdrawn, but low in achievement mastery and independence. Beyond this period, the aggressive elements appeared to drop out and restrictiveness led to a passive, dependent girl. But in adulthood, though one does not criticize one's mother, anger is easily aroused and justified retaliation strong. A consistent consequence in adulthood for girls of restrictive mothers was low criticism of *mother,* and for boys, low criticism of *father.*

These most interesting findings imply some complex interactions of age and sex variables. Early restrictiveness appears to have far greater inhibiting power than later restrictiveness. Restrictiveness at later ages, whether it succeeds in producing a conforming-dependent child or not, is likely to generate more hostility in the child, albeit, controlled hostility. At these later ages, the child is more likely to be aware of the "unfairness" of a restrictive parent and resent excessive control. Also at the later age, the child is more capable of retaliating with aggression, even though it is eventually inhibited. The data further imply that boys are more likely to fight against a restrictive mother successfully. It would be nice to know to what degree father enters into this successful battle.

Restrictiveness versus Permissiveness in a Hostile Context

A proportionately large number of studies have explored the consequences of restrictiveness versus permissiveness in groups of parents who are primarily warm or hostile. Others have measured both restrictiveness versus permissiveness and some aspect of warmth versus hostility and examined the interactions of the two. In general, the studies show that permissiveness combined with hostility maximizes aggressive, poorly controlled behavior, while restrictiveness combined with hostility maximizes self-aggression, social withdrawal, and signs of internal conflict.

Parents of delinquents repeatedly have been shown to have poor affectional relations with their children and to use poor disciplinary techniques. While delinquency is not a homogeneous psychological category, one might expect differences between delinquents and non-delinquents to have some relevance for understanding the antecedents of aggressive and poorly controlled behavior. One of the earliest studies to stress the importance of parental discipline was that by Healy and Bronner (1926). Although they lacked control data, they noted a high incidence (40 percent) of parental neglect and lack of exercise of control (lax about discipline) among 4,000 court-referred delinquents. Later studies by Burt (1929), the Gluecks (1950), McCord and associates (1959), and Bandura and Walters (1959) have essentially shown that mothers of delinquents are very likely not to attempt to exert much control over their children, place few restrictions on them, and do not enforce obedience. These studies have consistently shown, however, that a relatively higher incidence of overly strict discipline occurs among fathers of delinquent boys. While fathers of delinquents on the average tend to be lax in discipline, there are some who use a brutal kind of strict control. In these families, mother is usually lax in discipline. Coupled with other findings on defective affectional relations, this evidence suggests that maximum generation of noncompliant, aggressive, and poorly controlled behavior occurs largely under lax-hostile conditions, that is, where hostility is generated and no controls are demanded from the child when he rebels.

A number of widely divergent studies of "normal" children lead to implications which are very similar to those from the delinquency studies. McCord and associates (1961) classified largely working-class mothers of boys into three levels of control (over, normal, subnormal). Overcontrol was defined as mother's insistence that the boy should be close at all times and submit completely to her direction. Normal control reflected concern with shaping the child's activities in some areas but granting freedom in others. Subnormal control reflected a neglecting or unconcerned attitude. Because lower-class parents tend to show less warmth, and the "permissive" category used was primarily neglect, we have considered these findings as fitting into the permissive-hostile group. The findings indicated that nonaggressive boys came most frequently from homes where mother was overcontrolling; assertive boys came most frequently from homes where mother used normal control; while aggressive boys came from homes with both subnormal control and overcontrol. In both this study and the delinquency studies, the occurrence of high rates of aggression or nonconformity has been associated with overly strict *and* overly permissive discipline. As we shall note later, the evidence suggests that overt aggression is likely to occur in the child with an overly strict parent only if the other parent is permissive or lax about discipline, that is, where there is one type of inconsistency (McCord et al., 1959, 1961). In brief, this study adds support to the notion that lax discipline can contribute to aggressiveness.

Meyers (1944) examined the effects of certain aspects of discipline under experimental conditions where the child was faced with a variety of conflicting commands from two adults. Nursery school teachers rated the parents on attitudes of rejection, dominance, submission, and overprotection. Dominance and submission were very similar in meaning to restrictiveness and permissiveness as we have used them here. Consistent with the delinquency studies, parents of the children who exhibited noncompliance in the experiment were higher on rejection and submission (hostile-lax) than other parents. Of further interest for understanding the effects of restrictiveness versus permissiveness, was the fact that parents who were both rejecting and submissive had children who were noncompliant; while parents who were rejecting and dominant had compliant children. Results of a similar nature, but focusing on aggression rather than noncompliance, were found by Sears and associates (1957). Both permissiveness for aggression to mother and punitiveness for aggression to mother were found to increase aggression, even though these two variables were negatively correlated with each other. Maximal aggression was associated with high permissiveness-high punishment (analogous to the lax-hostile condition of the delinquency studies or Meyers' submissive-rejecting condition).

Several studies suggest that more neurotic-like conflicts are generated under a restrictive-hostile condition. Although these studies are in no sense replications, their implications are consistent with each other. First, in the follow-up study mentioned earlier, R. R. Sears (1961) showed that low permissiveness-high punishment (restrictive-hostile) leads to maximum self-aggression (self-punishment, suicidal tendencies, accident proneness) for twelve-year-old boys. In an early study of self-reports of 230 graduate students, Watson (1934) related self-descriptions to the students' reports of parental discipline on a strictness versus permissiveness dimension. Watson (1957) noted later that his definition of strictness was probably confounded with severe punishment and rejection. The way in which his students' reports fit other findings for restrictive-hostile parents supports this hunch. Students with parents in the strictest quartile reported more hatred and constraint in relations to parents, more rejection of teachers, poorer relations with classmates (more quarrels and more shyness), more unsatisfactory love affairs, more worry, anxiety, and guilt, more unhappiness and crying, and more dependence on parents. It is difficult to understand why they also reported better grades and stronger ambition, unless this represented some sort of compensatory striving for acceptance. Lewis (1954), Rosenthal, Finkelstein, Ni, and Robertson (1959), and Rosenthal, Ni, Finkelstein, and Berkwits (1962) all present evidence from clinical studies that inhibited, neurotic children tend to have more constraint or excessive control in their family backgrounds than aggressive or delinquent children. By and large, these studies suggest that the combination of restrictiveness and hostility fosters considerable resentment, with some of it being turned against the self, or, more generally, experienced as internalized turmoil and conflict.

Restrictiveness versus Permissiveness in a Warm Context

Watson (1957) has carried out one of the few studies to investigate directly the consequences of strictness and permissiveness in intact families offering an adequate level of warmth to the child. Consistently strict and consistently permissive families were selected through nominations from parents, teachers, and social workers, and were finally screened after home interviews by social workers. Parent self-ratings and the children's ratings of their parents' discipline confirmed the classifications with a high degree of accuracy. The children were evaluated through direct observation under experimental conditions, and through projective techniques (doll play, thematic stories, and Rorschach). The results showed that children reared in a warm-permissive home were more independent (ease of assuming responsibility for own behavior), more friendly in interaction with adults (cooperation), moderately persistent in the fact of an impossible task (rather than either extreme), more creative, and less hostile on projective measures. Children reared in a warm-restrictive home were more likely to be dependent, unfriendly, to be either very high or very low in persistence, less creative, and to show more fantasy hostility. The similarity of these results to the general patterning of the findings in the study by Kagan and Moss is more than striking.

Maccoby (1961) pursued another aspect of the effects of warmth and permissiveness. Using the same children followed up by Sears at age twelve, she studied the antecedents of the tendency to enforce rules with peers. Maccoby found that parents who had been restrictive in the early years (evaluated when the child was five) had boys who were strict rule-enforcers at age twelve. Rule-enforcing boys also showed less overt aggression (teacher ratings), less misbehavior when the teacher was out of the room, and were highly motivated to do school work. On examining the interactions with warmth, she found maximum rule enforcement when mother was warm and restrictive, and the least rule enforcement when mother was warm and permissive. The results for girls were again perplexing, and suggest that we are going to have to do some different thinking about development in girls. The rule-enforcement measures for girls were associated with more misbehavior when the teacher was out of the room, and in other ways contained more aggressive rather than conforming implications. Consistent with this was the fact that mothers' punitiveness rather than restrictiveness predicted rule enforcement for girls. Maccoby's results for boys are consistent with the findings by R. R. Sears (1961) of least aggression in boys when mother was low in permissiveness and low in punitiveness (restrictive-warm), and with Meyers' (1944) findings of maximum conformity when mother was dominant and accepting (restrictive-warm).

There are a few studies to suggest that permissiveness in a warm context can also facilitate aggressive behavior, but perhaps of a different character, which might better be called social assertiveness. Baldwin (1949) related the nursery school behavior of children to home-observation ratings of mothers. Children from homes high in democracy (warmth, permissiveness, and rationality) were higher on socially outgoing behaviors of the hostile and domineering kinds as well as the friendly kind (as noted by Watson). In contrast to the aggression of children with hostile parents, however, the aggressing and bossing of children from democratic homes was quite successful and led to acceptance by the group. A somewhat related finding comes from a study by Levy (1943). When he divided his overprotective mothers into an indulgent type (warm, permissive, emotionally involved), and a dominant type (warm, restrictive, emotionally involved), he found that where mother was mainly indulgent, the child was rebellious, aggressive, disrespectful, and disobedient at home, but a model of deportment in school. Where mother was dominating, the child was more submissive, dependent, timid in school, neat, obedient, and polite. While both of these studies leave much to be desired in determining just which parental antecedents relate to the child behaviors, they both suggest the possibility that the kind of aggression which emerges from a warm-permissive environment is more easily turned on and off in response to reinforcing conditions, rather than being an uncontrolled, reflexive, emotional reaction.

Levin (1958) has suggested the possible importance of another dependent variable in thinking about the consequences of warmth and permissiveness. Levin measured the frequency with which children used adult dolls as agents of action in doll play (adult-role taking). The maximum adult-role taking occurred under the combination of warmth and permissiveness. If adult-role taking is assumed to reflect a positive modeling of the parent and the learning of adult ways of doing things, these findings are theoretically consistent with the greater independence (Watson) and achievement mastery (Kagan and Moss) noted earlier to be associated with permissiveness.

Summary: Restrictiveness versus Permissiveness

The research literature indicates a number of consistent consequences of restrictive and permissive approaches to child training. This dimension reflects the degree to which control is exerted (or not exerted) over the child, but the manner in which control is achieved can vary considerably. The consensus of the research suggests that both restrictiveness and permissiveness entail certain risks. Restrictiveness, while fostering well-controlled, socialized behavior, tends also to lead to fearful, dependent, and submissive behaviors, a dulling of intellectual striving and inhibited hostility. Permissiveness on the other hand, while fostering outgoing, sociable, assertive behaviors, and intellectual striving, tends also to lead to less persistence and increased aggressiveness.

Longitudinal analysis suggests that early restrictiveness by mother (prior to age three) leads more consistently to conforming, dependent behavior than later restrictiveness. Both boys and girls show some aggressive reactions (although of an inhibited form) to mothers' later restrictiveness.

The interactions of restrictiveness versus permissiveness with warmth versus hostility are particularly informative. Some of the salient findings are summarized in the accompanying table. The counter-aggression generating properties of hostility are apparent in the child of both permissive-hostile and restrictive-hostile parents. In the former, the aggression is expressed directly with little control. In the latter, the aggression is expressed in certain safe areas

Interactions In The Consequence of Warmth Versus
Hostility and Restrictiveness Versus Permissiveness

	Restrictiveness	Permissiveness
Warmth	Submissive, dependent, polite, neat, obedient (Levy) Minimal aggression (Sears) Maximum rule enforcement, boys (Maccoby) Dependent, not friendly, not creative (Watson) Maximal compliance (Meyers)	Active, socially outgoing, creative, successfully aggressive (Baldwin) Minimal rule enforcement, boys (Maccoby) Facilitates adult role taking (Levin) Minimal self-aggression, boys (Sears) Independent, friendly, creative, low projective hostility (Watson)
Hostility	"Neurotic" problems (clinical studies) More quarreling and shyness with peers (Watson) Socially withdrawn (Baldwin) Low in adult role taking (Levin) Maximal self-aggression, boys (Sears)	Delinquency (Gluecks, Bandura and Walters) Noncompliance (Meyers) Maximal aggression (Sears)

(with peers), but is more likely to be inhibited and turned against the self, or be revealed in manifestation of internal conflict. On theoretical grounds, the restrictive-hostile condition would be expected to produce the most defensive identification or identification with the aggressor. The many parallels between the effects of this condition with the results of the authoritarian personality studies should be apparent.

The findings for the warm-permissive condition are consistent with the recommendations of child-rearing specialists concerned with maximizing socially outgoing characteristics and individuality. The child with warm-permissive parents is socialized mainly through love, good models, reasons, and a trial-and-error learning of how his actions (which are a bit uncontrolled at times) have an impact on others.

A detailed examination of the processes by which permissiveness and restrictiveness have their effects has yet to be undertaken. A step in this direction is the experimental research on the effects of permissiveness which comes from a series of studies of doll-play techniques (Hollenberg and Sperry, 1951; P. S. Sears, 1951; Yarrow, 1948). When the child's behavior is measured over a series of experimental sessions under warm-permissive, interaction conditions, a general increase in a variety of response patterns is found. Such results are consistent with the common-sense notion that permissiveness serves as a generalized reinforcer for a wide range of responses, just as restrictive attitudes appear to have a generalized inhibitory effect. Future research might well address itself to a more careful examination of how breadth of control (variety of areas in which control is demanded), intensity of control, mode of control, and age of the child influence the generality of inhibited behavior in the child. The present research implies that all of these factors are important, but does not permit one to specify their relative importance. Research might also give closer consideration to the relative effectiveness of father and mother as inhibitory agents.

Consequences of Inconsistent Discipline

The concept of consistency in discipline is multifaceted and quite poorly understood, although everyone is quite ready to agree that inconsistency is *bad* for children. It is reasonable to assume that consistent behavior by the parent will increase the degree of predictability of the child's environment and lead to more stable behavior patterns. A problem arises, however, in understanding the effects of inconsistency, since inconsistency can take many forms, and research has by and large neglected to examine the effects of different types of inconsistency. Certain behaviors may be permitted at one time and not at others on a capricious basis, or because mother is present at one time and not another, or because mother's moods change from one time to another, or because one parent is present and not the other. Inconsistency might also be expected to have different effects as a function of the patterns of rewards and punishments utilized. For example, threatening punishment and not following through could have different effects from rewarding a behavior at one time and punishing it at another, or punishing at one time and doing nothing the next time. A kind of inconsistency can also arise when there is a discrepancy between what the child is rewarded for doing, what he is told to do, and what he sees others doing.

Confusion may also arise about the term *consistency,* depending upon the standards for judgment of what constitutes consistency. One parent might be literally and rigidly consistent, and another might be consistent with her rational goals for the child, though showing behavioral variability. Subtleties of this sort have not been closely examined.

Research on inconsistency has taken several approaches. Some have derived a conglomerate rating of the general stability of the parent-child interactions; some have evaluated the consistency over time for a single parent; and others have contrasted the severity of demands placed on the child by one parent with those of the other.

Probably the clearest and most consistent evidence on inconsistency comes from the delinquency studies (Andry, 1960; Bandura and Walters, 1959; Burt, 1929; Carr-Saunders, Mannheim, and Rhodes, 1944; Glueck and Glueck, 1950; McCord et al., 1959). These studies have repeatedly shown a higher incidence of erratic or inconsistent discipline, both within and between parents, to contribute to antisocial behavior. The evidence from McCord and associates (1959) is particularly clear in demonstrating that intra-parental inconsistency makes a contribution to crime rates in addition to that produced by a lack of warmth. A subsequent study of nondelinquent boys (McCord et al., 1961) also revealed greater consistency in discipline for mothers of nonaggressive boys than for mothers of aggressive boys.

Three additional studies have investigated the effects of inconsistency produced by differences in the parents' approach to discipline. Read (1945) provides suggestive evidence that when one parent of nursery school children is strict and the other permissive, more "unfavorable behavior" (aggression?) is displayed by the child than when both parents are strict or permissive. Considering only the cases where low demands are placed on the child, McCord and associates (1961) found that when one parent was punitive and the other was nonpunitive, boys were more likely to be aggressive than when both parents were punitive or nonpunitive. A similar positive association between inter-parental inconsistency and crime rates was demonstrated in an earlier study (McCord et al., 1959).

A few other consequences of inconsistency (not clearly defined) are suggested in studies by Terman and associates (1938) and by Sanford and associates (1943). Terman found that a category of irregular discipline (in contrast to strict or permissive) tended to be selected as descriptive of their upbringing by persons who later scored low on a marital happiness scale. Sanford defined a syndrome which he called "unstable home" in his study of a group of five- to fourteen-year-olds. Unstable home was defined in terms of the use of capricious discipline and overstimulation of the child. Families high on "unstable home" would repeatedly arouse the child to a high pitch through fatigue effects and overstimulation, and then punish the child for the resulting behavior. Unstable home was positively associated with anxious emotionality, low social feelings, and low conscientiousness.

Inconsistent discipline apparently contributes to "maladjustment," conflict, and aggression in the child. There is obviously a need for more carefully controlled research on different kinds of inconsistency, and a need to articulate the processes by which types of inconsistency affect the child.

A Look to the Future

It is painfully apparent that the social scientists who have set for themselves the task of unraveling the consequences of child-rearing practices are faced with a problem with infinite complexities. The literature reviewed implies that the research strategy has been one of the first establishing the more salient themes and then moving cautiously toward the variations on the themes produced by a more complex interaction of variables. To illustrate more concretely the potential rewards of pursuing these more complex interactions, we would like to close this review by summarizing a rather stimulating analysis by Bronfenbrenner (1961a). His data are based on teacher's ratings of responsibility and leadership for 192-tenth-grade boys and girls. Evaluations of parental child-rearing practices were obtained from the adolescents themselves, who by and large have been shown to be rather accurate observers of the parents.

Starting on familiar ground, Bronfenbrenner first found that rejection, neglect, and lack of discipline from father were associated with irresponsible behavior in boys. High levels of responsibility were related to warmth and nurturant attitudes, especially from mother, and with *moderately* strong discipline, especially from father. Bronfenbrenner also found that *too much* discipline impeded the development of responsibility. For girls, a dramatically different picture emerges. While rejection and neglect lead to low responsibility as for boys, the presence of strong *paternal* discipline is particularly debilitating, much more so than for boys. Again, the effect is curvilinear, but highest responsibility in girls is associated with a low-moderate level of discipline rather than the high-moderate level found for boys. There appear to be optimal levels of authority, with the optimum level higher for boys than for girls.

The results for leadership gave a similar picture with a slight change in focus. Rejection, neglect, parental absence, and protectiveness all related to low leadership for both sexes. For boys, leadership was facilitated by high nurturance, warm relations with parents, and principled discipline; however, these same factors served to discourage leadership in girls and foster dependency.

As noted earlier, girls receive considerably more affection and less physical punishment than boys. With greater earlier affection and less punitive or more love-oriented discipline, there is a risk of oversocialization in girls (parental power is high). The familiar findings that girls are more obedient, cooperative, anxious, and dependent are consistent with this analysis. Boys, on the other hand, are more likely to receive less affection, have greater demands for independence placed on them, and be disciplined with techniques which have less inhibitory power. With less affection, greater discipline is required to achieve a given effect. The net result, according to Bronfenbrenner, is a greater risk of undersocialization in boys. The upshot of this thinking is the hypothesis that the optimal balance of affection and control is different for the two sexes. The danger for girls is an overdose of both and for boys an underdose of both. These dangers are probably conditioned by sex differences in sensitivity, sex-typed parent-child relations, and sex-typing training goals.

Bronfenbrenner also examined the relative amount of authority wielded by each parent, apart from type of discipline used, and found this to relate to the child's behavior. Thus, paternal authority was found to facilitate responsibility in boys and impede it in girls. Taking this one step farther, both responsibility and leadership are facilitated by relatively greater salience of the same-sexed parent. The evidence indicates, however, that too much dominance of either parent leads to lower levels of responsibility and leadership (Bronfenbrenner, 1961b).

Implications

It is apparent that the consequences of disciplinary practices cannot be fully understood except in the context of the warmth of the parent-child relation, the prior history of disciplinary practices and emotional relations, the role-structure of the family, and the social and economic conditions under which a particular family unit is living. In view of these complexities, it also becomes apparent that many of the generalizations drawn from the research literature must be restricted to the kinds of populations studied. In essence, this means that our knowledge is most firm where mothers of working- and middle-class families are involved. Because of the difficulties in obtaining the cooperation of families at the lowest class levels, and fathers of all class levels, our knowledge is less complete for these sub-groups. Obviously, these gaps need to be pursued. It should also be noted that research has tended to focus initially on extreme practices. The majority of parents do not fall at these extremes and typically use a large variety of mixed procedures in discipline. There are probably many routes to being a "good parent" which vary with the personality of both the parents and children and with the pressures in the environment with which one must learn to cope. Analysis of the purer examples provided by extreme groups aids in understanding basic principles, but still leaves one somewhat at a loss when more complex interactions are involved.

Many potential readers of this chapter are faced daily with the problems of evaluating the adequency of parents as parents. Such evaluations are particularly crucial when there is a question of removing a child from a home or placing him in a foster home. The development of the Parent Attitude Research Instrument (PARI) by Schaefer and Bell (1958) has seemed to some to offer a hopeful procedure for aiding in their decisions. The failure even to mention research on the PARI in this review should not be interpreted as an oversight. With very few exceptions, the research with this instrument has not supported its usefulness (in its present form) for making valid predictions about parents. There is some research on questionnaire methods in progress which may eventually aid in such practical decisions, but the stage of practical utility is probably ten years off. On the other hand, research covered in this review does offer some practical suggestions for conceptualizing parental behavior in terms of a few elemental dimensions (and related consequences) which can be of aid in sensitizing one to things to look for in forming judgments about parents.

Some rather basic convictions about the consequences of various modes of child rearing have received support in this review. The importance of warmth and permissiveness in facilitating the growth of sociable, independent children has found repeated support. The debilitating effects of parental hostility in its many forms is certainly apparent. Even here, however, it should be noted that it is primarily extreme forms of hostility which have been demonstrated to have undesirable consequences. It is not yet clear to what degree a certain amount of openly hostile interaction between parent and child may actually facilitate the child's ability to cope with the realities of independent living in our society. The preliminary work by Bronfenbrenner is particularly provocative in suggesting that we should perhaps be thinking more in terms of optimal levels rather than "this is good and that is bad." In this same vein, caution should be exercised in supposing that use of love-oriented techniques of discipline is "good" and use of power-asserting techniques is "bad." This review has focused on specifying consequences, not evaluating their desirability. Illustrations of different values which might be placed on these various approaches to discipline are not difficult to find. Acceptance of boys by their peers in our culture requires an ability to react to provoked attack with an adequate counterattack. Disciplinary procedures which strongly inhibit or fail to provide models for such behavior, could foster adjustment problems for boys with their peers. Needless to say, one could go too far in generating feelings of anger and aggressive responses, as suggested by the delinquency studies. In evaluating the potential "goodness" and "badness" of love-oriented methods, there appears to be no evidence that the positive love-oriented methods (use of praise and reasons) have undesirable consequences. However, there is a possibility that the use of threats to the love relationship (negative love-oriented methods) may be so powerful a control method that the development of independence is jeopardized. The research also has suggested both "desirable" and "undesirable" consequences of more extreme forms of both restrictiveness and permissiveness. It is apparent that the task of the professional serving in a consultant role to parents requires considerable wisdom in judging the potential implications of a series of complexly interacting processes.

Possible further implications for those concerned with attempts to modify the behavior of parents and children can be drawn from the research findings and the speculation about the processes by which certain consequences in the child occur. First, where both mothers and fathers have been studied, most of the research has shown the father's influence on the child's behavior to be at least equal to that of the mother. Such findings should help to reinforce the growing trend toward inclusion of the father in treatment efforts. Next, where the disciplinary approach to the child does not seem to be producing the desired effects, this review suggests that it might be profitable to give attention to a detailed analysis of what the parent is rewarding and punishing, the timing of punishment in relation to what the child does, the degree of frustration involved, the clarity with which expectations are communicated to the child, the consistency of reinforcement within and between parents, and the types of models for the child implied by the parents' behavior. In many instances it is possible that making the parent more aware of how his or her behavior is having an impact on the child can motivate a change in the parent's handling of the child. As an aside, it should be pointed out that the effectiveness of various educational procedures in modifying parent behavior has not been adequately researched. A summary of the studies that have been made is presented by Brim (1959, pp. 290–317).

Scientific knowledge on discipline is progressing rapidly or slowly, depending on one's perspective. From the viewpoint of history, the gains in systematic knowledge over the past thirty years have been close to the spectacular. From the viewpoint of persons who must daily face the complex and seemingly impossible problems of troubled families, the gains must appear to border on the trivial.

References

Allinsmith, B. B. "Expressive styles: II. Directness with which anger is expressed," in D. R. Miller and G. E. Swanson, eds., *Inner Conflict and Defense.* New York: Holt, Rinehart, 1960, 315–336.

* Additional reference.

Allinsmith, W. "Moral standards: II. The learning of moral standards," in D. R. Miller and G. E. Swanson, eds., *Inner Conflict and Defense.* New York: Holt, Rinehart, 1960, 141–176.

Allinsmith, W., and T. C. Greening. "Guilt over anger as predicted from parental discipline: a study of superego development," *American Psychologist, 10* (1955), 320 (Abstract).

Andry, R. G. *Delinquency and Parental Pathology.* London: Metheun, 1960.

Aronfreed, J. "The effects of experimental socialization paradigms upon two moral responses to transgression," *J. Abnormal Soc. Psychol., 66* (1963), 437–448.

Aronfreed, J. "The nature, variety, and social patterning of moral responses to transgression," *J. Abnormal Soc. Psychol., 63* (1961), 223–240.

* Aronfreed, J. "The origin of self-criticism," *Psychol. Rev.,* in press.

Aronfreed, J., R. A. Cutick, and S. A. Fagan. "Cognitive structure, punishment, and nurturance in the experimental induction of self-criticism," *Child Development, 34* (1963), 281–294.

Baldwin, A. L. "The effect of home environment on nursery school behavior," *Child Development, 20* (1949), 49–61.

Baldwin, A. L., J. Kalhorn, and F. Breese. "Patterns of parent behavior," *Psychol. Monograph, 58* (1945), No. 3 (Whole No. 268).

Bandura, A. "Relationship of family patterns to child behavior disorders," Progress Report, USPHS, Project No. M-1734, Stanford University, 1960.

Bandura, A. "Social learning through imitation," in M. R. Jones, ed., *Nebraska Symposium on Motivation, 1962.* Lincoln: University of Nebraska Press, 1962.

Bandura, A., D. Ross, and S. A. Ross. "Transmission of aggression through imitation of aggressive models," *J. Abnormal Soc. Psychol., 63* (1961), 575–582.

Bandura, A., and R. H. Walters. *Adolescent Aggression.* New York: Ronald Press, 1959.

Becker, W. C., D. R. Peterson, L. A. Hellmer, D. J. Shoemaker, and H C. Quay. "Factors in parental behavior and personality as related to problem behavior in children," *J. Consult. Psychol., 23* (1959), 107–118.

Becker, W. C., D. R. Peterson, Z. Luria, D. J. Shoemaker, and L. A. Hellmer. "Relations of factors derived from parent-interview ratings to behavior problems of five-year-olds," *Child Development, 33* (1962), 509–535.

Brim, O. G. *Education for Child Rearing.* New York: Russell Sage Foundation, 1959.

Bronfenbrenner, U. "Socialization and social class through time and space," in E. E. Maccoby, T. M. Newcomb and E. L. Hartley, eds., *Readings in Social Psychology.* New York: Holt, Rinehart, 1958, 400–425.

Bronfenbrenner, U. "Some familial antecedents of responsibility and leadership in adolescents," in L. Petrullo and B. M. Bass, eds., *Leadership and Interpersonal Behavior.* New York: Holt, Rinehart, 1961 (a).

Bronfenbrenner, U. "Toward a theoretical model for the analysis of parent-child relationships in a social context," in J. C. Glidewell, ed., *Parental Attitudes and Child Behavior,* Springfield, Ill.: Charles C Thomas, 1961 (b).

Burt, C. *The Young Delinquent.* New York: Appleton-Century, 1929.

Burton, R. V., E. E. Maccoby, and W. Allinsmith. "Antecedents of resistance to temptation in four-year-old children," *Child Development,* 32 (1961), 689–710.

Carr-Saunders, A. M., H. Mannheim, and E. C. Rhodes. *Young Offenders.* New York: Macmillan, 1944.

Dollard, J., N. E. Miller, L. W. Doob, O. H. Mowrer, and R. Sears. *Frustration and Aggression.* New Haven: Yale University Press, 1939.

* Droppleman, L. F., and E. S. Schaefer. "Boys' and girls' reports of maternal and paternal behavior." Paper read at American Psychological Association, New York, August, 1961.

* Emmerich, W. "Parental identification in young children," *Genet. Psychol. Monographs,* 60 (1959), 257–308 (a).

* Emmerich, W. "Young children's discriminations of parent and child roles," *Child Development,* 30 (1959), 404–420 (b).

Eron, L. D., T. J. Banta, L. O. Walder, and J. H. Laulicht. "Comparison of data obtained from mothers and fathers on childrearing practices and their relation to child aggression," *Child Development,* 32 (1961), 457–572.

Estes, K. W. "An experimental study of punishment," *Psychol. Monographs,* 57 (1944), No. 263.

Finch, H. M. "Young children's concepts of parent roles," *J. Home Economics,* 47 (1955), 99–103.

Freud, S. *New Introductory Lectures on Psychoanalysis.* New York: Norton, 1933.

* Gardner, L. P. "An analysis of children's attitudes toward fathers," *J. Genet. Psychol.,* 70 (1947), 3–28.

Glueck, S., and E. T. Glueck. *Unraveling Juvenile Delinquency.* Cambridge: Harvard University Press, 1950.

Grinder, R. E. "Parental childrearing practices, conscience, and resistance to temptation of sixth grade children," *Child Development,* 33 (1962), 803–820.

Grinder, R. E., and R. E. McMichael. "Cultural influence on conscience development: resistance to temptation and guilt among Samoans and American Caucasians," *J. Abnormal Soc. Psychol.,* 66 (1963), 503–506.

* Hawkes, G. R., L. G. Burchinal, and B. Gardner. "Preadolescents' views of some of their relations with their parents," *Child Development,* 28 (1957), 393–399.

Healy, W., and A. F. Bronner. *Delinquents and Criminals: Their Making and Unmaking.* New York: Macmillan, 1926.

Heinicke, C. M. "Some antecedents and correlates of guilt and fear in young boys." Unpublished doctoral dissertation, Harvard University, 1953.

Hill, W. F. "Learning theory and the acquisition of values," *Psychol. Rev.,* 67 (1960), 317–331.

Hoffman, M. L. "Childrearing practices and moral development: generalizations from empirical research," *Child Development,* 34 (1963), 295–318.

Hoffman, M. L. "Power assertion by the parent and its impact on the child," *Child Development,* 31 (1960), 129–143.

Hoffman, M. L., and H. D. Saltzstein. "Parent practices and the child's moral orientation." Paper read at the American Psychological Association, Chicago, September, 1960.

Hollenberg, E., and M. Sperry. "Some antecedents of aggression and effects of frustration in doll play," *Personality*, 1 (1951), 32–43.

* Kagan, J. "The child's perception of the parent," *J. Abnormal Soc. Psychol.*, 53 (1956), 257–258.

* Kagan, J., B. Hosken, and S. Watson. "Child's symbolic conceptualization of parents," *Child Development*, 32 (1961), 625–636.

* Kagan, J., and J. Lemkin. "The child's differential perception of parental attributes," *J. Abnormal Soc. Psychol.*, 61 (1960), 440–447.

Kagan, J., and H. A. Moss. *Birth to Maturity: the Fels Study of Psychological Development*. New York: Wiley, 1962.

* Kohn, M. L. "Social class and parent-child relationship: an interpretation," *Amer. J. Sociol.*, 68 (1963), 471–480.

* Kohn, M. L., and E. E. Carroll. "Social class and the allocation of parental responsibilities," *Sociometry*, 23 (1960), 372–392.

Lambert, W. W., L. M. Triandis, and M. Wolf. "Some correlates of beliefs in the malevolence and benevolence of supernatural beings: a cross-societal study," *J. Abnormal Soc. Psychol.*, 58 (1959), 162–169.

Levin, H. "Permissive childrearing and adult role behavior," in D. E. Dulany, R. L. DeValois, D. C. Beardsley, and M. R. Winterbottom, eds., *Contributions to Modern Psychology*. New York: Oxford University Press, 1958, 307–312.

LeVine, B. B. "Punishment techniques and the development of conscience." Unpublished doctoral dissertation, Northwestern University, 1961.

Levy, D. M. *Maternal Overprotection*. New York: Columbia University Press, 1943.

Lewis, H. *Deprived Children*. London: Oxford University Press, 1954.

Maccoby, E. E. "The generality of moral behavior," *American Psychologist*, 14 (1959), 358 (Abstract).

Maccoby, E. E. "The taking of adult roles in middle childhood," *J. Abnormal Soc. Psychol.*, 63 (1961), 493–503.

McCord, W., J. McCord, and A. Howard "Familial correlates of aggression in non-delinquent male children," *J. Abnormal Soc. Psychol.*, 62 (1961), 79–93.

McCord, W., J. McCord, and I. K. Zola. *Origins of Crime*. New York: Columbia University Press, 1959.

MacKinnon, D. W. "Violations of prohibitions," in H. A. Murray, ed., *Explorations in Personality*. New York: Oxford University Press, 1938, 491–501.

Meyers, C. E. "The effect of conflicting authority on the child," *University Iowa Stud. Child Welf.*, 20 (1944), 31–88, No. 409.

* Miller, D. R., and G. E. Swanson. *Inner Conflict and Defense*. New York: Holt, Rinehart, 1960.

Radke, M. "Relation of parental authority to children's behavior and attitudes," *University Minnesota Inst. of Child Welf. Monograph*, (1946), No. 22.

Read, K. H. "Parents' expressed attitudes and children's behavior," *J. Consult. Psychol.*, 9 (1945), 95–100.

Roff, M. "A factorial study of the Fels Parent Behavior Scales," *Child Development,* 20 (1949), 29–45.

Rosenthal, M. J., M. Finkelstein, E. Ni, and R. E. Robertson. "A study of mother-child relationships in the emotional disorders of children," *Genet. Psychol. Monographs,* 60 (1959), 65–116.

Rosenthal, M. J., E. Ni, M. Finkelstein, and G. K. Berkwits. "Father-child relationships and children's problems," *AMA Arch. Gen. Psychiat.,* 7 (1962), 360–373.

* Roy, K. "Parents' attitudes toward their children," *J. Home Economics,* 42 (1950), 652–653.

Sanford, R. N., M. M. Adkins, R. B. Miller, and E. Cobb. "Physique, personality, and scholarship: a cooperative study of school children," *Soc. Res. Child Development Monograph,* 8 (1943), No. 1.

Schaefer, E. S. "A circumplex model for maternal behavior," *J. Abnormal Soc. Psychol.,* 59 (1959), 226–235.

Schaefer, E. S. "Converging conceptual models for maternal behavior and for child behavior," in J. C. Glidewell, ed., *Parental Attitudes and Child Behavior.* Springfield, Ill.: Charles C Thomas, 1961.

Schaefer, E. S., and R. Q. Bell. "Development of a parental attitude research instrument," *Child Development,* 29 (1958), 339–361.

Sears, P. S. "Doll play aggression in normal young children: influence of sex, age, sibling status, father's absence," *Psychol. Monographs,* 65 (1951), No. 6.

Sears, R. R. "The relation of early socialization experiences to aggression in middle childhood," *J. Abnormal Soc. Psychol.,* 63 (1961), 466–492.

Sears, R. R., E. E. Maccoby, and H. Levin. *Patterns of Child Rearing.* Evanston, Ill.: Row, Peterson, 1957.

Sears, R. R., L. Rau, and R. Alpert. "Identification and child training: the development of conscience." Paper read at the American Psychological Association, Chicago, September, 1960.

Sears, R. R., J. W. M. Whiting, V. Nowlis, and P. S. Sears. "Some childrearing antecedents of aggression and dependency in young children," *Genet. Psychol. Monographs,* 47 (1953), 135–234.

Skinner, B. F. *The Behavior of Organisms.* New York: Appleton-Century, 1938.

Symonds, P. M. *The Psychology of Parent-Child Relationships.* New York: Appleton-Century, 1939.

Takala, M., T. Nummenmaa, and U. I. Kauranne. "Parental attitudes and child-rearing practices: a methodological study," *Acta Academiae Paedogogicae Jyvaskylaensis,* 19 (1960), 1–75.

* Tasch, R. J. "The role of the father in the family," *J. Exp. Educ.,* 20 (1952), 319–361.

Terman, L. M., et al. *Psychological Factors in Marital Happiness.* New York: McGraw-Hill, 1938.

Unger, S. M. "Antecedents of personality differences in guilt responsivity," *Psychol. Rep.,* 10 (1962), 357–358.

Unger, S. M. "On the development of guilt-response systems." Unpublished doctoral dissertation, Cornell University, 1960.

Watson, G. "A comparison of the effects of lax versus strict home training," *J. Soc. Psychol.,* 5 (1934), 102–105.

Watson, G. "Some personality differences in children related to strict or permissive parental discipline," *J. Psychol.,* 44 (1957), 227–249.

Whiting, J. W. M., and I. L. Child. *Child Training and Personality.* New Haven: Yale University Press, 1953.

Yarrow, L. J. "Effect of antecedent frustration on projective play," *Psychol. Monographs,* 62 (1948), No. 6.

4
Father Dominance and Sex-Role Development in Kindergarten-Age Boys
Henry B. Biller

Every family has an internal structure characterized
by mother-father relationships as well as by parent-child
relationships. It has long been believed that the larger
structural context has some impact upon a child's
developing psychological system and, in particular, that
the relative power of mother and father affects the course of
child development. One of the interesting conclusions
in the following study is that the structures that objectively

exist in the family may be less important to children than the structures that the children believe exist. A distinction between the psychological and the objective structures is in evidence even at early ages, and it is the belief about parental structure that correlates most with personality variation.

The major hypotheses pertaining to the boy's sex-role development have been derived from theories of identification. These hypotheses postulate the importance of the father behaving in a particular way if his son is to identify with him and become masculine. Freudian theory (e.g., Fenichel, 1945) emphasizes the importance of the father being punitive and threatening; status envy theory (e.g., Whiting, 1960), the father being the primary consumer of resources; learning theory (e.g., Mowrer, 1950), the father being affectionate and rewarding; role theory (e.g., Parsons, 1955), the father being a primary dispenser of both rewards and punishments. Similar to role theorists, social power theorists (e.g., Bandura and Walters, 1963) stress that the parent who most controls valued resources is the most likely to be imitated. From each of these theories it could be predicted that the more the father is dominant (in terms of the particular theory's emphasized function), the more likely the boy will behave in a masculine manner.

Abridged from Henry B. Biller, "Father Dominance and Sex-Role Development in Kindergarten-Age Boys," in *Developmental Psychology*, 1 (1969), 87–94. Reprinted by permission of the American Psychological Association and the author.

This study was supported by Public Health Service Fellowship 1-Fl-MH-32, 808-01 from the National Institute of Mental Health. Computer services were generously supplied by the Duke University Computing Center. This paper is based on parts of a PhD dissertation submitted to the Graduate School of Arts and Sciences at Duke University and further data analysis. Additional data collected in the dissertation research are reported elsewhere (Biller, 1968). The author wishes to express his appreciation to Lloyd J. Borstelmann and Darwyn E. Linder of Duke University and David L. Singer of Teachers College, Columbia University, for their valuable suggestions; to the kindergarten directors, teachers, children, and parents who participated in this study; and to David Sherwood for interviewing parents and Pam Parker for scoring interview tapes.

A possible shortcoming of hypotheses derived from these theories of identification is that they do not differentiate among different aspects of sex role. Biller and Borstelmann (1967), attempting to conceptually refine distinctions discussed by Lynn (1959), consider three different aspects of sex role: sex-role orientation, sex-role preference, and sex-role adoption. Sex-role orientation (O) relates to the way an individual basically views himself in terms of maleness and/or femaleness. Sex-role preference (P) refers to the individual's preferential set toward socially defined symbols or representations of sex role. Sex-role adoption (A) pertains to the individual's masculinity and/or femininity as viewed by members of his society.

Most of the investigations relating to the impact of the father-son relationship on sex-role development were stimulated by hypotheses derived from theories of identification. The results of several studies (Freedheim, 1960; Heilbrun, 1965; Moulton, Burnstein, Liberty, and Altucher, 1966; Mussen and Distler, 1959; Mussen and Rutherford, 1963) suggest that when the boy views his father as more dominant than his mother, the boy's masculine development is facilitated. In a study measuring relative dominance of parents by placing them in decision-making situations, Hetherington (1965) found that boys from father-dominant homes scored more masculine on a projective sex-role test (IT Scale) than boys from mother-dominant homes. Such studies seem to be most supportive of hypotheses derived from the role and social power theories of identification. However, these studies have used only very restricted measures of sex-role development and do not provide evidence as to whether the father's behavior and/or the boy's perception of the father's behavior have differential effects depending on the aspect of sex role considered.

The present investigation was designed to explore the relationship among kindergarten-age boys' perceptions of father dominance, their fathers' dominance in father-mother interaction, and different aspects of the boys' sex-role development.

Method

Subjects

The subjects in the first phase of the study were 186 Caucasian boys attending private kindergarten classes in urban and suburban areas of Durham, North Carolina. The boys ranged in age from 4 years,

8 months, to 6 years, 2 months, with a mean age of 5 years, 5 months ($SD = 3.82$ months). Families ranged in socioeconomic status (SES) from upper lower class to upper middle class, with a high representation from the middle class. The SES ratings were made in terms of a 5-point scale of father's occupation, based on the work of Warner, Meeker, and Eells (1960). In the second phase of the study parents of 48 of the boys were interviewed to assess father dominance in father-mother interaction. These parents were selected on the basis of their sons' sex-role patterns. Taking into account high or low status on each of the three aspects of sex role, there was a random selection of 6 boys from each of the eight possible sex-role patterns. Of the 48 sets of parents who were chosen to participate, only 3 did not, and by further random selection they were replaced. The 48 boys whose parents were selected ranged in age from 4 years, 11 months, to 6 years, with a mean age of 5 years, 5 months ($SD = 3.64$ months) and their families were similar to the original group in terms of SES.

General procedure

The study was initially described to kindergarten directors, teachers, and parents as an investigation of varieties of boys' play. Several pre-experimental hours were spent at each school getting acquainted with the children. Children were seen individually for 10- to 15-minute sessions in private and relatively quiet rooms. Measures of O and P and perception of parental dominance were given during separate sessions. Teachers' ratings were used to assess A. Parents were sent letters asking for their cooperation in the parent interview phase of the study. These letters were signed by both the investigator and the director of the kindergarten which their son was attending. Parents were then contacted in a random order to set up interviews which took place in their homes at their convenience.

Measures of Sex Role

Sex-role orientation. Both figure drawings and a dramatic fantasy game were used to assess O. The child was asked to draw a person (DAP) and after he had designated its sex (he was asked who the drawing represented), he was instructed to draw a person of the opposite sex. With kindergarten-age children modes of differentiation of sex are usually limited to hair detail and/or gross distinction in clothing. A scoring system was developed in pilot work which was assumed to reflect differing levels or points of masculinity of O on a hypothetical continuum. The four levels of masculinity were: drawing a male first and differentiating (6 points), drawing a male first but not differentiating (4 points), drawing a female first but not differentiating (2 points), and drawing a female first and differentiating (1 point). There was a tendency for drawing a male first to be related to differentiating male and female figures ($x^2 = 3.80$, $p < .05$).

The other measure of O was an extensively modified version of Brown's IT Scale (Brown, 1956). In order to make the IT figure more sexually neutral in appearance, following a suggestion by Hall (Brown, 1962), only the face was presented rather than the whole body. The IT figure was referred to as "a child playing a make-believe game," a game in which "the child can be anybody or do anything in the whole world." The child designated who IT was being and what IT was wearing and doing from among various sets of pictures including people (Indian Chief or Indian Princess; man or woman), wearing apparel (men's clothes or women's clothes; men's shoes or women's shoes), and tasks (working with building tools or cooking utensils; fixing broken objects or washing and ironing). A point was scored for each masculine designation and 2 additional points (1 each) were scored if the boy, when questioned, gave the child a boy's name and said the child would become a father. Split-half reliability computed by the Spearman-Brown formula was .89.

Sex-role preference. Both a toy-preference and a game-preference task were used to assess P. Following Anastasiow's (1964) procedure the boy was asked to choose which toys he would like to play with the most. Anastasiow graphically reproduced five masculine toys (toy soldier, 4 points; fire engine, 3 points; gun, 2 points; truck, 1 point; blocks, 0 points) and five feminine toys (doll, 5 points; dishes, 4 points; beads, 3 points; purse, 2 points; comb and brush, 1 point) and developed a procedure in which there were 45 paired comparisons. In the present study, as would be expected, masculine and feminine scores were highly negatively correlated (—.78), and it was decided to subtract feminine scores from masculine scores in computing total toy-preference scores.

Game preference was also measured through picture choice. Pictures of the same two boys playing four masculine games (archery, baseball, basketball, and football) and four feminine games (hop-scotch, jacks, dancing, and jumprope) which had been found to be highly sex typed by Rosenberg and Sutton-Smith (1964) were drawn on 3×5 inch cards. The boy was shown two games at a time and asked to choose which game he would like to play the most. There were 16 choice situations; every masculine game was paired with every feminine game, and 1 point was given for each masculine choice. Split-half reliability computed by the Spearman-Brown formula was .78.

Sex-role adoption. A rating scale of masculinity of A was designed to assess the boy's relative assertiveness, aggressiveness, competitiveness, independence, and activity directed toward physical prowess and mastery of the environment. Items assessing lack of masculinity in terms of the boy's relative passivity, dependency, and timidity were also included. There were 16 items in all, 9 assumed to be characteristic of high masculinity, 7 of low masculinity. Concrete descriptions were given of each behavior to be rated (e.g., "is active and energetic, on the move, plays hard"; "leads other children, organizes play activities, assigns tasks to others"; "is timid around others, is fearful when introduced to new adults and children, fears physical contact"). Each boy was rated on each item in terms of a 5-point scale, very frequently, frequently, sometimes, seldom, and never. Each item was scored either 0, 1, 2, 3, or 4. For example, for the 9 items assumed to be characteristic of high masculine A, 4 points were scored when the behavior was checked as very frequently occurring, no points when it was checked as never occurring. Two teachers' ratings were available for 165 of the 186 subjects and in these cases an average A score was computed. Interrater reliability for total scores ranged from .75 to .96.

Measures of Father Dominance

Child interviews. The questions were similar to those Freedheim (1960) used for assessing childrens' perceptions of father dominance. The questions were selected and modified through pilot work, so that they were suitable for kindergarten-age children, and questions in the area of competence were added. There was a total of 20 items: 5 each for decision making (e.g., "Who is the boss at home?" "Who says which TV program your family watches?"), competence (e.g., "Who in your family knows the most about animals?" "If a light bulb in your house goes out, who puts in a new one?"), nurturance (e.g., "Who gives you the most gifts and toys?" "Who takes you the most places you want to go?"), and limit setting (e.g., "Who tells you what time to go to bed?" "Who tells you how to behave at meals?"). If the boy named the father in answering a question, 4 points were scored, and if he named the mother, no points were scored. If he responded by saying "Both" or "Don't Know," a more specific statement was asked for (i.e., "Who does it the most?"). If he then said "Father," 3 points were scored and if he said "Mother," 1 point was scored. If he still did not designate a particular parent, 2 points were scored. Split-half reliability computed by the Spearman-Brown formula was .81.

Parent interviews. Father dominance in father-mother interactions was inferred from Farina's (1960) interview technique. A research assistant who had no information concerning the boys in the study conducted the interviews. Each parent was first asked individually how he would respond to certain hypothetical problem situations concerning child behavior. After the mother and father had responded individually to the problem situations, they were then brought together, presented with the same problem situations and asked to come to joint agreements. (Farina's problem situations were modified to make them appropriate for parents of 5-year-old boys.) The following are some of the problem situations:

As you look out the window you see your son angrily knock a girl off her tricycle. Your husband [wife] has punished your son for something he did. As he walks by now you hear him mumble a nasty description about his father [mother].

Twice in the last hour you have told your son to pick up his toys. As you look around now you see that he's stopped working and is now looking off into the air. You ask him a third time but he refuses to pick up his toys.

A second research assistant with no knowledge of the data from other phases of the study transcribed and scored the tape-recorded interviews. Father dominance in terms of any specific index could be scored a maximum of 12 times, once for each situation. Each time the father spoke first, spoke most, or spoke last, a point was scored. Each time the mother passively accepted the father's decision a point was scored, and each time the father passively accepted the mother's decision a point was subtracted. Each time, in terms of the final solution, the mother moved more toward acceptance of the father's decision than he moved toward acceptance of her decision, a point was scored.

Five randomly selected interview tapes were independently scored by the author. Similar to Farina's findings, there was virtually perfect interscorer agreement. There were some slight disagreements concerning the exact number of seconds a particular parent talked and concerning the classification of certain parental solutions, but these disagreements did not affect the father-dominance score.

Results

Relations Among the Measures of Masculinity

It was expected that the relationships among measures of the same aspect of sex role would be higher than relationships among measures of different aspects of sex role. The results conformed with such expectations. . . . Small positive but significant relationships [were found] among the different aspects of sex role consistent with previous studies and a multiaspect conception of sex-role development (Biller and Borstelmann, 1967). An overall O score was computed which allowed for approximately equal weighting of DAP and IT scores. A similar procedure was followed in combining the toy-preference and game-preference scores into an overall P score.

Relations Among the Measures of Father Dominance

The results concerning the boys' perceptions of their parents were similar to previous studies with young children (Dubin and Dubin, 1965). Fathers were perceived to be generally more dominant, . . . decision making, . . . and competent than mothers. Mothers were perceived as significantly more limit setting . . . but not as more nurturant than fathers. (The nurturance items in the present study did not involve caretaking where mothers tend to be more dominant but were concerned with positive attention giving.) Although there were large individual differences among families in the father-mother interactions, there was no overall tendency for either paternal or maternal dominance. The boys' perception of father dominance was significantly related ($r = .46$) . . . to their fathers' dominance in father-mother interaction. The specific areas of perceived father dominance showed generally low but positive relationships with father dominance in father-mother interaction ($r = .29$ for decision making; $r = .22$ for competence; $r = .27$ for limit setting; $r = .11$ for nurturance).

Father Dominance and Masculinity

A strong relationship was found between the degree boys perceive their fathers as dominant and the boys' masculinity.[1] For all three aspects of sex role, a high level of perceived father dominance was associated with a higher degree of masculinity than either the medium or low levels, and the medium level was associated with a higher degree of masculinity than the low level (see Table 1). With respect to size of relationship with perceived father dominance, the order was O ($r = .58$), P ($r = .34$), and A ($r = .24$). The relationships were similar when the individual measures of O and P were considered.

The specific areas of perceived father dominance generally were more strongly related to O than to P or A. Perceived father decision making correlated .46 with O, .39 with P but only .19 with A. Per-

TABLE 1. Means and Standard Deviations of Sex-Role Scores in Relation to Perceived Father Dominance

Dominance	N	M	SD
Orientation			
High	59	27.17	9.72
Medium	67	16.90	11.78
Low	60	8.18	8.66
Preference			
High	59	18.29	8.86
Medium	67	13.47	8.84
Low	60	9.63	8.82
Adoption			
High	59	43.10	9.08
Medium	67	38.45	10.19
Low	60	35.38	9.83

1. Tables presenting the results of analyses of variance were presented in the original article, as well as the results of numerous separate tests of significance. —[EDITOR]

ceived father competence correlated .36 with O but only .20 with P and .21 with A. Perceived father nurturance and perceived father limit setting showed significant correlations only with O ($r = .29$ for nurturance; $r = .27$ for limit setting).

In terms of the relationship between perceived father dominance and sex-role development, the 48 boys whose parents were interviewed were similar to the total subject group.

As can be seen in Table 2, father dominance in father-mother interaction was also found to be related to the boy's sex-role development. A high degree of father dominance was related to high O and high P but there was little difference in O and P between boys with low and medium levels of father dominance. There was only a slight tendency for a low degree of father dominance in father-mother interaction to be associated with low A. Correlations indicated low but fairly consistent relationships between father dominance in father-mother interaction and the aspects of sex role; $r = .30$ with O, $r = .24$ with P, and $r = .20$ with A. The relationships were similar when the individual measures of O and P were considered.

Discussion

The degree to which the boy views his father as dominant seems to influence his sex-role development, but the effect seems somewhat dependent on which aspect of sex role is being considered. In terms of

Table 2. Means and Standard Deviations of Sex-Role
Scores in Relation to Father Dominance
in Father-Mother Interaction

Dominance	N	M	SD
Orientation			
High	16	26.00	12.42
Medium	15	12.33	11.25
Low	17	13.17	14.20
Preference			
High	16	18.06	10.49
Medium	15	11.80	7.90
Low	17	10.29	8.20
Adoption			
High	16	41.81	10.95
Medium	15	40.27	11.87
Low	17	38.06	11.87

degree of association with perceived father dominance, the order was O, P, and A. It may be that sex-role development progresses in a relatively stage-like manner; O development may, to some extent, precede P development; and P development may, to some extent, precede A development. The boy may be more influenced in the earlier stages of sex-role development by familial interactions than he is in later stages when his personal characteristics, such as his physique, and his interactions with peers and other adults attain more significance (Biller and Borstelmann, 1967).

The role theory (e.g., Parsons, 1955) and the social power theory (e.g., Bandura and Walters, 1963) hypotheses seemed to be supported more than other identification theory hypotheses in that the specific areas of perceived father dominance appeared to have an additive influence on sex-role development. When perception of father dominance was considered in terms of its components, father dominance in decision making and competence seemed relatively more important than father dominance in nurturance and limit setting.

The parent interview measures of father dominance seemed to be assessing the degree to which the father played a masculine role in his family, at least in his interactions with his wife. By being the family decision maker, the father seems to make himself more discriminable from the mother, along with increasing the incentive value of the masculine role. A high degree of father dominance in father-mother interaction seemed to facilitate O and P development.

Father dominance in father-mother interaction showed consistent but weaker relationships with sex-role development than did the boy's perception of father dominance. The boy's behavior seems much determined by his particular perception of reality and it may be that his view of the father is the most veridical measure. The boy's perception of his father may also be influenced by his mother's behavior. In father-mother interaction some mothers encouraged their husbands to make decisions while others appeared to prevent their husbands from serving as adequate models by constantly competing with them for the decision-making role.

Other analyses of the interview tapes have suggested the seeming complex influences of family interactions on the boy's sex-role development. Several of the boys who were not very masculine had fathers who were dominant in terms of father-mother interaction and generally seemed masculine, but also appeared to be controlling and restrictive of their sons' behavior. For instance, this type of dominant father seemed to punish his son for disagreeing with him. The boy's masculine development appears most facilitated when his father is dominant (a masculine model) and also allows and encourages the boy to be dominant. It seems that such a situation is particularly important in A development. It also seemed that in families where the mother and father were competing for the decision-making function, boys were often very restricted. It may be that in some families when the mother does not allow her husband to be dominant he is more apt to attempt to dominate his son in a restrictive and controlling manner. Much more research concerning the effects of family dynamics needs to be done if one is to better understand the sex-role development process.

References

Anastasiow, N. S. "Success in school and boys' sex role patterns," *Child Development,* 36 (1964), 1053–1066.

Bandura, A., and R. H. Walters. *Social Learning and Personality Development.* New York: Holt, Rinehart, 1963.

Biller, H. B. "A multiaspect investigation of masculine development in kindergarten age boys," *Genet. Psychol. Monographs,* 76 (1968), 89–138.

Biller, H. B., and L. J. Borstelmann. "Masculine development: An integrative review," *Merrill-Palmer Quart.,* 13 (1967), 253–294.

Brown, D. G. "Sex role preferences in children: Methodological problems," *Psychol. Rep.,* 11 (1962), 477.

Brown, D. G. "Sex role preferences in young children," *Psychol. Monographs,* 70 (1956), 14 (Whole No. 421).

Dubin, R., and E. R. Dubin. "Children's social perceptions: A review of research," *Child Development,* 36 (1965), 809–838.

Farina, A. "Patterns of role dominance and conflict in parents of schizophrenic patients," *J. Abnormal Soc. Psychol.,* 61 (1960), 31–38.

Fenichel, O. *The Psychoanalytic Theory of Neurosis.* New York: Norton, 1945.

Freedheim, D. K. "An investigation of masculinity and parental role patterns." Unpublished doctoral dissertation, Duke University, 1960.

Heilbrun, A. G., Jr. "An empirical test of the modeling theory of sex role learning," *Child Development,* 36 (1965), 789–799.

Hetherington, E. M. "A developmental study of the effects of sex of the dominant parent on sex role preference, identification, and imitation in children," *J. Person. Soc. Psychol.,* 2 (1965), 188–194.

Lynn, D. B. "A note on sex differences in the development of masculine and feminine identification," *Psychol. Rev.,* 66 (1959), 126–135.

Moulton, P. W., E. Burnstein, P. Liberty, and N. Altucher. "The patterning of parental affection and dominance as a determinant of guilt and sex typing," *J. Person. Soc. Psychol.,* 4 (1966), 356–363.

Mowrer, O. H. *Learning Theory and Personality Dynamics.* New York: Ronald Press, 1950.

Mussen, P. H., and L. Distler. "Masculinity, identification and father-son relationships," *J. Abnormal Soc. Psychol.,* 59 (1959), 350–356.

Mussen, P. H., and E. Rutherford. "Parent-child relations and parental personality in relation to young children's sex role preferences," *Child Development,* 34 (1963), 589–607.

Parsons, T. "Family structure and the socialization of the child," in T. Parsons and R. F. Bales, eds., *Family, Socialization, and Interaction Process.* Glencoe, Ill.: Free Press, 1955.

Rosenberg, B. G., and B. Sutton-Smith. "The measurement of masculinity and femininity in children: An extension and revalidation," *J. Genet. Psychol.,* 104 (1964), 259–264.

Warner, W. L., M. Meeker, and K. Eells. *Social Class in America.* New York: Harper, 1960.

Whiting, J. W. M. "Sorcery, sin, and the superego: A cross-cultural study of some mechanisms of social control," in M. P. Jones, ed., *Nebraska Symposium on Motivation.* Lincoln: University of Nebraska Press, 1960.

5

The Study of Ordinal Position:
Antecedents and Outcomes
Edward E. Sampson

Structure and composition of families are a function of
sibling relationships as well as of parental relationships. A
great deal of research attention has been given to the
difference between single-child families and multiple-child
families and to the effect of birth order in multiple-child
families. Such factors are believed to affect child
development because birth order is correlated with such
matters as the experience of the parents, the relative status

and dominance among siblings, and the availability of different kinds of models to be imitated. Sampson reviews the literature on birth order effects and points out those effects which seem to be found consistently.

Everybody, regardless of scientific bent, would undoubtedly be willing to agree that order of birth plays a role in influencing personality and behavior. The parent is cognizant of the fact that his own actions, anxieties, abilities, and perhaps aspirations change as a function of the sex of his child and the order of its birth. An adult who reflects upon his own childhood experiences may recall many instances of differential treatment as a function of his sex and ordinal position. Scientific psychology has been interested for some decades in the effects of ordinal position on intellectual achievement and on social adjustment. A review article by Jones (1931) suggested that during the period 1881–1931 over 250 studies were conducted, focusing primarily on two outcome variables: physical traits and the incidence of disease. The paper reported 88 references, for the most part discussing the factor of intelligence. After reviewing this extensive array of literature Jones stated that, "The emotional or motivational 'average score' for a given birth rank has in itself no explanatory significance and may serve merely to obscure the operation of diverse and sometimes opposing factors" (p. 237).

In 1937, Murphy, Murphy, and Newcomb summarized over 40 studies (including some mentioned by Jones) dealing with a more extensive array of variables, yet still concentrating heavily on the factors of intelligence and adjustment. After examining these studies, most of which indicated rather conflicting findings, the authors stated that the results were inconclusive or even contradictory because, "the objective fact of ordinal position without regard to its meaning to the child, to the siblings, and to the parents, is sure to yield meager psychological results." They continued, suggesting that, "His (the child's)

Abridged from Edward E. Sampson, "The Study of Ordinal Position: Antecedents and Outcomes," *Progress in Experimental Personality Research,* vol. 2, edited by Brendan A. Maher (New York: Academic Press, 1965), 175–228. Reprinted by permission of Academic Press, Inc., and the author.

psychological position in the family is of utmost importance for the development of social behavior, but 'psychological position' is by no means completely dependent on birth order" (pp. 362–363).

If we ask three broad questions relevant to the area—"Does ordinal position make any difference?"; "If so, what are these differences?"; "Why do we find such differences?"—we note that, for the most part, this earlier work was directed toward answering the first two questions, leaving the third to armchair speculation and post hoc interpretation of oftentimes insignificant findings. Furthermore, as of 1937, the answer to the first questions yielded so many inconsistencies that, for awhile, concern with ordinal position disappeared.

A few individuals continued their work within the older mode of ordinal position research, computing rates of delinquency, schizophrenia, etc., for different ordinal positions. We encounter few studies dealing with the issues raised by the third question, and these focused specifically on the relationship between parental behavior and developmental trends in the child. For the most part, they were less concerned with ordinal position than with the broad array of general socialization variables.

A newer, more systematic search for ordinal position effects began with the series of publications by Koch (1954; 1955; 1956a, b, c, d; 1957). It was not until 1959, however, with the publication of Schachter's *The Psychology of Affiliation,* that ordinal position took its place among the legitimate foci of psychological investigation. The focus had shifted, with the controlled psychological experiment replacing the correlational field surveys of the past, and with the variables of anxiety and affiliation replacing intelligence and adjustment.

Personality Variables

It has already been implied in the preceding section that ordinal position should produce different kinds of personality organization as a function of the differential environmental experiences. In this section we shall consider in turn some of the major variables of personality which have been more recently examined in the research literature.

Intellectual Functioning

An attempt is made to separate those studies which deal mainly with measures of intelligence or some aspect of intellectual capacity from those which deal with the outcome variables of intellectual achievement or eminence. The latter concerns will be discussed [later] in this chapter.

As indicated previously, the concern with differential intellectual functioning has been a major focus of the work on ordinal position since its inception. Theoretically, one might suspect that the firstborn would have an advantage intellectually over the later born. West (1960) cited Faris's "isolation theory," which suggested that minimal interaction with sibs may produce qualities favorable to the development of scientists who, we assume, have a higher level of intelligence. West also suggested that other factors which are related to ordinal position, for example, the availability of money and the favoring of the first, might produce a higher level of scientific intellect. The previous section suggested that the firstborn receives initially a greater amount of parental attention and verbal stimulation, which might also lead to a higher intellectual development. The earlier demands and expectations of the parents might also serve to motivate the first to achieve intellectually, as might the more adult-oriented concern of the first as compared with the second born. Not all theoretical accounts, however, point in the direction of favoring the first over the second. Thus, for example, the assumed overprotection of the first (which does not seem fully warranted by the data), which leads to greater dependency and conformity, does not sound like the kind of behavior often thought to mark the intelligent, presumably independent, curious, even creative person. It might well be expected, then, that the kind of "school-bookish" intelligence that most tests measure would favor the firstborn, whereas the second born might be favored in the more creative intellectual pursuits.

Jones's (1931) review indicated some conflicting empirical findings with respect to intelligence and ordinal position. In some of the later work, however, there appeared to be a more consistent indication favoring the firstborn child. Both Koch (1954) and Altus (1962), using different kinds of subjects—Koch used young children from two-sib families, whereas Altus used male and female college students—found that firstborn males scored higher on verbal abilities than later born males, but that there was no difference between first and later males in mathematical aptitude. Altus did find, however, that the first female was higher on mathematical aptitude than the later female, although this was not a significant trend. Pierce (1959) reported that high-achieving high school students in a sample of 10th and 12th graders were predominantly firstborn or only children. On the other hand, Schoonover (1959), using a sample of elementary school children from Michigan, found no difference between the older and younger sibs in intelligence or achievement as measured by deviations from norms for their chronological age. She suggested that her results agreed with the earlier results of Hsiao (1931), and Jones and Hsiao (1928), but disagreed with those of Thurstone and Jenkins (1929), Willis (1924), and, as we have seen, with those of both Koch (1954) and Altus (1962).

Two separate studies have indicated that the sex of his sibling is an important determinant of an individual's intelligence. Koch (1954) found that those with a male sibling scored higher on the verbal test than those with a female sib. This agreed with Schoonover (1959), who stated that sibs with brothers have higher scores than sibs with sisters in all mental and achievement measures. With respect to age spacing, Schoonover reported that this made no apparent difference. Similarly, it did not appear to be a significant contributor to Koch's data. Family size does seem to be a factor, however, at least according to Pierce (1959).

Most studies indicate that the firstborn attains a higher level of eminence, fame, and intellectual outcome than the later born. This adds to the total weight of findings, which suggest that there is a relationship between ordinal position and intelligence, appearing to favor the firstborn, especially if he comes from a small family and is either an only child or has a younger brother to spur him on.

Need for Affiliation

Until the 1959 publication by Schachter, little work had been concerned with affiliative needs in persons of differing birth rank. Schachter's significant findings, indicating that firstborn persons, when anxious, tended to affiliate more than later born persons, inspired numerous studies relating affiliation as a need, or as a behavioral response to ordinal position. In this section, we mainly examine those studies bearing directly on the measure of affiliation as a need. . . .

In the studies already surveyed employing either a projective measure of the need for affiliation [e.g., the TAT or the French Test of Insight (French, 1958)] or some variety of paper-and-pencil test (e.g., Edwards Personal Preference Scale), we find inconsistent results. Rosenfeld (1964) administered the TAT or the French Test of Insight to a series of subjects in five independent studies; his samples varied from psychology students and dormitory residents at the University of Kansas to high school seniors in Detroit. He found no significant main effect of ordinal position or sex, and no significant interactions using measured need for affiliation as a dependent variable. Employing Edwards Personal Preference Scale on a group of Berkeley high school students from two-sib families, we obtained data (Sampson and Hancock, 1962) that similarly indicate no significant difference in the need for affiliation as a function of ordinal position, sex of subject, or sex of sibling.

These results, however, are to be contrasted with those of Dember (1963), who found that the firstborn scored higher on the need for affiliation than the later born. Although not employing a projective test, Gerard and Rabbie (1961), using paid college student subjects, found that significantly more later born preferred to wait alone when under fear arousal than firstborn. Other studies . . . [described elsewhere] also generally indicated this kind of affiliative behavior for the firstborn (e.g., Radloff, 1961; Sarnoff and Zimbardo, 1961; Schachter, 1959; Zimbardo and Formica, 1963). We have previously reported the study by Conners (1963), the results of which indicated that among a sample of fraternity men, the firstborn scored *lower* on TAT measured need for affiliation than later borns.

Turning from studies employing test measures for affiliation, we find that Patterson and Zeigler (1941), using a sample of both schizophrenics and normal controls, found that the firstborn were significantly below the group in ratings as "good mixers." This finding was contradicted by the studies of Schooler and Scarr (1962), and Schooler and Raynsford (1961), which indicated that among a female sample of chronic schizophrenics, the first is more sociable, especially under stress (Schooler and Raynsford). This is complicated by the results of Bossard and Boll (1955), which described the later born as more sociable, and those of Hillinger (1958), which indicated that the firstborn is more introverted than the second.

If we consider only those studies which presumably have employed the same kind of projective measure of the need for affiliation (i.e., Rosenfeld's studies, the Dember study, and the Conners study), we find one set of results indicating no significant ordinal position effect (Rosenfeld), one indicating that firstborn score higher (Dember), and one indicating that second born score higher (Conners). Both Rosenfeld's and Dember's samples contained men and women, while Conners used only fraternity men. The precise conditions of measurement were specified only by Rosenfeld, who indicated that the test was administered under neutral conditions. It is likely that thought about affiliation was aroused under the fraternity measurement conditions in Conners' study, but it is unknown what kind of affiliative arousal existed in Dember's study. As Schachter and others have indicated, only under a specific emotional arousal do firstborn prefer to affiliate more than the second. It is possible, therefore, that the neutral conditions of Rosenfeld's study and the probably neutral conditions of Dember's study produced only slight but often nonsignificant differences in the favor of the firstborn. It should be noted that the majority of the directional differences in Rosenfeld's studies favored the firstborn over the later in high-need affiliation. On the other hand, when a more direct arousal of affiliation exists, as it possibly did among Conners' sample of fraternity men, the second born express greater affiliative concern in their fantasy behavior than the first. It is possible that under conditions which arouse specific fear or dependency needs, the firstborn desire to affiliate more than the second (cf. Gerard and Rabbie, 1961; Radloff, 1961; Sarnoff and Zimbardo, 1961; Schachter, 1959); when affiliation itself is directly aroused, the second born express more fantasy concern over affiliation than the first; and when the conditions of arousal are neutral, there is little or no difference between the first and the second born in affiliative fantasy or behavior. These are, however, simply speculations offered to account for some of the inconsistencies which have emerged in the empirical results. Their confirmation awaits direct testing in a single study.

Our conclusion at this point is that, as yet, no unequivocal relationship has been demonstrated between ordinal position and the *measured need* for affiliation; as we shall see later, the picture with respect to *behavior* which may be interpreted as involving affiliation is more clearly in favor of the firstborn.

General Anxiety

Concern with anxiety and ordinal position has two major roots. On the one hand, some earlier theoretical speculation centered about the potential for neuroticism of the firstborn child; he was thought to be overprotected, spoiled, subjected to anxious and inconsistent parental behavior, etc. This approach would lead one to expect the firstborn to be more anxious than the later born. On the other hand, we have the more recent concern, again inspired by Schachter's 1959 book, which suggests a relation between ordinal position and affiliative responses to anxiety and fear arousal. In this section, we attempt to concentrate mainly on measures of anxiety, either physiological or self-report. . . .

As with many of the personality measures, the picture with respect to anxiety is by no means consistent. Pauline S. Sears (1951) found that mothers rated the firstborn of a like-sexed pair as more fearful, worrisome, and anxious than the second. Reaching a somewhat similar conclusion, Macfarlane et al. (1954) reported mothers' ratings of their children which indicated that the firstborn child, especially the girl, is rated as displaying greater tension and withdrawal than the second born girl. A somewhat similar pattern was observed for the male, especially with respect to withdrawal. In the more directly experimental literature, Yaryan and Festinger (1961) indicated that the firstborn among a sample of female high school students were rated as less comfortable than the later born prior to taking an expected test. Consistent with this was the Schachter finding (1959) that fear-arousing situations arouse more anxiety in the first than in the second born among female college students.

Up to this point, it appears as if the firstborn is more generally anxious than the later born. However, Weller (1962) found no difference between first and second (among a sample of college females) in aroused anxiety, where this refers to the difference between pre- and post-experimental arousal, as measured by an adjective checklist. He did find, however, that in the high-anxiety condition of the experiment (where subjects were led to expect a high level of pain), the later born subjects entered the experiment with higher anxiety than either the firstborn or only children. Moore (1964) reported no difference between first and later born college students on a self-report measure of anxiety. Rosenfeld reported that the later born had higher measured test anxiety in four of his five studies. And finally, we have found in our data (Sampson and Hancock, 1962) that on a measure of test anxiety administered to Berkeley high school students from two-sib families, the firstborn reported less anxiety than the second born, regardless of their own sex or the sex of their siblings.

If we put these data together, we find that although mothers generally describe their first as more anxious than their later born child, two studies indicate that the firstborn have higher anxiety than the later (Schachter, 1959; Yaryan and Festinger, 1961); three indicate that the second born have higher anxiety than the first (Rosenfeld, 1964, unpublished; Sampson and Hancock, 1962, unpublished; Weller, 1962); and two indicate no difference (Moore, 1964; Weller, 1962). On this basis, it appears that there is no clear conclusion about the relationship between ordinal position and anxiety. However, at least with respect to test anxiety, which is presumably linked to academic achievement, the later born appears more anxious than the firstborn. If we consider the tentative conclusions concerning intelligence and intellectual achievement (i.e., school success) discussed [elsewhere in this chapter] the greater test anxiety of the later born may be a realistic self-report appraisal of his academic difficulties.

Dependency-Submissiveness versus Independence-Dominance

On the theoretical side, as we have already mentioned, the hypothesis is that the firstborn child should be more dependent than the later born, presumably because of (a) parental overprotection, (b) parental inexperience, and (c) parental inconsistency (Schachter, 1959; Sears et al., 1957). Each of these is assumed to frustrate the firstborn child's dependency needs and lead to a higher level of the need. On the other hand, however, it has been suggested that as compared with the later born, the firstborn child is expected to take the dominant role in family interaction (Sletto, 1934), to be a responsible parent surrogate (Rosen, 1961; Sampson, 1962), and to be a responsible adult earlier (Bakan, 1949; Bossard and Boll, 1955; Davis, 1959; Rosen, 1961). It might be hypothesized that both kinds of pressures are operating on the firstborn child, the result of which is to develop some degree of *dependency conflict* within the firstborn rather than a more simply conceived high need for dependence or a high need for independence.

If we use the scheme proposed by Kasl, Sampson, and French (1964), we may refer to two separate dimensions, each having an approach and an avoidance region. One dimension involves a need for dependence, the other, a need for independence. Conceptualized in this manner, an individual may be thought as having a high need to approach dependence *and* a high need to approach independence, thus providing him with a particularly difficult conflict over dependency. This would be contrasted to the individual who, for example, may be characterized as having a high need to approach dependence *and* a high need to avoid independence. The latter individual is driven in similar directions by these separate forces, whereas the former individual is the victim of two opposing driving forces: the classic conflict situation.

Although none of the studies we report deals specifically with this conceptualization of a *dependency conflict,* it is well to keep this in mind in attempting to understand the results to be reported both in this section and in the important outcome section on conformity behavior. . . . Thus, for example, what appear to be conflicting results from two different studies might better be seen in terms of this broader framework in which, under certain conditions (not yet specified), high *n* approach dependence is aroused in the firstborn, while under other conditions, high *n* approach independence is aroused.

In the literature reviewed by Murphy et al. (1937), two studies (Bender, 1928; Eisenberg, 1937) indicated that the firstborn and the only child score higher on a measure of ascendance or dominance. Using the old Bernreuter, Abernethy (1940) found that the only child was more self-sufficient and dominant than children in the other ordinal positions, and the eldest child was more dominant than the middle child. Our own data (Sampson and Hancock, 1962), obtained using the Autonomy measure from the Edwards Personal Preference Scale, indicate a significant main effect favoring the firstborn over the second born, regardless of the subject's own sex or the sex of his sibling.[1]

A somewhat complicating factor is suggested by the Koch data (1956d), which indicate that in the same-sex sibling pairs, the second born is more insistent on his rights than the first (and here we assume that "insistence" is an expression of some degree of independence), whereas in cross-sex pairings, the second is *less* insistent than the first.

---

1. Admittedly, in this section as in the others pertaining to measures and conceptions of personality variables, we are sloughing off the issue involving the relationship between the various measures. For the sake of some degree of simplicity, however, we must begin somewhere, even with the tenuous assumption that these are generally tapping the same underlying disposition.

On the side favoring the second born, we find the data of Pauline Sears (1951) in which the mothers rated the second child as negativistic and stubborn and the first as dependent. The data of Macfarlane et al. (1954) are somewhat consistent with the Sears data; however, they found the term negativism as descriptive of both the later born (male) and the firstborn (female). Although we shall not dwell on this point further in this section, this similarity between the second male and first female, and between the first male and second female, still appears again, particularly in the outcome section on conformity. . . . Using teachers' ratings of dependency among a sample of 3–6 year olds, Haeberle (1958) found that the first had higher dependency scores than the later born, and girls had generally higher dependency scores than boys. She also reported that more firstborn have dependency problems. This is consistent with our earlier scheme outlining the dependency conflict for the firstborn.

Although seemingly less directly concerned with dependence-independence, Moore (1964) reported no difference between the firstborn and the later born on an Acquiescence Scale, and Singer (1964) reported no difference between the first male and the later male on the Mach V scale, a measure of interpersonal manipulation.

Our tally at this point suggests five studies favoring the high dominance of the firstborn, four favoring the dominance of the later born, and two studies involving related variables, favoring neither. Neither the view which maintains that parental overprotection and inexperience frustrate the firstborn child's dependency needs and produce a person high in this need, nor its opposite, emphasizing the independence and responsibility of the firstborn, receive support. The dependency conflict scheme as presented above may be more correct; yet until we can specify the conditions under which one need or the other predominates, we are forced to make the less refined statement that we would expect no simple relationship between ordinal position and the need for independence. We would expect, however, a greater concern with the general issue of dependence-independence among the firstborn as compared with the second born. And, furthermore, we would expect that a projective fantasy measure would tap this level of involvement better than a more objective index. It should be mentioned that preliminary work with just such a projective (Kasl et al., 1964) failed to produce any significant results involving ordinal position in a female college student sample. It may well be, however, that a female sample is least useful for testing the dependency conflict paradigm, as they should be subjected to less pressure than the male on the "approach independence" side of the scheme.

Impulse Control, Aggression, and Superego Development

If we think of the control of aggression as partly a supergo function, we have the speculative account offered by Storer (1961). He suggests that the firstborn male develops a harsher superego than the second born, and is thus less self-sufficient than the later born, but more able to exercise impulse control and delay gratification. From this reasoning, one might expect the firstborn to be better able to withhold the expression of their aggressive impulses.

We already have a theoretical, but not a firm empirical, basis for expecting the firstborn to experience greater frustration as a function of inconsistent parental demands. Perhaps, to follow a frustration-aggression hypothesis, the firstborn also houses a greater reservoir of unexpressed frustration-produced aggression. When we combine the preceding with the assumed parental restrictiveness of the firstborn (cf. Lasko), we have a picture of a more controlled, less directly aggressive child.

The empirical data are generally consistent with the preceding expectation, although not unequivocally so. In the review presented by Murphy et al. (1937) are four studies dealing with some form of aggression. Two of these reported nonsignificant ordinal position effects with respect to anger (Stratton, 1934) and explosiveness (Wile and Noetzel, 1931). One reported a higher degree of anger among the firstborn (Stratton, 1927). The remaining Goodenough and Leahy, 1927) indicated that the firstborn is low in aggression, while the only child is high. When we add to this earlier work some of the later studies, the trends emerge somewhat more distinctly. Pauline Sears (1951), in her study of doll play aggression in normal young children, found that the only child and the younger child were equal in total aggressive activity, but both the first male and the first female child were *less* aggressive than the younger. This difference was statistically significant for the females, and is a trend for the males. Sears also reported one M.A. thesis which indicated that mothers rated their second child as physically aggressive, negativistic, and stubborn (Dean, 1947), and one based on observations of 3–6-year-old children's behavior in a school setting which suggested that the first showed the least amount of aggression (Gewirtz, 1948). We may add to this picture the Patterson and Zeigler (1941) finding, obtained on a sample of both schizophrenic and control adults, that the firstborn were *below* the remainder on aggressive behavior. Wile and Davis (1941) found that the nonfirstborn and the only child had the highest frequency of aggressive behavior in a sample of spontaneously delivered individuals. By contrast, in an instrumentally delivered sample, the firstborn had the highest frequency of aggressive behavior, with the only child coming next. Koch (1955) reported that the first male child in a two-child family, where the younger child was a sister, was rated by the teachers as low in aggressiveness. Haeberle (1958) found that the later born were characterized by low temper control. She also suggested that the later born with a sibling of the same sex had less impulse control than one with a sibling of the opposite sex. Along this same line, Macfarlane et al. (1954) characterized the later born male as having temper tantrums, being negativistic, and destructive, while the firstborn is timid. For females, however, it was the firstborn who was characterized as having temper tantrums and being negativistic, and also as being timid.

On the negative side of the above picture, but somewhat consistent with the Macfarlane et al. descriptions, Koch reported (1955) that the first female was more aggressive and competitive than the later female and the first male. In addition, the first female was described as being more quarrelsome. In her sample of female college students, Abernethy (1940) reported that the firstborn was more aggressive than subjects having older siblings, particularly in families of four or more. It should be noted that on the side favoring high firstborn aggression, the samples generally have involved firstborn females. However, as some of the previous studies have also involved samples of females (e.g., P. Sears, 1951) and have shown just the opposite finding, it does not seem feasible to do more than note this as a possible factor of importance.

With respect to more directly aggressive behavior, it does appear that in general, the firstborn child is less aggressive than the second born. This relationship appears stronger for the male than for the female samples.

Need for Achievement

The need for achievement enters the picture via an assumed relationship of ordinal position with training in independence and responsibility. The work of Winterbottom (1958) and of Krebs (1958) suggested a positive relation between early training in independence and the development of the need for achievement. Rosen (1961) suggested a rather similar point. He assumed that the firstborn child received not only a more intense, but also an earlier training in independence and responsibility, and that this training led to a higher need for achievement. The writer (Sampson, 1962) reported results using a projective measure of n achievement (French Test of Insight) which indicated that the firstborn had a higher need for achievement than the later born, especially among females. Using a similar form of that test, Rosenfeld (1964) reported similar results for certain aspects of his sample, but the contrary for most of his data (i.e., later born have a higher need for achievement than firstborn). His data generally indicated complex interactions among sex, ordinal position, and stimulus items.

In the original interpretation of what appeared to be a sex difference (Sampson, 1962), it was suggested that the firstborn female is more involved than the firstborn male in role behaviors which demand independence and responsibility. Bossard and Boll (1955) reached a similar conclusion, suggesting that at least within the large family system, the oldest child is most often described as the responsible member of the family, with the oldest daughter being seen as the most responsible. In a more recent study using Berkeley high school students from two-sib families and employing both a projective measure of n achievement and the Edwards Personal Preference Scale self-report measure, the firstborn had a significantly higher need for achievement than the later born, but only on the self-report measure; the projective differences were not significant (Sampson and Hancock, 1962).

In the same study, the firstborn, regardless of sex, preferred to take less extreme risks. This finding is consistent with the Atkinson model (Atkinson, Bastian, Earl, and Litwin, 1960; Atkinson and Litwin, 1960), which suggests that persons high in the need for achievement will prefer moderate rather than extreme risks. Thus once again we have data suggesting that the firstborn has a higher need for achievement than the second born. Elder (1962) reported that the firstborn had higher academic achievement motivation with respect to grades than did the youngest children in the family. Similarly, Pierce (1959) reported that the firstborn child or the only child was more often a high-achieving student in high school.

On the negative side, in addition to aspects of Rosenfeld's work, Moore (1964) reported no differences between first and later born college students on a self-report measure of achievement. Although no negative evidence with respect to the need for achievement itself, our more recent Berkeley study found that the firstborn reported that they were involved in *later* independence training than the second. Our subjects were given the Winterbottom scale and asked to complete it themselves, much as one might have parents do. These are retrospective reports of high school students, and thus may not reflect the actual training itself. Nevertheless, these data are not consistent with what we have assumed to be the intervening link between ordinal position and the development of the need for achievement.

Generally speaking, although some negative evidence complicates matters, there does appear to be some consistency in the data with respect to measured need for achievement. In addition, when we later examine the outcome variable of fame and eminence, which we assume is influenced by an individual's motivation to achieve, we shall see that the direction favors the firstborn. Thus we tentatively conclude that the firstborn is higher in need for achievement than the later born.

Authoritarianism

There appear to be only two studies relating ordinal position to measured authoritarianism, employing the F scale. Both indicate that there are no differences between first and later born persons on authoritarianism (Stotland and Dunn, 1962; Greenburg, Guerino, Lashen, Mayer, and Piskowski, 1963).

Self-Esteem

... [T]here is a theoretical rationale which suggests that the firstborn will have lower self-esteem than the later born. Presumably, because he must identify more directly with the powerful and capable adults rather than with less distant and skillful sibs, the firstborn child develops this lesser sense of self-esteem.

For the most part, the earlier work did not deal with what is now referred to as self-esteem, but with introversion and dissatisfaction with oneself. Busemann (1928) found that the only child and children from small families reported themselves to be introverted and dissatisfied with themselves. Goodenough and Leahy (1927) reported that the firstborn was more introverted and less self-confident than the later born. We have previously mentioned Hillinger's findings (1958) that the first were more introverted than the later born.

Recent work adds to this picture. Zimbardo and Formica (1963), using male college undergraduates, indicated that the firstborn had lower self-esteem than the later born. Stotland and Dunn (1962) however, using both male and female undergraduates, found no difference in self-esteem among firstborn, later born, and only children. In another study, Stotland and Cottrell (1962) found results which they felt *implied* that the firstborn and the only child had lower self-esteem than later born; this was not directly measured, but only inferred from behavior in the experimental setting.

In their study, Stotland and Dunn measured self-esteem through a Q sort, while Zimbardo and Formica used three measures: Janis and Field's two scales of Social Inhibition and Feelings of Inadequacy, plus a scale devised by Sarnoff and Zimbardo (1961). The differences in modes of measurement as well as in the samples employed could, of course, account for the difference in results. The evidence, when viewed overall, however, offers some tentative support to the hypothesis that the firstborn child develops a lower level of self-esteem than the later born child.

Outcome Variables

In this section we examine "outcome" or dependent variables of ordinal position research. For the most part, these involve behavioral differences between persons of different ordinal position. In many instances, this research has developed empirically, simply seeking to discover in what ways persons of different ordinal positions differ. In other instances, however, specifically derived hypotheses are tested. In either case, the findings in this section are viewed usefully in terms of the linkages they provide to earlier theoretical considerations, both at the level of parental behavior and attitudes and at the second level of personality attributes. When appropriate and possible, we shall indicate these linkages.

Social and Intellectual Achievement, Eminence, and Fame

If we were to identify the ingredients of social and intellectual eminence, we might turn to the factors of ability and motivation. With respect to ability, it seems reasonable to assume that a high level of intellect would contribute to eminence. With respect to motivation, it seems reasonable to assume that a high level of achievement motivation would be relevant for one's attainment of a position of social eminence. From the previous results involving intelligence, achievement, and ordinal position, we have some evidence favoring the firstborn child's attaining a position of social and intellectual eminence. The data with respect to achievement motivation itself were rather equivocal, some studies indicating that the firstborn had a higher need for achievement than the second born, and other studies indicating the reverse; the data involving intelligence were generally consistent in favoring the first ordinal position.

As we examine the material in this section, we note an overwhelming array of data which favor the firstborn individual or the only child. In their review, Murphy et al. (1937) pointed to the study of Ellis (1926) which suggested that, in all but large families, it is the eldest child who achieves fame (in large families, it is the youngest), and of Guilford and Worcester (1930) which suggested that the only child is superior in occupational status and in marks in school. Their review presented one study (Bohannon, 1898) which indicated that the only child ranks lower on school success than other ordinal positions. In addition, they presented a study by Busemann (1928) which indicated that children with sibs rank higher in school performance than only children.

To these earlier studies, we may add the more recent findings. Schachter (1963) cited the Cattell and Brimhall work of 1921 which found that more American men of science are firstborn than one would expect. Schachter continued by citing his own data, which indicate that (a) more students taking introductory psychology are firstborn than one would expect; (b) more graduate students in psychology and education are firstborn; (c) more medical students are firstborn; (d) there is the same percentage of firstborn in high school as in the general population; (e) the firstborn have a higher high school grade-point average than the later born. All of these data point to the predominance of the first ordinal position in higher education and in seeking advanced degrees. Supporting the Schachter results, Cobb and French (1964) found that the first position is over-represented among medical students. In addition, they suggested that the advantage of the oldest over the youngest son increases with the size of the sibship and is an especially great difference for families in which the father's level of occupation is low relative to his level of education. They interpreted this finding as suggesting that the father's own frustrated achievement motivations have been strongly projected onto his first son. Yasuda (1964) reported that first sons (note: this includes positions other than simple firstborn) hold better jobs than younger sons, and that first sons had more education than younger sons. Visher (1948) suggested that more leading American scientists were the first child than expected by chance. Chen and Cobb's review (1960) reported that a higher proportion of the firstborn are of recognized intellectual attainment. Pierce (1959) reported that high-achieving high school students are first or only children. Pierce (1959) also found that more small families than large families produce high-achieving children. West (1960), studying a sample of scientists in research organizations, found the greatest frequency of research scientists among the first, fifth, and sixth orders, with depressed frequencies among the second, third, and fourth positions. West also suggested that the bigger the family, the less probable that it will produce a research scientist. This appears to be consistent with Pierce's conclusion favoring the small over the large family. Lees (1952) reported that in his sample of men in England, more of the eldest won scholarships and attended the university than the later born. Finally, Elder (1962) reported that the firstborn have higher academic achievement than the youngest children.

On the basis of this survey, it appears rather consistently that the firstborn child (and, probably, especially the firstborn male) is more likely to achieve social and intellectual eminence. The firstborn indeed may not only be holding the expectations of his parents to achieve social status and success, but also may have been subjected to other conditions which are beneficial in motivating a person to reach high: e.g., (1) the absence of a sibling for a period of time with the consequent orientation toward the adult world; (2) the accelerated verbal and intellectual training; (3) the early demands for responsibility; (4) the early period of complete attention and then its sudden withdrawal, setting the person on his own to strive to win the high level of approval and affection he once held; (5) the inconsistency in training which on the beneficial side may increase the first child's ability to tolerate novelty, variation, and ambiguity, while at the same time he seeks its elimination, a condition possibly requisite to a scientific approach.

Conformity and Interpersonal Manipulation

In the case of the outcome variable of conformity, we are sufficiently distant from the assumed intervening psychological mechanisms that prediction is difficult. We might assume a relationship between the variables of dominance-submission and conformity. However, no clear relationship exists between ordinal position and dominance; thus it is difficult to utilize dominance in predicting conformity behavior. One might next assume that the need for achievement is related to conformity. In an earlier article (Sampson, 1962), this possibility was suggested. Again, we find the data relating ordinal position to the need for achievement sufficiently inconsistent to make this connection tenuous. Dependency, and specifically affiliative dependency, has been offered as a possible intervening factor. Yet, other than a tentative postulate of dependency-conflict for the firstborn, this line of argument does not stand up too strongly.

Not only is the picture with respect to any intervening mechanism rather confused, but the meaning of the outcome variable of conformity is highly complex. What is the meaning of the behavior which we label conformity? Is the subject changing his judgmental position or his attitude in order to be more correct, as determined by agreement with a group consensus? If this is the meaning of conformity, then one might expect the person high in need achievement to "conform" in order to be correct, and the person high in need affiliation to "conform" in order to be in agreement with those others with whom he would like to affiliate. Does nonconformity refer to maintaining one's own position or changing actively in opposition to some advocated position (Sampson, 1960; Willis and Hollander, 1964)? Once again, the meaning here is important for interpreting the results as well as for offering predictions about conforming or nonconforming behavior.

Now that the stage has been set, we can examine the available literature relating ordinal position to conformity, realizing that should any consistency in findings occur, there will still remain a rather difficult problem of interpretation.

Goodenough and Leahy (1927) reported that the firstborn is more suggestible than the later born. Becker and Carroll (1962) indicated that the firstborn among a sample of young boys at a playground yielded more in an Asch-type influence situation than did the later born. In a later study (Becker and Lerner, 1963) the results were less clear. As in the Becker and Carroll study, conformity was measured by yielding in an Asch-type situation. In the more recent study, however, one condition received a high payoff for each correct judgment and the other condition, a low payoff. The authors reported that with a low payoff, there was no difference between first and later born; i.e., small payoffs led to decreased yielding for both first and later born. However, with high payoffs, the later born subjects conformed (yielded) more than did the firstborn subjects. What seems of particular interest in this study is not that its results are opposite to the earlier studies, but rather that it suggests the importance of the reward structure of the experimental situation in affecting the outcome. In this study, reward structure was specifically manipulated experimentally; in the majority of studies, the precise nature of this structure is an unknown, making it difficult to understand the results without somehow inferring the subject's perception of it.

In a study of the effects of dormitory roommates, Hall and Willerman (1963) found that the firstborn was more susceptible to the grade-influence effects of the roommate than was the later born, whereas the later born were more influential over roommates' grades than were the firstborn. In other words, only if his roommate is a later born does a student benefit from his high grades; and then he benefits most if he is himself a firstborn. One might suppose that with respect to grade influences, we are dealing with a situation of high reward. If this supposition is correct, then the Hall and Willerman findings are at odds with the Becker and Lerner findings. However, the nature of the influence situations themselves are sufficiently different to jeopardize comparison. Yielding in an Asch-type situation and yielding (if it may even be called that) to the long-term indirect influence of one's roommate do not appear to embody comparable psychological meanings.

Staples and Walters (1961) found a directional result similar to Hall and Willerman's as well as to Becker and Carroll's study. In an autokinetic influence situation, they found that the firstborn (when anxious) were more suggestible than the later born. Their subjects were female college students. On the other hand, Moore (1964), using a sample of male college students, reported no difference between the first and later born on the autokinetic test. Taken together, the latter two findings might well suggest an interaction effect between sex and ordinal position. Some of the writer's own data are relevant to this point.

In an earlier study (Sampson, 1962), it was suggested that among males, the first conformed more than the later born, whereas among females, the first conformed less than the later born. In that study, the samples involved both college students and Coast Guard recruits, and conformity generally involved following the requests of someone in an authority position. The results which Schachter reported (1959), based on a study by Ehrlich, were presented then to support our findings with respect to the male subjects. In an effort to replicate the 1962 study, but this time in a single, well-controlled situation, another study was undertaken with Francena Hancock. High school students from two-sib families were used. The sample represented all possible combinations of subject sex, sibling sex, and ordinal position. In addition, it was limited to a sib age spacing of from 1 to 4 years. Subjects were presented with two related tasks involving judgmental conformity. In the first task, they were requested to estimate (in writing) the number of dots held up before them by the E.[2] In the second task, they were to estimate the height of a line drawn in the middle of a triangle. Estimates were then handed in. Approximately 15 minutes later, the E casually announced the general consensus of the group as to the number of dots and the height of the triangle. The subjects were then provided with an opportunity to record their estimates again. Subjects were run in a large classroom in groups averaging about 50 persons. An index of conformity was computed based on the combined judgments on the two estimation tasks, and the data subjected to

2. I would like to thank Dwight Harshbarger, who served as the major experimenter in this data collection. I would also like to thank Wayne Sailor, without whose ability in handling computer programming on the IBM 7090, the series of highly complex three-way analyses of variance with unequal N's, could never have been accomplished.

a three-way analysis of variance. In this manner, the main effects of (a) ordinal position, (b) subject sex, (c) sibling sex, and all possible interactions were determined. The results indicated that the firstborn "conformed" more than the later born. A further examination of the means for the separate groups lent some support to the findings of the 1962 study. That is, while the firstborn males "conformed" much more than the later born males, this difference in "conformity" was relatively slight for the females. Thus, among males especially, ordinal position was significantly related to "conformity behavior," but among females there seemed to be little if any relationship; if anything, the firstborn females "conformed" less than the later born females.

The word "conformity" is put in quotations to indicate that it is important to examine the possible meaning of conformity in this context. The sample of Ss employed was attending a high school located in a college community. Many of them undoubtedly were planning to attend the university [and if we follow Schachter (1963), particularly the firstborn]. Because the experiment was introduced as being under the sponsorship of the Psychology Department of the University of California, many of them might have felt particular pressure to perform well, i.e., to answer correctly. Thus, when they heard that their judgments were "out of line" and, therefore, perhaps in error, they changed in order to be correct. Those who changed most were the firstborn, presumably those most likely to be attending the university. In the second place, "conformity" in this context has the meaning of agreeing with one's peers. If the firstborn is more involved in affiliative behavior directed toward his peers, his action of changing his judgment is then but another affiliative gesture on his part, another effort to seek peer approval.

We have previously alluded to the somewhat striking similarity between the firstborn male and the second born female, and between the second born male and the firstborn female. We originally suggested this similarity in 1962 (Sampson, 1962), and based it on the similar conformity behavior of these groups. Once again, in this Berkeley study, we encountered a similar patterning, with the firstborn male and the second born female conforming more, and the second born male and the firstborn female conforming less. We suggested earlier that some of the characterization presented by Macfarlane et al. (1954) seems to be congruent with this finding. There are two further studies of relevance, both involving what we have referred to as interpersonal manipulation, and both of which seem to reach rather similar conclusions.

In a fascinating study, Singer (1964) related ordinal position to a measurement of Machiavellianism and to grade-point average. His results suggested a differential style of interpersonal manipulation (Machiavellianism) employed by first and later born as a function of their sex. Among males, Singer reported a higher correlation between Mach V scores and college grade-point average (GPA) for the later born than for the firstborn, although the first male and the later male both have approximately the same Mach V score. He interpreted this finding as suggesting that the second born male is more adept, smooth, and skillful at interpersonal manipulation than the firstborn male, although the first male shares equally with the later male the desire to manipulate. For females, on the other hand, Singer found a different mode of interpersonal strategy. The firstborn female is the more successful interpersonal strategist as compared with the later born female. Her form of strategy, however, involved using her good looks to "work on" the instructor. Thus, for example, the firstborn female tends to sit in front of the class, to see the instructor after class, and to visit the instructor during his office hours, significantly more than does the later born female. If we summarize these results, Singer is suggesting that the second male and the first female are similar in their skillful interpersonal manipulative abilities, while the first male and second female are equally unskilled in manipulation.

Sutton-Smith et al. (1964) reported a rather similar patterning in the strategy preferences (as inferred from occupational interests) for first and later born persons of the same-sex sib pairs. In all male sib pairs, the firstborn preferred to achieve success by means of a style using "strategy," whereas the second born preferred an achievement style of "power." In all female sib pairs, however, the reverse held. As Sutton-Smith et al. used the terms, "power" as a success style generally refers to physical power, whereas "strategy" as a style refers to the determination of one's outcomes through rational decisions rather than sheer power.

The parallel between the findings of Sutton-Smith et al. and of Singer lies more in the fact that the first male and second female are seen to be similar (as are the second male and the first female) than in the precise interrelationship of the manipulative styles. However, it is possible that the true nature of the manipulation to achieve a high

GPA, described by Singer as characteristic of the second male and the first female, does actually involve more a style of power than one of strategy.

What are of interest, however, are the emerging facts which suggest that, as compared with the first male and the second female, the second male and the first female are (1) more resistant to peer group influence, (2) more successful interpersonal manipulators to achieve grades, and (3) more oriented toward an achievement style based on power than one based on a rational-thinking strategy. Some rather striking implications for the ordinal position literature also emerge from this collection of findings. In the first place, they suggest the extreme importance of treating separately males and females in research on ordinal position. A simple combination of all firstborns regardless of sex, and a comparison with all second and later born regardless of sex, adds considerably to the error in comparison and to the confusion in understanding the outcome. In the second place, they suggest the need to examine more closely and systematically the underlying conditions which produce this similarity. In other words, what is there in common about the early training and experiences of the firstborn female and the second born male, or the first male and second female, that might produce a similarity of response to a social influence situation? This line of investigation would lead one to examine studies involving sex differences in child rearing (cf. Sears et al., 1957), a topic which is not germane to this review.

Although in examining the range of studies involving conformity and interpersonal manipulation we have pointed to the importance of the sex-by-ordinal position interaction, we should not ignore the fact that all studies reviewed do not simply confirm this conclusion. Thus, some studies employing both sexes (e.g., Hall and Willerman, 1963) found support for greater influencibility of the firstborn, apparently regardless of sex. The safest conclusion would be that the possibility of an interaction cannot be overlooked, given the nature of some of these findings.

Sociability and Social Acceptance

On the basis of previous theoretical considerations, but less firmly from empirical findings, one would expect the firstborn to be more concerned with affiliating with others. Thus one might expect him to be more friendly and generally sociable, assuming he is concerned with such affiliative matters. However, as we have seen from the Singer study (1964), the firstborn (male), although concerned with affiliation and sociability, might not be sufficiently adept interpersonally to handle himself in appropriate ways with other people. Thus, he might try to be sociable, but find his inept advances met with rejection by these others. The latter possibility makes it difficult to present any simple predictive statement relating ordinal position to sociability. We shall examine the relevant data.

Sells and Roff (1963) had grade school classes rate same-sex members as most and least liked. They reported that the only and the youngest are more highly ranked by the peer group than the oldest child. The middle child is least accepted. Schachter (1963) indicated that the first is *less liked* than the later born in fraternities and sororities. Bossard and Boll (1955) suggested that the later born is described as popular, sociable, and well liked. Patterson and Zeigler (1941) reported that the first are not rated as "good mixers." To round out this picture further, we may recall the Hillinger data (1958), which indicated that the firstborn was more introverted, and thus, presumably, less sociable than his later born counterpart. The data thus far indicate that the later born child is more sociable and more accepted by his peer group than is the firstborn.

If we add to this picture the Dittes' finding (1961), which suggests that the firstborn is significantly more vulnerable to variations in positive regard expressed by others, the implications of these sociability data become even more apparent. The firstborn is sensitive to others' evaluation of him, and yet is more likely to be rejected by these others. This picture of the firstborn jibes closely with Singer's description of the "poor soul" who would like to be interpersonally suave and manipulative, but who simply cannot handle himself with others. In this instance, he would like to affiliate and belong, but is not easily accepted by others, and responds significantly to this apparent rejection by other persons.

The picture with respect to sociability is not without its inconsistencies. Koch's data (1956d, 1957) indicated that the first female is rated as being more friendly than the second female. Koch also suggested that there is no relation between ordinal position and the number of friends one has. The latter finding for the young children in Koch's sample is somewhat akin to Singer's data with respect to college females, in which he reported that later born females and firstborn females date about equally (Singer, 1964).

As a general statement of results, however, a picture emerges of the somewhat more sociable and more highly peer-rated later born child.

Anxiety and Affiliative Behavior

One of Schachter's major findings (1959) indicated that, when he is anxious, the firstborn desires to affiliate more than does the second born. However, in the absence of such anxiety, there is no difference in the affiliative preferences of first and later born individuals. Two interpretative rationales were offered for the general tendency to affiliate when anxious. The first stressed the idea that simply being with others provides a means of receiving comfort and protection when one is afraid. The second suggested that being with others provides an opportunity to evaluate an ambiguous emotional state by means of a social comparison process. Which of these two is the "correct" process has formed the focus of much of the experimentation involving anxiety and affiliation, with each experimenter adding a slightly new twist to his experimental procedure in order to provide a more adequate test, e.g., informing the Ss of their emotional state presumably to eliminate this as a determinant of their desire to affiliate (Dittes and Capra, 1962; Gerard and Rabbie, 1961). Precise conclusions regarding the issue of social comparison versus social reassurance are more difficult to make (cf. Pepitone, 1964, who reaches a similar conclusion from his review of these data) than are conclusions pertaining more directly to the issue of ordinal position.

In general, most of the experimental work has strongly and rather consistently indicated that the firstborn, when anxious, responds in a more affiliative manner than the later born. Wrightsman (1960) found that "waiting together" was an effective means for reducing anxiety as compared with "waiting alone," particularly for Ss who were firstborn. Waiting together or alone appears to make little difference for later born individuals. Gerard and Rabbie (1961) reported many detailed and complex findings involving alone-to-gether preferences and actual GSR readings of emotional arousal. Although almost every S in their sample preferred the "together" condition when anticipating a fear-arousing situation, and although

111

their data generally support a social comparison interpretation of affiliative behavior, the ordinal position effects tend to support the hypothesis favoring firstborn subjects. Dittes and Capra (1962), while rejecting a social comparison explanation in favor of one involving social reassurances and esteem enhancement, found that the firstborn who was allowed to feel uncertain about his reaction to an emotion-arousing threat showed greater affiliative preference than the firstborn who was informed about the similarity of his reaction to others. Later born Ss, on the other hand, reportedly showed the opposite reaction. Radloff (1961) suggested that the firstborn affiliate only when dependency related needs are aroused. As a demonstration of this, Radloff aroused experimentally the need to have one's opinion evaluated. His data indicate that this experimental manipulation produced significant differences in affiliative tendencies for the firstborn subjects, but nonsignificant differences for the later born. As a final indication of this affiliative preference, Sarnoff and Zimbardo (1961) reported results which supported Schachter's original hypothesis that the firstborn affiliate when anxious.

In addition to this preceding series of studies involving anxiety and affiliation, a related set of studies concerned with volunteering for experimentation was undertaken. In 1961, Capra and Dittes found that 76% of the volunteers for a small group experiment were first-born. These results were interpreted as support for a hypothesis favoring the affiliative tendencies of the firstborn subject. It might be added that such findings could be taken as support for a social comparison theory in which the firstborn is seen as demanding more points of reference for self-evaluation than the later born, and thus is generally more likely to volunteer in order to learn about himself. This is particularly relevant when we look at the Suedfeld finding (1964) which indicates that 79 percent of those volunteering for a sensory deprivation experiment were firstborn. Weiss, Wolff, and Wistley (1963) had subjects volunteer for group, individual, or isolation studies under a condition in which they were simply asked for a yes-no answer or in which they were asked to rank these three kinds of experimental contexts. Their results indicated that there was a trend for the firstborn to volunteer *less* for the group experiment. However, with the ranking measure, the firstborn ranked group experiments first significantly more than did the later born.

If we combine these results, they are somewhat equivocal in their interpretation. In the first place, as Schachter (1963) had indicated, more firstborn appear to enter college and to take introductory psychology than later born; thus one would expect more of them to be around to volunteer for any experiment, especially when the solicitation takes place in an introductory psychology class. In the second place, the results themselves do not clearly support an affiliate interpretation, as the firstborn appear to volunteer or select studies without an excessive regard for their affiliative potential. Finally, it does seem that there are more meaningful ways to assess the affiliative preferences of the different ordinal positions than the procedure of soliciting volunteers for a variety of experiments. Undoubtedly, much more than affiliative preference enters to determine such behavior; it is even doubtful that any sense of affiliation is even present.

Empathy and Identification

For the most part, the studies to be reported in this section have been under the senior authorship of Ezra Stotland. Stotland's concern with the variables of empathy, identification, and self-esteem and with their relation to ordinal position are particularly relevant to the conceptual framework which stresses the function of sibs as models for comparison of behaviors and feelings. In this respect, therefore, the material in this section is of relevance to the social comparison interpretation of the anxiety-affiliation data of the preceding section. The material here is also relevant to the issue involved in peer group conformity, a behavior which may be interpreted in terms of a process of social comparison and consensual validation of social reality (cf. Festinger, 1950, 1954; Schachter, 1951; Sampson and Brandon, 1964).

The general research paradigm employed in these studies involves the use of a model who performs some task on which he succeeds or fails. The similarity of experience of the model and the S is frequently manipulated and measures are obtained of the $S's$ empathy or identification with the model.

Stotland and Cottrell (1962) presented data which suggest that when the S is allowed to interact with the model, the later born Ss see a greater self-other similarity than do the firstborn. In another study, Stotland and Dunn (1962) suggested that Ss who are firstborn or only children do not show a tendency to identify with the model. In a further study, Stotland and Dunn (1963) presented the S and the model with the same initial test and then placed the model in a failure situation. Later born Ss showed significantly more empathy under these conditions than did the firstborn. Empathy was determined both by the $S's$ self-ratings of anxiety and by a measure of palmar sweating. Only on the self-report measure, however, was such empathy manifest. When S did not think that he and the model took the same initial test, these authors reported no difference in empathy between the first and the later born Ss (Stotland and Dunn, 1963). Additionally, these authors found that the later born Ss identified more with the model (i.e., rated their ability and the model's ability as similar) when they shared the same initial experience than when the S thought that he and the model took different initial tests. However, the firstborn and the only child identified with the model regardless of the similarity or difference of initial experience.

In a rather complex study, Stotland and Walsh (1963) attempted to determine the relation between ordinal position and empathy, where the attribute to be acquired was the level of anxiety of the model. In the earlier Stotland and Cottrell study, the attribute to be acquired was the model's level of performance on a counting task. Their data indicate a general support of the preceding work. Their major hypothesis, namely that second born Ss show greater empathy than do first or only children, was supported by trends in their data, although the differences were not statistically significant. An additional finding suggested that the later born were more attracted to another person who had suffered anxiety than were the firstborn. They referred to this as sympathy.

It appears from the work of Stotland and his associates that the second born tend to identify more with others than the firstborn, presumably because they react "as if they were still in a family of peers, which was their initial experience in life" (Stotland and Walsh, 1963, p. 614). This peer orientation of the later born as compared with the more adult orientation of the firstborn is consistent with other interpretations of ordinal position differences (cf. McArthur, 1956).

It is of interest to note, however, what appears to be a differential *use* of others on the part of the firstborn and the later born individual. When anxious himself, the firstborn turns to others for comparison or solace. Yet, when the other is anxious, the second born is more able to empathize with and appreciate the plight of the other. Perhaps this differential relatedness to others has something to do with higher peer group ratings of the later born. That is, the later born seems more sympathetic toward others and somewhat more understanding of their positions, a condition which may more easily lead to a bond of friendship than the more dependent use of others which characterizes the behavior of the firstborn.

References

Abernethy, Ethel M. "Data on personality and family position," *J. Psychol.*, 10 (1940), 303–307.

* Adler, A. *Social Interest: A Challenge to Mankind*. Trans. by J. Linton and R. Vaughan. London: Faber and Faber, 1945.

Altus, W. D. "Sibling order and scholastic aptitude," *American Psychologist*, 17 (1962), 304.

* Armstrong, C. P. "Delinquency and primogeniture," *Psychol. Clin.*, 22 (1933), 48–52.

Atkinson, J. W., and G. H. Litwin. "Achievement motive and test anxiety conceived as motive to approach success and motive to avoid failure," *J. Abnormal Soc. Psychol.*, 60 (1960), 52–63.

Atkinson, J. W., J. R. Bastian, R. W. Earl, and G. H. Litwin. "The achievement motive, goal setting, and probability preferences," *J. Abnormal Soc. Psychol.*, 60 (1960), 27–36.

Bakan, D. "The relationship between alcoholism and birth rank," *Quart. J. Stud. Alc.*, 10 (1949), 434–440.

* Baker, H. J., F. J. Decker, and A. S. Hill. "A study of juvenile theft," *J. Educ. Res.*, 20 (1929), 81–87.

* Baldwin, A. L. "Differences in parent behavior toward three- and nine-year old children," *J. Pers.*, 15 (1946), 143–165.

Becker, S. W., and Jean Carroll. "Ordinal position and conformity," *J. Abnormal Soc. Psychol.*, 65 (1962), 129–131.

Becker, S. W., and M. J. Lerner. "Conformity as a function of birth order and types of group pressures," *American Psychologist*, 18 (1963), 402.

* Becker, W. C., D. R. Peterson, L. A. Hellmer, D. J. Shoemaker, and H. C. Quay. "Factors in parental behavior and personality as related to problem behavior in children," *J. Consult. Psychol.*, 23 (1959), 107–118.

* Bellrose, D. "Behavior problems of children." Master's essay, Smith College School for Social Work, Northampton, Mass., 1927.

Bender, I. F. "Ascendance-submission in relation to certain other factors in personality," *J. Abnormal Soc. Psychol.*, 23 (1928), 137–143.

* Bennett, I. *Delinquent and Neurotic Children*. New York: Basic Books, 1960.

* Additional reference.

* Berman, H. H. "Order of birth in manic-depressive reactions," *Psychiat. Quart.,* 7 (1933), 430–435.

* Blatz, W. E., and F. A. Bott. "Studies in mental hygiene of children: I. Behavior of public school children—a description of method," *J. Genet. Psychol.,* 34 (1927), 552–582.

Bohannon, F. W. "The only child in a family," *Pedag. Sem.,* 5, (1898), 474–496.

* Bossard, J. H. S., and Eleanor S. Boll. "Personality roles in the large family," *Child Development,* 26 (1955), 71–78.

Bossard, J. H. S., and Eleanor S. Boll. *The Large Family System.* Philadelphia: University of Pennsylvania Press, 1956.

* Breckenridge, S. P., and E. Abbott. *The Delinquent Child and the Home,* 1912.

* Brim, O. G., Jr. "Family structure and sex role learning by children," *Sociometry,* 21 (1958), 1–16.

* Brofenbrenner, U. "Socialization and social class through time and space, in E. E. Maccoby, T. M. Newcomb, and E. L. Hartley, eds., *Readings in Social Psychology,* 3rd ed. New York: Holt, Rinehart, 1958, 400–425.

* Burt, C. *The Young Delinquent.* New York: Appleton-Century, 1925.

Busemann, A. "Die Familie als Eriebnis-milieu des Kindes," *Z. Kinderforsch,* 36 (1928), 17–82 (a).

Busemann, A. "Geschwisterschaft, Schultuchtigkeit und Charakter," *Z. Kinderforsch,* 34 (1928), 1–52 (b)

* Campbell, A. A. "A study of the personality adjustments of only and intermediate children," *J. Genet. Psychol.,* 43 (1933), 197–206.

* Carman, A. "Pain and strength measurements of 1507 school children in Saginaw, Michigan," *Amer. J. Psychol.,* 10 (1899), 302–398.

Chen, Edith, and S. Cobb. "Family structure in relation to health and disease," *J. Chron. Dis.,* 12 (1960), 544–567.

Cobb, S., and J. R. P. French, Jr. "Birth order among medical students." Unpublished mimeographed report, University of Michigan, Ann Arbor, 1964.

* Conners, C. K. "Birth order and needs for affiliation," *J. Pers.,* 31 (1963), 408–416.

* Damrin, Dora F. "Family size and sibling age, sex, and position as related to certain aspects of adjustment," *J. Soc. Psychol.,* 29 (1949), 93–102.

Davis, A. "American status systems and the socialization of the child," in C. Kluckhohn and H. A. Murray, eds., *Personality in Nature, Society, and Culture.* New York: Knopf, 1959, 567–576.

Dean, Daphne A. "The relation of ordinal position to personality in young children." Unpublished master's thesis, State University of Iowa, Iowa City, 1947.

Dember, W. M. "Birth order and need affiliation," *American Psychologist,* 18 (1963), 356.

Dittes, J. E. "Birth order and vulnerability to differences in acceptance," *American Psychologist,* 16 (1961), 358.

Dittes, J. E., and P. C. Capra. "Affiliation: comparability or compatibility," *American Psychologist,* 17 (1962), 329.

116

* Dugdale, R. I., *The Jukes* (new edition). New York: Putnam, 1910.

* Durkheim, F. *Division of Labor.* Glencoe, Ill.: Free Press, 1947.

Eisenberg, P. "Factors related to feelings of dominance." Paper delivered at Annual Meeting, Eastern Branch, American Psychological Association, 1937.

Elder, G. H., Jr. "Family structure: the effects of size of family, sex composition, and ordinal position on academic motivation and achievement," in *Adolescent Achievement and Mobility Aspirations* (mimeo). Chapel Hill, N. C.: Institute for Research in Social Science, 1962, 59–72.

Ellis, H. *A Study of British Genius* (new edition). Boston: Houghton, 1926.

Festinger, L. "Informal social communication," *Psychol. Rev.,* 57 (1950), 271–282.

* Festinger, L. "Motivation leading to social behavior," in R. Jones, ed., *Nebraska Symposium on Motivation.* Lincoln: University of Nebraska Press, 1954.

* Foster, S. "A study of the personality make-up and social setting of fifty jealous children," *Ment. Hyg.,* 11 (1927), 53–77.

* Freedman, Deborah S., R. Freedman, and P. K. Whelpton. "Size of family and preference for children of each sex," *Amer. J. Sociol.,* 66 (1960), 141–146.

* French, E. G. "Development of a measure of complex motivation," in J. W. Atkinson, ed., *Motives in Fantasy, Action, and Society.* Princeton, N. J.: Van Nostrand, 1958, 242–248.

* Friedjung, J. "Die Pathologie des einzigen Kindes," *Wien klin. Wschr.,* 24 (1911), 42.

Gerard, H. B., and J. M. Rabbie. "Fear and social comparison," *J. Abnormal Soc. Psychol.,* 62 (1961), 586–592.

Gewirtz, J. L. "Dependent and aggressive interaction in young children." Unpublished doctoral dissertation, State University of Iowa, Iowa City, 1948.

* Glass, D. D., M. Horowitz, I. Firestone, and J. Grinker. "Birth order and reaction to frustration," *J. Abnormal Soc. Psychol.,* 66 (1963), 192–194.

Goodenough, F. I., and A. M. Leahy. "The effect of certain family relationships upon the development of personality," *J. Genet. Psychol.,* 34 (1927), 45–72.

Greenberg, H., R. Guerino, M. Lashen, D. Mayer, and D. Piskowski. "Order of birth as a determinant of personality and attitudinal characteristics," *J. Soc. Psychol.,* 60 (1963), 221–230.

* Gregory, I. "An analysis of familial data on psychiatric patients: parental age, family size, birth order, and ordinal position," *Brit. J. Prev. Soc. Med.,* 12 (1958), 42–59.

Guilford, R. B., and D. A. Worcester. "A comparative study of the only and non-only children," *J. Genet. Psychol.,* 38 (1930), 411–426.

Haeberle, Ann. "Interactions of sex, birth order, and dependency with behavior problems and symptoms in emotionally disturbed preschool children." Paper read at Eastern Psychological Association, Philadelphia, 1958.

Hall, R. I., and B. Willerman. "The educational influence of dormitory roommates," *Sociometry,* 26 (1963), 291–318.

* Hawkes, G. R., L. Burchinal, and B. Gardner. "Size of family and adjustment of children," *Marriage and Family Living,* 20 (1958), 65–68.

* Henry, A. F. "Sibling structure and perception of disciplinary roles of parents," *Sociometry*, 20 (1957), 67–74.

Hillinger, F. "Introversion und Stellung in der Geschwisterrcihe" ("Introversion and rank position among siblings"), *Z. Exp. Angew. Psychol.*, 5 (1958), 268–276.

* Hion, V. "Sur actiologic, symptomataologie und pathogenese des stotterns," *Folia Neuro-Esthon.*, 12 (1932), 190–195.

* Hooker, H. F. "The study of the only child at school," *J. Genet. Psychol.*, 39 (1931), 122–126.

Hsiao, H. H. "The status of the firstborn with special reference to intelligence," *Genet. Psychol. Monographs*, 9 (1931), Nos. 1–2.

Jones, H. E. "Order of birth," in C. Murchison, ed., *A Handbook of Child Psychology*. Worcester, Mass.: Clark University Press, 1931, 204–241.

Jones, H. E., and H. H. Hsiao. "A preliminary study of intelligence as a function of birth order," *J. Genet. Psychol.*, 35 (1928), 428–433.

Kasl, S. V., E. E. Sampson, and J. R. P. French, Jr., "The development of a projective measure of the need for independence: a theoretical statement and some preliminary evidence, *J. Pers.*, 32 (1964), 566–586.

Koch, H. L. "Attitudes of young children toward their peers as related to certain characteristics of their siblings," *Psychol. Monographs*, 70 (1956), No. 19 (Whole No. 426) (d).

Koch, H. L. "Children's work attitudes and sibling characteristics," *Child Development*, 27 (1956), 289–310 (c).

Koch, H. L. "The relation in young children between characteristics of their playmates and certain attributes of their siblings," *Child Development*, 28 (1957), 175–202.

Koch, H. L., "The relation of certain family constellation characteristics and the attitudes of children toward adults," *Child Development*, 26 (1955), 13–40.

Koch, H. L. "The relation of 'primary mental abilities' in five- and six-year olds to sex of child and characteristics of his sibling," *Child Development*, 25 (1954), 209–223.

Koch, H. L. "Sibling influence on children's speech," *J. Speech Dis.*, 21 (1956), 322–328 (b).

Koch, H. L. "Sissiness and tomboyishness in relation to sibling characteristics," *J. Genet. Psychol.*, 88 (1956), 231–244 (a).

Krebs, A. M. "Two determinants of conformity: age of independence training and achievement," *J. Abnormal Soc. Psychol.*, 56 (1958), 130–131.

* Krout, M. H. "Typical behavior patterns in twenty-six ordinal positions," *J. Genet. Psychol.*, 54 (1939), 3–29.

* Lasko, Joan Kalhorn. "Parent behavior toward first and second children," *Genet. Psychol. Monographs*, 49 (1954), 96–137.

Lees, J. P. "The social mobility of a group of eldest born and intermediate adult males," *Brit. J. Psychol.*, 43 (1952), 210–221.

* Levy, D. M. "Maternal overprotection and rejection," *Arch. Neurol. Psychiat.*, 25 (1931), 886–889.

McArthur, C. "Personalities of first and second children," *Psychiatry,* 19 (1956), 47–54.

Macfarlane, Jean W., Lucile Allen, and Marjorie P. Honzik. "A development study of the behavior problems of normal children between 21 months and 14 years," *University of California Publ. in Child Development,* 2 (1954).

* Martensen-Larsen, O. "The family constellation analysis and male alcoholism," *Acta Genet. Statist. Med.,* 7 (1957), 441–444.

* Mead, G. H. *Mind, Self, and Society.* Chicago: University of Chicago Press, 1934.

* Moore, R. A., and Freida Ramseur. "A study of the background of one hundred hospitalized veterans with alcoholism," *Quart. J. Stud. Alc.,* 21 (1960), 51–67.

Moore, R. K. "Susceptibility to hypnosis and susceptibility to social influence," *J. Abnormal Soc. Psychol.,* 68 (1964), 282–294.

Murphy, G., L. B. Murphy, and T. Newcomb. *Birth Order. Experimental Social Psychology.* New York: Harper, 1937, 348–363.

* Navratil, L. "On the etiology of alcoholism," *Quart. J. Stud. Alc.,* 20 (1959), 236–244.

* Orbison, Miriam E. "Some effects of parental maladjustment on firstborn children," *Smith College Stud. Soc. Work,* 16 (1956), 138–139.

* Parsley, M. "The delinquent girl in Chicago: the influence of ordinal position and size of family," *Smith College Stud. Soc. Work,* 3 (1933), 274–283.

Patterson, R., and T. W. Zeigler. "Ordinal position and schizophrenia," *Amer. J. Psychiat.* 98 (1941), 455–456.

Pepitone, A. *Attraction and Hostility.* New York: Atherton Press, 1964.

* Phillips, E. L. "Cultural vs. intropsychic factors in childhood behavior referral," *J. Clin. Psychol.,* 12 (1956), 400–401.

Pierce, J. V. "The educational motivation of superior students who do and do not achieve in high school," United States Office of Education, Department of Health, Education, and Welfare, November, 1959.

* Plank, R. "The family constellation of a group of schizophrenic patients," *Amer. J. Orthopsychiat.,* 23 (1953), 817–825.

Radloff, R. "Opinion evaluation and affiliation," *J. Abnormal Soc. Psychol.,* 62 (1961), 578–585.

Roe, A. *The Making of a Scientist.* New York: Dodd, Mead, 1953.

Rosen, B. C. "Family structure and achievement motivation," *Amer. Soc. Rev.,* 26 (1961), 574–585.

Rosenfeld, H. "Relationships of ordinal position to affiliation and achievement motives: direction and generality." Unpublished report, 1964.

* Rosenow, C. "The incidence of firstborn among problem children," *J. Genet. Psychol.,* 37 (1930), 145–151.

* Rosenow, C., and Anne H. Whyte. "The ordinal position of problem children," *Amer. J. Orthopsychiat.,* 1 (1931), 430–434.

* Ross, B. M. "Some traits associated with sibling jealousy in problem children," *Smith College Stud. Soc. Work,* 1 (1931), 363–378.

Sampson, E. E. "An experiment on active and passive resistance to social power." Unpublished doctor's dissertation, University of Michigan, Ann Arbor, 1960.

Sampson, E. E. "Birth order, need achievement, and conformity," *J. Abnorm. Soc. Psychol.,* 64 (1962), 155–159.

Sampson, E. E., and A. C. Brandon. "The effects of role and opinion deviation on small group behavior," *Sociometry,* 27 (1964), 261–281.

Sampson, E. E., and F. T. Hancock. "Ordinal position, socialization, personality development, and conformity." Unpublished National Inst. Mental Health Grant (M-5747-A), 1962.

Sarnoff, I., and P. Zimbardo. "Anxiety, fear, and social affiliation," *J. Abnormal Soc. Psychol.,* 62 (1961), 155–159.

* Schachter, S. "Birth order, eminence, and higher education," *Amer. Soc. Rev.,* 28 (1963), 757–767.

* Schachter, S. "Deviation, rejection, and communication," *J. Abnormal Soc. Psychol.,* 46 (1951), 190–207.

Schachter, S. *The Psychology of Affiliation.* Stanford, Calif.: Stanford University Press, 1959.

* Schooler, C. "Birth order and schizophrenia," *Arch. Gen. Psychol.,* 4 (1961), 91–97.

Schooler, C., and S. W. Raynsford. "Affiliation among chronic schizophrenics: relation to intrapersonal and background factors," *American Psychologist,* 16 (1961), 358.

Schooler, C., and Sandra Scarr. "Affiliation among chronic schizophrenics: relation to intrapersonal and birth order factors," *J. Pers.,* 2 (1962), 178–192.

Schoonover, Sarah M. "The relationship of intelligence and achievement to birth order, sex of sibling, and age interval," *J. Educ. Psychol.,* 50 (1959), 143–146.

Sears, Pauline S. "Doll play aggression in normal young children: influence of sex, age, sibling status, father's absence," *Psychol. Monographs,* 65 (1951), No. 6 (Whole No. 323).

* Sears, R. R. "Ordinal position in the family as a psychological variable," *Amer. Soc. Rev.,* 15 (1950), 397–401.

Sears, R. R., Eleanor F. Maccoby, and H. Levin. *Patterns of Child Rearing.* New York: Harper, 1957.

* Sears, R. R., J. W. M. Whiting, V. Nowlis, and Pauline S. Sears. "Some child-rearing antecedents of aggression and dependency in young children," *Genet. Psychol. Monographs,* 47 (1953), 135–234.

Sells, S. B., and M. Roff. "Peer acceptance-rejection and birth order," *American Psychologist,* 18 (1963), 355.

Singer, J. E. "The use of manipulative strategies: Machiavellianism and attractiveness," *Sociometry,* 27 (1964), 128–150.

* Slawson, J. *The Delinquent Boy: A Socio-psychological Study.* Boston: Badger, 1926.

Sletto, R. F. "Sibling position and juvenile delinquency," *Amer. J. Sociol.,* 39 (1934), 657–669.

* Smalley, R. E. "The influence of differences in age, sex, and intelligence in determining the attitudes of siblings toward each other," *Smith College Stud. Soc. Work,* 1 (1930), 23–39.

* Smart, R. G. "Alcoholism, birth order, and family size," *J. Abnormal Soc. Psychol.,* 66 (1963), 17–23.

* Stagner, R., and E. T. Katzoff. "The personality as related to birth order and family size," *J. Appl. Psychol.,* 20 (1936), 340–346.

Staples, F. R., and R. H. Walters. "Anxiety, birth order, and susceptibility to social influence," *J. Abnormal Soc. Psychol.,* 62 (1961), 716–719.

Storer, N. W. "Ordinal position and the Oedipus complex," *Lab. Soc. Relat. Harvard University Bulletin,* 10(2) (1961), 18–21.

Stotland, E., and N. B. Cottrell. "Similarity of performance as influenced by interaction, self-esteem, and birth order," *J. Abnormal Soc. Psychol.,* 64 (1962), 183–191.

Stotland, E., and R. E. Dunn. "Empathy, self-esteem, and birth order," *J. Abnormal Soc. Psychol.,* 66 (1963), 532–540.

Stotland, E., and R. E. Dunn. "Identification, opposition, authority, self-esteem, and birth order," *Psychol. Monographs,* 76 (1962), No. 9 (Whole No. 528).

Stotland, E., and J. A. Walsh. "Birth order and an experimental study of empathy," *J. Abnormal Soc. Psychol.,* 66 (1963), 610–614.

* Stout, Ann M. "Parent behavior toward children of differing ordinal position and sibling status." Doctoral thesis, University of California, Berkeley, 1960.

Stratton, G. M. "Anger and fear: their probable relation to each other, to intellectual work, and to primogeniture," *Amer. J. Psychol.,* 39 (1927), 125–140.

Stratton, G. M. "The relation of emotion to sex, primogeniture, and disease," *Amer. J. Psychol.,* 46 (1934), 590–595.

* Stuart, J. C. "Data on the alleged psychopathology of the only child," *J. Abnormal Soc. Psychol.,* 20 (1926), 441.

Suedfeld, P. "Birth order of volunteers for sensory deprivation," *J. Abnormal Soc. Psychol.,* 68 (1964), 195–196.

Sutton-Smith, B., J. M. Roberts, and B. G. Rosenberg. "Sibling associations and role involvement," *Merrill-Palmer Quart.,* 10 (1964), 25–38.

Thurstone, L. L., and R. I. Jenkins. "Birth order and intelligence," *J. Educ. Psychol.,* 20 (1929), 640–651.

* Thurstone, L. L., and T. G. Thurstone. "A neurotic inventory," *J. Soc. Psychol.,* 1 (1930), 3–30.

Visher, S. S. "Environmental backgrounds of leading American scientists," *Amer. Soc. Rev.,* 13 (1948), 66–72.

Weiss, J., A. Wolff, and R. Wistley. "Birth order, recruitment conditions, and preference for participation in group vs. non-group experiments," *American Psychologist,* 18 (1963), 356.

Weller, L. The relationship of birth order to anxiety," *Sociometry,* 25 (1962), 415–417.

West, S. S. "Sibling configurations of scientists," *Amer. J. Sociol.,* 66 (1960), 268–274.

Wile, I. S., and R. Davis. "The relation of birth to behavior," *Amer. J. Orthopsychiat.*, 11 (1941), 320–334.

Wile, I. S., and A. B. Jones. "Ordinal position and the behavior disorders of young children," *J. Genet. Psychol.*, 51 (1937), 61–63.

Wile, I. S., and E. Noetzel. "A study of birth order and behavior," *J. Soc. Psychol.*, 2 (1931), 52–71.

Willis, C. B. "The effects of primogeniture on intellectual capacity," *J. Abnormal Soc. Psychol.*, 18 (1924), 375–377.

Willis, R. H., and E. P. Hollander. "An experimental study of three response modes in social influence situations," *J. Abnormal Soc. Psychol.*, 69 (1964), 150–156.

Winter, L. *Mass. State Hosp. Bulletin,* 1897, 463.

Winterbottom, M. R. "The relation of need for achievement to learning experiences in independence and mastery," in J. W. Atkinson, ed., *Motives in Fantasy, Action, and Society.* Princeton, N. J.: Van Nostrand, 1958, 453–478.

Witty, P. A. " 'Only' and 'intermediate' children of high school ages," *Psychol. Bulletin,* 31 (1934), 734.

Wrightsman, L. "Effects of waiting with others on changes in level of felt anxiety," *J. Abnormal Soc. Psychol.*, 61 (1960), 216–222.

Yaryan, R. B., and L. Festinger. "Preparatory action and belief in the probable occurrence of future events," *J. Abnormal Soc. Psychol.*, 63 (1961), 603–606.

Yasuda, Saburo, "A methodological inquiry into social mobility," *Amer. Soc. Rev.*, 29 (1964), 16–23.

Zimbardo, P., and R. Formica. "Emotional comparison and self-esteem as determinants of affiliation," *J. Pers.*, 31 (1963), 141–162.

Part II
Peers and Intimates

As a person reaches adulthood, contacts with parents and siblings tend to be replaced by close relationships with friends and with one's mate. The first three chapters in this section (6, 7, and 8) indicate some ways that peers and associates contribute to character and psychological functioning. The last two selections in this section focus more specifically on mateship as a crucial factor in adult development and adjustment.

In our society, an adult's associates are acquired largely through organizational memberships, and the articles concerned with organizations and institutions in the next section can be studied to extend understanding of peer effects. Chapter 14 is especially important in this regard since it explicitly outlines the principles of Differential Association as a theory of interpersonal influence.

No person remains constant throughout adulthood, but in the short run a person does maintain relatively stable perspectives and habits that structure his responses to the various life situations. Accordingly, much of the research on adults has focused on the fit between persons and their circumstances. This concern with psychological adjustment is evident in the last three chapters of this section (8, 9, and 10), and again in Chapters 13, 24, and 26.

6

Immediate and Long-Term Effects of Experimentally Induced Social Influence in the Modification of Adolescents' Moral Judgments

William G. Le Furgy and Gerald W. Woloshin

As children grow older they develop more mature ways of thinking and of accounting for their own and others' behaviors. To a large degree this maturation is a simple function of age, older children having broader perspectives and more mature orientations. Yet this chapter indicates that the basic developmental process can be accelerated and retarded by social influences. Peer groups can influence a child to think in broader, deeper ways or, on the other hand, can lead a child to regress to more shallow, egoistic thinking. Such a finding may be especially important in accounting for the differences in moral orientation that occur by social class and by nationality, as discussed in Chapter 18.

While the qualitative differences in the moral judgments of children at various stages of development have been systematically characterized (Kohlberg, 1963; Turiel, 1969), the mechanisms by which the child progresses from one stage to the next are less well understood. Piaget (1932) described the initial stage of the child's moral development as "heteronomous" or the morality of constraint. During this period the child tends to reify the prohibitions and sanctions of the adult world. He perceives rules as sacred and immutable. This moral realism gradually gives way to a more relativistic view as the child acquires the cognitive capacities to discriminate social from physical reality. Because social interaction with peers demands reciprocity and an appreciation of the motives and intentions of others, rules come to be viewed as man-made, emerging from group consensus, and subject to consensually validated change. Their value is no longer seen as intrinsic, but as instrumental in securing and maintaining order.

Explanations of how the child makes the transition from one stage of moral development to the next have relied heavily upon Piaget's (1932) early speculations concerning the induction of cognitive disequilibrium arising from continued interaction between the child

Reprinted from William G. Le Furgy and Gerald W. Woloshin, "Intermediate and Long-Term Effects of Experimentally Induced Social Influence in the Modification of Adolescents' Moral Judgments," in *Journal of Personality and Social Psychology,* 12 (1969), 104–110. Reprinted by permission of the American Psychological Association and the authors. Footnotes have been numbered.

This work was partially supported under National Science Foundation Contract Number G4848. The authors would like to express their gratitude to Irving H. Sears for his assistance in the standardization of the stimulus items and in the running of subjects.

and his social environment. While no investigations have employed face-to-face interaction with peers, several studies have attempted to induce modifications in children's moral judgments by simulating interactions with peers and adults in the laboratory. Characteristically, experimenters have been content to rely upon the child's appreciation of the role-playing efforts of an adult model or hypothetical peer models.

Turiel (1966) attempted to modify moral judgment by exposing adolescents to a role-playing procedure designed to shift the judgments of the children away from their dominant stage of moral reasoning. During the experimental treatments the experimenter assumed the roles of friends from whom the subject was to solicit advice. Following Kohlberg's (1963) concept of a six-stage sequence of moral development [see Chapter 18 in this volume], the level of this advice was varied from one stage below to one or two stages above the subject's dominant stage. Exposure to advice one stage above the child's dominant stage was found to be most effective in producing change. Rest, Turiel, and Kohlberg (1968), in a related study, found children to express preferences for styles of reasoning above their predominant stage of moral development. The child's progression to these advanced stages was found to be a complex interaction of his own spontaneously expressed style of reasoning and the highest level of moral logic that he could comprehend.

Bandura and McDonald (1963) employed a variety of modeling and reinforcement procedures to alter specific aspects of children's moral judgments. A series of Piaget-type stories, that contrasted a well-intentioned act resulting in considerable material damage with a selfishly motivated act which resulted in minor consequences, was used to assess the children's orientation with regard to Piaget's dimension of objective-subjective morality. By having their subjects respond alternately with a preinstructed adult model, Bandura and McDonald were able to demonstrate short-term, but significant, shifts from the children's initial styles of moral judgment. Crowley (1968), by using more carefully standardized story items and a more intensive training procedure, was able to show dramatic shifts in the moral judgments of first-graders from an objective to a subjective orientation. These modifications in orientation were sustained over a period of 18 days.

The success of procedures such as those above in modifying children's styles of moral judgment have been relatively modest with regard to both their extent and duration. Despite the fact that both Piaget (1932) and Kohlberg (1963) imply that the child's inter-action with his peers plays a crucial role in his development of in-creasingly sophisticated styles of moral judgment, no studies have employed social influence procedures, in their experimental manipu-lations. Asch (1951) demonstrated that the addition of a second confederate to a single original model magnified the impact of the immediately induced social influence by a factor of 4.63. The addi-tion of a third confederate increased the compliance effect by a factor of 12.12 over the single model situation. Whether or not such ampli-fication generalizes to the long-term social learning aspects of the effect is a central issue of the present study. The majority of investi-gations concerned with social influence have concentrated on short-term conformity effects, specific to the immediate situation in which the social influence has been applied. The long-term effect of social influence as a variable in social learning has not been systematically explored (Blake and Mouton, 1961). A number of studies have found that alterations in subjects' behaviors that occur under induced social influence generalize to subsequent situations in which the subject is alone and not exposed to external pressures (Bovard, 1948; Deutsch and Gerard, 1955; Rohrer, Baron, Hoffman, and Swander, 1954; Schachter and Hall, 1952; Sherif, 1935). Such social learning effects appear to be at least a partial function of the extremity and certainty of the subject's initial position (Duncker, 1938; Gerard, 1954; Marinho, 1942; Schonbar, 1945).

The present study was designed to exploit the effectiveness of social influence procedures on the moral judgments of young ado-lescents. The experiment attempted to explicate the mechanisms of developmental transition by specifying the relationships of peer in-fluences on children of two distinct levels of moral development.

Method

Subjects

Fifty-three seventh- and eighth-grade students from the Princeton, New Jersey, junior high school served as subjects in the study. The 27 boys and the 26 girls (mean [age] $= 13.6$) were selected at random from the class roles. They came to the laboratory, on a volunteer basis, in response to a letter sent to their homes. The children were paid $4 for their participation in the four phases of the study.

Stimulus Items

The dependent measure devised for use in this study consisted of a moral relativism scale (the R scale) designed to assess the subject's position along the moral realism-moral relativism dimension. The scale was composed of 35 items in story form similar to those used by Kohlberg (1963). Taken as a whole, the 35 stories encompassed each of the 11 aspects of Piaget's moral sequence as characterized by Kohlberg (1963). Each story poses a moral dilemma in which the protagonist is confronted with a choice between two mutually exclusive alternatives, each having equal social desirability. Typically, these dilemmas offer a choice between obedience to a legal or social norm and a deviant response in favor of a set of extenuating circumstances: for example, an individual finds a sum of money—should he return it in the face of the fact that his wife needs an operation? Should a student seek illegal help on a term paper to prevent his being flunked by an unfair teacher, etc.[1] Children who consistently decided in favor of the prevailing legal or social authority were designated realistic. Children who systematically resolved these conflicts in favor of the extenuating circumstances were designated as relativistic. The 35 items used in this study were selected on the basis of a standardization procedure in which a large number of items were administered to over 200 children between the ages of 8 and 16 years. Significant sex differences were found. Girls of all ages showed a significantly greater tendency to select alternatives in favor of moral realism. On the 35 items, girls averaged 21.39 realistic responses; while boys averaged 14.35.[2] For the present study, the 35 items were distributed among four equivalent forms of the R scale with a mean interform reliability of .72.

1. The complete scale of 35 story items may be obtained from the authors upon request.

2. It has been suggested by Klinger, Albaum, and Hetherington (1964) that such sex differences may be related to the fact that the protagonists of moral judgment story items are typically male. The stories used in the present study were subsequently counterbalanced for sex of protagonist and readministered to a second large sample of children. The tendency of girls to respond in a morally realistic direction remained unaffected by this balanced presentation.

Design and Procedure

The experimental procedure was divided into four phases, each carried out on a different day. On the first day the children were administered a 10-item pretest form of the R scale. These scores were standardized in order to make comparisons between the sexes feasible. Twenty-nine children scoring above the population mean were assigned to the relativistic treatment condition. The 24 children scoring below the mean were assigned to the realistic condition. The children were invited back to the laboratory on the following day in groups of 6 for the social influence phase of the study. Each returning group was composed of subjects of the same sex and classification on the R scale. For this phase of the study the subjects were taken to six adjacent cubicles in a different part of the building. They were provided with a headset and microphone and given the following instructions: "Now you are going to hear some more stories like the ones you heard yesterday. Only this time we are going to let you hear each other's answers." Twenty story items were then read to the subjects by the experimenter through the headphones. After each story the subjects heard what they believed to be their fellow subjects' responses.

What the subjects actually heard were the prerecorded responses of a set of confederates of the same age and sex as the subjects. The responses of these confederates were consistently contrary to the subject's initial position on the R scale. For six of these social influence stories the subjects were exposed to the responses of all five confederates before they were allowed to give their answers. For four of the stories the subjects were in the fifth response position. For five of the stories the subjects were in the fourth position. For the sake of credulity, the subjects were requested to respond once in the first position, once in the second position, and three times in the third position. The 20 story items, presented to the subjects in this manner, were used only during the social influence phase and did not appear in other phases of the study. The control subjects received the same treatment except for the fact that they were not exposed to the responses of the confederates. Immediately following the social influence phase, the subjects were asked to respond privately to a second 10-item form of the R scale. One week later the subjects were asked to return to the laboratory and were administered a third 10-item form of the R scale. In all phases of the experiment, except the social influence phase, the subjects responded in private and were assured that their responses would be kept anonymous. Over the next few months, as the subjects had occasion to return to the laboratory, they were given the original 10-item pretest. The mean elapsed time between the first and second administration of the pretest was 100 days. At this point the study was concluded and its purposes and procedures fully explained to the subjects.

Results

Compliance to Social Influence

The effects of the experimentally induced social influence were evaluated by computing the difference between the subjects' scores on the pretest and social influence forms of the R scale. For the relativistic children, these difference scores for the control group showed random fluctuations from zero point. The experimental group showed significant displacements in the direction of the applied social influence. Experimental boys and girls showed mean deviations of —1.55 and —1.06 (standard score units), respectively, from their pretest scores. An analysis of variance of these difference scores for the relativistic subjects showed the main effect of the induced social influence to be significant. . . .

Analogous results were found in the conformity behavior of the realistic children. While the difference scores of the control subjects fluctuated randomly about the zero point, the experimental boys and girls showed respective mean difference scores of 2.77 and 3.87 (standard score units). Analysis of variance showed the main effect of social influence to be highly significant. . . . In both analyses neither the sex nor the interaction effects approached significance. The absence of sex differences may have resulted from the relatively high rate of conformity for all of the experimental subjects. When exposed to social influence, both boys and girls yielded to the majority view on an average of 16 out of a possible 20 trials.

At the conclusion of the social influence phase, the subjects were asked to respond privately to the immediate posttest form of the R scale. Figure 1 presents the mean movement from pretest position for the relativistic subjects on each of the three successive post tests.

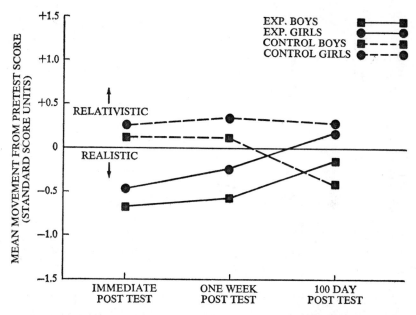

FIGURE 1. Mean movement from original position for the relativistic children during the posttest phases of the experiment.

Both boys and girls in the experimental treatment show movement in the direction of the applied social influence during the immediate and 1-week post test. However, these effects appear to have regressed to zero by the final post test 100 days later. Analysis of variance of these data reveals the interaction between time and experimental treatment to be significant. . . . This interaction implies a significant difference between the control and the experimental groups for the immediate and 1-week post tests with a reduction of this difference by the final testing session. However, this interpretation is qualified by the drop in final posttest scores for boys in the control group.

Figure 2 presents the mean movement of the realistic children from their initial pretest orientations for each of the posttest phases. Despite the fact that the control group showed a slight movement toward a more relative orientation as the subjects became adapted to the experimental procedure, both boys and girls in the experimental

131

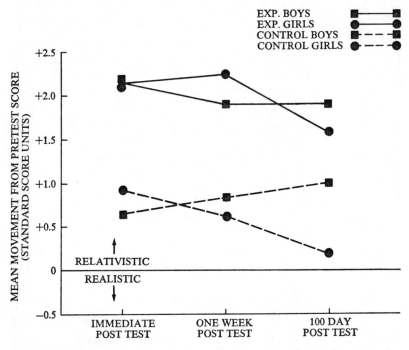

FIGURE 2. Mean movement from original position for the realistic children during the posttest phases of the experiment.

group showed dramatically stronger shifts in the direction of moral relativism. These shifts appeared to remain undiminished over the 100 days of the experiment. An analysis of variance found this main effect to be significant. . . . Neither sex nor interaction effects were significant. When faced with social influence, both realistic and relativistic children showed significant yielding and subsequent modifications in their styles of moral judgment. There remains the question of the extent of the relationship between such experimentally induced peer influence and long-term modifications in styles of moral judgment. Correlations (r) were obtained for the experimental subjects between the extent of their conformity to social influence and the subsequent modifications in their R scale scores on the three post tests. These coefficients were .88 for the immediate post test, .85 for the 7-day post test, and .76 at 100 days.

Discussion

Turiel (1968) in his criticism of the Bandura and McDonald (1963) procedure emphasized his contention that their method served to induce changes only in "isolated surface responses" that were not representative of changes in the children's underlying conceptualizations. In an earlier paper, Turiel (1966) cited duration over time and indirect change on nonexperimentally treated items as necessary criteria for structural or fundamental change in judgmental style. The present study, by employing stimulus items that range across all of the relevant aspects of Piaget's conception of autonomous morality, by inducing exclusively indirect, generalized change lasting up to 100 days, by demonstrating the differential effectiveness of attempts to induce progressive over retrogressive change, should fall within the limits of such demands.

It has been suggested by Langer (1967) and Turiel (1969) that subjects may be able to detect a "pattern" in the response alternatives of the various stimulus items and thus respond in accord with the demand characteristics of the experimental situation. Aside from the fact that the dilemmas used in the present study were complex and not obviously similar, the subjects seemed unaware of the extent and the fact of their conformity. Correlations between their personal estimates of their conformity and the actual number of times that they yielded to social influence were insignificant. Even had the subjects perceived some unidimensional consistency in the confederates' responses, there was no immediately obvious reason for them to continue to respond in this mode once the pressure to conform had been removed, and they were once again allowed to respond in private.

The results of the study document the fact that adolescents of both sexes and moral orientations will respond to immediate, face-to-face peer pressures with dramatic shifts away from their initial orientations. The differential effectiveness of this influence over time tends to confirm the work of other investigators (Smedslund, 1961a, 1961b; Turiel, 1966) who have found children to be consistently more susceptible to efforts designed to induce progressive rather than retrogressive change. While children who are more advanced in their development of a morally relative orientation are no less able to resist immediate social pressures than are their morally realistic counterparts, it is theoretically significant that they do not show comparable long-term effects. Disequilibrium induced by peer pressure in a developmentally advanced direction may be resolved through the subject's accommodation in the direction of this influence. The lessened long-term effectiveness of analogous social influence applied in a developmentally regressive direction is subject to a somewhat more tentative interpretation. Once the normative influences had been removed and the subjects allowed to respond privately, the accommodation of the relativistic children to the majority view was quite modest and appeared to be readily dissipated in the course of their everyday experiences over the 100 days of the experiment. The fact that the relativistic children returned gradually to their initial pretest position suggests that their exposure to regressive social influence did have some temporary residual effects. This return of the relativistic subjects to their initial judgmental styles accounts for the gradual reduction of the correlations between initial conformity and long-term change in moral orientation. These results suggest that pressure to conform, when it is applied in a developmentally relevant domain, need not automatically imply fundamental long-term changes in orientation. While such social influence may serve to modify immediate and short-term performance, the salience of induced conformity for social learning may depend upon its relevance to the developmental status of the subjects.

References

Asch, S. E. "Effects of group pressure upon the modification and distortion of judgments," in H. Guetzkow, ed., *Groups, Leadership, and Men.* Pittsburgh: Carnegie Press, 1951.

Bandura, A., and F. J. McDonald. "Influence of social reinforcement and the behavior of models in shaping children's moral judgment," *J. Abnormal Soc. Psychol.*, 67 (1963), 274–281.

Blake, R. R., and J. S. Moulton. "Conformity, resistance, and conversion," in I. A. Berg and B. M. Bass, eds., *Conformity and Deviation.* New York: Harper, 1961.

Bovard, E. W., Jr. "Social norms and the individual," *J. Abnormal Soc. Psychol.*, 43 (1948), 62–69.

* Crowley, P. M. "Effect of training upon objectivity of moral judgment in grade-school children," *J. Person. Soc. Psychol.*, 8 (1968), 228–232.

* Additional reference.

Deutsch, M., and H. B. Gerard. "A study of normative and informational social influences upon individual judgment," *J. Abnormal Soc. Psychol.*, 51 (1955), 629–636.

Duncker, K. "Experimental modification of children's food preferences through social suggestion," *J. Abnormal Soc. Psychol.*, 33 (1938), 489–507.

Gerard, H. B. "The anchorage of opinions in face-to-face groups," *Human Relations*, 7 (1954), 313–326.

Klinger, E., A. Albaum, and M. Hetherington. "Factors influencing the severity of moral judgments," *J. Soc. Psychol.*, 63 (1964), 319–326.

Kohlberg, L. "The development of children's orientations toward a moral order: I. Sequence in the development of moral thought," *Vita Humana*, 6 (1963), 11–33.

Langer, J. "Disequilibrium as a source of development." Paper presented at the meeting of the Soc. Res. Child Development, New York, April, 1967.

Marinho, H. "Social influence in the formation of enduring preferences," *J. Abnormal Soc. Psychol.*, 37 (1942), 448–468.

Piaget, J. *The Moral Judgment of the Child.* London: Kegan Paul, Trench, Trubner, 1932.

Rest, J., E. Turiel, and L. Kohlberg. "Level of moral development as a determinant of preference and comprehension of moral judgments made by others." Unpublished manuscript, University of Chicago, 1968.

Rohrer, J. H., S. H. Baron, E. L. Hoffman, and D. V. Swander. "The stability of autokinetic judgments," *J. Abnormal Soc. Psychol.*, 49 (1954), 595–597.

Schachter, S., and R. Hall. "Group-derived restraints and audience persuasion," *Human Relations*, 5 (1952), 397–406.

Schonbar, R. A. "The interaction of observer-pairs in judging visual extent and movement," *Arch. Psychol.*, 41 (1945), No. 299.

Sherif, M. A. "A study of some social factors in perception," *Arch. Psychol.*, 27 (1935), No. 187.

Smedslund, J. "The acquisition of conservation of substance and weight in children: II. External reinforcement of conservation of weight and of the operations of addition and subtraction," *Scandinavian J. Psychol.*, 2 (1961), 71–84 (a).

Smedslund, J. "The acquisition of conservation of substance and weight in children: III. Extinction of conservation of weight acquired 'normally' and by means of empirical controls on a balance," *Scandinavian J. Psychol.*, 2 (1961), 85–87 (b).

Turiel, E. "An experimental test of the sequentiality of developmental stages in the child's moral judgments," *J. Person. Soc. Psychol.*, 3 (1966), 611–618.

Turiel, E. "Developmental processes in the child's moral thinking," in P. Mussen, J. Langer, and M. Covington, eds., *New Directions in Developmental Psychology.* New York: Holt, Rinehart, 1969.

7

Social Interaction
and the Self-Concept
Melvin Manis

In symbolic interactionism (a social psychological theory
founded by social philosopher George Herbert Mead), one
of the basic tenets is that a person's notion of self grows out
of interaction with others and is largely a reflection of the
way others view the self. This chapter provides evidence that
opinions of others are indeed an important influence on
the self-concept—people judge us by our behavior—and in
turn, we tend to see our selves in terms of others'

judgments. This process explains in part how relationships with others are stored and how they affect later behavior, even when these others are absent.

Science progresses when two or more supposedly unrelated sets of phenomena can be explained by reference to a single set of governing principles. Inasmuch as the self-concept may be defined, in common-sense fashion, as the organized collection of attitudes, opinions, and beliefs an individual holds about himself, it would be reasonable to expect that it will be influenced by those factors that have previously been shown to influence other kinds of beliefs and opinions. In short, it is at least initially justified to assume that the self-concept is not essentially different from any other set of attitudes, opinions, or beliefs collected by an individual about any given object or topic.[1]

Most beliefs or opinions are acquired or learned in the course of interactions between people. This form of social influence or social learning is most marked in areas where direct and independent empirical investigation is most difficult. Sherif's famous experiment on the autokinetic phenomenon (16) is a dramatic illustration that the things an individual sees and believes about the external world are largely dependent upon the opinions of others. As an extension of this general principle, it is to be expected that the things which an individual sees and believes about himself are, to an extent, determined by what others believe about him. Such a view is clearly in ac-

Reprinted from Melvin Manis, "Social Interaction and the Self-Concept," in *Journal of Abnormal and Social Psychology,* 51 (1955), 362–376. Reprinted by permission of the American Psychological Association and the author. Footnotes have been renumbered.

This paper has been adapted from a dissertation which was submitted in partial fulfillment of the requirements for the Ph.D. The author wishes to express his gratitude to his advisor, J. McV. Hunt, and to Ross Stagner, for help and encouragement in the preparation of this study.

1. In this paper such terms as attitude, opinion, belief, and perception are used synonymously since they are all ultimately hypothetical constructs which are inferred from overt responses to observable situations.

cordance with the writings of Cameron (3), Cooley (5), Mead (11), Newcomb (13), Rogers (15), Sullivan, and Snygg and Combs (17).

Confirmation and Attitude Change[2]

In general, an individual feels that a belief is "proper" or "valid" to the extent that it commands confirmation (or agreement) from others. In the words of Festinger: "If there are other people around him who believe the same thing, then his opinion is, to him, valid. If there are not others who believe the same thing, then his opinions are, in the same sense, not valid" (8, p. 5).

Since we all soon learn that we may be punished for holding "invalid" beliefs, we are continually "checking" our opinions against the views of others. When, because of a lack of confirmation, we find that one of our beliefs is "incorrect," we seek to remedy the situation by either changing our view, or by changing the views of others, so as to "legitimatize" our own position.

In "checking" and "correcting" his beliefs, an individual relies more upon some people than others. These people may be regarded as his reference individuals and it is against the yardstick of their opinions that he measures the validity of his own beliefs. In particular, most people "check" their beliefs by comparing them with the opinions of their friends.

When an individual's friends do not confirm his beliefs, he will seek to increase confirmation by (a) exerting pressure on them to change their views, (b) "correcting" his own "mistaken" impressions, or (c) simultaneously following both these courses of action. In any case, regardless of the particular mechanism which is chosen, the individual will attempt to create a state of affairs in which he and his friends are in general agreement. That is, he will attempt to bring about an increase, in confirmation.

When two friends disagree about some political matter, they will probably discuss their views openly and in this manner will achieve some measure of agreement. Similarly, when an individual's self-concept is not confirmed by the views of his friends there should be an eventual increase in agreement. The analogy between the two

---

2. The propositions which are advanced in this section are drawn largely and adapted from the work of Festinger and his associates (8).

situations is not perfect, however, for our cultural values generally prohibit us from frankly telling another person our opinion of him, nor can he tell us his frank opinion of himself. But this does not preclude the possibility of communication, since our impressions or beliefs about an individual are, to some extent, communicated to him through our actions. That is, we tend to respond to him in a fashion which is consonant with our perception of him. Conversely, an individual is probably able to communicate his self-concept to others through this same behavioral medium.

Hypotheses for This Study

Confirmation—Change and Friendship

Hypothesis I. According to our theory and the results of numerous experiments on the social conditions of belief (9, 16), increases in confirmation (or agreement) should, and do, occur when the conflicting views concern some external matter such as football, perceived movement, or the like. If the self-concept is, in fact, not essentially different from these externally directed beliefs, similar increases in confirmation should occur. This leads to the prediction that: I. *Over a period of time there will be an increase in agreement between the individual's self-perception and his friends' perceptions of him.*

Hypothesis II. In the preceding section we made the assumption that people influence, and are more influenced by, their friends than their nonfriends. In an experiment on "The Exertion of Influence through Social Communication," Back (2) has confirmed an hypothesis which is similar to this assumption. He found that cohesive groups, defined as those which are highly attractive to their members, exert more influence on the beliefs of their members than do noncohesive groups. As obvious extrapolation of this finding is the prediction that friendship groups exert more influence over their members' beliefs than do groups which are composed of individuals who have not chosen each other as friends.

If the members of a group are able to influence each others' beliefs, they should, over a period of time, be able to diminish any disagreement which exists between them. If they cannot influence one another, they should be relatively powerless to resolve such conflicts.

We can, therefore, quantify the influence that the members of a group exert over one another in terms of their ability to settle disagreements. Thus, if the members of friendship groups have more influence over each others' beliefs than do the members of groups which are composed of nonfriends, it may be hypothesized that: II. *Over a given period of time, there will be a greater increase in agreement between an individual's self-concept and his friends' impressions of him, than there will be between the individual's self-concept and his nonfriends' impressions of him.*

Confirmation and Changes of the Self-Concept

Hypothesis III. It is our contention that through their actions toward him, an individual's self-concept is affected by those whose opinion he values. To be more concrete, an individual's self-concept can be either altered or reinforced by his friends, depending upon whether or not their actions toward him tend to confirm his existing self-image. According to our theory, changes in the self-concept should, by and large, be aimed at increasing the agreement between the individual's self-concept and the way he is perceived by his friends. We, therefore predict, that: III. *Over a period of time, changes in the individual's self-concept will tend to increase the agreement between his self-concept and his friends' perceptions of him.*

Hypothesis IV. If an individual is more strongly influenced by his friends than by his nonfriends, this should be manifested in the respective abilities of friends and nonfriends to influence the content of his self-concept. This leads to the hypothesis that: IV. *During a specified period of time, the content of an individual's self-concept will be more influenced by his friends' views of him than by his nonfriends' views of him.*

Confirmation and Changes in Others' Perceptions of the Individual

Hypothesis V. When an individual's self-concept is not confirmed by his friends, he may, by behavioral means, strive to alter their impressions of him. Since our culture prohibits an individual from openly discussing his own self-concept, he may try to influence others by acting, whenever possible, in a fashion which he believes to be consonant with his own self-concept and at odds with their opinions of him. If, for example, the individual believes himself to be mature despite the disagreement of others, he may try to change their views by consistently and repeatedly acting toward them in what he conceives to be a mature manner. In this fashion he will attempt to "convince" them of the validity of his self-concept. This leads to the hypothesis that: V. *When an individual's friends change their opinions of him, these changes will tend to increase the agreement between his self-concept and his friends' perceptions of him.*

Hypothesis VI. If an individual is more strongly motivated to receive confirmation from his friends than from his nonfriends, he might be expected to exert correspondingly greater effort in his attempts to alter their views of him. Accordingly, he should be more successful in getting them to accept his beliefs about himself as valid. This leads to the hypothesis that: VI. *During a given period of time, an individual will be more successful in influencing his friends to accept his self-concept as valid than he will be in similarly influencing the opinions of his nonfriends.*

Method

Subjects. The Ss in this study were 101 male students at the University of Illinois. The overwhelming majority of them were midyear freshmen who had entered the University five weeks before the start of the experiment. Their ages ranged from 17 to 26, although most were between 17 and 19.

These men lived together in a dormitory-style building which had been temporarily divided into rooms by a series of metal lockers. Nearly all of the men were assigned to these rooms on a random basis. There were a few, however, who had known each other before the start of the semester and who had asked to be placed in the same room. There were usually four men in each room. For the purposes of this study, groups were formed by pairing adjacent rooms, making a total of eight men in most of the various groups.

Testing procedures. The Ss described each member of their group, including themselves, on 24 bipolar rating scales. These scales were derived from Cattell's (4) factor analysis of Allport and Odbert's adjective trait list (1). Cattell's study resulted in 12 relatively inde-

141

pendent factors. Of these, the eight which accounted for the most variance were represented by three items each. Synonyms were substituted for the original terms when, in the judgment of E,[3] Cattell's items seemed too complex for our Ss. Because of their origin in the Allport-Odbert trait list, the items which were selected may be assumed to sample virtually all of the important descriptive dimensions on which people within our culture vary.

Following his self-description, his description of an "ideal self," and his descriptions of others, each S made sociometric choices from among the members of his group. The descriptive items and the sociometric questionnaires were administered twice, with a six-week period intervening between the two administrations. At the time of the first test administration the Ss had lived together for a period of five weeks.

Sociometric data. The sociometric data were used to select a *friend* and a *nonfriend* for each of the Ss. The friend was defined as that person within his group whom S had mentioned most frequently in the first sociometric questionnaire. The person who was selected also had to be mentioned by S as one of his five best friends on campus in the first sociometric questionnaire. The nonfriend was defined as the roommate to whom S had given the fewest sociometric votes on Test I. The people who were selected on the above criteria also had to satisfy certain requirements for stability of friendship or nonfriendship, as revealed by the sociometric data of Test II.

It seemed desirable to select the nonfriend from within S's room, rather than from within his group as a whole, to ensure that the frequency of contact between Ss and friends and Ss and nonfriends would be roughly comparable.

The criteria of friendship that are discussed above sometimes resulted in a situation in which two Ss chose the same person as a friend. In such cases the two friendship pairs could not be considered independent of one another since one individual was common to both. This lack of independence would violate one of the assumptions of our statistical tests. To solve this problem it was decided to eliminate all Ss who had chosen the same person as a friend save for the S who had given him the greatest total of sociometric votes. A similar procedure was adopted for those instances in which two or more Ss chose the

3. The instrument used in this study is similar to that developed by Helper (10).

same person for a nonfriend. Here, however, the *S* who had given this nonfriend the lowest total number of sociometric votes was retained and the others eliminated.

When these eliminations had been completed, there remained a sample of 36 independent friendship pairs and a sample of 28 independent pairs of nonfriends. All of the statistical tests to be reported were performed using these two samples.

Results and Discussion[4]

The concept of confirmation, or agreement, is central to each of the hypotheses which has been developed above. Operationally, this concept is defined by the value of the D statistic between an individual's self-description and his friend's (or nonfriend's) description of him (6, 14). It should be noted that the value of this D, which might be termed a confirmation score, is inversely related to the amount of confirmation which the individual receives; that is, small D's indicate more confirmation than do large ones.

Hypothesis I. Over a period of time there will be an increase in agreement between the individual's self-perception and his friend's perception of him.

A comparison of the confirmation scores received at Test I with the confirmation scores received at Test II shows the latter smaller than the former and the difference permits rejection of the null hypothesis. . . . Closer inspection of the data reveals, however, that this increase in agreement is significant only for those 19 *S*-friend pairs in which the *S*s described themselves more positively than they were described by their friends. . . .[5] The 17 remaining *S*-friend pairs, in which the *S*s described themselves less positively than their friends had described them, showed a trend in the hypothesized direction, but this trend was not significant. . . .

Hypothesis II. Over a period of time, there will be a greater increase in agreement between an individual's self-concept and his friends' im-

4. The *p* values reported here are for one-tailed tests. These are used because the direction of each anticipated trend was specified prior to the collection of the data. [Numerical values of the significance tests have been deleted.— EDITOR]

5. Operationally speaking, the *S*s who described themselves more positively than their friends had described them were those whose self-descriptions were more similar to their "ideal selves" than were their friends' descriptions of them.

pressions of him than there will be between the individual's self-concept and his nonfriends' impressions of him.

Increases in confirmation were measured by the difference between the S's two confirmation scores. The amount by which the second D was smaller than the first was interpreted as an index of the increase in confirmation, since a small D indicated more confirmation than a large D. In those cases where the D at Test II was larger than the D at Test I, the obtained difference was given a negative sign.

The amount by which confirmation could increase in any S-friend (or S-nonfriend) pair was dependent upon its initial level, since, to cite an extreme example, there could be no increase in confirmation if there were no initial disagreement. For this reason Ss were matched on the basis of their first confirmation score when comparing them in terms of the amount by which confirmation had increased. Figure 1 shows the mean increase in confirmation for these matched groups of S-friend and S-nonfriend pairs. For purposes of graphic clarity a constant has been added to each mean to raise them all to a positive value.

Note that in 8 of the 10 pairs of matched groups the mean increase in confirmation for S-friend pairs exceeds the mean increase in con-

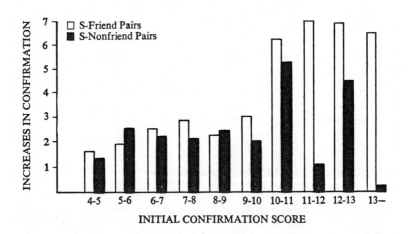

FIGURE 1. Comparison of Increases in Confirmation for S-Friend Pairs and S-Nonfriend Pairs with Groups Matched on the Basis of Initial Confirmation Scores.

firmation for *S*-nonfriend pairs. An analysis of these 10 pairs of values by means of Wilcoxon's Signed Ranks Test (18) resulted in rejection of the null hypothesis. . . . The results which have been obtained are thus consonant with our theoretical prediction.

To put our hypothesis to a more severe test, the *S*-friend pairs were split into two groups, the *positive* and the *negative,* as were the *S*-nonfriend pairs.[6] The increase in confirmation for corresponding *S*-friend and *S*-nonfriend groups was then compared. These additional tests were performed to control for the possibility that the overall significance test reported above was in some way contaminated by the fact that the *S*-friend and *S*-nonfriend groups differed in their respective proportions of *positive* and *negative* pairs.

Since, as discussed above, the initial confirmation level determines the amount of possible increase in confirmation for any *S*-friend (or *S*-nonfriend) pair, it was again deemed advisable to take this source of variance into account. It was, however, impossible to utilize the previously described method for matching subgroups on the basis of their initial confirmation scores. Instead, an analysis of covariance design was adopted in which the increases in confirmation were compared after the variance due to differences in the initial confirmation scores had been accounted for.

The results showed that the increase in confirmation for the *positive* group of *S*-friend pairs exceeded the increase in confirmation for the *positive* group of *S*-nonfriend pairs. . . . A similar comparison between the two *negative* groups showed no essential difference. Apparently increases in confirmation are more marked for *S*-friend pairs than for *S*-nonfriend pairs, providing the *S*s' self-concepts are relatively favorable. When the *S*s' self-concepts are relatively unfavorable, this tendency disappears.

Hypothesis III. Over a period of time, changes in the individual's self-concept will tend to increase the agreement between his self-concept and his friends' perceptions of him.

---

6. In what follows here, the term *positive S*-friend (or *S*-nonfriend) pairs refers to those pairs in which the *S*'s initial self-descriptions was more favorable than was his friend's (or nonfriend's) initial description of him. *Positive S*s, or *S*s with "relatively favorable" self-concepts, will refer to those whose self-descriptions satisfied this requirement. Conversely, *negative* pairs will be those for whom the reverse was true. *Negative S*s, or those with "relatively unfavorable" self-concepts, will be *S*s whose self-descriptions were unflattering as judged by this criterion.

Operationally, Hypothesis III predicts that the individual's second self-description will be more similar to his friend's first description of him than his first self-description was. Analysis of the data by means of the Wilcoxon Signed Ranks Test lends support to this prediction and permits rejection of the null hypothesis. . . .

Although the above finding indicates that the Ss' self-concepts were influenced significantly by their friends' perceptions of them, it is possible that this trend was primarily due to effects obtained with the *negative* Ss. That is, perhaps the only Ss whose self-concepts were influenced were those who would increase their self-esteem by echoing the views of their friends, while the other Ss remained uninfluenced by their friends' relatively unflattering estimates of them. To investigate this possibility the S-friend pairs were again split into *negative* and *positive* groups and the data from each of these groups were analyzed separately using the Wilcoxon test. As expected, the *negative* group of Ss were significantly influenced by their friends' estimates of them. . . . For the *positive* group of Ss, the results were less clear-cut. Although the trend was in the predicted direction, it did not reach significance. . . .

The individual's self-concept is apparently influenced by his friend's perception of him, providing this friend perceives him in a more ideal light then he perceives himself. If the friend perceives him in relatively unfavorable terms, his influence is not felt to any significant degree. Although one may conclude that this nonsignificant trend is solely due to chance variation, it is possible that it represents the beginning of a "real" effect which would have achieved significance if there had been a longer interval between testing sessions. In short, perhaps the individual's self-concept can be influenced by his friends' opinions of him whether they be positive or negative, although it may take somewhat longer before he will accept a negative perception of himself as being valid. The psychoanalytic concept of resistance seems particularly pertinent here.

There is another possible explanation for this finding. It may be that when people have relatively unfavorable impressions of those who have chosen them for friends, they tend to disguise their true feelings, since our culture generally prohibits open expression of negative reactions in such a situation. This would make it difficult for the *positive* Ss to get any accurate knowledge of what their friends think of them and would, therefore, reduce the extent to which these friends would influence their self-concepts. It might be hypothesized, however, that with the passage of time, the Ss' knowledge of their friends' attitudes toward them would become increasingly accurate and would be paralleled by a corresponding increase in the influence which these friends would exert.

Hypothesis IV. During a specified period of time, people will be more influenced by their friends' views of them than by their nonfriends' views of them.

The extent to which each S's self-concept was influenced by his friend's (or nonfriend's) opinion of him was quantified by subtracting the D between his second self-description and his friend's (or nonfriend's) first description of him from the initial confirmation score. . . .

For reasons which have been discussed in connection with Hypothesis II, it was necessary to match groups of Ss on the basis of their initial confirmation scores when testing Hypothesis IV. This comparison of matched groups is graphically depicted in Figure 2, where once again, for purposes of graphic clarity, a constant had been added to each point to raise them all to positive numbers.

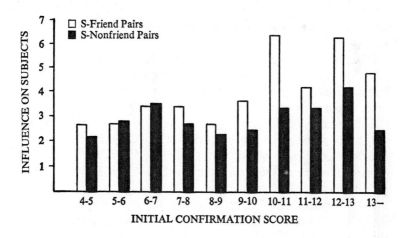

FIGURE 2. Comparison of Influence Exerted on Ss' Self-Concepts by Friends and Nonfriends with Groups Matched on the Basis of Initial Confirmation Scores.

Note that in eight of the ten pairs of groups, the friends exerted more influence over the individual's self-concepts than did the nonfriends. The difference between these ten pairs of matched groups is highly significant. . . . This finding provides empirical support for the proposition that an individual's self-concept is more affected by the views of his friends than by the views of his nonfriends.

One might argue, however, that the Ss' self-concepts were not more amenable to influence by their friends because of the greater cohesiveness of the S-friend pairs, but because, by and large, the Ss were perceived in a more favorable light by their friends than by their nonfriends. That is, within the S-friend group there was a greater proportion of *negative* Ss than there was in the S-nonfriend group. This fact would tend to favor the S-friend pairs in any overall significance test such as the one reported above, since it has already been shown that Ss are more likely to have their self-concepts influenced by those who view them in a relatively flattering light than by those who view them with relative disfavor. To control for this contaminating factor the S-friend pairs were again split into *negative* and *positive* groups, as were the S-nonfriend pairs. Corresponding S-friend and S-nonfriend groups were then compared to see if, as predicted, the friends had influenced the Ss' self-concepts more than had the nonfriends. An analysis of covariance design was again used to control for any differences in the amount of initial confirmation.

The results showed no significant difference between the amount of influence exerted on the two groups of *negative* Ss. That is, friends and nonfriends were equally successful in influencing the self-concepts of Ss who had described themselves in relatively unflattering terms.

In the case of the *positive* Ss, however, there was a tendency for the friends to be more influential than were the nonfriends. . . . This finding resulted from the fact that the *positive* Ss tended to accept their friends' opinions of them even though these opinions were relatively unflattering, while the Ss in the corresponding S-nonfriend group showed some tendency to rebel against the unfavorable opinions of nonfriends. However, neither of these trends was statistically significant.

People are apparently equally willing to accept the estimates of them held by friends and nonfriends, providing these estimates are relatively flattering to them. If they are perceived by others in a relatively unflattering light, however, they seem to accept the views of friends more readily than the views of nonfriends.

Hypothesis V. When an individual's friends change their opinions of him, these changes will tend to increase the agreement between his self-concept and his friends' perceptions of him.

Operationally, this hypothesis predicts that the D between S's first self-description and his friend's second description of him will be smaller than the D between the S's first self-description and his friend's first description of him. That is, on the assumption that the beliefs which make up the self-concept are like other beliefs learned in social interaction (8, 9), we predict that S's views will influence the views of his friend—the friend's attitude towards S will become increasingly similar to S's initial self-concept.

Analysis of the data fails to support this hypothesis. When the S-friend pairs were split into *positive* and *negative* groups, the same non-confirmatory results were obtained. It, therefore, appears that the individual is unable to "convince" others of the validity of his self-concept. Thus these data would appear to support only the "looking-glass" derivation of the self-concept described by Cooley (5) and Mead (11), and not the more general assumption, made initially in this study, that the self-concept is essentially no different from any other set of opinions or beliefs. The self-concept appears to be a special case in which influence is exerted in one direction only: from the other to the self, not from the self to the other. There are a number of possible explanations for this.

Perhaps the results obtained derive from the fact that, contrary to common assumption, people do not act in accordance with their self-concepts. Because of distortions caused by unconscious factors there may be a low correlation between their self-concepts and their overt behavior. They cannot, therefore, clearly communicate their self-concepts to others through their actions. This, in turn, precludes the possibility of successfully "convincing" others of the validity of these self-perceptions.

On the other hand, one may reason that the individual's self-concept is rarely regarded by others as being a valuable source of accurate information for forming an opinion about him. Even if his self-image is communicated to them, they may be relatively uninfluenced by it because of their suspicion that his beliefs about himself are distorted.

Hypothesis VI. During a given period of time, an individual will be more successful in influencing his friends to accept his self-concept as valid than he will be in similarly influencing the opinions of his non-friends.

The extent to which each S was successful in influencing others' opinions of him was quantified by subtracting the D between his first self-description and his friend's (or nonfriend's) second description of him from the confirmation score which was obtained in Test I. Thus, for a given S-friend pair, S would have been maximally successful in influencing his friend if the friend's second description of him had been altered so as to make it coincide with his (S's) initial self-image.

For reasons which were discussed earlier, indices of the type described above cannot exceed the individual's first confirmation score. S-friend and S-nonfriend pairs were, therefore, divided into subgroups and then matched on the basis of their initial confirmation score, as in Figure 1 and Figure 2. The results showed no consistent trend favoring either the friends or the nonfriends; neither group was influenced by their Ss' self-concepts.

When the S-friend and the S-nonfriend pairs are subdivided into *positive* and *negative* groups, the results are essentially unchanged. While the *positive* groups show some tendency . . . for the friends to be more strongly influenced by the Ss' self-concepts than were the nonfriends, this is almost solely due to the fact that the Ss' self-concepts were rejected more strongly by their nonfriends than they had been originally. This may have occurred as follows: The non-friends, recognizing that these Ss have rejected them, may have perceived them (Ss) in an increasingly unfavorable light. Since these Ss' self-descriptions were originally more favorable than their nonfriends' descriptions of them, this would result in increased disagreement.

Generally speaking, the results of this study support the theories of Cooley (5) and Mead (11). The Ss' self-concepts were significantly influenced by their friends' opinions of them, particularly when they were perceived by these friends in a relatively favorable light. On the other hand, the friends' perceptions of the Ss were not significantly influenced by the Ss' self-images. Increases in agreement within S-friend pairs were primarily due to changes in the Ss' self-concepts, rather than to changes in the friends' perceptions of the Ss.

The results with respect to the cohesion (or friendship-nonfriend-ship) variable were less clear-cut and the predicted differences appeared only in comparisons of *Positive Ss*. Thus the Ss' self-images were more affected by the views of friends who saw them in a relatively unfavorable light than by the views of nonfriends who had similarly unfavorable attitudes toward them. In addition, the *positive*

Ss influenced their friends' views of them more than they influenced the views of their nonfriends, although this resulted primarily from the fact that with the passage of time the nonfriends seemed to increase their disagreement with these Ss' self-images. Finally, there was a greater increase in confirmation for the *positive* S-friend pairs than for the *positive* S-nonfriend pairs. This result was not surprising, in view of the fact that increases in confirmation may be conceived of as being roughly related to the summated effects of (a) the influence exerted on S's self-concept, and (b) the influence which S is able to exert on the other person's perception of him. Since the *positive* S-friend pairs exceeded the *positive* S-nonfriend pairs on each of these "component" variables, it was to be expected that the two groups would also differ in terms of their respective increases in confirmation.

Summary

This study was based on the assumption that the self-concept is not essentially different from other collections of beliefs. The self-descriptions of a group of Ss were compared with others' estimates of them and certain perceptual changes were predicted. Predictions were also made regarding the effects of group cohesion on these hypothesized changes. Following a six-week period during which the participants in the study interacted freely, a retest was administered and the predictions checked. The results were in accord with the theories of Cooley (5) and Mead (11), but offered only partial support for the contention that the self-concept is no different from other beliefs; although the Ss' self-concepts were influenced by others' perceptions of them, there was no tendency for the self-estimates to affect the views of one held by others. Finally, the cohesion variable affected the results in a complex fashion which was related to the relative favorableness of the S's self-description.

References

1. Allport, G. W., and H. S. Odbert. "Trait-names: a psycho-lexical study," *Psychol. Monographs,* 47 (1936), No. 1 (Whole No. 211).

2. Back, K. "The exertion of influence through social communication," in L. Festinger, K. Back, S. Schachter, H. H. Kelley, and J. Thibaut, eds., *Theory and Experiment in Social Communication.* Research Center for Group Dynamics, University of Michigan (Rep. Stud. under ONR, 1950).

3. Cameron, N. *The Psychology of Behavior Disorders*. New York: Houghton, 1947.

4. Cattell, R. B. *Personality: A Systematic, Theoretical, and Factual Study*. New York: McGraw-Hill, 1950.

5. Cooley, C. H. *Human Nature and the Social Order*. New York: Charles Scribner, 1922.

6. Cronbach, L. J., and Goldine C. Gleser. "Assessing similarity between profiles," *Psychol. Bulletin*, 50 (1953), 456–473.

7. Edwards, A. L. *Experimental Design in Psychological Research*. New York: Holt, Rinehart, 1950.

8. Festinger, L. "Informal social communication," in L. Festinger, K. Back, S. Schachter, H. H. Kelley, and J. Thibaut, eds., *Theory and Experiment in Social Communication*. Research Center for Group Dynamics, University of Michigan (Rep. Stud. under ONR, 1950).

9. Festinger, L., and J. Thibaut. "Interpersonal communication in small groups," in L. Festinger, K. Back, S. Schachter, H. H. Kelley, and J. Thibaut, eds., *Theory and Experiment in Social Communication*. Research Center for Group Dynamics, University of Michigan (Rep. Stud. under ONR, 1950).

10. Helper, M. M. "Learning theory and the self-concept," *J. Abnormal Soc. Psychol.*, 41 (1955), 184–194.

11. Mead, G. H. *Mind, Self, and Society*. Chicago: University of Chicago Press, 1934.

12. Moses, L. E. "Non-parametric statistics for psychological research," *Psychol. Bulletin*, 49 (1952), 122–145.

13. Newcomb, T. M. *Social Psychology*. New York: Dryden, 1950.

14. Osgood, C. E., and G. H. Suci. "A measure of relation determined by both mean difference and profile information," *Psychol. Bulletin*, 49 (1952), 215–262.

15. Rogers, C. R. *Client-Centered Therapy*. New York: Houghton, 1951.

16. Sherif, M. *The Psychology of Social Norms*. New York: Harper, 1936.

17. Snygg, D., and A. W. Combs. *Individual Behavior*. New York: Harper, 1949.

18. Wilcoxon, F. "Individual comparisons by ranking methods," *Biometrics Bulletin*, 1 (1945), 80–82.

8

Interaction and Adaptation: Intimacy as a Critical Variable

Marjorie Fiske Lowenthal
and Clayton Haven

Friends and intimates help one to survive life crises not only
by contributing solutions to objective problems, but also
by serving as an emotional resource that helps to maintain
psychic adjustment. In this study the focus is on confidants
—persons with whom one shares one's most intimate
problems and joys. The results of this chapter add meaning
to the truism that "people need people," but more
importantly, it suggests that some persons may be less
affected by life change than others because of their
richer social life.

This paper is a sequel to previous studies in which we noted certain anomalies in the relation between traditional measures of social deprivation, on the one hand, and indicators of morale and psychiatric condition, on the other, in studies of older populations. For example, lifelong isolates tend to have average or better morale and to be no more prone to hospitalization for mental illness in old age than anyone else, but those who have tried and failed to establish social relationships appear particularly vulnerable.[1] Nor, with certain exceptions, do age-linked trauma involving social deprivation, such as widowhood and retirement, precipitate mental illness.[2] While these events do tend to be associated with low morale, they are by no means universally so. Furthermore, a voluntary reduction in social activity, that is, one which is not accounted for by widowhood, retirement, or physical impairment, does not necessarily have a deleterious effect on either morale or on professionally appraised mental health status.[3]

In analyzing detailed life histories of a small group of the subjects making up the samples for these studies, we were struck by the fact that the happiest and healthiest among them often seemed to be people who were, or had been, involved in one or more close personal relationships. It, therefore, appeared that the existence of such a relationship might serve as a buffer against age-linked social losses and thus explain some of these seeming anomalies. The purpose of the present study is to explore this possibility. In doing so, we shall first illustrate how two rather conventional measures of interaction

Abridged from Marjorie Fiske Lowenthal and Clayton Haven, "Interaction and Adaptation: Intimacy as a Critical Variable," in *American Sociological Review*, 33 (1968), 20–30. Reprinted by permission of the American Sociological Association and the authors.

This research program has been supported primarily by NIMH Grant MH-09145. Dr. Alexander Simon, Chairman of the Department of Psychiatry and Medical Director of Langley Porter Neuropsychiatric Institute, and Professor Lowenthal, are co-principal investigators. The authors wish to express their thanks to Professor Leo Lowenthal, Dr. Donald Spence, Dr. Thomas Trier, and especially Dr. Margaret Clark for their critical reviews of the manuscript.

1. Marjorie Fiske Lowenthal, "Social Isolation and Mental Illness in Old Age," *American Sociological Review*, 29 (February, 1964), 54–70.

2. Marjorie Fiske Lowenthal, "Antecedents of Isolation and Mental Illness in Old Age," *Archives of General Psychiatry*, 12 (March, 1965), 245–254.

3. Marjorie Fiske Lowenthal and Deetje Boler, "Voluntary vs. Involuntary Social Withdrawal," *Journal of Gerontology*, 20 (July, 1965), 363–371.

and role status are related to three measures of adaptation which represent different frames of reference. Taking advantage of the panel nature of the data, we shall further document these relationships by analyzing the effect of social gains and losses on adaptation. We shall then show how the presence or absence of a confidant serves as an explanatory variable in the overall trends and deviations noted in the relationships between the more conventional social measures and adaptation. Finally, we shall describe briefly the characteristics of those who do and do not have a confidant, and discuss the implications of these findings for adult socialization and adaptation.

The Concept of Intimacy. As we explored the literature prior to analyzing our own material on intimacy, we were struck by the paucity of references to the quality, depth, or reciprocity of personal relationships in social science materials. In their studies of the relationship between social interaction and adjustment, sociologists traditionally have been concerned with the concepts of isolation and anomie, often gauged or inferred from low rankings on quantitative indicators of social roles and contacts; that is, with questions such as how many roles a person fills, how much of his time is spent in interaction with others, and the relationship to the subject of persons with whom this interaction takes place. Several of these studies have established a modest relationship between social isolation and maladjustment.[4] With a few exceptions noted below, they have not taken into account the quality or intensity of the individual's relationships with others.

Psychologists have been concerned with dyadic relationships, including the parental and the marital, but although there are references in the literature to Freud's possibly apocryphal mention of the capacity for love as a criterion of mental health, one finds little research directly related to qualities or behavior reflecting the capacity for intimacy or reciprocity. Nor do the traditional personality tests often tap characteristics relevant to such concepts. Some research on animal and human infants, however, has explored this dimension. Harlow and Zimmermann[5] have shown that infant monkeys spend a great deal more time with a cloth mother surrogate than with a wire surrogate, regardless of which mother provides the milk. They conclude, as have

---

4. For a selected review of this literature, see Lowenthal (1964), *op. cit.*
5. Harry F. Harlow and Robert R. Zimmermann, "Affectional Responses in the Infant Monkey," *Science,* 130 (1959), 421–432.

Spitz and Wolf in their studies of human infants,[6] that the need for love is instinctual. Ferreira,[7] drawing on his own research and that of Bowlby,[8] concludes that the need for intimacy is "primary and of an instinctual nature . . . the intimacy need may represent a more basic instinctual force than oral or even nursing needs."

It is primarily the psychoanalysts and the analytically oriented psychologists who, largely on the basis of clinical insights, have stressed this capacity or need, often implying that from its development and fulfillment grow all other forms of social growth and constructive social action. One of the fundamental precepts of Angyal's theory[9] is that "existing in the thought and affection of another really is a very concrete level of existence. . . ." He goes on to say that the establishment and maintenance of such a close relationship is "the crux of our existence from the cradle to the grave." Erikson postulates the capacity for intimacy as one of the major developmental tasks of life, ideally to be achieved in the establishment of a close relationship with a person of the opposite sex in late adolescence and early adulthood.[10] While our data support this view, it seems clear that there are other viable forms of intimacy which are not necessarily experienced as substitutes for, or supplements to, a stable heterosexual relationship.

In the light of the general paucity of research on the problem of intimacy, it is not surprising that it has not been systematically explored in relation to older populations. Rosow's important study of friendship patterns under varying age-density conditions[11] does not take the depth of these relationships into account. Arth,[12] in his study

6.　Rene A. Spitz and Katherine M. Wolf, "Anaclitic Depression," *Psychoanalytic Study of the Child,* vol. 2 (New York: International Universities Press, 1946), 313–342.

7.　A. J. Ferreira, "The Intimacy Need in Psychotherapy," *American Journal of Psychoanalysis,* 24 (November, 1964), 190–194.

8.　John Bowlby, "The Nature of the Child's Tie to His Mother," *International Journal of Psychoanalysis,* 39 (September–October, 1958), 350–373.

9.　Andras Angyal, *Neurosis and Treatment: A Holistic Therapy* (New York: Wiley, 1965), 19.

10.　Erik H. Erikson, "Identity and the Life Cycle," *Psychological Issues,* Monograph 1 (New York: International Universities Press, 1959).

11.　Irving Rosow, *Social Integration of the Aged* (New York: Free Press of Glencoe, 1967).

12.　Malcolm Arth, "American Culture and the Phenomenon of Friendship in the Aged," in Clark Tibbitts and Wilma Donahue, eds., *Social and Psychological Aspects of Aging* (New York: Columbia University Press, 1962), 529–534.

of friendships in an aging population, is concerned with "close" friendships, but he does not define closeness. Blau's pioneering study of structural constraints on friendships of the aged[13] documents the importance of prevailing age-sex-marital status patterns in the establishment of friendships, but it does not discuss the quality or intensity of these relationships.

Obviously, this is a delicate area to explore with field research methods, and our own approach was a simple—if not crude—one. The analysis rests largely on responses to the question: "Is there anyone in particular you confide in or talk to about yourself or your problems?" followed by a description of the identity of the confidant. Still, the findings tend not only to confirm the insights of clinicians and the rather sparse observations of other researchers, but also to clarify some of the puzzling deviations we have noted in our own work in regard to the relationship between social measures, on the one hand, and adaptation, on the other.

The Sample

The sample on which this report is based consists of 280 sample-survivors in a panel study of community-resident aged, interviewed three times at approximately annual intervals. The parent sample included 600 persons aged sixty and older, drawn on a stratified-random basis from 18 census tracts in San Francisco. The sample of 280 remaining at the third round of interviewing is about equally divided in terms of the original stratifying variables of sex, three age levels, and social living arrangements (alone or with others). As might be expected, the panel differs from elderly San Franciscans (and elderly Americans), as a whole, by including proportionally more of the very elderly, more males, and more persons living alone. Largely because of the oversampling of persons living alone, the proportion of single, widowed, and divorced persons, and of working women, is higher than among elderly Americans in general. Partly because of the higher proportion of working women, their income level was higher than average (44 percent having an income of over $2,000 per year, compared with 25 percent among all older Americans). The proportion of foreign born (34 percent) resembles that for older San Franciscans in

13. Zena Smith Blau, "Structural Constraints on Friendships in Old Age," *American Sociological Review,* 26 (June, 1961), 429–440.

general (36 percent), which is considerably more than for all older Americans (18 percent). While some of these sample biases may tend to underplay the frequency of the presence of a confidant, we have no reason to believe that they would influence findings from our major research question, namely, the role of the confidant as an intervening variable between social resources and deprivation and adaptation.

Measures of Role, Interaction, and Adaptation. The two conventional social measures to be reported here are number of social roles[14] and level of social interaction.[15] Men tend to rank somewhat lower than women in social interaction in the younger groups, but up through age 74, fewer than 17 percent of either sex rank "low" on this measure (defined as being visited [only] by relatives, contacts only with persons in dwelling, or contacts for essentials only).[16] Isolation increases sharply beginning with age 75, however, and in that phase women are slightly more isolated than men (32 percent compared with 28 percent), possibly because of the higher proportion of widows than of widowers. In general, because they are less likely to be widowed and more likely to be working, men have more roles than women at all age levels, and this discrepancy becomes particularly wide at 75 or older, when 40 percent of the men, compared with only 15 percent of the women, have three or more roles. Among men, a low level of social interaction and a paucity of social roles tend to be related to low socioeconomic status, but this does not hold true for women.

The principal measure of adaptation in this analysis is a satisfaction-depression (or morale) score based on a cluster analysis of answers to 8 questions.[17] For a subsample of 112, we shall also report ratings of psychiatric impairment by three psychiatrists, who, working independently, reviewed the protocols in detail but did not see the sub-

14. Roles include parent, spouse, worker, churchgoer, and organization member.

15. Ranging from "contributes to goals of organizations" to "contacts for the material essentials of life only." All measures of interaction and adaptation reported here pertain to the second round of follow-up.

16. Only a few of the tables drawn upon for this paper are presented in the text; others are available on request.

17. The distribution of individual cluster scores was dichotomized at the median: persons falling below the median are called "depressed," and persons falling above the median are called "satisfied." Questions pertained to the sense of satisfaction with life, happiness, usefulness, mood, and planning.

jects.[18] We thus have a subjective indicator of the sense of well-being, and a professional appraisal of mental health status. A third measure, opinion as to whether one is young or old for one's age, is included to round out the adaptation dimension with an indication of what might be called the respondent's opinion as to his relative deprivation—that is, whether he thinks he is better or worse off than his age peers.

As is true for the social indicators, there are age, sex, and class differences in regard to these adaptation measures which we shall have to bear in mind in analyzing the relationship between these two dimensions. Among men, morale deteriorates evenly with advancing age, from somewhat over one-third "depressed" among those under 65 to about three-fifths among those 75 or older. The youngest women are more depressed than the youngest men (47 percent depressed), but there is no increase—in fact there is a slight decrease—in depression among the 65–74 year old women. The oldest women, however, are nearly as depressed as the oldest men. There are no consistent age or sex trends in regard to whether the subject thinks he is young or old for his age—a slight majority of both sexes at all age levels consider themselves young.

Mental health status, as judged by psychiatrists, indicates that if all age groups are combined, men are psychiatrically more robust than women. This is especially true for the oldest group (75 or older), where four-fifths of the men, compared with only two-fifths of the women, are considered unimpaired. The sex difference is reversed, however, in the middle age range (65–74), where men are judged to be more impaired than women (44 percent, compared with 29 percent rated impaired). While at first glance this discrepancy might be interpreted as a consequence of psychic crises relating to retirement, detailed analysis of a large psychiatrically hospitalized older sample[19] indicates that retirement rarely precipitates psychiatric disorder. But this same analysis does demonstrate clearly that physical deterioration in the elderly is frequently accompanied by psychiatric impairment. The sharp reversal of sex differences in mental health status in the

18. One-third (38 persons) were judged impaired, the majority (30 persons) only mildly so. Seven were rated moderately, and one severely impaired.

19. Marjorie Fiske Lowenthal, Paul L. Berkman and Associates, *Aging and Mental Disorder in San Francisco: A Social Psychiatric Study* (San Francisco: Jossey-Bass, 1967); A. Simon, M. Fiske Lowenthal, and L. Epstein, *Crisis and Intervention* (San Francisco: Jossey-Bass, 1970).

middle age group may, therefore, be associated with the earlier onset of physical impairment among men. The fact that the death rate for men between 65 and 74 is considerably greater than for women may, in turn, on the principle of survival of the fittest, account for the oldest men's (75 or more) again being judged of more robust mental health than women.

In view of the association between physical and mental health in the elderly, and of the association between poor health and low socioeconomic status, it is not surprising that there is also some relationship between low socioeconomic status and psychiatric impairment, though this association is more marked for men than for women. Low morale, on the other hand, is related to low socioeconomic status among both men and women.[20]

Relationship between Social Measures and Adaptation. . . . There is a clear and consistent relationship between social resources and good morale, and between social deprivation and low morale. Low social interaction, in particular, is strongly related to depression. While high ranks on both social measures contribute to the sense of relative privilege (feel young for age), a low rank is not related as consistently to a sense of relative deprivation as it is to poor morale. A high rank on the two social measures is more closely associated with professional ratings of good mental health than with the respondents' own reports on mood and sense of relative advantage or deprivation. A low rank on social measures, however, is not consistently or markedly related to a rating of impairment. In other words, social resources and social deficits appear to influence self-appraisals of mood, comparison of self with others, and professional appraisals of adaptation in different ways. Social roles and high interaction are apparently considered to

20. The index of current economic position is based on a combination of monthly rent, annual income, and the Tryon Index of San Francisco census tracts. The Tryon Index, with scores ranging from zero (low) to 10 (high), is based on proportions of persons in professional or managerial occupations, with college education, and self-employed, the proportion of dwelling units with one or fewer persons per room, and the proportion of domestic and service workers. See Robert C. Tryon, *Identification of Social Areas by Cluster Analysis* (Berkeley: University of California Press, 1955). The lowest quartile consists of persons who scored below the median on all three measures (the medians were: income, $2,500; rent, $60; Tyron score, 4.5), and the highest quartile consists of persons who scored above the median on all three socioeconomic measures.

be indicators of, or associated with, mental health—but their absence is not necessarily construed as indicative of impairment. The pattern of association between the social indicators and morale is just the reverse. Social deficits—at least as indicated by the social interaction measure—are more highly correlated with a depressed state than are social resources correlated with a satisfied state. The sense of relative privilege is enhanced by social advantage, but social disadvantage does not necessarily evoke a sense of relative deprivation, at least insofar as this sense is reflected by feeling average or old for one's age.

If we compare these social indicators, as reported at the second follow-up, with those reported at the first follow-up approximately one year earlier, we find that several changes took place. These trends were on the order of those noted for other variables used in the panel questionnaire.[21] Social interaction and role status closely resemble each other with respect to change, with 14 and 15 percent, respectively, "improving," and 20 and 21 percent, respectively, "deteriorating." The broad patterns of relationship between change in social resources and the three indicators of adaptation resemble those [discussed above]. Social losses are related to poor morale, but gains are not related to high morale. Gains are, however, highly correlated with good psychiatric status, though again decrements are not so strongly associated with poor status. Improvements in role and social interaction are related to a sense of relative advantage, as indicated by feeling young for one's age, but losses do not markedly contribute to a sense of relative deprivation (feeling old). This again suggests that a professional's judgment of mental impairment rests on factors other than the absence of indicators of health; an individual's subjective sense of well-being does not automatically result from supplying the role and interaction deficits that often are associated with low morale.

On the other hand, maintaining the status quo in social interaction and role is related to good adaptation, regardless of which indicator of adjustment is used. In fact, on four of the six correlations, stability proves to be more highly associated with good adaptation than does "improvement." At the same time, we note that sizeable proportions of those who suffered social decrements are well-adapted, ranging from one-third to over half, depending on the adaptation measure

21. Lowenthal and Berkman, *op. cit.*

used. Clearly, our conventional measures alone do not fully explain the relation between the individual's position and behavior in his social milieu, on the one hand, and his adjustment, on the other.

Pursuing our hypothesis with regard to the potential importance of a confidant as a buffer against social losses, we turn to Table 1, which shows the current presence or absence of a confidant, and recent losses, gains, or stability in intimate relationships, in conjunction with the three adaptation measures. As the first column shows, the presence of a confidant is positively associated with all three indicators of adjustment. The absence of a confidant is related to low morale. Lack of a present confidant does not, however, have much bearing on the individual's sense of relative deprivation, or on the psychiatric judgments of mental impairment. We suggest, though with the present data we cannot fully document, two possible explanations for these findings. First, as we have previously noted,[22] there are some lifelong isolates and near-isolates whose late-life adaptation apparently is not related to social resources. The sense of relative deprivation, at least for older persons, no doubt applies not only to current comparisons with one's peers, but also to comparisons with one's own earlier self. This would contribute to an explanation of the fact that some older people without a confidant are satisfied. They do not miss what they never have had. Our second explanation echoes the old adage that it is better to have loved and lost than never to have loved at all. The psychiatrists, in rating mental health status, may take *capacity* for intimacy into account, as indicated by past relationships such as marriage or parenthood. The respondent, in a more or less "objective" comparison of himself with his peers, may also take these past gratifications into account. However, such recollections may well be less serviceable on the more subjective level of morale and mood.

The right side of the table, showing change and stability in the confidant relationship, dramatically exemplifies the significance of intimacy for the subjective sense of well being: the great majority of those who lost a confidant are depressed, and the great majority of those who maintained one are satisfied. Gaining one helps, but not much, suggesting again the importance of stability, which we have noted in relation to the other social measures. Maintenance of an intimate relationship also is strongly correlated with self-other compari-

22. Lowenthal (1964), *op. cit.*

Table 1. The Effect of a Confidant on Adaptation

| | Current Presence of Confidant | | Change in Confidant Past Year | | |
	Yes	No	Gained	Lost	Maintained same confidant
	%	%	%	%	%
Psychiatric status					
Unimpaired	69	60	(60)	(56)	80
Impaired	31	40	(40)	(44)	20
Opinion of own age					
Young	60	62	42	49	61
Not young	40	38	58	51	39
Morale					
Satisfied	59	41	44	30	68
Depressed	41	59	56	70	32

sons and with psychiatrists' judgments, though losses do not show the obverse. This supports our suggestion that evidence of the *capacity* for intimacy may be relevant to these two more objective indicators of adaptation.

The great significance of the confidant from a subjective viewpoint, combined with the fact that sizeable proportions of people who showed decrements in social interaction or social role nevertheless were satisfied, raised the possibility that the maintenance of an intimate relationship may serve as a buffer against the depression that might otherwise result from decrements in social role or interaction, or from the more drastic social losses frequently suffered by older persons, namely widowhood and retirement. To test this hypothesis, we examined the morale of changers on the interaction and role measures in the light of whether they did or did not have a confidant.

The Intimate Relationship as a Buffer Against Social Losses. As Table 2 shows, it is clear that if you have a confidant, you can decrease your social interaction and run no greater risk of becoming depressed than if you had increased it. Further, if you have no confidant, you may increase your social activities and yet be far more likely to be depressed than the individual who has a confidant but has lowered his interaction level.[23] Finally, if you have no confidant and retrench in your social life, the odds for depression become overwhelming. The findings are similar, though not so dramatic, in regard to change in social role: if you have a confidant, roles can be decreased with no effect on morale; if you do not have a confidant, you are likely to be depressed whether your roles are increased or decreased (though slightly more so if they are decreased). In other words, the presence of an intimate relationship apparently does serve as a buffer against such decrements as loss of role or reduction of social interaction.

What about the more dramatic "insults" of aging, such as widowhood or retirement? While a few people became widowed or retired during our second follow-up year (and are, therefore, included among

23. Parallel analyses of the other two adjustment measures are not included here. The psychiatric ratings are available for only a subsample of 112 (and cells would become too small). The indicator of opinion of own age reflects trends similar, though not so marked, as those shown here, except for increase in role status, where the absence of a confidant does not contribute to a negative opinion.

Table 2. Effect on Morale of Changes in Social Interaction and Role Status, in the Presence and Absence of a Confidant

	Social Interaction						
	Increased				Decreased		
	Has Confidant		No Confidant		Has Confidant		No Confidant
	%		%		%		%
Morale							
Satisfied	55		(30)		56		13
Depressed	45		(70)		44		87

	Role Status						
	Increased				Decreased		
	Has Confidant		No Confidant		Has Confidant		No Confidant
	%		%		%		%
Morale							
Satisfied	55		(42)		56		(38)
Depressed	45		(58)		44		(62)

the "decreasers" in social role), there were not enough of them to explore fully the impact of these age-linked stresses. We, therefore, have checked back in the life histories of our subjects and located persons who retired within a seven-year period prior to the second follow-up interview or who became widowed within this period. Though our concern is primarily with social deficits, we added persons who had suffered serious physical illness within two years before the second follow-up contact, since we know that such stresses also influence adaptation.

. . . The hypothesis is confirmed in regard to the more traumatic social deprivations. An individual who has been widowed within seven years, and who has a confidant, has even higher morale than a person who remains married but lacks a confidant. In fact, given a confidant, widowhood within such a comparatively long period makes a rather undramatic impact on morale. Among those having confidants, only 10 percent more of the widowed than of the married are depressed, but nearly three-fourths of the widowed who have no confidant are depressed, compared with only about half, among the married, who have no confidant.[24] The story is similar with respect to retirement. The retired with a confidant rank the same in regard to morale as those still working who have no confidant; those both retired and having no confidant are almost twice as likely to be depressed as to be satisfied, whereas among those both working and having a confidant, the ratio is more than reversed.

Although relatively few people (35) developed serious physical illness in the two-year period prior to the second follow-up interview, it is nevertheless amply clear that a confidant does not play a mediating role between this "insult" of aging and adjustment as measured by the depression-satisfaction score. The aged person who is (or has recently been) seriously ill is overwhelmingly depressed, regardless of whether or not he has an intimate relationship. Superficially, one might conclude that this is a logical state of affairs. A social support—such as an intimate relationship—may serve as a mediating, palliative, or alleviating factor in the face of social losses, but one should not expect it to cross system boundaries and serve a similar role in the

24. This finding suggests the need for far more detailed questioning on the confidant relationship than we were able to undertake. It may well be that some married persons assumed that the question pertained to confidants other than spouses.

face of physical losses. On the other hand, why doesn't one feel more cheerful, though ill, if one has an intimate on whom to rely for support, or to whom one can pour out complaints? At this point we can only conjecture, but one possible explanation is that serious physical illness is usually accompanied by an increase in dependence on others, which in turn may set off a conflict in the ill person more disruptive to his intimate relationships than to more casual ones. This may be especially true of dependent persons whose dependency is masked.[25] A second possibility is that the assumption of the sick role may be a response to the failure to fulfill certain developmental tasks. In this event, illness would be vitally necessary as an ego defense, and efforts of intimates directed toward recovery would be resisted.[26] A third possibility is that illness is accompanied by increased apprehension of death. Even in an intimate relationship, it may be easier (and more acceptable) to talk about the grief associated with widowhood or the anxieties or losses associated with retirement than to confess one's fears about the increasing imminence of death.

Characteristics of Persons Having a Confidant; Confidant Identity. In turning to the question of who does, and who does not, maintain an intimate relationship, we found sex and marital status differences that were not unexpected, and some discrepancies with respect to age and socioeconomic status that seemed, at first glance, puzzling. Despite the fact that there were about twice as many widows as widowers in this sample, women were more likely to have a confidant than were men (69 percent, compared with 57 percent). Age trends are irregular. Both persons under 65 and those 75 and older were less likely to have a confidant than the 65 to 74 year olds. Women are more likely than men to have an intimate relationship at all age levels, and the differences between the sexes are especially pronounced in those under 65, where nearly three-fourths of the women and only half the men reported that they have a confidant. These findings tend to support those of Arth[27] and Blau[28] in regard to the social capacities and ad-

25. Alvin Goldfarb, "Psychodynamics and the Three-Generation Family," in Ethel Shanas and Gordon F. Streib, eds., *Social Structure and the Family: Generational Relations* (Englewood Cliffs, N. J.: Prentice-Hall, 1965), 10–45.

26. Lowenthal and Berkman, *op. cit.*

27. Arth, *op. cit.*

28. Blau, *op. cit.*

vantages of women. The married are notably more likely to have a confidant than those who are not; single persons are most deprived on this score, and the widowed fall between. Persons above the median on our socioeconomic measure are considerably more likely to have a confidant than those below it, and the differences are more marked for men than women. Education makes surprisingly little difference for either sex, but occupational differences are marked for men.

As to the identity of the confidant, among the nearly two-thirds of the sample who do have a confidant, the identity of this person is fairly evenly distributed among spouse, child, and friend. Siblings or other relatives as confidants are comparatively rare. Among women in general, husbands are least frequently mentioned, while wives are the most important for men. This is not only because women are more likely to be widowed, for if we look only at those who are married, or still married, men at all age levels are more likely to report a spouse than are women. Women are about twice as likely as men to mention a child or another relative, and more likely to name friends.

In view of the frequently noted class differences in social inter-action,[29] it does not surprise us that more than half again as many of those above the median on our socioeconomic measure have a confidant than do those below the median. The generally reported wider range of friendship patterns among the higher socioeconomic groups does not prepare us for the class differences in the identity of confidants reported by this older sample, however. More than three times as many of the higher class report a spouse than do those of lower socioeconomic status (28 percent compared with 8 percent). While this tendency holds among both sexes, the discrepancies are most dramatic among men (36 compared with 2 percent). Conversely, more than twice as many of the low socioeconomic group report a friend, and again it is men who account entirely for the discrepancy. Women of higher status are slightly more likely to have a friend as confidant than are women of lower status. Analysis of detailed life history interviews available for a subsample provide some evidence that the lesser importance of the spouse as confidant among the men of the lower socioeconomic group is connected with problems of masculine role and identity, low-status males considering close association with women a sign of male weakness. This he-man theory gains

29. *Ibid.;* Rosow, op. cit.

some support in the fact that among men, not having a confidant is more related to blue collar occupational status than it is to little schooling. Men in the blue collar occupations, whether skilled or un-skilled, would obviously—at least in the United States—have less opportunity to associate with women than would white collar males.

In these same life history studies, we have noted some examples of "a regression or escape into intimacy" with advancing age. That is, people who have maintained both intimate and other types of social relationships may, on retirement, for example, or after the departure of children from the home, withdraw to a situation where a close relationship with the spouse is, in effect, the only social contact. But this is by no means the rule. In general, the more complex the social life, the more likely is there to be an intimate relationship, no doubt, in part, because of the larger pool of social resources from which a confidant may be drawn. Among persons having three or more social roles, for example, three-fourths have a confidant, whereas among those having two or fewer social roles, only slightly more than half have a confidant. Similarly, two-thirds of those on the highest level of social interaction have an intimate relationship, while the majority of those whose interaction is limited to being visited by relatives do not. Such resources, however, are more important for men than for women.

9

Marriage Research and Conflict: An Integrative Review

William A. Barry

Marriage, by its ubiquity, is immensely important in the everyday lives of most people, and thus it is astonishing how little research attention has been given to it. It seems plausible that such an intense relationship must have major effects on the personalities and characters of husband and wife, yet relatively little is known about this. In this chapter, Barry reviews the research that has been done, reflecting the predominant concern of studies so far on the correlation between individual personalities and marriage adjustment.

. . . It would appear that homogamy (like choosing like) is a basic norm in mate selection [Tharp, 1963]. Homogamy obtains not only in regard to cultural and social variables (race, age, religion, ethnic origin, and social class) but also in regard to personality variables as measured by tests. Tharp sharply and decisively demolishes Winch's (1958) research purporting to show that need complementarity and not homogamy was the norm for mate selection from a pool of eligibles. Need-complementarity theory may not yet be dead, however, since the careful work of Bermann and Miller (1967) on roommate choices indicates that in stable relationships, need complementarity, at least in regard to certain needs, does prevail whereas it tends not to in unstable relationships. This kind of careful research has yet to be applied to marriage in an attempt to test Winch's hypotheses. The thoughtful theorizing of Rosow (1957) might also lead to a mode differentiated and careful use of a need-complementarity theory of mate selection. But as of now homogamy has a clear hold on the field.

If homogamy is the norm, there is still the question of how it works as a factor in mate selection. Do people look for likes consciously? Or can some other factor explain homogamous choices? Katz and Hill (1958) reviewed a number of studies demonstrating that residential propinquity is a strong factor in mate selection. These authors then try to raise residential propinquity to the level of a theory explaining mate selection, but the theory seems to reduce to the trivial observation that one must meet one's future spouse in order to select him or her. In spite of this stricture, propinquity, if understood as the social circle within which one moves, probably does account for much of the homogamy reported.

Propinquity in this sense might also explain Warren's (1966) findings, based on a national cross-sectional clustered sample of males, about the importance of the factor of educational level for homoga-

Abridged from William A. Barry, "Marriage Research and Conflict: An Integrative Review," in *Psychological Bulletin*, 73 (1970), 41–47. Reprinted by permission of the American Psychological Association and the author.

During most of the research for this paper, the author was supported by National Institute of Mental Health pre-doctoral fellowship 5-FL-MH-29,083 (MTLH). In its final preparation he was supported by United States Public Health Service research grant Communication Patterns, MH-10975, Harold L. Raush, Principal Investigator. The author expresses his gratitude to Harold L. Raush for his critical reading of earlier versions and his very helpful suggestions.

171

mous marriages. These findings can be explained by postulating that educational level defines to a great extent the social milieu where prospective mates meet. Propinquity on some basis thus narrows the field of eligibles to a relatively homogeneous group of people, but the question still remains as to how John chooses Jane from this group of eligibles.

One promising middle-level theory has been proposed by Coombs (1966). His thesis, based on an extensive review of social psychological research on interpersonal attraction, is that value consensus fosters mutually rewarding interaction and leads to interpersonal attraction. The theory posits that: (a) persons with similar background learn similar values; (b) interaction between such persons is mutually rewarding since they share a universe of discourse which fosters communication and understanding with a minimum of tension and ego threat; (c) these rewards leave a feeling of satisfaction with the partner and a desire to continue the relationship whence homophily and homogamy follow. Coombs tested the theory by running a dance pairing computer-selected college students of varying degrees of value consensus. Given the initial homogeneity of the whole sample (i.e., all were students at the same school), the fact that he got results in the hypothesized direction (i.e., the greater the value consensus, the greater the tendency to continue the relationship) is an a fortiori argument for the theory. The earlier findings of Kirkpatrick and Hobart (1954), of Udry, Nelson, and Nelson (1961), and of Kerckhoff and Davis (1962) are also consistent with the theory. Note that the theory does not necessarily posit conscious selection on the basis of similar values; it merely assumes that similar values (or perceived similar values) foster rewarding interaction. Note, too, that the evidence for both general and specific theory applies only to the college educated or middle class.

Obviously, value-consensus theory presents a cognitive approach to understanding mate selection. Clinicians and personality theorists of a dynamic persuasion will be ill at ease with the neglect of dynamic factors such as unconscious motivation, defenses, and object-relations schemata in this theory. Psychoanalytic theory, for one, speaks of displacement of cathexis from the cross-sex parent to nonrelatives on the basis of some characteristic or set of characteristics common to the parent and the final love object (Flügel, 1950); but, as Tharp (1963) pointed out, only sporadic and generally unsuccessful attempts to test this hypothesis have been made. One can only sympathize with the researcher who tries to sort out the factors which might be involved. Is it the tilt of the nose, a characteristic gesture, a quality of the voice, etc., which pulls Jane out of the crowd for John?

A convergence of cognitive and dynamic orientations might well be found in concentration on object-relations theory. Coombs (1966) pointed out that in the research on interpersonal attraction, assumed similarity of values has been found to be more highly correlated with attraction than actual similarity. Thus, it can be postulated that one assimilates the initially attractive person to one's positively evaluated object-relations schema where the other is imaged as concordant in values. One could further hypothesize that the outcome will at least partly depend on the degree of differentiation of the schema. If it is undifferentiated, there may be a tendency to see all attractive people as sharing one's own values, and thus one may not be able to ascertain whether values do in fact coincide sufficiently. If in fact values do not coincide and if marriage eventuates, conflict is probably inevitable (a point documented later). If, on the other hand, the schema is more differentiated, then one can test for compatibility of values and attitudes before marriage. We shall return to this point later.

Studies of Marital Adjustment

Background factors associated with marital adjustment. Reuben Hill (Waller and Hill, 1951, p. 358) lists the following background factors associated with marital adjustment in various studies (number of confirmations and disconfirmations in parentheses): happiness of husband's parents' marriage (5, 1), husband's close attachment to his father (3, 0), husband's childhood residence in the country (3, 0), husband's age at marriage (3, 2), husband's educational level (3, 3). Of interest in this list is the frequency with which the husband's background is found to be related to marital adjustment, a point stressed by Burgess and Cottrell (1939) on the basis of their study.

The split of three confirmations and three disconfirmations on husband's educational level can now be adjudicated on the basis of a number of studies (Hillman, 1962; Hollingshead, 1955; Williamson, 1952, 1954) culminating in Bernard's (1966) definitive work based on the 1960 census data. It is beyond doubt that by any measure of socioeconomic status (income, occupation, or education) there is a positive correlation between such status indices and endurance of marriage (Bernard, 1966) or reported happiness with marriage (Gurin, Veroff, and Feld, 1960). All of the studies cited find the clearest evidence for such a relation with regard to the husband's rather than the wife's status.

Personality factors associated with marital adjustment. Burgess and Wallin (1953) summarize the findings of the earliest investigators regarding the relationship between personality variables and marital adjustment (as measured by adjustment tests). The happily married are characterized as emotionally stable, considerate of others, yielding, companionable, self-confident, and emotionally dependent. The unhappily married show opposite characteristics.

Studies comparing happily married to unhappily married couples on personality tests measuring neurotic traits support the conclusion that there is a correlation between neurotic traits in the individual and marital unhappiness [Terman et al., 1938; Burchinal et al., 1957; Dean, 1966]. In all three investigations the wives have slightly higher correlations between personality test scores and marital happiness.

There have been two longitudinal studies of engaged couples who were followed through marriage. Burgess and Wallin (1953) reported correlations of .25 for men and .18 for women between Thurstone Neurotic Inventory scores before marriage and marital adjustment scores on the follow-up. More interesting and significant is the study by Uhr (1957) using Kelly's (1955) data from a follow-up after almost 18 years of marriage. Uhr divided the couples into happily and unhappily married groups. He reported that the husbands in the unhappy group 18 years after marriage were, at the time of engagement, significantly more neurotic in tendency, more introverted, and more self-conscious (as measured by the Bernreuter Personality Inventory) than the happy husbands. On the other hand, the wives who were unhappy 18 years after marriage differed at engagement from the happy wives on only one variable of the Bernreuter (being less sociable). The longitudinal studies indicate that at the beginning of marriage, at any rate, the husband's personality traits are more strongly related to later happiness in marriage than are the wife's.

One of Uhr's other findings lends some credence to the developmental problems upon whose solution depends the course of future development (Havighurst, 1953). After 18 years of marriage the unhappy husband's scores on the Bernreuter had improved so that they did not differ significantly from the happy husbands except in now being significantly less sociable. There were no significant differences between happy and unhappy wives. It may be, as Uhr intimates, that the personality weaknesses of the unhappy husbands hindered the couples' early adjustment to marriage, thus leading to unhappiness in marriage and difficulty with later tasks of marital development, as the developmental task theory hypothesizes. The unhappy husbands' increase in postive self-report as measured by the Bernreuter may be due to positive extramarital experiences with jobs, etc. There is also a possibility that the increase reflects a tendency to see themselves as healthier than they are.

Both Burchinal, Hawkes, and Gardner (1957) and Dean (1966) report that while husbands' marital adjustment scores correlate negligibly, if at all, with their wives' scores on personality inventories, the wives' marital adjustment scores vary positively and significantly with the husbands' personality scores. Moreover, Dean notes that the variable which correlated highest with both the husbands' and the wives' marital adjustment scores was wives' positive rating of their husbands' emotional maturity (.52 and .55, respectively). Thus, if both the husband and wife rate him positively on a personality inventory, the marriage tends to be happy.

A cautionary note seems in order. Corsini (1956b) reported that the only significant correlation between understanding of the spouse (prediction of the spouse's responses to a number of statements in a Q sort) and marital happiness occurred for his sample of 20 couples when the husband was the object of the understanding. Amazingly enough, this relation was maintained even when the husbands and wives were randomly paired, that is, those wives who "predicted" the randomly selected husband's Q sort well were happy and so were these husbands. There seems to be a stereotyped conception of the "good" husband which is shared by both husbands and wives. No such stereotype appears for wives. Corsini thus argues that the relevant relationship is between marital happiness and a culturally shared conception of what a husband should be. No one has replicated Corsini's findings, and, unfortunately, no one has seen fit to follow his lead and test significant findings for couples against randomly paired couples. Until this is done, we cannot be sure whether the correlations noted above are spurious or real indicators of a relationship between the personality strengths of husbands and marital happiness.

175

Tharp (1963), having reviewed the studies of Dymond (1954), Corsini (1956a, 1956b), and Luckey (1960a, 1960b) on interpersonal perception among spouses, concludes that marital happiness is related to the wife's perception of the husband being congruent with his self-perception. This congruence relates to culturally accepted definitions of what a good husband ought to be. But none of these studies found a relationship between marital adjustment and the congruence of the husband's perception of his wife with her self-perception. A more recent study by Kotlar (1965) corroborates this generalization. Moreover, in his study, even though the husbands in happy marriages did not differ from their counterparts in unhappy marriages in self-ratings of dominance (Leary Interpersonal Check List), their wives rated them significantly higher on this dimension than the wives in the unhappy marriages rated their husbands. Kotlar concludes that the important factor may not be congruence of perception but the motivation to perceive the husband as above average in fulfilling his marital role. These studies on interpersonal perception fit Corsini's reasoning about the stereotyped conception of the husband's role. What is intriguing, however, is the question of why wives in happy marriages see their husbands as above average and further what the functional connection is between happiness in marriage and such perception. It is, of course, also possible that the husbands in unhappy marriages overrate themselves and that their wives' perceptions are more veridical.

A number of studies have shown that similarity of personality is related to marital adjustment (Blazer, 1963; Corsini, 1956a; Dymond, 1954; Pickford, Signori, and Rempel, 1966). Levinger and Breedlove, (1966) have corroborated Byrne and Blaylock's (1963) suggestion that assumed similarity of attitudes may provide an index of marital satisfaction. Levinger and Breedlove report that assumed similarity of attitudes is more highly correlated with husbands' marital satisfaction than with wives'. Again the longitudinal nature of Uhr's (1957) study sheds light on the possible reasons for these positive associations. Kelly (1955), reporting on the same data but without dividing the couples into happy and unhappy groups, had shown that husbands and wives do not tend to become any more similar after 18 years of marriage than they were at the time of engagement. Uhr, however, reports that over all 72 variables studied the happy husbands and wives were more *different* from one another at the time of engagement than were the unhappy couples. But after 18 years of marriage the happy spouses are more alike, the unhappy ones more unlike one another. And the nature of these changes is consistent with what we have been noting in all these studies. The most consistent in their responses over the 18-year period are the happy husbands, followed by the unhappy wives. Thus, the changes that occur seem to be by the happy wives in the direction of their husbands and by the unhappy husbands in the direction away from their wives.

A pattern seems to be emerging from these data. Factors pertaining to the husband appear to be crucial to marital success. Background factors generally considered to lead to a stable male identity, such as happiness of the husband's parents' marriage and the husband's close attachment to his father, are related to happiness in marriage. The higher the husband's socioeconomic status and educational level, the greater the marital happiness. The more stable and nonneurotic the husband portrays himself on personality inventories at the time of marriage and the more consistent he is in such self-portrayal over the course of the marriage, the happier the marriage. The higher the wife rates him on emotional maturity as well as on fulfilling his role as husband in conformity to cultural expectations, the happier the marriage. The more the wife comes to resemble her husband on attitude and personality inventories over time, the happier the marriage. It would appear—to generalize a bit—that a solid male identification, established through affectional ties with the father and buttressed by academic and/or occupational success and the esteem of his wife, is strongly related to happiness in marriage for the couple.

References

Bermann, E., and D. R. Miller. "The matching of mates," in R. Jessor and S. Feschbach, eds., *Cognition, Personality, and Clinical Psychology.* San Francisco: Jossey-Bass, 1967.

Bernard J. "Marital stability and patterns of status variables," *J. Marriage and the Family,* 28 (1966), 421–439.

Blazer, J. A. "Complementary needs and marital happiness," *Marriage and Family Living,* 25 (1963), 89–95.

Burchinal, L. G., G. R. Hawkes, and B. Gardner. "Personality characteristics and marital satisfaction," *Social Forces,* 35 (1957), 218–222.

Burgess, E. W., and L. S. Cottrell. *Predicting Success or Failure in Marriage.* Englewood Cliffs, N. J.: Prentice-Hall, 1939.

Burgess, E. W., and P. Wallin. *Engagement and Marriage*. Philadelphia: Lippincott, 1953.

Byrne, D., and B. Blaylock. "Similarity and assumed similarity of attitudes between husbands and wives," *J. Abnormal Soc. Psychol.*, 67 (1963), 636–640.

Coombs, R. H. "Value consensus and partner satisfaction among dating couples," *J. Marriage and the Family*, 28 (1966), 166–173.

Corsini, R. J. "Multiple predictors of marital happiness," *Marriage and Family Living*, 18 (1956), 240–242 (a).

Corsini, R. J. "Understanding and similarity in marriage," *J. Abnormal Soc. Psychol.*, 52 (1956), 327–332 (b).

Dean, D. G. "Emotional maturity and marital adjustment," *J. Marriage and Family*, 28 (1966), 454–457.

Dymond, R. "International perception and marital happiness," *Canadian J. Psychol.*, 8 (1954), 164–171.

Flügel, J. C. *The Psychoanalytic Study of the Family*. London: Hogarth, 1950.

Gurin, G., J. Veroff, and S. Feld. *Americans View Their Mental Health: A Nationwide Interview Survey*. New York: Basic Books, 1960.

Havighurst, R. J. *Human Development and Education*. New York: Longmans, Green, 1953.

Hillman, K. G. "Marital instability and its relation to education, income, and occupation: an analysis based on census data," in R. F. Winch, R. McGinnis, and H. R. Barringer, eds., *Selected Studies in Marriage and the Family*, rev. ed. New York: Holt, Rinehart, 1962.

Hollingshead, A. B. "Class differences in family stability," in M. B. Sussman, ed., *Sourcebook in Marriage and the Family*. New York: Houghton, 1955.

Katz, A. M., and R. Hill. "Residential propinquity and marital selection: a review of theory, method, and fact," *Marriage and Family Living*, 20, (1958), 27–35.

Kelly, E. L. "Consistency of the adult personality," *American Psychologist*, 10 (1955), 659–681.

Kerckhoff, A. C., and K. E. Davis. "Value consensus and need complementarity in mate selection," *Amer. Soc. Rev.*, 27 (1962), 295–303.

Kirkpatrick C., and C. Hobart. "Disagreement, disagreement estimate, and non-empathetic imputations for intimacy groups varying from favorite date to married," *Amer. Soc. Rev.*, 19 (1954), 10–19.

Kotlar, S. L. "Middle-class marital role perceptions and marital adjustment," *Sociology and Social Res.*, 49 (1965), 283–294.

Levinger, G., and J. Breedlove. "Interpersonal attraction and agreement: a study of marriage partners," *J. Person. Soc. Psychol.*, 3 (1966), 367–372.

Luckey, E. B. "Marital satisfaction and congruent self-spouse concepts," *Social Forces*, 39 (1960), 153–157 (a).

Luckey, E. B. "Marital satisfaction and parent concepts," *J. Consult. Psychol.*, 24 (1960), 195–204 (b).

Pickford, J. H., E. I. Signori, and H. Rempel. "Similar or related personality traits as a factor in marital happiness," *J. Marriage and the Family*, 28 (1966), 190–192.

Rosow, I. "Issues in the concept of need complementarity," *Sociometry,* 20 (1957), 216–233.

Terman, L. M., P. Buttenwieser, L. W. Ferguson, W. B. Johnson, and D. P. Wilson. *Psychological Factors in Marital Happiness.* New York: McGraw-Hill, 1938.

Tharp, R. G. "Psychological patterning in marriage," *Psychol. Bulletin,* 60 (1963), 97–117.

Udry, F. R., H. A. Nelson, and R. Nelson. "An empirical investigation of some widely held beliefs about marital interaction," *Marriage and Family Living,* 23 (1961), 388–390.

Uhr, L. M. "Personality changes during marriage." Unpublished doctoral dissertation, University of Michigan, 1957.

Waller, W. W., and R. Hill. *The Family: A Dynamic Interpretation.* New York: Dryden, 1951.

Warren, B. L. "A multiple variable approach to the assortative mating phenomenon," *Eugenics Quart.,* 13 (1966), 285–290.

Williamson, R. C. "Economic factors in marital adjustment," *Marriage and Family Living,* 14 (1952), 298–301.

Williamson, R. C. "Socioeconomic factors and marital adjustment in an urban setting," *Amer. Soc. Rev.,* 19 (1954), 213–216.

Winch, R. F. *Mate Selection: A Study of Complementary Needs.* New York: Harper, 1958.

10
Power, Status, and Love
Theodore D. Kemper

Levels of affection and degree of control were seen to be important aspects of parent-child relationships in Chapter 3. In this chapter, Kemper uses similar variables to analyze relationships among adults. In particular, he proposes that adult relationships can be characterized by the respective statuses of the persons (i. e., the amount of esteem that each gives the other) and by their respective powers or capabilities to enforce demands. Different combinations of status and power are seen to yield qualitatively different relationships. The chapter is largely theoretical and its ideas await empirical tests, but it places adult relationships within a conceptual framework that already is well-documented, that is continuous with the frameworks for analyzing other types of relationships, and that gives fresh perspective to the study of marriage and marriage adjustment.

In recent years, a cumulative body of evidence gathered from a variety of sources has suggested that social behavior might be fruitfully understood as stemming from at least two basic dimensions. Depending on the type of data, these dimensions have been variously labeled *individual prominence and achievement* and *sociability* (Carter, 1954); *assertiveness* and *likeability* (Borgatta, Cottrell, and Mann, 1958; Borgatta, 1964); *authoritarian-control* and *hostility-rejection* (Zuckerman, 1958); *control* and *affection* (Schutz, 1958); *autonomy versus control* and *love versus hostility* (Schaefer, 1959); *interpersonal deprivation versus interpersonal seeking* (Longabaugh, 1966). Despite the variations in dimensional labels and the nuances of difference implied, the two relational themes contained in these concepts are (1) control of one actor by another, and (2) the degree of positive orientation of actors to each other. There is good sociological sense in subsuming the two sets of labels under the standard sociological rubrics of *power* and *status*.

Power may be understood, in the Weberian sense, as one actor realizing his will over the opposition of other actors (Weber, 1947). Social relations in which power is a feature are thus marked by various degrees of *involuntary compliance,* or dynamically, attempts are made to gain compliance by means of coercion, threat, and punishment.

Prepared especially for this volume. Mr. Kemper is Associate Professor, Department of Sociology, Queens College of the City University of New York.

Status, on the other hand, may be understood as *voluntary compliance* with respect to the desires, wishes, and requests of another. This includes the manifold forms of deference and prestige, concrete material rewards such as money or goods of value, intimate expressive accessibility either in emotional or physical forms, etc.

Although other dimensions of relationship have been proposed, the power and status dimensions appear to be universal emergents, reported in all studies. Other dimensions appear to be functions of the particular task in which the persons or groups under observation are engaged (cf. Longabaugh, 1966). It is possible, thus, to take a speculative leap as follows: if power and status relations are the two basic dimensions of social behavior, then all common parlance terms for social relationships may be comprehended by positioning actors in a two-dimensional power-status space, i.e., relationships as diverse as totalitarianism and romantic love could be explicated, at this level of abstraction, by locating the actors in the space consisting of power and status coordinates.

In this chapter, we shall concentrate on the analysis of a single type of relationship in power-status terms, namely *love*. We will propose a typology of love relationships as well as some developmental paths taken by love relations under certain conditions. Some consequences for the actors are then treated.

Types of Love

Discussions of love are usually frustrated by the criticism that there are many different kinds of love, and that different conclusions must be drawn depending on which type of love we are talking about. Fromm (1956), for example, mentions *brotherly* love, *motherly* love, *erotic* love, *self*-love, and love of *God*. This is certainly a plausible, but not necessarily an exhaustive list. Until some analytic paradigm is available from which the various types of love can be derived, discussions of love must necessarily be limited by the uncertainty concerning those other conceptual types of love not yet discovered. In this section we wish to propose such a paradigm, which can then provide a comprehensive basis for analytical investigations of the various kinds of love.

To begin, we will propose a very simple assumption, namely, that if we wish to identify a relationship between two actors as somehow involving love, then *at least* one of the actors must receive extremely high *status* from the other actor. Thus, if A loves B, then B receives extremely high status from A. How high is somewhat open to question. Does it mean that A would die for B if the circumstances required? This is possible; although for most people this is a rare test of love and thus does not assist us in defining love for the great mass of humans. We can perhaps resolve the ambiguity by suggesting that the status must be implicitly limitless.

If we accept the assumption just proposed, i.e., that a love relationship implies at least one actor with extremely high status, we have a means of discovering how many different types of love relationships are possible. We do this by plotting all of the dyadic possibilities between two actors in the power-status space in which one or both actors are extremely high in status. Power in this case is left to vary freely and will assist in generating the various types of love. Table 1 shows that there are seven possibilities.

Before discussing these types of love, it is important to recall the definitions of power and status. The former represents punishment or the threat of it and may include anything from a raised eyebrow or an omitted salutation to homocide. Status on the other hand means the voluntary compliance with the actual or suspected desires of the other.

Examination of Table 1 shows that we present only extreme or ideal types. It is possible, of course, that except for at least the one actor who is very high in status, the power and status position of the other actor can vary unrestrictedly, as can the power position of the higher status actor. Thus, it is conceivable that the actor who has less power and status could have a moderate amount of both rather than

Table 1. Seven Types of Love

Type	Actor A		Actor B	
	Power	Status	Power	Status
1: Romantic love	High	High	High	High
2: Psychoanalytic transference	High	High	Low	High
3: Brotherly love	Low	High	Low	High
4: Infidelity	High	High	High	Low
5: Love of God; or infatuation	High	High	Low	Low
6: Adulation by fans	Low	High	Low	Low
7: Parent-infant	Low	High	High	Low

having none at all, and this is probably a frequent case that might perhaps be added as an empirical instance of some importance. Yet we believe that little is changed fundamentally for theoretical purposes by treating only the ideal types. Baudelaire (1947) suggests that love is like a surgical operation, in which the one who loves more is like the patient under the knife of the one who loves less. Thus, if Baudelaire is correct, even a small differential in loving makes a vast difference. Since, too, the power and status scales are continual, it is empirically possible for infinite gradations of love relationship to exist. We cannot, however, deal with more than the ideal types of love; otherwise, no analysis is possible. Let us look now at the seven types of love.

1. Romantic Love

A reciprocated relationship between two actors, where each gives the other high status and both have high power, is, in our view, what is commonly designated as romantic love. The mutual involvement of the parties is of such an order that each can punish the other severely for real or imagined transgressions in order to insure absolute conformity in the future, as well as to assuage the hurt feelings of the past. To be romantically involved is to wield power as well as pleasure, and occasionally to be a victim. The "romantic agony" in which the loved object is also a threat is indeed an agony, since it is an approach-avoidance or cognitive imbalance phenomenon. The very instability of such situations reveals, indeed, how precarious romantic love must be. The fact that romantic love is the only relationship in which both actors are extremely high in both power and status, i.e., at the very ends of the two relational scales, explains why this form of relationship is both so significant in human affairs as well as so constant a theme of man's concern.

2. Psychoanalytic Transference

The type of love in which one actor is high in both power and status while the other is high in status only is a most unusual one, and while it may occur in the ordinary course of social life, it is rare indeed. The closest we can come to an institutionalized relationship of this type is the case of psychoanalytic transference. There the analysand de-

velops a strong attachment for the analyst, endowing him, in his surrogate role for an earlier love object, with very high status and power.
The analyst may not, theoretically, as well as therapeutically, return
the love in kind, but the analysand must be valued, thus he receives
high status from the therapist. The critical point here is that the analysand not be given power, for then he and the analyst are romantically
involved, as in the first of the love relationships discussed above.

3. Brotherly Love

The millennial hope of man, as well as, obviously, his vain dream,
has been to order social life on the basis of brotherly love, when "they
shall beat swords into ploughshares" and "neither shall they learn
war any more." Sociologically, it would entail that all men be high
in status, and equally low in power. Compliance would be willing;
self-interest would metamorphose into the other's interest; and disagreement, should it arise, would be adjudicated by mechanisms that
neither invoke power nor require it. If there is an abiding problem for
men, it is surely focused here: how to let go of power and accord each
other status. Ethical injunctions dating back thousands of years have
advised men that this is their salvation, yet have not, at the same time,
provided the theory or the means by which the transformation from
power to status can be accomplished. It is a bold hope that social
science can uncover enough of the wellspring of human action to make
it possible to devise the means by which the low power, high status
goal can be attained.

4. Infidelity

The very fragility of romantic love should not astonish us, nor should
we be amazed that it most often evanesces. One form of the disinte-
gration of romantic love is infidelity. The deceived partner still accords
high power and status to the unfaithful one, but the latter no longer
accords status to the other. The usually clandestine nature of infidelity
is a warrant of the unsuspecting partner's power and not of his or her
status. Discovery usually leads to punishment for the unfaithful one.
Though infidelity is a normative form, with relatively large percentages of American men and women engaging in explicit acts of infidelity (Kinsey et al., 1948, 1953), the inherent dangers of the game

militate against an extended duration of this form of relationship. Thus, it usually constitutes a transitional phase in the passages of the relationship from one of love to another which is not love.

5. Love of God or Infatuation

In some relationships there is such a disparity between the subjective or objective positions of the two actors, that the relationship is largely one-sided. Sudden infatuations are of this order, where a mere glance is sufficient to inflame the sentiments of one person while the other is unaware of the excitement he stimulates or the actual power and status he holds. The ultimate form of dualism of this kind of love is often found in the love of God. In various ways men are commanded to love God, and it is believed that God loves man. The two, however, can scarcely be equated. God's power and status are infinitely greater than man's, according to the doxologies of most western religious traditions. God demands from man, not merely extremely high status, but *hyper-status,* while man can only hope for, though not demand, high status from God.

6. Adulation by Fans

The most attenuated form of the love relationship is found in the case where the power and status of one partner is low and only the status of the other partner is high. Prototypical of this form of love is the relationship between fans and their idol. Though one thinks immediately of the crescendoes of adulation which performers are able to evoke from their fans, the relationship is essentially weak because the bonding is unidirectional, marked by the high status of only one of the actors and by the inability of either actor to exert power over the other on an individual basis. Collectively, however, fans do command very great power. When the relationship is seen in that form, it is no longer the same, for it becomes a parent-infant love relationship (which will be discussed next). When fans gain power, gained usually by wielding it, there is little chance that they can return to the relative innocence of adulation. It is one of the apparent effects of power, that once used it stains a relationship in a manner difficult to erase or to forget.

7. Parent-Infant

The newborn infant is, in the overwhelming majority of cases, accorded virtually supreme status. No need or desire is denied the neonate. Every cry is heard and heeded. Sociologically, it is a fine position to hold vis-à-vis another. The *other,* in this case, is usually the mother who is bereft of status. Virtually nothing is given to or done for her by the infant. Of course, this is because the infant is not aware of mother's interest nor does it know the appropriate symbol system required to detect mother's wants, etc. Mother does, however, have one resource when all else is lacking, namely power. Her physical and psychological superiority can in most cases prevail over the infant. Certain infant tactics which may gain it power, as prolonged shrieking, crying, etc. do not succeed; if they did, the relationship would deteriorate to type four discussed above, namely infidelity. Mothers, therefore, are willing to accept the low status part of the bargain. As the child grows older, the relationship changes in most cases to one of the other forms and over time probably passes through a number of forms, not excluding romantic love. The best outcome from the point of view of both parties, if such an evaluation may be ventured here, is probably brotherly love. All other outcomes ultimately lead to dissatisfaction or stultification for one or both of the actors.

Dynamics of Status Conferral

If, as we have proposed, love involves one or both parties who are extremly high in status, it is critical to our understanding of "falling in love," staying in love, and falling out of love, to know how status comes to be accorded in the first place. Indeed an answer to this question will also provide us with an answer, in part, as to how status comes to be withdrawn.

The key to the entire issue, in our view, is that *according status is involuntary.* We mean here that true willingness to comply with the wishes, needs, and interests of another, especially at the very high levels implied by love, is not an act under the rational, volitional control of the actor who is according the status.

We mean by "involuntary" simply that the actor does not respond with his head as it were, but with his heart or gut, i.e., truly expressively. The meaning of expressive can be understood to say that involuntary feelings necessarily lead to involuntary behaviors. This is not to say that expressiveness will emanate at all. One may find one-self in love with someone else's wife and come to the very rational decision to contain one's feelings and never express them. Thus, it is possible to decide volitionally in most cases whether or not to behave toward the other in terms of high status conferral. But whether one feels love, or not, in the first place, is, in this view, an involuntary matter.

This insight, which we believe is crucial to an understanding of the status dimension of social relations, we obtain from the important work of Hamblin and Smith (1966). Their interest was in testing a theory of status prediction. Graduate students evaluated professors on various characteristics such as merit of publication, merit of teaching, professional demeanor, cordiality, appearance, and likableness. These bases of evaluation were employed in a multiple regression analysis to predict professorial status as the dependent variable. Hamblin and Smith hypothesized that status might operate analogically to psycho-physical responses of a nonvoluntary nature, where the magnitude of the response is an exponential function of the magnitude of the stimulus:

$$R = cS^n, \text{ or multivariate, } R = cS_1{}^{n1}S_2{}^{n2} \ldots S_k{}^{nk}$$

Here R equals the status of the professor, c is a constant and S_i are the evaluation stimuli, such as merit of publications, etc., and n is the exponent. When the multivariate multiplicative equation is transformed into a logarithm, it reads,

$$\log R = \log C + n_1 \log S_1 + n_2 \log S_2 + \ldots + n_k \log S_k$$

The exponents are now equivalent to regression coefficients. Hamblin and Smith were able to account for 98 percent of the variance in the dependent variable, professorial status, by means of this model. Support for the involuntary nature of status conferral was provided by this successful application of the psychophysical multiplicative model. This remarkable outcome, however, is no more so than the statement which prepares the ground for it:

> Genuine status giving is problematical because having feelings of approval, respect, or esteem for someone appears to be beyond the individual's direct choice. In fact, the evidence suggests that all feelings, including those of approval, respect, or esteem, are part

of a class of nonvoluntary responses. As with all nonvoluntary responses, these feelings are presumably controlled by the unconditioned or the conditioned stimuli which elicit them. Apparently, an individual must provide the valued attributes and behavior which produce in the other the feelings of approval, respect, or esteem; then and only then may these feelings be communicated as genuine status. (Hamblin and Smith, p. 184)

We would demur only in that the communication of the feeling is not involuntary. Though one cannot will to love another, one can will whether or not this feeling is to be broadcast.

Status, then, is accorded to a person when he exhibits some behavior or characteristic which stimulates the other to confer status. This is somewhat like the phenomenon of releasing-stimuli described by ethologists (Lorenz, 1952). Involuntary status conferral is also akin to what Zetterberg (1966) describes as "emotional overcomeness."

We may now ask what kinds of behavior or trait can evoke status conferral. Though the number of possibilities here is indeed infinite, we would say that each culture institutionalizes certain standards and transmits them as values. There is, for example, nothing inherently wrong with feet or shoes acting as objects to evoke admiration and love, but because a culture does not elevate feet or shoes for status conferral it is only for the rare fetishist that bizarre objects may have this power. There are also sex differences which may be considered worthy of status—for women in western societies: beauty, devotion, loyalty, purity (at one time largely in the sexual sense), modesty, dependency; for men: strength, competence, handsomeness, wealth, sensitivity, dependability, intellect, artistry. For both sexes, the characteristics are not wholly independent of each other. For example, sensitivity and artistry, or artistry and competence, are not orthogonal. The point, however, is that some configuration of characteristics is proposed, sometimes explicitly, sometimes implicitly, by the culture. as being worthy of status accord. Individuals, of course, with their partially idiosyncratic socialization experiences (Brim, 1960) are differentially implanted with the standards that define who among the opposite sex is worthy of status, and what is worthy of status in one's own behavior and traits. The psychoanalytic tradition (Flügel, 1950) is even more explicit about what characteristics of the love object cue off involuntary status accord: the loved one is deemed to be a replica in some sense of the first love object, namely mother or father.

When another manifests behavior or traits that are in conformity with the internalized standard, status accord is automatically triggered. We admire the other, respect him, like him, defer to him, etc. But this is not yet love. For we love only one or at most a few, though we may respect or admire many. This is a pivotal matter, for it is conjectural whether the limited extensity of love (Sorokin, 1954) is the reflection of inherent limits on the accordance of very high or extremely high status due to the *nature* of men, or whether it is a limit imposed by the fact that by chance alone very few others who are capable of cueing off the very highest status accord are within our ken at any one time. A possible reason for the latter, if it is the true explanation of the limited extensity of love, may be that the other does not release the very highest status accord unless that other conforms to the internalized standards in not merely one, but in a number of characteristics. Thus, he may not only be handsome, but competent, sensitive, and dependable. She is not only beautiful, but modest, loyal, pure. The well-known "halo-effect" may then be depended upon to cast a proper glow over the remaining characteristics of the other. At this point we have another who is a paragon with respect to perhaps all of the standards of virtue that were internalized. How can one fail to grant extremely high status to such a person? Conclusively, loving that person is in no sense an act of will.

If one accords status to another because he or she reflects so many of these desirable characteristics and acquires others by halo, it is understandable that status will be withdrawn if those characteristics are no longer manifested and are not replaced by others. Additionally, if the status grantor's internalized standards change in the course of time, status will be withdrawn unless the other exhibits deserving behavior or traits in the new areas of evaluation. Finally, in addition to manifesting the panoply of desirable traits deserving status, a person may neutralize his status by exhibiting traits that are unworthy in the other's eyes. For example, he is handsome, witty, wealthy, and sensitive, but he derives his income from criminal activity. Or despite many good qualities, she is a compulsive gambler or an alcoholic. Just as in the case of status-accord, the disesteemed traits lead to an *involuntary* withdrawal of status. In general, the content of the standards for involuntary status conferral and withdrawal are crucial for an understanding of the dynamics of how love relationships change; this will be discussed extensively below.

Power and Dependency

We shall discuss now a fundamental aspect of the operation of power in social relations which also has a bearing on the management of love relations. Several authors have discussed the relationship between *power* and *dependency* (Blau, 1955, 1964; Thibaut and Kelley, 1959; Emerson, 1962). Emerson has done perhaps the most to work out the theory of how power and dependency are related. In a neat and highly plausible formulation, Emerson proposes that power and dependency are inversely related, that is, the power of A over B equals the dependency of B on A. In symbolic terms, $P_{AB} = D_{BA}$. Also, the power of B over A equals the dependency of A on B, or $P_{BA} = D_{AB}$. Within certain limits this is a highly satisfactory proposition. It is, however, entirely *structural* in nature. This is to say that it reflects only the outcome and does not take account of the dynamics or process.

The outcome of any relationship in the power dimension may indeed be A over B, because B depends on A more than A depends on B. But in the course of the struggle during which the structural outcome is decided, B, the more dependent actor, may have initiated more power plays than A. The rationale here is that the more dependent an actor is, as long as he is not in a state of total dependence, the more likely he is to employ power to get what he needs when it is not forthcoming. Ultimately, his dependency may require that he settle for what the other is willing to give him, i.e., he has less power in the relationship, but the dependency may provoke him to use more power acts more frequently.

From this process perspective, the formulation would be: the probability (Pr) of A using Power acts (PA) against B equals the dependency of A on B. Similarly for B, the probability of B using power acts against A equals the dependency of B on A; or $\Pr \left\{ PA_{AB} \right\} = D_{AB}$ and $\Pr \left\{ PA_{BA} \right\} = D_{BA}$. This result is in a sense a reversal of the structural position on power and dependency presented by Emerson and others. In our view, this process view of the probability of power acts is crucially implicated along with structural power in the dynamics of how love relationships degenerate, all too often, into their opposite, namely, conflict and hatred.

Given the definitions of love by Goode (1959) and Orlinsky (in press) cited above, a connection between sexual desire and power can be suggested. The nexus, we believe, is the exclusive dependency on the other for the massive gratification at least ideally involved in sexuality. The monogamous relationship, essentially a bilateral monopoly on sexuality, is, thus, especially prone to generating dependency in the sexual area, and, by derivation, power. Cultures in which sexual fidelity is neither seriously prescribed nor practiced, do not engender relational power in the sexual sphere. Dependency, however, is conceivable on any ground on which one actor derives gratification from another; therefore, relationships in which dependency is entailed for whatever reason generate power: *structural* power in the sense of $P_{AB} = D_{BA}$ and what may be called *process* power, defined in terms of the probability, $Pr \left\{ PA_{AB} \right\} = D_{AB}$, as described above.

Power, Status, and Love

We shall attempt now to weave together the various strands of the foregoing presentation to provide a theoretical answer as to why love dies. It is indeed perplexing, and to those involved usually painful, as to why two persons bound by ties of love can wind up by hating each other. We believe that the power and status definition of love, the involuntary nature of status conferral, and the relationship between power, power acts, and dependency are the basis for an adequate answer to this question.

The principal assumption of this part of the analysis is that, in general, to receive status is considered good and desirable by most persons, and that power or punishment, if used against them, is considered undesirable. We are excluding from consideration here pathological types, e.g. masochists, since they represent reversals of the usual response pattern.

It will be further assumed here that the most deeply felt love relationship is the romantic type, as described above, in which both actors have extremely high power and status. This level is not usually attained at once, although literary reportage frequently wastes no time in bringing the principals to this point. Perhaps more realistically, the love relationship may begin, on one or the other side, as an instance of adulation by fans (type six discussed above). In fortunate instances where the adulation is or becomes mutual, the relationship passes into the brotherly love model of type three. In less fortunate instances, where the love is not requited, it may die or, as is often the case, the less attainable the object, the more desirable it becomes (see Blau's discussion, 1964), and the relationship is elevated to the level of an infatuation (type five). This now involves, for the first time, power. In the bilateral adulation case, anchored temporarily in the vicinity of brotherly love, the recognition of mutual dependency—frequently at first, but not always, contingent on sexuality—propels the relationship into full-blown romantic love. Now both actors in the drama have high power and status.

There is much subjective evidence that the romantic condition inspires the sentiment that each will love (i.e., confer extremely high status) the other eternally. There is also much objective evidence to deny this subjective conclusion. The record suggests that instead of taking root permanently at the high power, high status mutuality of romantic love, the relationship very frequently develops in the direction of continued high power with a moderate-to-considerable loss of status on one or both sides. In the case of one-sided status loss, we have the relationship of infidelity (type four), and in a large number of cases the infidelity is explicitly sexual, although, of course, it need not be. Although the reduction of the sexual dependency of the unfaithful partner implies a loss of power for the duped one, this is more than compensated for by the latter's gain in power (potentially) if the infidelity is exposed. In the case of mutual status loss, each is "unfaithful" to the other, and this may or may not involve sexual infidelity. In this case, most conclusively, the relationship can no longer be called love, according to the definitions of this paper. Neither of the parties is now accorded extremely high status by the other.

In some proportion of the cases, varying apparently by phases of the life cycle (Rollins and Feldman, 1970), the romantic love relationship reverts to an earlier form in which power is reduced on both sides. A return to the brotherly love position, according to the assumptions which head this section, is the best possible outcome. Power is reduced and status conferral remains high. It is difficult to tell what proportion of love relations actually fit this outcome, despite the data by Rollins and Feldman (1970) cited above. This is because no measurements of power and status were obtained, but only subjective estimates of happiness. There ought, however, to be some rough correspondence between subjective happiness and the low power, high status condition.

Since a very substantial proportion of love relationships manifest high power and lowered status outcome, it is of great interest to understand how this may occur. We suggest that the standards for status conferral themselves may be involved in either of two major ways in the destruction of a love relationship. First, the standards employed by males may confer status for merely transitory aspects of the female, such as beauty and sexual appeal. Second, the standards employed by the female may preclude involuntary status conferral in the first place if they are based on instrumental calculation, a marketplace orientation which relates more to power than to status. Kephart (1967) found, for example, that women more than men are more likely to marry someone they don't love. In such instances, what would our understanding of power, status, dependency, power plays, and involuntary status conferral lead us to predict?

Let us first examine the case of the couple where the male has responded to internalized standards of the more transitory kind. Two bases exist for a relatively rapid decline in the level of male status conferral. First is the transitory nature of the original status conferral ground, i.e., the relatively speedy satiation with beauty and sexuality, or the fading of these in the flesh. Second is the fact that females are in general ranked lower than males in the culture. While falling in love may create a surge of egalitarianism or even reversal of adjudged superiority, attenuation or loss of the grounds for this unwontedly high status reduces the female to her former, lesser status. Thus, while she obviously continues in most cases to command higher status from her husband (or lover) than do other women, she is, after all, *just* a woman and partakes, therefore, in the generally lower status of women.

The male's withdrawal of status which constitutes phase one, can happen in innumerable ways from failing to open the door for her to failing to wait until she is ready for orgasm. The withdrawal of status conferring acts once generously and gladly given, is experienced as a loss. It is something like taking a cut in salary (another form of status grant), and the fact that it may happen gradually is no less disturbing. Some empirical support for the early decline of status accord by males is provided by Rubin (1969), who collected data from dating and engaged couples. Though males are more loving in the earliest phase of the relationship there is an alternation with their girlfriends in who loves more over time, and by the time the relationship is 18 months old or more there is a definite downward trend in the males' love scores (cf. also, Pineo, 1961; Marlow, 1968; Rossi, 1968).

The second phase is entered when the woman resorts to the most frequent device for maintaining and regaining status, namely process power, an unusually ineffective interaction. The flagging attentions of the male are usually commented on (a mild taste of power), complained about (a somewhat stronger taste of power), and, if fruitless, ignited into tirades (a full-blown taste of power). But to what avail? The man's status withdrawal was as little calculated as the initial status conferral. Power acts on the part of the wife can only make her less attractive than she is already, yet the sense of loss of the accustomed status level drives her to the use of power.

Baum (in press) has suggested that the greatest strains in marriage occur in those phases of the life cycle when the male is most involved in working out his career and the female is engaged primarily in caring for young children. Divorce rates would tend to substantiate at least the chronology of this argument (Jacobson, 1950). Nonetheless, we may argue that the two bases for male status withdrawal, namely the fading of the initially attractive, but often transitory qualities in the woman, and the re-devaluation of female interests, pursuits, activities, etc. in conformity with the prevailing cultural image are what lead to the interpersonal deterioration that marks what is obviously for many couples an admittedly difficult period. There is no inherent reason why career involvement should lead to status withdrawal from the wife, nor why child care should lead to power plays against the husband.

Although we do not have direct evidence for status withdrawal on the part of the husband, data presented by Rollins and Feldman (1970) show that between 50 and 100 percent of the wives are more likely than the husbands to report negative feelings arising one or more times a month from husband-wife interaction, at least until the fifth phase of the life cycle (oldest child under 21 years). These negative feelings we surmise are due in part to the husband's status withdrawal. In addition, the husband begins to use power.

Phase three is launched by the male's retaliation for the power used against him. This often involves the use of structural power which exists to a greater or lesser degree due to the objective dependency of females during the early child-rearing phases. This dependency, in Emerson's formulation, discussed above, makes possible the ultimate victory in coercive terms of the one who is less dependent. Where he had previously only insulted her by withdrawing status, he now adds injury by using his power in retaliation. His perspective on the matter is not rational, but partakes of a common response pattern, viz. power is visited on those who employ power against one. Where power on the woman's part might have been effective when the couple were in a romantic love relationship, it now only releases the use of his power in retaliation which in turn causes his status to decline in her estimation. Barry (1968) reports that troubled marriages are especially marked by the use of coercion by husbands.

This is the beginning of phase four, and here we are, by definition, no longer speaking of a love relationship. That is, once the husband and wife no longer confer extremely high status on one another, and the husband has resorted to coercion, we are dealing with another form of relationship, in which power not status is the pivotal variable. Compliance between the partners is ordered not voluntarily, but coercively. If the relationship continues as a series of power exchanges, status-conferral is less and less possible or likely. As we have spelled out in an assumption previously, men and women do not like power to be used against them. It is rare that a victim of power (barring pathology) can bring himself to grant status to his tormenter. This is true despite religious injunctions of western tradition dating back more than 2,000 years. There is little left to be said about the devolution of the love relationship into the archetypical pattern of power-driven nation-states. Whether or not such relationships endure de facto (for example, in the case of marriage), depends in part on other matters which cannot be gone into here.

We have proceeded in the foregoing discussion of the devolution of a love relationship on the assumption that while the male's standards for status conferral are transitory, the female's are not (nor are they instrumental and, therefore, inauthentic). We turn now to the probable outcome of the latter case, where the female's standards are inauthentic. The ultimate details differ little from what has just been discussed. Only the origin of the devolution differs.

It must be understood that the security motive that leads a woman to marry a man she does not love, though she may like him, is in part made possible by the perception that *she* is loved, i.e., she can feel secure because he confers on her unlimited status. That this status may be based on transitory standards is usually unknown to both parties. But when the status is withdrawn this is perceived as extremely threatening. This may be understood as follows.

In cases of female instrumental calculation, the relationship does not attain to romantic love, but falls immediately into the cell of infidelity. This means that the male has high structural power due to the female's acceptance of dependency while, in the ordinary case at the outset, she has both high power and status. When, due to transitory selection standards and lower valuation of women, the male begins to withdraw status, the female's instrumental plan is demolished. Not only is security threatened, but the compensation for the psychic costs of intimacy with a person one does not love, i.e., the status he conferred, is now also diminishing.

If we add to this the inevitable recognition on the male's part of the inauthenticity of the relationship from the female's part, i.e., the fact that he was never granted the status that the culture legitimates, there is an immediate ground for use of power on his part. Thus, all the ingredients of relational devolution are present, except in a heightened and more advanced stage.

From the foregoing it appears that the solution to the problem of deterioration in love relationships involves several factors: the standards for involuntary status conferral, the relative valuation of males and females in the culture, and the disastrous consequences of dependency, i.e., the creation of both structural and processual power. Some considerable revisions of culture, social structure, and division of labor as they relate to males and females may be seen as necessary before these problems can be mitigated.

Oblove

In the preceding, we have examined love relationships in terms of personal and cultural standards of selection and of the dynamics of power. Now we must examine another basis of flawed love relationship involving explicitly dispositional aspects of the actors. Dependency, which we have seen is implicated with power in love relationships, may be viewed not only in relational terms, but also as part of the personalities of the actors. An additional danger in love relationships is found here. Despite very strong, even passionate levels of manifest emotion, the relationship may involve not love, but pseudo-love, which we shall call *oblove* (the latin prefix 'ob' means against). Oblove is based on *need* for the other, but it implies nothing about giving to the other, which was our definition of love at the outset. Thus, one may oblove another and, mistakenly, due to the intensity of arousal, believe one is in love and persuade the other of this too. But oblove, based on need, is dependency, and dependency implies power, and power implies not loving but punishing. We have already seen the consequences of that.

Maslow (1959) has also differentiated between love and oblove, calling them *being*-type love and *deficiency*-type love. Fromm (1956), too, has discussed the matter from the point of view of self-love. In his formulation, a sufficient degree of *self-love* would preclude oblove. An additional insight is afforded by the love-oblove distinction.

Oblove expresses a *need* and is, therefore, a description of the psychological state of an actor. Love, on the other hand, is a matter of giving by one actor to another and is, therefore, a description of the relationship between the actors. In a well-worn Freudian term, oblove is narcissistic in that its fundamental concern is to satisfy the want in the self. A loving relationship, however, binds two actors together into a relational unit.

Effects on the Actors

We have set forth above a typology of love as well as some grounds for the development of romantic love and its devolution. It is of some interest to see what effects the various phases of relationship have on the actors themselves. In terms of indices of satisfaction, Rollins and Feldman (1970) provide data (some cited above) which show a declining level of satisfaction for both husbands and wives over the life cycle, with a curvilinear pattern of recovery of satisfaction in the later stages. This recovery phenomenon is due in part to changing outlooks and opportunities for gratification in the later phases of the life cycle. But the data are in part confounded by the loss of the cumulative subset of couples who divorce. Thus, by the later stages of the life cycle most of the divorces that are going to take place have already done so. Therefore, the residual pool of marriages, we can assume, are happier on the average than the earlier pool.

The curvilinear phenomenon of satisfaction over the life cycle is also shown in the work of Burr (1970) who relates satisfaction to such matters as the handling of finances, social activities, household tasks, degree of companionship, and sexual activity. A sustained difference between husbands and wives in the level of satisfaction over the entire life cycle is found only in regard to satisfaction with household tasks. Here men are clearly more satisfied than their wives.

In his extensive analysis of the literature, Barry (1970) suggests that the pivotal actor in the development of satisfactory or unsatisfactory relationships in the marriage appears to be the husband. Background factors of the husband, particularly whether or not he came from a happy home (Waller and Hill, 1951), are predictive of marital adjustment for both husbands and wives.

It is possible to speculate that husbands who come from unhappy homes have several disadvantages accruing to them in relation to their own marriages. Assuming identification with the father, the husband was exposed to a model who employed a good deal of power against the mother and provided relatively little status. The husband thus learned to relate to females with high power and low status, i.e., in a non-loving way. Standards for status conferral may also become distorted since, in a conflictive setting, it may become difficult to appreciate the qualities of the mother that would make for adequate standards. Should the son side with the mother in the conflict, a rejection of father and masculinity may develop—not to the point of homosexuality—but to the point of excessive dependency on the mother, and, perhaps, on any female. This implies a reversal of the standard cultural roles of male vis-à-vis female, and there are many females who would feel uncomfortable in such a role reversal. The husband from the generally happy home fortunately avoids these problems which can only exacerbate the difficulties of culturally induced transitory standards, and the normal issues of power and dependency.

Some support for these notions is found in the work of Uhr (1957) whose data show that husbands in unhappy marriages of some 18 years' duration were more likely than happy husbands to have entered marriage as somewhat neurotic, introverted, and self-conscious men (as measured by the Bernreuter personality inventory). Wives in these marriages differed initially from the wives in happy marriages in that they were less sociable initially.

It is useful to learn, however, that a retest of both husbands and wives in the eighteenth year of marriage showed that unhappy husbands differed from happy husbands only in the fact of their lower sociability, while wives did not differ at all. While there is again the confounding discussed above due to loss of the couples whose marriages were so troubled that they divorced, it is apparent that personality effects are minimized over the life cycle for marriages that survive. This is due apparently to certain changes in the degree of congruence of the husbands and wives in the happy and unhappy marriages (Uhr, 1957). Over time, the data show, the wives in happy marriages became *more* like their husbands. For the unhappy couples, the husbands became *less* like their wives.

In general, contrary to the complementarity hypothesis (Winch, 1958), the data on personality of husbands and wives suggest that mates in happy marriages are more similar to each other than those in unhappy marriages (Cattell and Nesselroade, 1967; Pickford, Signori, and Rempel, 1966). Barry (1970) suggests that developmental trends in personality over the course of the marriage, as demonstrated by Uhr (1957), may explain the growth of similarity.

These outcomes can be explained in straightforward fashion by the application of the power/status theory. In happy couples, continued, high-status conferral by one partner is matched by similar, high-status conferral by the other. In each case, the traits of the one that triggers the status conferral are *also* accompanied by gratifications received from the other. Further, for each mate there are qualities admired by the other and therefore little power is used by one to alienate the other from those qualities. This would seem to be an ideal situation for modeling the qualities of the other.

Among the unhappy couples the initially admired attributes are accompanied by inadequate status and (probably) high power. The dynamics of stimulus generalization in cases of punishment suggest that the qualities of the other will be rejected for modeling (Hilgard, 1953).

The data cited also show a higher degree of accommodation on the part of wives than husbands over the course of the marriage, and this would help to explain the generally higher levels of negative feelings of women over the life cycle. This is true despite the fact that in generally happy marriages there is a desire to accommodate. The need for women to make the change, however, may be seen to be a function structurally, of lower power, in the relationship. We have cited the higher security-dependency factor in women's marriage choices, and consequently their greater vulnerability to the husband's power. In general, husbands seem to be happier when they have more power in the marriage (see Kemper, 1966), since this not only enables them to command greater compliance of their mates but also this relational superiority conforms with the cultural image of the deserved ranking of the sexes.

Summary

We have sought in this chapter to set forth a typology of love relationships based on a speculative understanding of the basic dimensions of all social relationships, namely, power and status. We postulated in addition some dynamic processes in terms of status conferral and withdrawal which affect the level of love. In conjunction with this, we reasoned further that the power factor was particularly interwoven with dependency in both a structural and processual sense. This relationship is seen as especially crucial for the devolution of romantic love relationships. The data cited support the contention that romantic love relationships do devolve into lowered levels of satisfaction for both spouses over the course of the life cycle, although there is an indication that satisfaction is curvilinear in nature.

Finally, we must realize that in the dynamics of the devolution of the romantic love relationship, whether by reason of crises occurring in various stages of the life cycle, or by virtue of the interpersonal dynamics of power and status relations, there is an interaction effect between these and the personal characteristics of the actors in the love drama. Husbands in particular appear to be the causal agents in determining the direction of the love relationship. And behind them hovers a culture which fosters transitory standards for status conferral and lesser ranking for women—both of these a breeding ground of trouble for a loving relationship.

References

Barry, William A. *Conflict in Marriage: A Study of Interactions of Newlywed Couples in Experimentally Induced Conflicts.* Doctoral dissertation, University of Michigan. Ann Arbor, Mich.: University Microfilms, No. 68–13 (1968), 273.

Barry, William A. "Marriage research and conflict: an integrative view," *Psychol. Bulletin,* 73 (1970), 41–54.

Baudelaire, Charles. *Intimate Journals*, trans. by Christopher Isherwood. Hollywood, Calif.: McRodd, 1947.

Baum, Martha. "Love and marriage: a study of engaged couples," *Sociol. Inquiry*, in press.

Bernreuter, R. G. *The Personality Inventory*. Palo Alto, Calif.: Consulting Psychologists Press, 1938.

Blau, Peter. *The Dynamics of Bureaucracy*. Chicago: University of Chicago Press, 1955.

Blau, Peter. *Exchange and Power in Social Life*. New York: Wiley, 1964.

Borgatta, Edgar F. "The structure of personality characteristics," *Behav. Science*, 9 (1964), 8–17.

Borgatta, Edgar F., Leonard S. Cottrell, Jr., and John H. Mann. "The spectrum of individual interaction characteristics and interdimensional analysis." Monograph Sup. 4, *Psychol. Rep.*, 4 (1958), 279–319.

Brim, Orville G., Jr. "Personality development as role learning," in Ira Iscoe and Harold Stevenson, eds., *Personality Development in Children*. Austin: University of Texas Press, 1960.

Burr, Wesley R. "Satisfaction with various aspects of marriage over the life cycle: A random middle class sample," *J. Marriage and the Family*, 32 (1970), 29–37.

Carter, Launor F. "Evaluating the performance of individuals as members of small groups," *Personnel Psychol.*, 7 (1954), 477–484.

Cattell, Raymond B., and John R. Nesselroade. "Likeness and completeness theories examined by 16 personality factor measures on stable and unstable married couples," *J. Person. and Soc. Psychol.*, 7 (1967), 351–361.

Emerson, Richard M. "Power-dependence relations," *Amer. Soc. Rev.*, 27 (1962), 31–41.

Flügel, J. C. *The Psychoanalytic Study of the Family*. London: Hogarth, 1950.

Fromm, Erich. *The Art of Loving*. New York: Harper, 1956.

Goode, William J. "The theoretical importance of love," *Amer. Soc. Rev.*, 24 (1959), 38–47.

Hamblin, Robert L., and Carole R. Smith. "Values, status and professors," *Sociometry*, 29 (1966), 183–196.

Hilgard, Ernest R. *Introduction to Psychology*. New York: Harcourt, Brace, 1953.

Jacobson, Paul H. "Differentials in divorce by duration of marriage and size of family," *Amer. Soc. Rev.*, 15 (1950), 235–244.

Kemper, Theodore D. "Mate selection and marital satisfaction according to sibling type of husband and wife," *J. Marriage and the Family*, 28 (1966), 346–349.

Kephart, William M. "Some correlates of romantic love," *J. Marriage and the Family*, 29 (1967), 470–479.

Kinsey, Alfred C. et al. *Sexual Behavior in the Human Male*. Philadelphia: Saunders, 1953.

Kinsey, Alfred C. et al. *Sexual Behavior in the Human Female*. Philadelphia: Saunders, 1948.

Longabaugh, Richard. "The structure of interpersonal behavior," *Sociometry,* 29 (1966), 441–460.

Lorenz, Konrad Z. *King Solomon's Ring.* New York: Thomas Y. Crowell, 1952.

Marlowe, Roy H. "Development of marital dissatisfaction of Mormon college couples over the early stages of the family life cycle." Unpublished master's thesis, Brigham Young University, 1968.

Maslow, Abraham. "Cognition of being in the peak experiences," *J. Genet. Psychol.,* 54 (1959), 43–66.

Orlinsky, D. E. "Love relationships in the life cycle: a developmental interpersonal perspective," in H. A. Otto, ed., *Love as a Growth Experience,* in press.

Pickford, John H., Edro I. Signori, and Henry Rempel. "Similar or related personality traits as a factor in marital happiness," *J. Marriage and the Family,* 28 (1966), 190–192.

Pineo, Peter C. "Disenchantment in the later years of marriage," *Marriage and Family Living,* 23 (1961), 3–11.

Rollins, Boyd C., and Harold Feldman. "Marital satisfaction over the family life cycle," *J. of Marriage and the Family,* 32 (1970), 20–28.

Rossi, Alice S. "Transition to parenthood," *J. Marriage and the Family,* 30 (1968), 26–39.

Rubin, Isaac Michael. "The social psychology of romantic love," Unpublished Ph.D. dissertation, University of Michigan, 1969.

Schaefer, Earl S. "A circumplex model for marital behavior," *J. Abnormal and Soc. Psychol.,* 59 (1959), 226–235.

Schutz, William C. *FIRO: A Three Dimensional Theory of Interpersonal Behavior.* New York: Holt, Rinehart, 1958.

Sorokin, Pitirim. *The Ways and Power of Love.* Boston: Beacon, 1954.

Thibaut, John W., and Harold A. Kelley. *The Social Psychology of Groups.* New York: Wiley, 1959.

Uhr, L. M. "Personality changes during marriage," Unpublished Ph.D. dissertation, University of Michigan, 1957.

Waller, Willard W., and Ruben Hill. *The Family: A Dynamic Interpretation.* New York: Dryden, 1951.

Weber, Max. *The Theory of Social and Economic Organization,* trans. by A. M. Henderson and Talcott Parsons. New York: Oxford University Press, 1947.

Winch, Robert F. *Mate Selection: A Study of Complementary Needs.* New York: Harper, 1958.

Zetterberg, Hans L. "The Secret Ranking," *J. Marriage and the Family,* 28 (1966), 134–142.

Zuckerman, M. et al. "Normative data and factor analysis of the parental attitude research instrument," *J. Consult. Psychol.* 22 (1958), 165–171.

Part III
Organizational and
Institutional Settings

In modern societies people spend vast amounts of time in organizational settings—sometimes by choice, sometimes by social fiat. The psychological impact of organizational settings is of special interest for this reason, but also because it is within organizations and institutions that society exerts its most direct control over the development of individuals by controlling both the structure of the organizations and the recruitment of different kinds of people into different kinds of settings.

The chapters in this section suggest some of the ways that organizational policies and patterns can become transformed into psychological effects. Chapters 11 and 13 focus on that most ubiquitous institution in our society— the school. Kohn and Schooler's extensive analysis in Chapter 12 suggests that the kind of work one does has far-reaching consequences for the development of personality and character, even though the magnitude of particular effects is relatively small. The last two chapters, 14 and 15, focus on organizations designed to rehabilitate, or resocialize, certain individuals.

Other relevant materials are in other sections. Chapter 17 shows that a relationship between education and democratic attitudes is stable over a range of nations and cultures; a correlation between education and field independence is noted in Chapter 19, and a peculiar effect of the college experience on moral thinking is discussed at length in Chapter 18. The unusual propensity of firstborns to attend college and achieve occupational success is discussed in Chapter 5. Chapter 20 indicates that movement into all-male work groups in a traditional society can have a major impact on psychological functioning, and that parallel processes may occur in our own society as a consequence of military service or of imprisonment.

11

The Impact of College: Epilogue

Kenneth A. Feldman
and Theodore M. Newcomb

Few institutions are so explicitly devoted to changing
people's minds as colleges. Thus this chapter, reviewing
research on college effects, may suggest some of the
ultimate limits and constraints operating on organizations
designed to produce personality change, at least those in
which participation is voluntary and the particular affiliation
is self-selected. The theoretical importance of personal
relationships is reinforced here again: peers in particular

seem to play a key role in personality change within the college environment. Also, it is found that, while important personality changes do occur as a consequence of college experiences, to a large degree colleges have the effect of accentuating what a person already is. The lack of dramatic personality conversions during college has contributed to recent rethinking concerning college impacts with more stress being put on the functioning of colleges as channels moving people into specific jobs and social circles where further socialization takes place.

In a sense, every student who ever attends any college undergoes some impact from the experience—even if he withdraws at the end of one "horrible week." Even if, following any number of years as a student, he shows no observable changes (say in scores on an achievement test or an attitude scale), it is possible that the college experience has reinforced and solidified certain characteristics that he had previously worn more lightly, and that might formerly have been only precariously established. Between his freshman and senior years, for example, he might have abandoned and then readopted his initial position concerning religion as a value. Such effects will probably not come to the attention of the researcher unless he has chosen to make intensive studies of individuals (see, for example, M. B. Smith et al., 1956). We have, however, had in mind a more restrictive notion of impact. We have searched the literature and compared various sets of findings with an eye to generalizations rather than to the infinite variety of individual processes that lie behind them. We have begun with general statements that apply to most colleges. Then we have offered a few propositions that apply to most colleges of certain kinds, to most students affected by certain aspects of college environments, or to most

Kenneth A. Feldman and Theodore M. Newcomb, "The Impact of College: Epiloque," *The Impact of College on Students,* vol. 1 (San Francisco: Jossey-Bass, Inc., 1969), 325–338. Reprinted by permission of the publisher and the authors. Footnote has been numbered.

students who have certain characteristics on entering college, and so on. When possible, we offered generalizations that assumed an interplay among whole sets of conditions. We have viewed colleges' impacts on their students through the often cloudy lenses of *effects that can in some sense be offered as generalizations*.[1]

Our first finding is very general indeed. Some uniformities can be found in impacts of American colleges and universities, although the particular content of the finding reported is surely time-bound as well as space-limited.

1. Freshman-to-senior changes in several characteristics have been occurring with considerable uniformity in most American colleges and universities in recent decades.

Declining "authoritarianism," dogmatism, and prejudice, together with decreasingly conservative attitudes toward public issues and growing sensitivity to aesthetic experiences, are particularly prominent forms of change—as inferred from freshman-senior differences. These add up to something like increasing openness to multiple aspects of the contemporary world, paralleling wider ranges of contact and experience. Somewhat less consistently, but nevertheless evident, are increasing intellectual interests and capacities, and declining commitment to religion, especially in its more orthodox forms. Certain kinds of personal changes—particularly toward greater independence, self-confidence, and readiness to express impulses—are the rule rather than the exception.

Such is the heavy preponderance of evidence from many institutions; but each nugget of data, taken singly, represents only an average trend in a particular college or university. Though individual changes are rarely reported, we can be sure that, in each population studied, some individuals—or perhaps many—swam against the current while others—conceivably a majority—changed little or none between entrance and graduation. These facts of statistical life are not changed by the equally solid fact that nearly all studies reveal the same preponderant direction of change: it is still only a prevalent tendency.

---

1. A few portions of this chapter are frankly impressionistic. Our own interpretations and fore-glimpses therein are not, we believe, inconsistent with the research findings considered in earlier chapters—but neither do they in every instance follow inevitably from those findings.

On the other hand, neither do these considerations alter the basic findings that each of the prevalent tendencies was in one direction rather than the other. (Suppose, for example, that our data had shown a preponderant freshman-to-senior change toward greater dogmatism and declining sensitivity to aesthetic experiences.) The preponderant shift, like Mount Everest, is there, it is in this direction and not that, and it is a challenge—to our understanding if not to our powers of survival in rarefied atmosphere.

Such evidence of net change does not, however, necessarily reflect impacts of colleges. It is to be expected that at least some individuals of college age who are not in college would, like their counterparts who are in college, show increasing openness to new experience and growing tolerance. Indeed, the available evidence on this point indicates that, as a preponderant trend, individuals who have not attended college (though eligible and acceptable) often change in the same directions as do students in college, though in lesser degree. The same culture-wide winds blow upon both populations, though college experience appears to hasten some kinds of changes, just as it may delay others.

In spite of the limitations of data on net changes, it seems altogether likely that some students in some colleges experience some changes that are *attributable* to the fact of being in college. And so our inquiry shifts to precisely such questions—*from* the demonstrations of preponderant trends *to* the analysis of particular conditions under which particular kinds of impacts can be demonstrated. This shift does not imply an abandoning of our search for generality, but rather the espousal of a different kind of general question: *under what conditions —regardless of where those conditions are found, and regardless of preponderant trends in contemporary American colleges in general— are particular kinds of impacts likely to occur?*

2. The degree and nature of different colleges' impacts vary with their student inputs—that is, entering students' characteristics, which differ among types of colleges in patterned ways.

The public images of colleges, together with their admission policies, have the consequence that their entering students have distinguishable sets of characteristics. This does not mean that all institutions attract equally homogeneous populations of students; indeed, degree of homogeneity itself may be an important distinguishing variable among colleges. Nor does it mean, of course, that every institution's student body is clearly distinguishable from all others in the distribution of its students' characteristics. But it is clear that there are important and measurable differences among types of colleges in this respect. In most of the characteristics for which data exist there is not a great deal of overlap, for example, between most private universities and most small, public colleges.

By and large, in institutions where most entering students have high capacity most of them will have family backgrounds of favored socio-economic status; the same students will, relative to those in other kinds of colleges, tend to be nonauthoritarian and to score high in intellectual dispositions. By the same token, student bodies that are generally low in any one of these characteristics will, in terms of prob-ability, be low in all or most of the others. The correlation is by no means perfect, but the pattern is unmistakable.

Some of these individual characteristics—family background, in particular—will be affected little or not at all by experience in college. Others, including authoritarianism, and political and religious orien-tations, for example, are clearly susceptible to change during college years. Such changes, according to the few currently available studies . . . are apt to increase rather than decrease the initial disparities among different colleges. In the absence of more complete data, we offer it only as a likely hypothesis that *those characteristics in which freshman-to-senior change is distinctive for a given college will also have been distinctive for its entering freshmen,* initial distinctiveness being in the same direction as subsequent change.

That impact is conditioned by input is hardly news, but the nature of the accentuating relationship that we hypothesize may illuminate one of the ways in which impact occurs. We suggest that two processes are at work. First, the prominence of initial characteristics—say re-ligious attitude in a sectarian college or vocational aspirations in a technical college—indicates a readiness on the part of a considerable number of individuals to move in directions compatible with those characteristics. This readiness is then reinforced by their discovery that many others share the same interests, which are thus socially reinforced.

Such an interpretation of differential impacts among different col-leges needs qualification. Accentuation is not, of course, the only process at work; this generalization, like the others, refers only to modal processes that distinguish some institutions from others. Students' initial interests may lapse, and quite new ones may be acquired—perhaps as adaptations of initial deviants to majority influence, or for any number of idiosyncratic reasons. Furthermore, in any except possibly the very small and highly homogeneous institutions, individual change tends to occur in different directions for different students, so that the process is not at all a monolithic one. But the fact remains, we suspect, that the kinds of college impacts that are massive enough to distinguish different colleges from one another are outcomes of the accentuation of initial distinctions.

3. Within the same college, experiences associated with the pursuit of different academic majors typically have effects over and beyond those that can be accounted for by initial selection into those major fields.

The accentuation processes by which such impact occurs are very similar to those that result in differentiation among colleges. Individuals who elect a particular major in a given institution are not a random assortment of all its students. The preponderance of evidence now available indicates that whatever characteristics distinguish entrants into different majors tend, especially if relevant to the academic field chosen, to become still more distinctive of those groups following the pursuit of the major.

The mere fact that the same individuals, as freshmen, typically become different in significant ways, as seniors, does not "prove" that changes reflect impact of college experiences. Two considerations make such an inference questionable: many individuals who do not go to college make similar changes; and the very characteristics that determine the decision whether or not to go to college may also predetermine the likelihood of change. But the finding that initial differences among students are accentuated, following subsequent experience in college, bypasses both of these considerations. Such an analysis makes it possible to hold constant the variables of capacity and desire to attend college, and also individuals' initial status on the variable hypothetically subject to change. This is most clearly shown in Huntley's data . . . : freshmen who initially scored highest in each value still further increased those scores if (as in most cases) they later selected a major relevant to that value—but, typically, not otherwise. Such a finding does not, of course, indicate that just going to college has a measurable impact, but it points to something more important—namely, a measured change that can reasonably be attributed to a particular combination of circumstances: a certain academic experience on the part of individuals already possessing certain characteristics. Other sources of impact also exist, presumably, but this one, at least, has been reasonably well demonstrated.

4. The maintenance of existing values or attitudes which, apart from certain kinds of college experience, might have been weakened or reversed, is an important kind of impact.

Perhaps the best illustration occurs in those studies showing the persistence of pre-induction attitudes on the part of students after they join fraternities or sororities. A common aspect of this phenomenon, and perhaps an essential one, is that students are selected for membership in the Greek societies, in large part, on the basis of possessing the characteristics that subsequently persist. At least one "crucial experiment" (Siegel and Siegel, 1957) . . . has shown that students who wished to join a sorority-like group, but could not do so, subsequently developed attitudes more closely resembling those of students with whom they continued to live. Meanwhile other students who did succeed in joining the preferred group tended to maintain their previous attitudes. Since the two groups differed, initially, not in attitudes but only in that members of one group drew lucky numbers permitting them to move, the effects of residential associates are clearly demonstrated.

This process of reinforcement or consolidation is less conspicuous than that of change in individuals' attitudes and values. But it represents just as real an impact, in the sense that, in the absence of the reinforcing or consolidating experiences, outcomes would have been different. Students, like other people, tend to meet or to seek out and associate with others who have similar attitudes and values. Insofar as this occurs, processes of consolidation are ubiquitous; we suspect that they are at once the most common and the least noticed sources of colleges' impacts on their students.

5. Though faculty members are often individually influential, particularly in respect to career decisions, college faculties do not appear to be responsible for campus-wide impact except in settings where the influence of student peers and of faculty complement and reinforce one another.

Based on evidence collected primarily during the early and middle years of the sixties, students typically report infrequent contact with faculty members at a personal level, nor do the majority of them indicate any strong desire for it. Many indivdual students do report experiences of intellectually exciting contacts with teachers, and sometimes even continuing personal friendships. For the most part, however, they expect such relationships to be professional—like those between patient and doctor, for example, only more frequent.

Their relative indifference to fraternalization with faculty members has something to do with students' consciousness of age and status differences, heightened by the symbolic significance of college as a milestone on the road from dependence on parental authority to maturity and autonomy. Students' recent and widespread expressions of concern about parietal rules (*in loco parentis*) and about their right to "a voice in decision making" represent, we suspect, not so much totally new attitudes as a new sense of freedom to voice them. The built-in differences between student and faculty culture are maintained, if in no other way, by the faculty's life-and-death power to grade students. Many students' first free association to the phrase "faculty member" might be something like "an automatic dispenser; you insert exams in the slot and it dispenses a grade."

At any rate, students perform a necessary function as socializers of one another—especially the younger by the older. Faculty can hardly expect to like the results of this kind of socialization if it occurs independently of their own endeavors, as if the two cultures were separated by a gulf.

6. The conditions for campus-wide impacts appear to have been most frequently provided in small, residential, four-year colleges. These conditions probably include relative homogeneity of both faculty and student body together with opportunity for continuing interaction, not exclusively formal, among students and between students and faculty.

Campus-wide impact presupposes not only a set of college influences, preponderantly favoring rather than opposing that effect, but also some degree of homogeneity on the part of its entering students. Until recently, at least, it has been a fact of life in American higher education that both of these conditions are more likely to be met in small, private colleges than in large, most commonly public ones. Many state universities attract a population almost as heterogeneous as the population of their states; their faculties are too large, and too thoroughly compartmentalized in departments, schools, colleges, and research centers, to exert uniform effects. Thus diverse influences—in quite different sub-environments within the megaversity—upon quite diverse student populations induce few *common* impacts, if any, beyond those that can be accounted for in terms of society-wide influences on young people who have somewhat superior capacities and more or less standard interests and aspirations in our society.

The "traditional" small, private colleges, on the other hand, are apt to have established images of their own—some of them nation-wide, some of them local. In either case, such institutions tend to attract both students and faculty who are familiar with the image, and favorably disposed to it. So it is that small colleges—inviting both informality and frequency of personal encounter, while providing relative homogeneity of student input and/or faculty influence—have had a potential for institution-wide impact that is typically lacking in large universities.

These considerations do not, of course, negate the possibility that certain sub-units or odd corners of larger universities have had marked impacts upon selected students. A university consisting of congeries of small loci of diverse impacts might, indeed, be the apotheosis of effective higher education. Such "local impacts" within large universities, however, have more often been attributable to good fortune, probably, than to systematic arrangements designed to make them occur.

7. In addition to the effects of campus-wide influences and the pressures of sub-environments, college impacts are conditioned by the background and personality of the student.

Presently available information suggests that the more incongruent a student is with the overall environment of his college the more likely he is to withdraw from that college or from higher education in general. We did not find much support, however, for the often-voiced notion that, for students who remain in college, change will be greatest for those whose backgrounds are initially the most discontinuous with the college environment. Our best guess at the moment is that a college is most likely to have the largest impact on students who experience a continuing series of not-too-threatening discontinuities. Too great a divergence between student and college, especially initially, may result in the student's marshalling of resistances. Too little might mean no impetus for change. From this point of view, a college's objectives might include that of inculcating a tolerance, or even a desire, for those discrepancies that can stimulate change and growth.

Students vary in the degree to which they are open to change—in terms either of their willingness to confront new ideas, values, and experiences non-defensively or of their willingness to be influenced by others. Current evidence suggests that the higher an entering student is on either of these dimensions, the greater is the impact of college. These traits need not be unchanging aspects of a student's personality —that is, they can be affected by experiences on the campus. Therefore, the amount and nature of college impacts are not necessarily predetermined by the student's initial degree of openness to change.

8. Attitudes held by students on leaving college tend to persist thereafter, particularly as a consequence of living in post-college environments that support those attitudes. Within-college changes, especially if accompanied by a general stance of openness to change, may be still further extended in response to new social and technological conditions.

The general finding that attitudes change little after college years cannot be attributed simply to "inherent inertia" or to some sort of early hardening of psychological arteries. The basic fact is that one's attitudes and values do not change whimsically, but in response to new information or to new ways of viewing one's world. The older one becomes, the less the *relative* impact of any particular set of new experiences. The unique thing about late-adolescence-merging-into-early-maturity is that at this stage of development one is, in our society, maximally motivated to achieve autonomy and at the same time minimally constrained to conform to the restrictions of adult roles. The typical consequence may well be this: if one does not change during this period one is not likly to change thereafter. Or, alternatively, if one has changed during these years one may have acquired a propensity for changing oneself in response to changes in the world outside oneself.

For many of its students, in sum, college-induced changes in attitudes and values are likely to persist. Most of them are not likely again to be so susceptible to new influences, and their college-acquired stances will, to some degree, continue to symbolize independence and adulthood. For some, at least, habits of being open to new information, and being influenced thereby, will result in persisting openness to further change; such an outcome, it may be argued, is one of the goals of a college education.

No single principle has emerged in so many different guises as that of accentuation—either, under certain conditions, of individuals' initially prominent characteristics or of initial differences among groups of students. In its general form, the proposition is as follows:

9. Whatever the characteristics of an individual that selectively propel him toward particular educational settings—going to college, selecting a particular one, choosing a certain academic major, acquiring membership in a particular group of peers—those same characteristics are apt to be reinforced and extended by the experiences incurred in those selected settings.

The proposition is intended to be a very broad one. It is too general, of course, to apply to every characteristic of every individual. It is intended, rather, to refer to characteristics that typically distinguish, say, eighteen-year-olds who do from those who do not go to college, or college students majoring in physics from those majoring in French. But it is not too general to be tested in the form of specific hypotheses in particular settings (as in comparatively small groups of academic majors at Union College). Also, the proposition is intended to include reinforcement or consolidation—without measured change (see proposition 4)—as well as further heightening of initially prominent characteristics.

Furthermore, the consequences of initial selection of a college or of a major, as asserted in the proposition, imply a certain degree of correctness on the part of the applicant to a particular college or a particular major, in estimating its suitability to his particular interests. Obviously, some such judgments are wide of the mark—quite aside from the fact that decisions about colleges and majors may be made on quite irrelevant grounds. Nevertheless, the empirical fact is that many colleges and probably most majors do attract and select students in ways that result in considerable homogeneity within their student populations.

What the general proposition really asserts is that *processes of attracting and selecting students are interdependent with processes of impact*. From this point of view, colleges' impacts begin before their students arrive. By the same token, those delayed processes of selection that result in student attrition must also be considered a form of impact: the disappearance of certain kinds of dropouts not only constitutes a message to those who remain; it also removes certain kinds of influence (in the form of deviant students) upon those who stay.

Insofar as the principle of accentuation is widely applicable, it carries some educational implications, especially about the possibility of narrowing student interests and increasingly homogeneous student bodies. If colleges select only certain kinds of young people, if particular colleges select only certain types within an already limited population, if departmental majors and student peer groups apply still more restrictive criteria of selection—then is it not inevitable that every student's world becomes increasingly narrowed, including only students and a few teachers like himself?

Put thus extremely, the facts belie the charge. While some degree of homogeneity characterizes every college's body of newly arrived students, the departing seniors are not necessarily more homogeneous. . . . Furthermore, accentuation of initial group differences is not invariably accompanied by increasing homogeneity of individual scores. (For example, at Union College where accentuation of initial major field differences was very strong, decreasing homogeneity within curricular groups with respect to the accentuated values was more common than increasing homogeneity.) Findings such as these do not suggest that the output of a succession of selective processes is a standard-model senior within each college or within each department. Rather, they point to pluralistic influences acting upon individuals who, though somewhat homogeneous in some respects, are diverse in many others. The possibility of narrow intensification of interests exists, of course, as we think it should, but far from every student follows that possible path.

More serious, perhaps, is the possibility that a good many prospective college students are *de facto* preordained to flow through certain academic channels without serious consideration of alternatives. Again, the available evidence sets the fear to rest. (To take one example, according to our most complete set of data, at Union College hardly more than one-third of the students selected majors in which their initially highest values were likely to be accentuated, in the sense of being further increased. For instance, only eleven of sixty-five students whose initially highest value was Aesthetic majored in humanities, although ten of these eleven raised their scores for this value still higher as seniors.) What the phenomenon of accentuation of initially prominent attributes reveals, then, must be stated conditionally: *if* students initially having certain characteristics choose a certain setting (a college, a major, a peer group) in which those characteristics are prized and nurtured, accentuation of such characteristics is likely to occur. Thus its prevalence in a given institution is determined by such considerations as the actual distinctiveness of each of the settings, the accuracy by which the distinctiveness is recognized, and the single-mindedness of the individuals entering that institution. The frequency of transfers from one college to another, from one prospective major to another, and from one residential or peer group to another, suggests that a student's earliest decisions do not ordinarily result in forms of accentuation that predetermine later choices.

Impacts, from this point of view, depend on the goodness of fit between student and institution—but this formulation conceals a paradox. If we assume that a college is likely to change its students, or that it should do so, then for any one of them, as of today, the personal characteristics for which he needs to find a good fit within his institution may be different from yesterday's. If changing and searching for new good fits are desirable experiences for a college student, then perhaps some colleges select and reward their students so narrowly that accentuation of initially prominent attributes becomes their only path to survival. Perhaps others select such heterogeneous bodies of students and provide for them settings which, educationally, are so poorly differentiated that experiences of accentuation are almost left to chance.

We suspect that, in fundamental ways, the twin experiences of self-discovery and finding a good fit involve a succession of accentuations, along with the discarding of poor fits. But colleges, too, can profit by self-discovery, and the study of its own patterns of providing accentuations is one path toward self-insight.

A Look Ahead

Tomorrow's settings for maximizing impacts on students will have to differ from yesterday's. It seems likely that the social and psychological conditions that have often been provided on small "intimate" campuses can be created within the larger (and often urban) universities increasing proportions of American students attending.

It is customary to attribute the shortcomings of undergraduate education in large American universities, along with many of the world's other ailments, to overpopulation. The increasing "prevalence of people," together with our addiction to democratic mass education, has overstuffed our universities, which have now become gargantuan anthills. Hence their computerized bureaucracy, their impersonality, and the impossibility of impacts that are educationally relevant. So goes the myth.

If, as we are told, myths serve collective functions, then perhaps the usefulness of this one is that it absolves educators from blame— but not the social scientists, who have presumably learned to distinguish between the effects of organizational size and of organizational structuring. One cannot inquire about the optimal size of a university without also asking about its modes of internal organization—the nature of its component parts and their interrelationships. University planners have, of course, given thought to matters of vertical organization, dealing with hierarchical levels of power and responsibility for making decisions in discriminable areas within the life of a modern multiversity. Their organizational charts typically resemble a truncated pyramid—cut off at the bottom; they do not have enough space at the bottom of the page for any level below the department chairmanship. We do not question the reality of such a vertical organization, but we wonder about its adequacy and its desirability. Our complaint is not merely that such vertical organizations may be overproliferated, but rather that they are too often expected to substitute for adequate forms of horizontal organization—that is, institutionalized arrangements concerning interrelationships at the same or immediately adjacent "levels." . . .

The size, in itself, of an institution devoted to higher education matters little if its internal organization is appropriate to its size. We have in mind *horizontal* organization in particular. At any given horizontal level, however, absolute size *does* matter. This assertion may be buttressed by another pair of rather general propositions:

1. Insofar as the goals of an organization prominently include psychological changes on the part of its members, as ends rather than only as means to other ends, its goals can be furthered by processes of mutual support and mutual stimulation among members of whom changes are expected. (Kurt Lewin put it this way: "It is often easier to change a whole group than a single individual.") This proposition, we suggest, applies *a fortiori,* though not exclusively, to changes in attitudes and values as contrasted, say, with the acquisition of information or dexterity.

2. The conditions that favor mutual stimulation and support must be described in interpersonal terms. They include, particularly, opportunity for continued interaction among the same individuals, allowing occasions for the discovery of mutual congeniality, preferably in varied settings—not just academic or just recreational or just residential, for example.

These proportions point quite directly to forms of horizontal organization such that, whatever the size of the institution, its human sources of stimulation and support (both students and faculty) will be distributed into as many centers as suggested by the following formula:

$$\frac{\text{Total population of the institution}}{\text{Optimal size of interpersonal environment}} = N \text{ of parallel units}$$

One may wonder, of course, whether such a form of horizontal organization might not be cumbersome. If, for example, a typical state mega-multiversity already includes a dozen or fifteen separate schools and colleges, would not a further division of even one of them (say the Arts College) into another dozen or so create an organization man's, or a university president's, nightmare? We are inclined to reply that if educational considerations are really superordinate, then administrative convenience is subordinate.

221

If basic educational practices of American colleges and universities have changed little during the past half century, neither have their forms of organization, and the two inertial trends are not unrelated. Our conversations with colleagues across the country suggest that there is no dearth of fresh and imaginative educational ideas, but a great deal of discouragement about the possibilities of "bucking the system." Faculty members tend to point to administrators, and vice versa, as the locus of resistance to changes. Both are right, in one sense, but both are wrong insofar as they assume that educational change must occur within existing forms of organization. Our own observation suggests that, given a single condition, new forms of horizontal organization invite, or at least facilitate, significant educational innovation. Indeed, one may go further: if new educational forms take interpersonal influence into account, then in contemporary American universities new organizational forms are a necessary means to educational ends.

The "single condition" that we have in mind, if such ends are to be achieved through such means, is a considerable degree of *local autonomy*. By way of analogy, it is a commonplace that conformity on the part of an individual is the enemy of creativeness. Just so, the exigencies of standard procedures within a single unit of a university are likely to abort creative innovations in education. Mere subdivision of a hypertrophied unit—say the Liberal Arts College of a state university—will not yield much innovation if each part is constrained to remain a miniature replica of the primeval parent. What is required is some sense of educational distinctiveness. Given a charter-built grant of autonomy, this kind of distinctiveness becomes possible.

References

Huntley, C. W. "Changes in study of value scores during the four years of college," *Genet. Psychol. Monographs,* 71 (1965), 349–383.

Huntley, C. W. "Changes in values during the four years of college," *College Student Survey,* 1 (1967), 43–48.

Siegel, A. E., and S. Siegel. "Reference groups, membership groups, and attitude change," *J. Abnormal Soc. Psychol.,* 55 (1957), 360–364.

Smith, M. B., J. S. Bruner, and R. W. White. *Opinions and Personality.* New York: Wiley, 1956.

12

Class, Occupation, and Orientation
Melvin L. Kohn and Carmi Schooler

Much of an organization's effect on individual personalities
occurs because that organization provides a particular set of
interpersonal relationships. Nevertheless, there is a long
tradition which supposes that the kinds of activities one
engages in also have an impact on personality and character,
and this chapter provides evidence in support of such an
idea. The effect of work activities seems to be small but
highly consistent in its effects on many different attitudes.

The authors of this chapter extend this argument by showing that while many of the attitudinal differences between social classes can be explained in terms of differences in educational background, an additional portion of the attitudinal variations between classes are a function of the different kinds of work done at different class levels.

This paper describes and interprets the relationship of social class to values and orientation. Its impetus comes from earlier research on class and parental values conducted in Washington, D. C. (Kohn, 1959) and in Turin, Italy (Pearlin and Kohn, 1966). Both studies found a distinct difference in emphasis between middle- and working-class parents' values for children—a higher valuation of self-direction by middle-class parents and of conformity to externally imposed rules by working-class parents. . . .

Our . . . important objective is to interpret the class relationship—to discover which of the many conditions of life associated with class position are most pertinent for explaining why class is related to values and orientation. The focus of this analysis is occupational conditions, particularly those that are conducive to, or restrictive of, the exercise of self-direction in work (cf. Kohn, 1963). Our principal hypothesis is that class-correlated differences in men's opportunities to exercise occupational self-direction—that is, to use initiative, thought, and independent judgment in work—are basic to class differences in values and orientation. Few other conditions of life

Abridged from Melvin L. Kohn and Carmi Schooler, "Class, Occupation, and Orientation," in *American Sociological Review,* 34 (1969), 659–678. Reprinted by permission of the American Sociological Association and the authors. Footnotes have been renumbered.

We are indebted, for critical advice and essential help, to our associates in this research—Lindsley Williams, Elizabeth Howell, Margaret Renfors, Carrie Schoenbach, and Mimi Silberman; to Paul Sheatsley, Eve Weinberg, Marilyn Haskell, and the staff of the National Opinion Research Center; and, for statistical advice, to Samuel Greenhouse, Elliot Cramer, and Jacob Cohen. For a more comprehensive discussion of the methods and findings presented in this paper, cf. Kohn, 1969.

are so closely bound up with social position as are those that determine how much opportunity, even necessity, men have for exercising self-direction in their work. Moreover, there is an appealing simplicity to the supposition that the experience of self-direction, in so central a realm of life as work, is conducive to valuing self-direction, off the job as well as on the job, and to seeing the possibilities for self-direction not only in work but also in other realms of life.

There is evidence in the Turin study that differences in men's experience of occupational self-direction largely explain class differences in parental values. The question now is whether these occupational experiences are important for explaining the relationships of class, not only to parental values, but also to values and orientations in general.

Research Methods

The research is based on interviews conducted for us by the National Opinion Research Center in the spring and summer of 1964. Thirty-one hundred men, representative of all men throughout the United States employed in civilian occupations, were interviewed (cf. Sudman and Feldman, 1965, for a general description of sampling methods). For most of the analyses that follow, the entire sample is used. The analysis of parental values, however, is limited to about half the men—those who have one or more children aged three through fifteen living at home. Each of these fathers was asked about his values for a specific child, randomly selected.

Of the men chosen to be in the study, 76 percent gave reasonably complete interviews, the median interview taking two and one-half hours. Few of the non-respondents seemed hostile or even suspicious; in the overwhelming majority of cases, they were either unavailable or insufficiently interested to give what they were told would be a very long interview. As far as can be learned from city directories in those cities where they exist, rates of non-response do not vary with occupational status.

About half the interview questions were directed to job, occupation, and career, the remainder to background information and to values and orientation. We shall discuss the contents of the questions, the concepts that guided the inquiry, and the indices developed to measure them, as they become relevant to the substantive analysis. The one exception is social class, which is of such great importance to all that follows that it had best be discussed now.

Social Class

We conceive of social classes as aggregates of individuals who occupy broadly similar positions in a hierarchy of power, privilege, and prestige (cf. Williams, 1960, p. 98). In this conception, class is multi-dimensional, embodying more than simply one or another of the items used to index it and more than any of the large number of social, cultural, and psychological variables with which it is correlated. Our index of social class is based on the two social variables that seem most important for defining class position in industrial societies—education and occupational position.

The index of class that we employ is Hollingshead's "Index of Social Position," a weighted combination of these two variables (cf. Hollingshead and Redlich, 1958, pp. 387–397). Hollingshead's classification of education is straightforward, but one might question his classification of occupational position. Essentially, he has modified the United States Census occupational classification (Edwards, 1938), making appropriate refinements, but validating the resulting classification only against expert opinion.

Duncan (1961) proposed an alternative system, also derived from the Census classification, but weighting the occupational categories to conform to the judgments of occupational prestige held by society at large. Given the evidence of consensus and stability in people's judgments of the relative prestige of occupations (Reiss et al., 1961; Gusfield and Schwartz, 1963; Hodge et al., 1964), Duncan's approach seems well justified. But the classification is dependent on the sometimes imprecise distinctions employed in the Census. Fortunately, the correlation between Duncan's and Hollingshead's occupational classifications, based on a random sample of 90 men in our study, is high enough (0.89) to indicate that they measure much the same thing. Where the two indices differ, it is usually because Duncan has had to use one of the grosser Census categories; the Hollingshead index generally seems more appropriate. We, therefore, retained Hollingshead's classification of occupational position, in effect having validated it against Duncan's conceptually well-buttressed but less precise alternative.

Values and Orientation

Parental Values

By values, we mean standards of desirability—criteria of preference (cf. Williams, 1960, pp. 402–403). By parental values, we mean those standards that parents would most like to see embodied in their children's behavior. Since values are hierarchically organized, a central manifestation of value is to be found in choice. For this reason, our index requires men to choose, from among 13 desirable characteristics . . . the three most desirable, the one most desirable of all, the three least important (even if desirable), and the one least important of all. This procedure makes it possible to place men's valuations of each characteristic along a five-point scale: 5=the most valued of all; 4=one of the three most valued, but not the most valued; 3=neither one of the three most valued nor one of the three least valued; 2=one of the three least valued, but not the least valued; and 1=the least valued of all. We must recognize that fathers are likely to accord high priority to those values that are not only important, in that failing to achieve them would affect the children's futures adversely, but also problematic, in that they are difficult of achievement. Our index of values measures conception of the "important, but problematic."

We find that the higher the fathers' class position, the more they value characteristics indicative of self-direction and the less they value characteristics indicative of conformity to external rules. That is, the higher the men's social class, the greater is their valuation of consideration, an interest in how and why things happen, responsibility, and self-control, and the less their valuation of manners, neatness and cleanliness, being a good student, honesty, and obedience. . . .

To secure a single index of self-direction *versus* conformity to externally imposed rules, we did a factor analysis of the set of value-choices; the first factor produced by this analysis clearly reflects this dimension.[1] Henceforth, we use scores based on this factor as the

1. This was an orthogonal principal component factor analysis, rotated to simple structure through the varimax procedure, based on the computer program presented by Clyde et al. (1966, p. 15). The first factor is the relevant one for present purposes; it contrasts neatness ($r=-0.62$), manners ($r=-0.56$), being a good student ($r=-0.35$), and obedience ($r=-0.34$), against an interest in how and why things happen ($r=0.51$), consideration ($r=0.43$), good

index of parental valuation of self-direction/conformity. It is correlated with social class, reaffirming that the higher the men's social
class, the more highly they value self-direction for their children; the
lower their class, the more highly they value conformity.

These findings confirm and extend the conclusions of the Washington (Kohn, 1959) and Turin (Pearlin and Kohn, 1966) studies. Not
only do middle-class parents have different values from those of
working-class parents, but the relationships between class and values
are consistently linear, from the highest to the nearly lowest socioeconomic strata of American society. . . . More detailed analyses . . .
show that the relationship of class to parental values is essentially
the same, whatever the age and sex of the child, in families of varying
size, composition, and functional pattern.

It should be noted that the correlations of class with the individual
values are no larger than 0.20; the correlation of class with the entire
set of values, as measured by the canonical correlation,[2] is 0.38; and
the correlation of class with valuation of self-direction or conformity,
as indexed by the factor scores, is 0.34. The magnitude of these correlations is only moderate; what makes them impressive is their
consistency.

Values for Self

To test our expectation that values for self are consonant with values
for children, we use a similar mode of inquiry—modifying the characteristics to be more appropriate for adults. . . . As anticipated,
characteristics indicative of self-direction—an interest in how and
why things happen, good sense and sound judgment, responsibility,
self-reliance, the ability to face facts squarely, and the ability to do
well under pressure—are more valued at higher social class levels.
There is evidence, too, that conformity is more valued at lower class
levels. But this evidence is limited, because in modifying the list, we
substituted only one "adult" characteristic—respectability—for four

---

sense (r=0.30), self-control (r=0.29), and responsibility (r=0.28). (A second
factor reflects the age of the child, contrasting characteristics more valued for
older children with those more valued for younger children.)

2. The canonical correlation is a multiple correlation of one or a set of independent variables to a set of dependent variables. More precisely, it is the maximum correlation between linear functions of the two sets of variables (cf.
Cooley and Lohnes, 1962, p. 35).

"child" characteristics—manners, obedience, neatness, and good student. Moreover, we narrowed—perhaps distorted—the connotations of honesty by changing it to truthfulness. Thus, the only way men could endorse conformity was to choose respectability.[3] At the lower class levels, more men did so—thereby providing the only possible evidence that conformity is more highly valued by men of lower social class position.

There is a second cluster of values associated with lower class position—centering around a high valuation of *competence,* as reflected in the ability to do many things well, success, and the ability to get along well with people. We think this represents an important theme, different from conformity, but also in contradistinction to self-direction.

This supposition is borne out by a factor analysis of the entire set of value-choices. Two factors embodying self-direction appear, one contrasting it to conformity, the other to competence. (The first factor is focused on judgment, contrasting reliance on one's own judgment with reliance on other people's judgments. The second is focused on performance, the contrast being between acting on the basis of one's own standards and acting competently.)[4] Both are significantly correlated with social class, albeit neither very strongly. It adds an essential modicum of information that the higher the men's class positions, the more self-directed are their values, with reference both to thought and to action.

Judgments About Work

It seems reasonable to assume that men judge jobs both in terms of the occupational conditions they might ideally want and of the alternatives that are realistically open to them. Again, as with values, judgments about jobs are constrained by what is thought important and what is thought problematic. Consonant with their greater valuation of self-direction, men of higher social class position should be better able

3. For this same reason—we think—the magnitude of the relationship of class to "values for self" is weaker than that to "values for children" (the canonical correlations being 0.27 and 0.38 respectively).

4. The first factor contrasts an interest in how and why things happen ($r=0.57$), good sense and sound judgment ($r=0.45$), and the ability to face facts squarely ($r=0.45$) with respectability ($r=-0.62$), truthfulness ($r=-0.43$), and success ($r=-0.33$). The second factor contrasts responsibility ($r=0.52$) and self-reliance ($r=0.40$) with the ability to get along well with people ($r=-0.68$) and the ability to do many things well ($r=-0.44$).

to take for granted such extrinsic aspects of the job as pay and security, and to focus instead on the possibilities it affords for self-expression and individual accomplishment. This expectation is given support in Inkeles's (1960, p. 9) analysis, which shows that among both Americans and refugees from the Soviet Union, men in higher status jobs are "more likely to be concerned about having a job which is interesting, stimulating, challenging, permits self-expression, and so on."

To learn about orientations to work, we asked men to evaluate the importance of various occupational conditions. Our data . . . confirm Inkeles's conclusion and extend it. Essentially, men of higher class position judge jobs more by intrinsic qualities; men of lower class position, more by extrinsic characteristics. That is, the higher the men's social class, the more importance they attach to how interesting the work is, the amount of freedom you have, the chance to help people, and the chance to use your abilities. The lower their class position, the more importance they attach to pay, fringe benefits, the supervisor, co-workers, the hours of work, how tiring the work is, job security, and not being under too much pressure.

That the extrinsic-intrinsic distinction is a central line of cleavage is substantiated by a factor analysis that differentiates an intrinsic from an extrinsic dimension in these judgments.[5] Social class is correlated with both dimensions. The correlation of class with men's interest in the extrinsic, though, is nearly twice as great as with their interest in the intrinsic. Class apparently matters more in determining whether men are forced to focus on the extrinsic than in determining whether they are free to focus on the intrinsic.

Social Orientation

We expect men of higher social class position to see society as so constituted that responsible individual action is practicable; men of lower social class position will be more likely to think that following the dic-

---

5. The first factor focuses on intrinsic qualities of jobs—how much opportunity the job provides for using one's abilities ($r=0.68$), how interesting the work is ($r=0.64$), and how much opportunity it offers to help people ($r=0.67$). The second factor focuses on the extrinsic benefits of the job, emphasizing hours of work ($r=-0.64$), fringe benefits ($r=-0.58$), how tiring the work is ($r=-0.58$), job security ($r=-0.57$), and not being under too much pressure ($r=-0.51$).

tates of authority is the course of wisdom. This distinction should be manifested in many ways, four of which seem especially pertinent: in how rigidly men define what is socially acceptable, in their definitions of appropriate moral standards, in how trustful they are of their fellowman, and in their stance toward change.

If orientations are consistent with values, men of higher social class position will be more open-minded in their views of the socially acceptable and in their tolerance of nonconformity, while men at lower class levels will hold a more authoritarian view of what is acceptable and more rigidly reject behavior that does not conform to the acceptable. This expectation is buttressed by past investigations that have found class to be related to "authoritarianism" (cf. Christie, 1954; Hyman and Sheatsley, 1954; Srole, 1956; Lipset, 1959; Kirscht and Dillehay, 1967, pp. 37–40); and by Stouffer's (1955) demonstration that intolerance of nonconformity is an essential ingredient of conformity.

The other aspects of social orientation that we investigated— standards of morality, trust, and stance toward change—deserve independent recognition. Self-direction implies the necessity for personally responsible moral standards; conformity requires only that one follow the letter—not necessarily the spirit—of the law. Self-direction also implies a certain degree of trust in one's fellowman and the belief that change can be for the good; a conformist orientation is more pessimistic.

The indices that we use to investigate the relationship of class to social orientation are derived from a factor analysis of a set of 57 questions, mainly of the "agree-disagree" and "how often?" types (only 53 items appear in the table reproduced here).[6] Table 1 gives

6. Fourteen analytically separable, but not necessarily empirically independent, aspects of orientation to society and to self were initially indexed. We borrowed from existing indices where possible (cf. Adorno et al., 1950; Srole, 1956; Rosenberg, 1957, 1962; McKinley et al., 1948 and the references therein), but modified or added questions to provide the necessary connotations. All fourteen indices met the usual criteria for unidimensional scales (Guttman, 1944, 1950; Ford, 1950; Menzel, 1953). Useful as the Guttman scaling technique is for eliminating questions that do not fall along a single dimension, it provides no definitive evidence that the retained questions all do fall along that dimension (cf. Schooler, 1968). Moreover, the set of scales might be redundant. To overcome these limitations, we subjected the entire battery of 57 questions, of which the scales were constituted, to a factor analysis. This analysis yielded twelve independent factors, nine of which are directly pertinent to the purposes of this paper and are used as indices.

Table 1. Principal Items of the Social Orientation and
Self-Conception Factors

	Loading[a]		Loading[a]

A. SOCIAL ORIENTATION

Factor 1. Authoritarian conservatism
    (Authoritarian–
      nonauthoritarian)

1. The most important thing to
teach children is absolute obedience to their parents. —.61
2. Young people should not be allowed to read books that are
likely to confuse them. —.58
3. There are two kinds of people in
the world: the weak and the
strong. —.58
4. People who question the old and
accepted ways of doing things
usually just end up causing
trouble. —.55
5. In this complicated world, the
only way to know what to do is
to rely on leaders and experts. —.52
6. No decent man can respect a
woman who has had sex relations before marriage. —.51
7. Prison is too good for sex criminals. They should be publicly
whipped or worse. —.51
8. Any good leader should be strict
with people under him in order
to gain their respect. —.45
9. It's wrong to do things differently from the way our fore-
fathers did. —.43
10. Once I've made up my mind, I
seldom change it. —.37
11. It generally works out best to
keep on doing things the way
they have been done before. —.33

Factor 2. Criteria of morality
    (Moral—amoral)

1. It's all right to do anything you
want as long as you stay out of
trouble. +.66
2. If something works, it doesn't
matter whether it's right or
wrong. +.57
3. It's all right to get around the
law as long as you don't actually
break it. +.54
4. Do you believe that it's all right

to do whatever the law allows,
or are there some things that are
wrong even if they are legal? +.51
5. It's wrong to do things differently from the way our fore-
fathers did. +.36

Factor 3. Trustfulness
    (Distrustful—trustful)

1. Do you think that most people
can be trusted? +.62
2. If you don't watch out, people
will take advantage of you. —.48
3. Human nature is really cooperative. +.42
4. It's all right to get around the
law as long as you don't break it. —.34

Factor 4. Stance toward change
    (Receptive—resistant)

1. Are you generally one of the
first people to try out something
new or do you wait until you see
how it's worked out for other
people? —.61
2. Are you the sort of person who
takes life as it comes or are you
working toward some definite
goal? +.43
3. It generally works out best to
keep on doing things the way
they have been done before. +.33

B. SELF-CONCEPTION

Factor 1. Self-confidence
    (Self-confident—diffident)

1. I take a positive attitude toward
myself. —.62
2. I feel that I'm a person of worth,
at least on an equal plane with
others. —.61
3. I am able to do most things as
well as other people can. —.60
4. I generally have confidence that
when I make plans I will be able
to carry them out. —.60
5. Once I've made up my mind, I
seldom change it. —.38

[a]Minus sign stands for "strongly agree" or "very frequently."

Table 1 (continued)

	Loading[a]		Loading[a]
6. Human nature is really coopera- tive.	—.36	2. How often do you feel downcast and dejected?	—.65
7. On the whole, I think I am quite a happy person.	—.33	3. How frequently do you find yourself anxious and worrying about something?	—.62
Factor 2. Self-deprecation (Self-deprecating— self-endorsing)		4. How often do you feel uneasy about something without know- ing why?	—.59
1. I wish I could have more respect for myself.	—.62	5. How often do you feel so rest- less that you cannot sit still?	—.58
2. At times I think I am no good at all.	—.55	6. How often do you find that you can't get rid of some thought or idea that keeps running through	
3. I feel useless at times.	—.54	your mind?	—.56
4. I wish I could be as happy as others seem to be.	—.53	7. How often do you feel bored with everything?	—.55
5. There are very few things about which I'm absolutely certain.	—.43	8. How often do you feel powerless to get what you want out of life?	—.50
		9. How often do you feel guilty for having done something wrong?	—.48
Factor 3. Attribution of responsibility (Fatalistic—accountable)		10. How often do you feel that the world just isn't very understand- able?	—.45
1. When things go wrong for you, how often would you say it is your own fault?	+.72	11. How often do you feel that there isn't much purpose to being alive?	—.40
2. To what extent would you say you are to blame for the prob- lems you have—would you say that you are mostly to blame, partly to blame, or hardly at all to blame?	+.68	**Factor 5.** Idea-conformity (Conforming— independent) 1. How often do your ideas and opinions differ from those of your friends?	+.74
3. Do you feel that most of the things that happen to you are the result of your own decisions or of things over which you have no control?	+.60	2. How about from those of other people with your religious back- ground?	+.70
Factor 4. Anxiety (Anxious—collected)		3. According to your general im- pression, how often do your ideas and opinions about im- portant matters differ from those of your relatives?	+.68
1. How often do you feel that you are about to go to pieces?	—.65	4. Those of most people in the country?	+.67

[a]Minus sign stands for "strongly agree" or "very frequently."

the exact wording of each component question that correlates 0.33 or more with each of these factors. In essence the four indices of social orientation are as follows.

Authoritarian conservatism. Men's definitions of what is socially acceptable—at one extreme, rigid conformance to the dictates of authority and intolerance of nonconformity; at the other extreme, open-mindedness.

Criteria of morality. A continuum of moral positions, from opportunistic to highly responsible.

Trustfulness. The degree to which men believe that their fellowman can be trusted.

Stance toward change. Men's receptiveness or resistance to innovation and change.

Class position is linearly related to all four aspects of social orientation. . . . The strongest correlation, by a very wide margin, is with authoritarian conservatism: the lower the men's social class position, the more rigidly conservative their view of man and his social institutions and the less their tolerance of nonconformity. The other aspects of orientation are less strongly correlated with social class, but the correlations are altogether consistent with our expectations. The lower the men's social class positions, the more likely they are to feel that morality is synonymous with obeying the letter of the law; the less trustful of their fellowman they are; and the more resistant they are to innovation and change.

Self-Conception

We expect men of higher class position to see themselves as more competent, more effective, more in control of the forces that affect their lives. We investigate five aspects of self-conception: self-confidence, self-deprecation, attribution of responsibility, anxiety, and idea-conformity.

The indices are derived from the same factor analysis as are those for social orientation (Table 1). They measure:

Self-confidence. The positive component of self-esteem: the degree to which men are confident of their own capacities.

Self-deprecation. The self-critical half of self-esteem: the degree to which men disparage themselves. (This empirical division of self-esteem accords well with the possibility that one can be simultaneously confident of one's capacities and critical of oneself.)

Attribution of responsibility. Men's sense of being controlled by outside forces or of having some control over their fate.

Anxiety. The intensity of consciously felt psychic discomfort.

Idea-conformity. The degree to which men believe their ideas mirror those of the social entities to which they belong.

The relationship of class to self-conception is not nearly as strong as is that of class to social orientation; apparently class is less relevant for how men view themselves than for how they view the external world. . . . But the findings are consistent with our expectations. The higher the men's social class position, the more self-confidence and the less self-deprecation they express; the greater their sense of being in control of the forces that affect their lives; the less beset by anxiety they are; and the more independent they consider their ideas to be.

Men's views of how effectively they function are significantly, but not strongly, associated with their social class positions, men at the top being more confident of their own capacities than are men lower in the social hierarchy.

Dimensions of Social Class

In interpreting the relationships of class to values and orientation,[7] the logical first step is to examine class itself, its components, and related aspects of stratification. This analysis yields four principal findings. The first is [that] . . . the class relationships are preponderantly linear, with virtually no significant curvilinear or higher order relationships, no sharp breaks, no departures from pattern. Therefore, in interpreting these class relationships, it is profitable to think of a continuous hierarchy of positions, not of discrete social classes.

Second, the two components of our index of class—education and occupational position—are each related, independently of the other, to almost all aspects of values and orientation, and these relationships are essentially additive. Thus, any explanation of the class relationships must take into account that both education and occupational position are involved.

7. We should note that these relationships are essentially invariant for all major segments of American society—regardless of race, religion, national background, region of the country, and size of community. It should also be noted that the class relationships remain significant when the age of the respondent and such artifacts of the interview procedure as the respondent's tendency to agree with statements put to him, his tendency to give extreme answers, the length of the interview, and his apparent attitude toward the interview, are controlled.

Third, such other aspects of stratification as income and subjective class identification bear only a small relationship to values and orientation when social class (as we have indexed it) is controlled. On the other hand, class is nearly as strongly related to values and orientation when income and subjective class identification are controlled as when they are not. Both income and class identification may prove important for explaining the relationship of class to other social phenomena, but they are not very important for values and orientation.

Finally, present social class position matters more for values and orientation than do class origins. Although we cannot overlook the obvious and critical fact that class origins play a major part in determining present class position, it is apparent that when men move into class positions different from those of their parents (and their grandparents), their values and orientation come to agree with those of their achieved class positions.

Occupational Conditions

We have narrowed the range of possibilities by finding that only those conditions of life that vary continuously with education and with occupational position can be of any great relevance for explaining the relationships of class to values and orientation. Many of the relevant conditions are implicated in men's occupational lives. Our further analysis is focused on the occupational conditions earlier hypothesized to be of critical import for explaining the class relationships—namely, the conditions determinative of the exercise of self-direction in work.

Occupational Self-Direction

Although many conditions of work are either conducive to or deterrent of the exercise of occupational self-direction, three in particular are critical.

First, a limiting condition: men cannot exercise occupational self-direction if they are closely supervised. Not being closely supervised, however, does not necessarily mean that men are required—or even free—to use initiative, thought, and independent judgment; it depends on how complex and demanding is their work.

A second and far more important condition for occupational self-direction is that the work, in its very substance, requires initiative, thought, and independent judgment. Work with "data" or with "people" is more likely to require initiative, thought, and judgment than is work with "things"; complex work with data or with people—synthesizing or coordinating data, teaching or negotiating with people—is especially likely to require initiative, thought, and judgment. Thus, occupational self-direction is most probable when men spend some substantial amount of their working time doing complex work with data or with people.

The third condition for occupational self-direction is that the work allows a variety of approaches; otherwise the possibilities for exercising initiative, thought, and judgment are seriously limited. The organization of the work must be complex; it must involve a variety of tasks that are in themselves complexly structured.

No one of these conditions is definitional of occupational self-direction. For example, even though most work with things does not require a great deal of self-direction, some work with things is highly self-directed—consider the sculptor. And work with data may not always be self-directed—consider routine office jobs. Nevertheless, each of these three occupational conditions tends to be conducive to the exercise of occupational self-direction, and the combination of the three both enables and requires it. Insofar as men are free of close supervision, do complex work with data or with people, and work at complexly organized tasks, their work is necessarily self-directed. And insofar as they are subject to close supervision, work with things, and work at simply organized tasks, their work does not permit self-direction.

The Relationship of Occupational Self-Direction
to Values and Orientation

We begin this phase of the analysis by ascertaining whether specific class-correlated occupational conditions are significantly related to values and orientation, independently of their relationship to social class. We do this to avoid spuriously explaining the relationship of *class* to values and orientation in terms of phenomena that can themselves be explained as functions of class. It is unimportant that the partial correlations—for occupational conditions controlled on social class—will necessarily be small; all that matters is that there be some statistically significant, independent association between a given occupational condition and one or, preferably, several aspects of values and orientation.

Closeness of supervision. The index here is a scale based on five questions about how much latitude men's supervisors allow and how supervisory control is exercised. Closeness of supervision, thus indexed, is associated with a constricted orientation. . . . Closely supervised men tend to value conformity for their children, to emphasize extrinsic benefits that jobs provide rather than opportunities for intrinsic accomplishment, to have standards of morality keyed to the letter rather than the spirit of the law, to be distrustful, to be resistant to innovation and change, to lack self-confidence, and to be anxious.

The substance of work with data, things, and people. The indices here are based on detailed inquiry about precisely what men do and how much time they spend working with data, with things, and with people. From this information, we rated the degree of complexity of men's work in each of the three realms, modeling our classifications on those used in the third edition of the *Dictionary of Occupational Titles* (United States Department of Labor, 1965).[8] We also rated the amount of time they spend working at each of the three types of activity and the overall complexity of their jobs.

Taking these seven indices of time and complexity of work with data, with things, and with people all together, we find . . . the substance of the work to be related to virtually all aspects of values and orientation. Doing complex work with data or with people is consistently associated with valuing self-direction and holding a consonant orientation; working with things is consistently associated with having conformist values and orientation.

The specifics of men's work with data, with things, and with people —the types of data with which they work, the tools they use, the

8. The *Dictionary's* ratings, based on *in situ* observations by trained occupational analysts, provide objective appraisals of typical job requirements for all major occupations. Our ratings for particular jobs prove to be highly consistent with the *Dictionary's* ratings for entire occupations. Although the third edition of the *Dictionary* appeared long after our survey was undertaken, our plans were based on it—thanks to the foreknowledge and advice provided by Sidney Fine, the originator of this very important classificatory system.

nature of their relations with the people with whom they interact— are relatively unimportant. What does matter for values and orientation is the complexity of work with data and with people, the time spent working with data, things, and people, and the overall complexity of the job. Each of these is independently relevant, and their multiple correlation with values and orientation is a bit greater than the correlation of any one of them.

The complexity of organization of work. Some jobs are endlessly repetitive, others offer a variety of different tasks or at least variety in the ways that essentially similar tasks can be performed. In some jobs, the "units" of which the stream of work is composed are nearly identical; in others, the units are complex entities—each with a structural integrity of its own—or the work is so highly diversified that it cannot be split meaningfully into units. Again the essence of the matter is complexity, but, in this case, from the perspective of the organization of the work. Simply organized jobs cannot allow much self-direction; complexly organized jobs require it.

Our indices here are based on men's appraisals of what constitutes "a complete job" in their occupation and of the repetitiveness of their work. These two aspects of the complexity of organization of work are independently related to values and orientation, their effects being additive. Men who work at complexly organized jobs tend to value self-direction for children, to emphasize intrinsic aspects of the job, to be open-minded and tolerant of nonconformity, to have moral standards that demand more than conformity to the letter of the law, to be receptive to change, and not to be self-deprecatory. . . .

In sum, each of the three conditions that are determinative of occupational self-direction—closeness of supervision; the substance of work with data, with things, and with people; and the complexity of organization of work—is consistently related to values and orientation, hence might help explain the class relationships. Moreover, each is significantly related to values and orientation independent of the other two. Of the three components of occupational self-direction, the substance of work with data, with things, and with people bears the strongest relationship to values and orientation; but closeness of supervision and the complexity of organization of work add to the total impact. As a result . . . occupational self-direction, independent of its close association with social class, is significantly related to almost all aspects of values and orientation with which we have dealt.

Other Facets of Occupation

Previous theoretical and empirical studies suggest many other class-correlated occupational conditions that might be related to values and orientation and, therefore, might help explain the class relationships.[9] We find, in fact, that several of these occupational conditions are related to values and orientation, independent of their relationship to social class—the principal ones being ownership, amount of competition, job security, size and supervisory structure of the firm or organization, position in the supervisory hierarchy, time pressure and the consequences of time pressure, and the average amount of overtime.

For present purposes, the primary importance of these findings lies not in their intrinsic interest but in the opportunity they afford for contrasting the conditions determinative of occupational self-direction with an alternative set of occupational conditions that we expect will not prove relevant for explaining the class relationships. This gives us a basis for a clear-cut test of our principal hypothesis: that the conditions determinative of occupational self-direction are highly relevant for explaining the relationships of class to values and orientation, and that other occupational conditions (even though related to values and orientation) are of little relevance for explaining these relationships.

The Relevance of Occupational Self-Direction for Explaining the Class Relationships

To test our hypothesis, we control (singly and in sets) all those occupational dimensions that have proved to be independently related to values and orientation, to see how much this reduces the class correlations. It must be emphasized that in dealing with these occupational conditions we are concerned, not with distinctions that cut across social class, but with experiences constitutive of class. The objective is

---

9. Our inquiry focused particularly on (a) ownership, job rights, and job security; (b) bureaucracy—as measured by the size and supervisory complexity of the employing firm or organization—and place in the supervisory structure; (c) the use and organization of time—including both the several facets of how work time is internally structured and how work time is separated from non-work time; (d) patterns of interpersonal relations in work; and (e) job satisfaction, occupational commitment, and subjective reactions to the job. Of the many occupational conditions studied, only those enumerated in the text proved to be independently related to values and orientation in a way that could be pertinent for explaining the class relationships. For the details of this analysis, cf. Kohn, 1969, Chapter 10.

to learn whether these constituent experiences are pertinent for explaining the class relationships. Our procedure is altogether hypothetical, for it imagines an unreal social situation—social classes that do not differ from one another in the occupational conditions experienced by their members. But it is analytically appropriate to use such hypothetical procedures, for it helps us to differentiate occupational conditions that are relevant for explaining the relationship of class to values and orientation from those that are not.

We need not discuss each occupational condition, for the major lessons of this analysis are sufficiently well documented by a summary presentation (Table 2). Most of the relationships of class to values and orientation are substantially attributable to the occupational conditions that are conducive to or restrictive of occupational self-direction, but not to the other occupational conditions. That is, controlling the conditions determinative of occupational self-direction greatly reduces the correlations of class to values and orientation—in almost all instances by half and in several by two thirds or more. Controlling the other occupational conditions has much weaker effects—in general, reducing the class correlations by less than one third. Controlling both sets of conditions reduces the correlations of class to values and orientation by no more than does controlling the conditions of occupational self-direction alone. Thus, the relationships of class to values and orientation are in large measure attributable to those conditions that are determinative of occupational self-direction.

This analysis can be pursued further by considering the relevance of occupational self-direction to each of the components of our index of class: education and occupational position. Is occupational self-direction pertinent primarily for explaining the relationships of *education* to values and orientation, primarily for explaining the relationships of *occupational position* to values and orientation, or equally for explaining both sets of relationships? The answer is that it is relevant to both, but more to occupational position than to education (Table 3). That is, the correlations of education to values and orientation are in small part attributable to occupational self-direction;[10] but the corre-

---

10. Since the object of this analysis is to see how controlling occupational self-direction affects the specifically educational component of the class relationships, occupational position is also controlled. Similarly, when we examine how controlling occupational self-direction affects the relationships of occupational position to values and orientation, education is controlled.

Table 2. Effects on the Class Correlations of Controlling Sets of Occupational Variables

	Initial correlation with social class[a]	Proportional reduction in the magnitude of the correlation when controlling:		
		Occupational self-direction[b]	Other occupational conditions[c]	All significant occupational conditions
A. *Parental Values*				
Self-direction/Conformity	.33**	.65	.33	.67
B. *Values for Self*				
Self-direction/Conformity	.16**	.56	.23	.54
Self-direction/Competence	.15**	.49	.25	.50
C. *Judgments about Work*				
Importance of Intrinsic Qualities	.19**	.94	.36	.94
Importance of Extrinsic Benefits	.35**	.57	.21	.58
D. *Social Orientation*				
Authoritarian Conservatism	.38**	.50	.21	.50
Criteria of Morality	.18**	.87	.32	.87
Trustfulness	.17**	.61	.22	.61
Stance toward Change	.15**	.95	.58	.99
CANONICAL CORRELATION	.48**	.56	.22	.56
E. *Self-conception*				
Self-confidence	.09**	.99	.64	.96
Self-deprecation	.09**	.87	.23	.86
Attribution of Responsibility	.12**	.45	.30	.49
Anxiety	.06**	.35	.10	.38
Idea-conformity	.13**	.57	.30	.60
CANONICAL CORRELATION	.22**	.57	.31	.60

[a] *Eta* or the canonical correlation. These figures differ slightly from those of preceding Tables because respondents for whom data were not complete are dropped. N > 2600, except for parental values, where N > 1285.

[b] Substance of the work with data, things, and people + closeness of supervision + complexity of organization of the work.

[c] Size and supervisory structure of the organization + time-pressure and its consequences + position in supervisory hierarchy + amount of competition + likelihood of loss of job or business + ownership status + amount of overtime.

**p < 0.01.

Table 3. Effects on the Educational and on the Occupational Position Correlations of Controlling Occupational Self-Direction

	Education (linear) Controlled on Occupational Position		Occupational Position (linear) Controlled on Education	
	Initial correlation[a]	Proportional reduction when controlling occupational self-direction	Initial correlation[a]	Proportional reduction when controlling occupational self-direction
A. *Parental Values*				
Self-direction/Conformity	.23**	.18	.09**	.83
B. *Values for Self*				
Self-direction/Conformity	.12**	.12	.05*	1.00
Self-direction/Competence	.13**	.11	.02	..
C. *Judgments about Work*				
Importance of Intrinsic Qualities	.04*	..b	.14**	.86
Importance of Extrinsic Benefits	.20**	.18	.15**	.70
D. *Social Orientation*				
Authoritarian Conservatism	.32**	.13	.05**	.98
Criteria of Morality	.08**	.44	.08**	.87
Trustfulness	.09**	.27	.08**	.70
Stance toward Change	.06**	.58	.05*	.00
CANONICAL CORRELATION	.36**	.15	.14**	.62
E. *Self-conception*				
Self-confidence	.05*	.31	.05*	.37
Self-deprecation	.03	..	.03	..
Attribution of Responsibility	.03	..	.05**	.43
Anxiety	.04*	..	.09**	.19
Idea-conformity	.08**	.19	.02	..
CANONICAL CORRELATION	.11**	.24	.12**	.24

[a]Respondents for whom occupational data are incomplete have been excluded.
[b]Proportional reduction not computed where the initial correlation is less than 0.05.
*p < 0.05.
**p < 0.01.

lations of occupational position to most aspects of values and orientation (with the notable exception of self-conception) are largely attributable to occupational self-direction.

One implication is that occupational position would cease to be relevant for most aspects of values and orientation if higher occupational position did not mean greater occupational self-direction. A second implication is that, although the magnitude of the correlations would be reduced, education would still be revelant for almost all aspects of values and orientation even if educated men were not so disproportionately situated in self-directed jobs. Why, then, is education pertinent? Our original hypothesis, to which we still adhere, was that educational level is pertinent to values and orientation insofar as education provides the intellectual flexibility and breadth of perspective that are essential for self-directed values and orientation; lack of education must seriously interfere with men's ability to be self-directed.

We do not have the data to test this hypothesis directly. We can, however, show that "intellectual flexibility" is involved in the relationship of education to values and orientation. As an approximate measure of intellectual flexibility, we rely on scores based on a single factor comprising several indices of how well men dealt with problems they encountered in the interview.[11] Scores on this measure of intellectual flexibility are correlated with education, hence with class, and are independently associated with most aspects of values and orientation.

11. The components of this factor (together with the factor loadings) are: (1) A rating of the adequacy of men's answers to the question, "Suppose you wanted to open a hamburger stand and there were two locations available. What questions would you consider in deciding which of the two locations offers a better business opportunity?" ($r=0.37$). (2) A rating of their answers to: "What are all the arguments you can think of for and against allowing cigarette commercials on TV? First, can you think of arguments *for* allowing cigarette commercials on TV? And can you think of arguments *against* allowing cigarette commercials on TV?" ($r=0.41$). (3) A measure of the frequency with which men agreed when asked agree-disagree questions ($r=0.52$). (4) Their summary scores on a portion of the Embedded Figures Test (cf. Witkin, 1962), which was given at the end of the interview ($r=0.67$). (5) The interviewers' appraisals of their intelligence ($r=0.60$). (6) Witkin's (1962) summary score for the Draw-A-Man test (administered at the end of the interview) ($r=0.75$). (7) The Goodenough estimate of intelligence (cf. Witkin, 1962), also based on the Draw-A-Man test ($r=0.78$). [See Chapters 1 and 19 of this volume for further discussions of "field independence."—EDITOR]

Controlling intellectual flexibility reduces many of the class correlations, notably the correlations with social orientation.[12]

Most importantly, the reductions in the class correlations are specific to the educational component of class; for example, controlling intellectual flexibility reduces the canonical correlation of education with social orientation by 40 percent, but it reduces the correlation of occupational position with social orientation by less than 10 percent. Although this finding is hardly definitive, it does strengthen the supposition that much of the importance of education for the class relationships lies in its contribution to the intellectual flexibility that we believe to be essential for self-directed values and orientation.

Conclusion

Much of the variation in men's values and orientation results from what we have to regard as idiosyncratic personal experience. Only a small proportion is attributable to the position men occupy in the general social structure. Still, social structure does have pronounced and consistent effects, and, of all aspects of social structure, class is by far the most important.

The higher their social class position, the more men value self-direction, and the more confident they are that self-direction is both possible and efficacious. The lower their social class position, the more men value conformity, and the more certain they are that conformity is all that their own capacities and the exigencies of the world allow. Thus, it would appear that men's values, their appraisals of their own abilities, and their understanding of the world are quite consistent. Self-direction is a central value for men of higher class position who see themselves as competent members of an essentially benign society. Conformity is a central value for men of lower class position who see themselves as less competent members of an essentially indifferent or threatening society. Self-direction, in short, is consonant with an orientational system premised on the possibilities of accomplishing what

12. Most class correlations are reduced by 25 percent to 50 percent when intellectual flexibility is controlled. All correlations except that with self-deprecation remain significant. It is not just that class is related to men's capacities to perceive and to judge, but that class shapes the reality that is there to be seen and to be judged.

one sets out to do; conformity, with an orientational system premised on the dangers of stepping out of line.

These relationships of class to values and orientation are substantially attributable to class-correlated variations in the degree to which jobs allow and require self-direction. More specifically, the job conditions determinative of occupational self-direction are of great importance for explaining the *occupational position* component of the class relationships, but are decidedly less important for explaining the *educational* component of these relationships. Occupational position seems to matter for values and orientation because it determines the conditions of self-direction that jobs provide or preclude; the critical facet of occupational position is that it is determinative of occupational self-direction. Education, on the other hand, seems to matter for values and orientation chiefly because it can be so very important for intellectual flexibility and breadth of perspective. Thus, the *class* relationships are built on the cumulative effects of educational training and occupational experience. The former is pertinent insofar as it provides or fails to provide the capability for self-direction, the latter insofar as it provides or fails to provide the experience of exercising self-direction in so consequential a realm of life as work.

We must acknowledge that nothing has been said about such issues as the relationship of occupational self-selection and of job mobility to values and orientation. The reinforcing processes by which jobs affect values and orientation, and values and orientation reflect back on jobs, are undoubtedly more complex than we have represented. The thrust of our discussion is not that all influence is in one direction, but rather that the occupational conditions attendant on class position are important in shaping men's values and orientation.

The processes by which men come to generalize from occupational to non-occupational realities need not be altogether or even mainly rational; all that we mean to assert is that occupation markedly affects men, not that men rationally decide on values and orientations to fit their occupational experiences.

In industrial society, where occupation is central to men's lives, occupational experiences that facilitate or deter the exercise of self-direction come to permeate men's views, not only of work and of their role in work, but also of the world and of self. The conditions of occupational life at higher social class levels facilitate interest in the intrinsic qualities of the job, foster a view of self and society that is conducive to believing in the possibilities of rational action toward purposive goals, and promote the valuation of self-direction. The conditions of occupational life at lower social class levels limit men's view of the job primarily to the extrinsic benefits it provides, foster a narrowly circumscribed conception of self and society, and promote the positive valuation of conformity to authority. Conditions of work that foster thought and initiative tend to enlarge men's conceptions of reality; conditions of constraint tend to narrow them.

References

Adorno, T. W., Else Frenkel-Brunswik, Daniel J. Levinson, and R. Nevitt Sanford. *The Authoritarian Personality*. New York: Harper, 1950.

Blalock, Hubert M., Jr. *Social Statistics*. New York: McGraw-Hill, 1960.

Blalock, Hubert M., Jr. *Causal Inferences in Nonexperimental Research*. Chapel Hill: University of North Carolina Press, 1964.

Christie, Richard. "Authoritarianism reexamined," in Richard Christie and Marie Jahoda, eds., *Studies in the Scope and Method of the Authoritarian Personality*. Glencoe, Ill.: Free Press, 1954, 123–196.

Clyde, Dean J., Elliot M. Cramer, and Richard J. Sherin. *Multivariate Statistical Programs*. Coral Gables, Fla.: Biometry Laboratory of the University of Miami, 1966.

Cohen, Jacob. "Some statistical issues in psychological research," in B. B. Wolman, ed., *Handbook of Clinical Psychology*. New York: McGraw-Hill, 1965, 95–121.

Cohen, Jacob. "Multiple regression as a general data-analytic system," *Psychol. Bulletin,* 70 (December, 1968), 426–443.

Cooley, William W., and Paul R. Lohnes. *Multivariate Procedures for the Behavioral Sciences*. New York: Wiley, 1962.

Duncan, Otis Dudley. "A socioeconomic index for all occupations," and "Properties and characteristics of the socioeconomic index," in Albert J. Reiss, et al., eds., *Occupations and Social Status*. New York: Free Press of Glencoe, 1961, 109–138, 139–161.

Edwards, Alba M. *A Social-Economic Grouping of the Gainful Workers of the United States*. Washington, D. C.: United States Government Printing Office, 1938.

Ford, Robert N. "A rapid scoring procedure for scaling attitude questions," *Public Opinion Quart.,* 14 (Fall, 1950), 507–532.

Gusfield, Joseph R., and Michael Schwartz. "The meanings of occupational prestige: reconsideration of the NORC scale," *Amer. Soc. Rev.,* 28 (April, 1963), 265–271.

Guttman, Louis. "A basis for scaling qualitative data," *Amer. Soc. Rev.,* 9 (April, 1944), 139–150.

Guttman, Louis. "The basis for scalogram analysis," and "The scalogram board technique for scale analysis," in Samuel A. Stouffer et al., eds., *Measurement and Prediction*. Princeton, N. J.: Princeton University Press, 1950, 60–90, 91–121.

Hodge, Robert W., Paul Siegal, and Peter H. Rossi. "Occupational prestige in the United States: 1925–1963," *Amer. J. Sociol.*, 70 (November, 1964), 286–302.

Hollingshead, August B., and Fredrick C. Redlich. *Social Class and Mental Illness: A Community Study*. New York: Wiley, 1958.

Hyman, Herbert H., and Paul B. Sheatsley. " 'The authoritarian personality': a methodological critique," in Richard Christie and Marie Jahoda, eds., *Studies in the Scope and Method of the Authoritarian Personality*. Glencoe, Ill.: Free Press, 1954, 50–122.

Inkeles, Alex. "Industrial man: the relation of status to experience, perception, and value," *Amer. J. Sociol.*, 66 (July, 1960), 1–31.

Kirscht, John P., and Ronald C. Dillehay. *Dimensions of Authoritarianism: A Review of Research and Theory*. Lexington: University of Kentucky Press, 1967.

Kohn, Melvin L. "Social class and parental values," *Amer. J. Sociol.*, 64 (January, 1959), 337–351.

Kohn, Melvin L. "Social class and parent-child relationships: an interpretation," *Amer. J. Sociol.*, 68 (January, 1963), 471–480.

Kohn, Melvin L. *Class and Conformity: A Study in Values*. Homewood, Ill.: Dorsey Press, 1969.

Labovitz, Sanford. "Some observations on measurement and statistics," *Social Forces*, 46 (December, 1967), 151–160.

Lipset, Seymour Martin. "Democracy and working-class authoritarianism," *Amer. Soc. Rev.*, 24 (August, 1959), 482–501.

McKinley, J. C., S. R. Hathaway, and P. E. Meehl. "The Minnesota multiphasic personality inventory: VI. the K scale," *J. Consult. Psychol.*, 12 (January–February, 1948), 20–31.

Menzel, Herbert. "A new coefficient for scalogram analysis," *Public Opinion Quart.*, 17 (Summer, 1953), 268–280.

Pearlin, Leonard I., and Melvin L. Kohn. "Social class, occupation, and parental values: a cross-national study," *Amer. Soc. Rev.*, 31 (August, 1966), 466–479.

Peters, Charles C., and Walter R. Van Voorhis. *Statistical Procedures and Their Mathematical Bases*. New York: McGraw-Hill, 1940.

Reiss, Albert J., Otis Dudley Duncan, Paul K. Hatt, and Cecil C. North. *Occupations and Social Status*. New York: Free Press of Glencoe, 1961.

Rosenberg, Morris. *Occupations and Values*. Glencoe, Ill.: Free Press, 1957.

Rosenberg, Morris. "The association between self-esteem and anxiety," *J. Psychiat. Res.*, 1 (September, 1962), 135–152.

Ryder, Robert G. "Scoring orthogonally rotated factors," *Psychol. Rep.*, 16 (June, 1965), 701–704.

Schooler, Carmi. "A note of extreme caution on the use of Guttman scales," *Amer. J. Sociol.*, 74 (November, 1968), 296–301.

Srole, Leo. "Social integration and certain corollaries: an exploratory study," *Amer. Soc. Rev.*, 21 (December, 1956), 709–716.

Stouffer, Samuel A. *Communism, Conformity, and Civil Liberties: A Cross-Section of the Nation Speaks its Mind.* New York: Doubleday, 1955.

Sudman, Seymour, and Jacob J. Feldman. "Sample design and field procedures," in John W. C. Johnstone and Ramon J. Rivera, eds., *Volunteers for Learning: A Study of the Educational Pursuits of American Adults.* Chicago: Aldine, 1965, 482–485 in Appendix 1.

United States Department of Labor. *Dictionary of Occupational Titles,* 3rd ed. Washington, D. C.: United States Government Printing Office, 1965.

Williams, Robin M., Jr. *American Society: A Sociological Interpretation,* 2nd ed. New York: Knopf, 1960.

Witkin, H. A., R. B. Dyk, H. F. Faterson, D. R. Goodenough, and S. A. Karp. *Psychological Differentiation: Studies of Development.* New York: Wiley, 1962.

13

Undermanning, Performances, and Students' Subjective Experiences in Behavior Settings of Large and Small High Schools

Allan W. Wicker

There is a long sociological tradition of supposing that overly segmented jobs lead to alienation and a sense of meaninglessness. This chapter provides a new look at the idea, and it appears that an opportunity for a variety of acts is indeed a healthful resource. While Karl Marx stressed the relationship between work and alienation, this study suggests that alienation can develop or be minimized in a broad variety of contexts, including recreational. The author further suggests that the presumed richness of rural life may be due to a greater diversity of activities and a greater need for the individual's participation than in larger, more specialized urban settings.

Recent research by Barker and his colleagues indicates that the number of students in a high school is related to the students' behaviors and subjective experiences in school extracurricular activities, such as theatrical productions, athletic events, and organization meetings. Students of small schools, vis-à-vis students of large schools, (*a*) enter more different kinds of activities, (*b*) hold more positions of responsibility in activities entered (Gump and Friesen, 1964; Wicker, 1967; Willems, 1965), (*c*) use more dimensions or constructs to describe school activities (Wicker, 1967), (*d*) experience more satisfactions "relating to being challenged, engaging in important actions, to being involved in group activities, and to achieving moral and cultural values (Barker and Gump, 1964, p. 197)," (*e*) report more internal and external pressures to attend and participate, including feelings of obligation to support the activities (Willems, 1964, 1967).

These studies support behavior setting theory (Barker, 1960). The *behavior setting* is an ecobehavioral unit whose characteristics include occurrence at a specifiable time and place, and systematic arrangement of people, other physical objects, and certain patterns of behav-

Abridged from Allan W. Wicker, "Undermanning, Performances, and Students' Subjective Experiences in Behavior Settings of Large and Small High Schools," in *Journal of Personality and Social Psychology*, 10 (1968), 255–261. Reprinted by permission of the American Psychological Association and the author.

This article is based on data collected for a doctoral dissertation submitted to the Department of Psychology of the University of Kansas. The author is indebted to Roger G. Barker, chairman of the dissertation committee, and to L. B. Kornreich, D. D. M. Ragle, and Edwin P. Willems for valuable comments on an earlier version of this paper. The cooperation of administrators of participating schools is gratefully acknowledged. Facilities of the University of Kansas Computation Center were used for some analyses. The research was supported by Public Health Service Grant 5 Fl MH-30, 582-02. Later analyses of data and the writing of this report were supported by a grant from the Graduate School of the University of Wisconsin, Milwaukee.

ior (Barker, 1968; Barker and Wright, 1954). The school activities are behavior settings.

The theory asserts that behavior settings must be supported by member participation if the settings are to continue to exist. Depending upon the number of people available to perform the essential functions, behavior settings may be *undermanned, optimally manned,* or *overmanned.* In undermanned settings, the setting functions are often in jeopardy, and occupants sense the possibility of losing the satisfactions the settings provide. This leads them to invest more time and effort than when occupants are numerous and behavior setting functions are not precarious. Often they take positions of responsibility and engage in a wide range of supportive behaviors. Under pressure to keep activities going, members seek to induce others to participate. Membership requirements are minimized, and attempts are made to bring available personnel to at least the minimal level of performance Feelings of involvement, success, failure, challenge, responsibility, and insecurity due to dependence upon others are common. In the present paper, the word *experiences* will denote students' feelings about their participation in behavior settings.

Barker and his associates have found that in small schools the number of students relative to the number of extracurricular behavior settings is much less than in large schools, suggesting that on the whole, the small school settings are relatively undermanned (Barker and Barker, 1964; Gump and Friesen, 1964; Willems, 1965, 1967). However, it seems likely that *some* settings or kinds of settings in small schools may be relatively *over*-manned, just as there may be *some* settings or kinds of settings in large schools which are *under*-manned, and the postulated experiences should occur only in those settings which are undermanned (high manpower needs relative to supply), regardless of the size of school in which the settings occur.

In the present study, students' experiences in high school extracurricular behavior settings are examined to test the following hypothesis. Students occupying settings characterized by many positions of responsibility relative to the manpower supply have more of the experiences postulated by the theory than students occupying settings characterized by few positions of responsibility relative to the manpower supply, regardless of whether comparisons are made between or within school size. . . .

A second focus of the present paper is the role of performances in accounting for differential experiences in settings. Students of large and small schools, who differ in average number of performances, also differ in average experiences (Barker and Gump, 1964). It may be that, regardless of school size or degree of undermanning in a setting, the experiences associated with undermanned settings occur only for the performers, and not for those who attend but do not responsibly participate. If this were true, the different average experiences of occupants of settings differing in degree of undermanning would be attributable to the relative frequency of performers in the settings.

Such a finding would tend to discount alternative explanations of the Barker group's findings in terms of rural-urban differences and other community size correlates. (In most of the studies, community size was not controlled, but varied with school size.) In addition, it would suggest that school size is important primarily because of its "channeling" function, that is, guiding students into settings which are (or are not) short of manpower and which, consequently, result (or do not result) in performances by the students.

Method

Subjects

Data were obtained from 107 juniors (eleventh grade) from four small high schools (number of juniors per school ranged from 17 to 49), and from 84 juniors from one large high school (number of juniors, 400). All students were tested in regular classes or study halls during school hours. Each school was the only public high school in its respective northeast Kansas community. Small school communities ranged in population from 450 to 1200; the large school community had 22,000 residents.

In some comparisons, students of large and small schools are matched on the basis of six variables shown by Willems (1964, 1965) to be related to student participation in extracurricular behavior settings: sex, status of father's occupation, father's education, mother's education, IQ, and grades in school for the preceding semester.

Questionnaire Materials

The information subjects provided is described below:

1. *Attendance and behavior in behavior settings.* Six different kinds of high school curricular activities were listed on a single sheet with a

brief description as varsity basketball game at home school (game), class or club business meeting (meeting), school play or musical production (play), informal dance at night (dance), class or club money-raising project (project), and school-sponsored or school-organized trip away from school (trip). Subjects were asked to write the name of one specific activity (behavior setting) of each kind they had attended, and then on a second sheet, for each such activity to describe what they had done there, particularly noting any job or special responsibility. Student behaviors in settings were categorized as performances if they involved leadership and/or carrying out setting functions, for example, competing as a member of the basketball team, ushering at a school play. Non-performances involve no particular responsibility, for example, watching a game.

2. *Experience rating scales.* An instrument in the general format of the semantic differential (Osgood, Suci, and Tannenbaum, 1957) was employed to measure subjects' experiences in settings they had attended. There were 27 scales, consisting of bipolar adjective pairs, for example, interesting-boring, or pairs of phrases, for example; I was active in what was going on—mostly I watched. Twelve of the scales were descriptions of personal experiences in settings, derived from behavior setting theory. One pole of each of these scales is given in Table 1. Subjects considered in turn each of the activities they had reported, and indicated their experiences in the settings by checking one of seven intervals between the poles of the scales.

Results

Within each school size, the index of undermanning for each kind of setting was the number of people who performed in the setting they named, divided by the number of people who attended a setting of that kind. . . .

. . . For five of the six kinds of behavior settings, undermanning is significantly greater in small than [in] large schools. Inspection of the undermanning indexes suggests that differences between schools are not constant. The differences are greatest for game and play, and there is a reversal for trip. . . .

The [subjective] experiences (listed in Table 1) are, as expected, generally more characteristic of students of small schools. And school size differences in experiences are more pronounced for those kinds

Table 1. Mean Experience Scale Ratings by Performers and Nonperformers of Large and Small Schools

Scale	Performer		Nonperformer		Significance levels
	Large school (n = 61)	Small school (n = 103)	Large school (n = 61)	Small school (n = 103)	
1. Helped me develop a skill or ability	3.4	2.6	4.5	4.5	a
2. Helped me have more confidence in myself	3.1	2.6	4.5	4.1	b
3. Gave me a chance to see how good I was	3.2	2.9	4.8	4.5	a
4. People depended on me: I was needed	2.6	2.6	5.0	4.9	a
5. I worked hard	2.8	2.1	4.6	4.4	b
6. I had an important job	3.0	2.5	5.3	5.3	a
7. I was worried about whether the activity would be a success	3.5	2.7	4.5	4.2	b
8. I was asked to go and help out	2.7	2.8	5.2	4.6	a
9. I was active in what was going on	2.2	1.8	4.6	3.5	c
10. I felt like I had really accomplished something	2.4	2.7	4.5	4.0	d
11. I spent much time	2.7	2.2	3.7	3.6	a
12. I worked closely with others	2.6	2.2	3.8	2.9	c

[a] School size, *ns*; performance level, $p < .001$; interaction, *ns*.
[b] School size, $p < .05$; performance level, $p < .001$; interaction, *ns*.
[c] School size, $p < .01$; performance level, $p < .001$; interaction, *ns*.
[d] School size, *ns*; performance level, $p < .001$; interaction, $p < .05$.

255

of settings for which there are also large differences in undermanning, for example, game and play. This finding supports the postulated experiences-undermanning relationship.

Comparisons of experiences within school size were made by testing mean scale ratings of settings of the two kinds most discrepant in undermanning: project and game for [the] large school, project and trip for [the] small school. In each instance, students' ratings of project settings should favor the undermanned pole of the experience scales. For each size, matched t tests were performed on ratings of all subjects who attended settings of the two genotypes.

For large school, 9 of the 12 scales showed significant differences in the expected direction; . . . for small school, the comparable figure was 11 out of 12. Thus, within the same school size there are large differences in average experiences of students when they occupy settings of kinds which are highly discrepant in degree of undermanning.

The next analysis examines the relationship of performance and experiences, and of school size and experiences when differences in performance are controlled. . . . The mean ratings and significance levels for the . . . testable effects are given in Table 1. The lower the mean rating, the closer it is to the pole of the experience scale listed in Table 1.

For all 12 scales, level of performance has a highly significant effect on experiences. Controlling for performance level eliminated school-size differences for 7 of the 12 scales. However, experiences of self-confidence (Scale 2), working hard (Scale 5), being concerned about the success of an activity (Scale 7), being active (Scale 9), and working closely with others (Scale 12) still characterized students of small schools more than those of large schools. This finding may be due to the fact that the control for performance level was not precise; no distinction was made between high level performances, that is, jobs involving considerable power over the setting such as playing on the basketball team, and low performances, that is, nonessential positions of low power such as selling concessions. A breakdown of performances of subjects in the present analysis reveals that 72 percent of the performances of students in small schools were high level, compared to 42 percent for students in large schools.

Finally, differences between performers and nonperformers in feelings of accomplishment (Scale 10) were greater for students in large than small schools.

Discussion

The present study has sought to refine the findings by Barker and his colleagues, who have dealt with the relationships of school size and (a) degree of undermanning in settings, (b) performances by students, and (c) students' experiences in settings. . . . While most large-school settings are overmanned, a few are undermanned; the opposite is true of the small school. Regardless of school size, students occupying overmanned settings are more likely to be nonperformers, although some will be performers. Occupants of undermanned settings are more likely to be performers. And since overmanned settings are more characteristic of large schools than small schools, the former will have fewer performances by the average student. Regardless of school size, most of the performers (but not the nonperformers) have the experiences postulated by Barker (1960). The average student in the large school, having fewer performances than his small school counterpart, also has fewer of the experiences. Thus school size is an important influence on students' experiences because of its relationship to the degree of undermanning of its settings and the consequent channeling of students into performance or nonperformance roles.

There are a number of convergences between the present findings in schools and research in industrial and laboratory settings. For example, students' level of responsibility in group tasks was shown to be positively related to their having certain experiences which presumably are satisfying. Reviews of research in industry indicate that job satisfaction is higher the greater the degree of control employees have over their work methods and work pace (Vroom, 1964) and the higher their position in the organizational hierarchy (Porter and Lawler, 1965). In a laboratory study Shaw (1960) found that students who were led to believe they had a large share of responsibility for a group project were willing to do more work than those who were told their share was small.

Second, in the present study level of responsibility was shown to be an important mediating variable in the relationship between school size and students' experiences in school activities. It is possible that the same variable mediates the consistently negative relationship between size of industrial sub-unit (e.g., work group) and job satisfaction (Porter and Lawler, 1965). As Shaw (1960) has pointed out, in situations where all workers have equal shares of responsibility, the share of the individual member will increase as group size decreases. Thus, the greater satisfaction of members of small work groups may be related to their greater responsibility for and control over group output and procedures. The role of degree of responsibility in the size-satisfaction relationship might be tested experimentally by varying members' shares of responsibility within each of several work groups of different size.

A third convergence stems from the finding that differences in experiences of students of large and small schools may be large or negligible, depending upon the kind of behavior setting. This is consistent with Porter and Lawler's observation that unless investigators clearly distinguish between sub-unit size and total organization size, "the effects of one type of size (e.g., total organization size) may be confounded by the effects of the other type of size (i.e., size of sub-units within total organizations) [p. 40]." In the present study, however, sub-units were examined in terms of degree of undermanning rather than size per se. . . .

References

Barker, R. G. "Ecology and motivation," *Nebraska Symposium on Motivation,* 8 (1960), 1–50.

Barker, R. G. *The Definition of Ecological Psychology: Concepts and Method for an Ecobehavioral Science.* Stanford, Calif.: Stanford University Press, 1968.

Barker, R. G., and L. S. Barker. "Structural characteristics," in R. G. Barker and P. V. Gump, eds., *Big School, Small School: High School Size and Student Behavior.* Stanford, Calif.: Stanford University Press, 1964.

Barker, R. G., and P. V. Gump, eds. *Big School, Small School: High School Size and Student Behavior.* Stanford, Calif.: Stanford University Press, 1964.

Barker, R. G., and H. F. Wright. *Midwest and Its Children: The Psychological Ecology of an American Town.* New York: Row, Peterson, 1954.

Gump, P. V., and W. V. Friesen. "Participation in non-class settings," in R. G. Barker and P. V. Gump, eds., *Big School, Small School: High School Size and Student Behavior.* Stanford, Calif.: Stanford University Press, 1964.

Osgood, C. E., G. J. Suci, and P. H. Tannenbaum. *The Measurement of Meaning.* Urbana: University of Illinois Press, 1957.

Porter, L. W., and E. E. Lawler. "Properties of organization structure in relation to job attitudes and job behavior," *Psychol. Bulletin,* 64 (1965), 23–51.

Shaw, D. "Size of share in task and motivation in work groups," *Sociometry,* 23 (1960), 203–208.

Vroom, V. H. *Work and Motivation.* New York: Wiley, 1964.

Wicker, A. W. "Students' experiences in behavior settings of large and small high schools: an examination of behavior setting theory," doctoral dissertation, University of Kansas. Ann Arbor, Mich.: University Microfilms, 1967, No. 68–644.

Willems, E. P. "Forces toward participation in behavior settings," in R. G. Barker and P. V. Gump, eds., *Big School, Small School: High School Size and Student Behavior*. Stanford, Calif.: Stanford University Press, 1964.

Willems, E. P. "Participation in behavior settings in relation to three variables: size of behavior settings, marginality of persons, and sensitivity to audiences," doctoral dissertation, University of Kansas. Ann Arbor, Mich.: University Microfilms, 1965, No. 66–6060.

Willems, E. P. "Sense of obligation to high school activities as related to school size and marginality of student," *Child Development,* 38 (1967), 1247–1260.

14

Differential Association and the Rehabilitation of Drug Addicts

Rita Volkman and Donald R. Cressey

People in an organization or group tend to develop some
degree of homogeneity in their attitudes and values. Social
psychologists have developed a Theory of Differential
Association to describe this process and the conditions
under which it is most likely to occur. Here the theory is used
to interpret processes in a therapeutic group concerned with
rehabilitating drug addicts. However, the same theory can be
used just as well to account for normal socialization or
socialization into deviant groups.

In 1955 Cressey listed five principles for applying Edwin Sutherland's theory of differential association to the rehabilitation of criminals.[1] While this article is now frequently cited in the sociological literature dealing with group therapy, "therapeutic communities," and "total institutions," we know of no program of rehabilitation that has been explicitly based on the principles. The major point of Cressey's article, which referred to criminals, not addicts, is similar to the following recommendation by the Chief of the United States Narcotics Division: "The community should restore the former addict to his proper place in society and help him avoid associations that would influence him to return to the use of drugs."[2]

Cressey gives five rules (to be reviewed below) for implementing this directive to "restore," "help," and "influence" the addict. These rules, derived from the sociological and social-psychological literature on social movements, crime prevention, group therapy, communications, personality change, and social change, were designed to show that sociology has distinctive, nonpsychiatric, theory that can be used effectively by practitioners seeking to prevent crime and change criminals. Sutherland also had this as a principal objective when he formulated his theory of differential association.[3]

Assuming, as we do, that Cressey's principles are consistent with Sutherland's theory and that his theory, in turn, is consistent with more general sociological theory, a test of the principles would be a test of the more general formulations. Ideally, such a test would involve careful study of the results of a program rationally designed to utilize the principles to change criminals. To our knowledge, such a test has not been made.[4] As a "next best" test, we may study rehabili-

Reprinted from Rita Volkman and Donald E. Cressey, "Differential Association and the Rehabilitation of Drug Addicts," in *American Journal of Sociology*, 69 (1963), 129–142. Reprinted by permission of the University of Chicago Press, and the authors.

1. Donald R. Cressey, "Changing Criminals: The Application of the Theory of Differential Association," *American Journal of Sociology*, LXI (September, 1955), 116–120. See also Cressey, "Contradictory Theories in Correctional Group Therapy Programs," *Federal Probation*, XVIII (June, 1954), 20–26.

2. Harry J. Anslinger, "Drug Addiction," *Encyclopaedia Britannica*, VII (1960), 677–679.

3. Edwin H. Sutherland and Donald R. Cressey, *Principles of Criminology*, 6th ed. (Philadelphia: Lippincott, 1960), 74–80.

4. See, however, Joseph A. Cook and Gilbert Geis, "Forum Anonymous: The Techniques of Alcoholics Anonymous Applied to Prison Therapy," *Journal of Social Therapy*, III (First Quarter, 1957), 9–13.

tation programs that use the principles, however unwittingly. Such a program has been in operation since 1958. Insofar as it is remarkably similar to any program that could have been designed to implement the principles, the results over the years can be viewed as at least a crude test of the principles. Since the principles are interrelated, the parts of any program implementing them must necessarily overlap.

"Synanon," an organization of former drug addicts, was founded in May, 1958, by a member of Alcoholics Anonymous with the assistance of an alcoholic and a drug addict. In December, 1958, Volkman (a non-addict) heard about the two dozen ex-addicts living together in an abandoned store, and she obtained permission of the Synanon Board of Directors[5] to visit the group daily and to live in during the weekends. In July, 1959, she moved into the girls' dormitory of the group's new, larger quarters and continued to reside at Synanon House until June, 1960. Cressey (also a non-addict) visited the House at Volkman's invitation in the spring of 1960; for one year, beginning in July, 1960, he visited the organization on the average of at least once a week. He deliberately refrained from trying to influence policy or program, and his theory about the effects of group relationships on rehabilitation were unknown to the group. Most of the interview material and statistical data reported below were collected by Volkman during her 1959–1960 period of residence and were used in the thesis for her Master's degree, prepared under the direction of C. Wayne Gordon.[6] As both a full-fledged member of Synanon and as a participant observer, Volkman attended about three hundred group sessions, a few of which were recorded. She was accorded the same work responsibilities, rights, and privileges as any other member, and she was considered one of Synanon's first "graduates."

The Subjects

Background data were available on only the first fifty-two persons entering Synanon after July, 1958. These records were prepared by

5. The Board at first was composed of the three original members. It is now made up of the founder (an ex-alcoholic but a non-addict) and seven long-term residents who have remained off drugs and who have demonstrated their strict loyalty to the group and its principles.

6. Rita Volkman, "A Descriptive Case Study of Synanon as a Primary Group Organization." Unpublished master's thesis, Department of Education, University of California, Los Angeles, 1961.

a resident who in July, 1959, took it upon himself to interview and compile the information. We have no way of determining whether these fifty-two persons are representative of all addicts. However, we believe they are similar to the 215 persons who have resided at Synanon for at least one month.

Age and sex distributions are shown in Table 1: 44 percent of the fifty-two were Protestant, 35 percent Catholic, 8 percent Jewish.[7] Racially, 27 percent were Negro, and there were no Orientals; 19 percent of the Caucasians were of Mexican origin and 13 percent were of Italian origin. Educational attainment is shown in Table 2. Although the data on early family life are poor because the resident simply asked, "What was your family like?" it may be noted that only five of the fifty-two indicated satisfaction with the home. Words and phrases such as "tension," "arguing," "bickering," "violence,"

Table 1. Age and Sex*

Age (In Years)	Males		Females		Total	
	No.	Percent	No.	Percent	No.	Percent
18–20	0	0	1	7	1	2
21–30	17	44	11	79	28	54
31–40	18	48	2	14	20	38
41–50	1	3	0	0	1	2
51–60	2	5	0	0	2	4
Total	38	100	14	100	52	100

*Median ages: males, 31.0; females, 27.5.

Table 2. Educational Attainment

	No.	Percent
Part grade school	1	2
Completed grade school	3	6
Part high school	24	46
Completed high school	11	21
Part college	13	25
Completed college	0	0
Total	52	100

7. In May, 1961, 20 percent of the residents were Jewish.

"lack of warmth," "went back and forth," and "nagged" were common.[8]

The sporadic and tenuous occupational ties held by the group are indicated in Table 3. This table supports the notion that addicts cannot maintain steady jobs because their addiction interferes with the work routine; it suggests also that these members had few lasting peer group contacts or ties, at least so far as work associations go. In view of their poor employment records, it might be asked how the addicts supported their addictions, which cost from $30 to $50 a day and sometimes ran to $100 a day. Only four of the men reported that they obtained their incomes by legitimate work alone; thirty (79 percent) were engaged in illegitimate activities, with theft, burglary, armed robbery, shoplifting, and pimping leading the list. One man and seven women were supplied with drugs or money by their mates or families, and five of these females supplemented this source by prostitution or other illegitimate work. Five of the fourteen women had no income except that from illegitimate activities, and none of the women supported themselves by legitimate work only.

Institutional histories and military service histories are consistent with the work and educational histories, indicating that the fifty-two members were not somehow inadvertently selected as "easy" rehabilitation cases. The fifty-two had been in and out of prisons, jails, and hospitals all over the United States. Table 4 shows that ten men

Table 3. Length and Continuity of Employment

No. of Years on One Job	Unsteady (Discontinuous or Sporadic)	Steady (Continuous)	Total
Under 1	36*	4	40
2–3	3	2	5
4–5	1	3	4
6 or over	2	1	3
Total	42	10	52

*Of this category 67 percent defined their work as "for short periods only."

8. Cf. Research Center for Human Relations, New York University, *Family Background as an Etiological Factor in Personality Predisposition to Heroin Addiction* (New York: the Author, 1956).

Table 4. Confinements in Institutions

No. of Confinements	No.		
	Male	Female	Total*
1– 3	9	6	15
4– 6	12	7	19
7– 9	8	0	8
10–12	0	1	1
13–15	2	0	2
Total confinements	166	59	225

*Three males indicated "numerous arrests," and four supplied no information. These seven were not included in the tally.

and one woman had been confined seven or more times; the mean number of confinements for males was 5.5 and for females 3.9. The table seems to indicate that whatever value confinement in institutions might have had for this group, it clearly did not prevent further confinements.

In sum, the pre-Synanon experiences of the fifty-two residents seems to indicate nonidentification with pro-legal activities and norms. Neither the home, the armed services, the occupational world, schools, prisons, nor hospitals served as links with the larger and more socially acceptable community. This, then, is the kind of "raw material" with which Synanon has been working.[9]

The Program

Admission. Not every addict who knocks on the door of Synanon is given admission. Nevertheless, the only admission criterion we have been able to find is *expressed willingness* to submit one's self to a group that hates drug addiction. Use of this criterion has unwittingly implemented one of Cressey's principles:

> If criminals are to be changed, they must be assimilated into groups which emphasize values conducive to law-abiding behavior and, concurrently, alienated from groups emphasizing values conducive

9.   Of the fifty-two members 60 percent first heard about Synanon from addicts on the street or in jails, prisons, or hospitals; about a fourth heard about it on television or read about it in a magazine; and the remainder were told of it by members or past members.

to criminality. Since our experience has been that the majority of criminals experience great difficulty in securing intimate contacts in ordinary groups, special groups whose major common goal is the reformation of criminals must be created.

This process of assimiliation and alienation begins the moment an addict arrives at Synanon, and it continues throughout his stay. The following are two leaders' comments on admission interviews; they are consistent with our own observations of about twenty such interviews.

1. When a new guy comes in we want to find out whether a person has one inkling of seriousness. Everybody who comes here is what we call a psychopathic liar. We don't take them all, either. We work off the top spontaneously, in terms of feeling. We use a sort of intuitive faculty. You know he's lying, but you figure, "Well, maybe if you get a halfway positive feeling that he'll stay. . . ." We ask him things like, "What do you want from us?" "Don't you think you're an idiot or insane?" "Doesn't it sound insane for you to be running around the alleys stealing money from others so's you can go and stick something up your arm?" "Does this sound sane to you?" "Have you got family and friends outside?" We might tell him to go do his business now and come back when he's ready to do business with us. We tell him, "We don't need you." "You need *us*." And if we figure he's only halfway with us, we'll chop off his hair.

It's all in the *attitude*. It's got to be positive. We don't want their money. But we may just tell him to bring back some dough next week. If he pleads and begs—the money's not important. If he shows he really cares. If his attitude is good. It's all in the attitude.

2. Mostly, if people don't have a family outside, with no business to take care of, they're ready to stay. They ain't going to have much time to think about themselves otherwise. . . . Now, when he's got problems, when he's got things outside, if he's got mickey mouse objections, like when you ask him, "How do you feel about staying here for a year?" and he's got to bargain with you, like he needs to stay with his wife or his sick mother—then we tell him to get lost. If he can't listen to a few harsh words thrown at him, he's

not ready. Sometimes we yell at him, "You're a goddamned liar!" If he's serious he'll take it. He'll do anything if he's serious.

But each guy's different. If he sounds sincere, we're not so hard. If he's sick of running the rat race out there, or afraid of going to the penitentiary, he's ready to do anything. Then we let him right in. . . .

This admission process seems to have two principal functions. First, it forces the newcomer to admit, at least on a verbal level, that he is to try to conform to the norms of the group, whose members will not tolerate any liking for drugs or drug addicts. From the minute he enters the door, his expressed desire to join the group is tested by giving him difficult orders—to have his hair cut off, to give up all his money, to sever all family ties, to come back in ten days or even thirty days. He is given expert help and explicit but simple criteria for separating the "good guys" from the "bad guys"—the latter shoot dope. Second, the admission process weeds out men and women who simply want to lie down for a few days to rest, to obtain free room and board, or to stay out of the hands of the police. In the terms used by Lindesmith, and also in the terms used at Synanon, the person must want to give up drug *addiction,* not just the drug *habit.*[10] This means that he must at least *say* that he wants to quit using drugs once and for all, in order to realize his potentials as an adult; he must not indicate that he merely wants a convenient place in which to go through withdrawal distress so that he can be rid of his habit for a short time because he has lost his connection, or for some other reason. He must be willing to give up all ambitions, desires, and social interactions that might prevent the group from assimilating him completely.

If he says he just wants to kick, he's no good. Out with him. Now we know nine out of ten lie, but we don't care. We'd rather have him make an attempt and *lie* and then get him in here for thirty days or so—then he might stick. It takes months to decide to stay. Most fish [newcomers] don't take us seriously. We know what they want, out in front. A dope fiend wants dope, nothing else. All the

10. Alfred R. Lindesmith, *Opiate Addiction* (Bloomington, Ind.: Principia Press, 1947), 44–66.

rest is garbage. We've even taken that ugly thing called money. This shows that they're serious. Now this guy today was sincere. We told him we didn't want money. We could see he would at least give the place a try. We have to find out if he's sincere. Is he willing to have us cut off his curly locks? I imagine cutting his hair off makes him take us seriously. . . .

Although it is impossible to say whether Synanon's selective admission process inadvertently admits those addicts who are most amenable to change, no addict has been refused admission on the ground that his case is "hopeless" or "difficult" or that he is "unreachable." On the contrary, before coming to Synanon, twenty-nine of the fifty-two addicts had been on drugs for at least ten years. Two of these were addicted for over forty years, and had been in and out of institutions during that period. The average length of time on drugs for the fifty-two was eleven years, and 56 percent reported less than one month as the longest period of time voluntarily free of drugs after addiction and prior to Synanon.

Indoctrination. In the admission process, and throughout his residence, the addict discovers over and over again that the group to which he is submitting is antidrug, anticrime, and antialcohol. At least a dozen times a day he hears someone tell him that he can remain at Synanon only as long as he "stays clean," that is, stays away from crime, alcohol, and drugs. This emphasis is an unwitting implementation of Cressey's second principle:

> The more relevant the common purpose of the group to the reformation of criminals, the greater will be its influence on the criminal members' attitudes and values. Just as a labor union exerts strong influence over its members' attitudes toward management but less influence on their attitudes toward say, Negroes, so a group organized for recreation or welfare purposes will have less success in influencing criminalistic attitudes and values than will one whose explicit purpose is to change criminals.

Indoctrination makes clear the notion that Synanon exists in order to keep addicts off drugs, not for purposes of recreation, vocational education, etc. Within a week after admission, each newcomer participates in an indoctrination session by a spontaneous group made up of four or five older members. Ordinarily, at least one member of the Board of Directors is present, and he acts as leader. The following are excerpts from one such session with a woman addict. The rules indicate the extreme extent to which it is necessary for the individual to subvert his personal desires and ambitions to the antidrug, anti-crime group.

> Remember, we told you not to go outside by yourself. Whenever anybody leaves this building they have to check in and out at the desk. For a while, stay in the living room. Don't take showers alone or even go to the bathroom alone, see. While you're kicking, somebody will be with you all the time. And stay away from new-comers. You got nothing to talk to them about, except street talk, and before you know it you'll be splitting [leaving] to take a fix together. Stay out of the streets, mentally and physically, or get lost now.
> No phone calls or letters for a while—if you get one, you'll read it in front of us. We'll be monitoring all your phone calls for a while. You see, you got no ties, no business out there any more. You don't need them. You never could handle them before, so don't start thinking you can do it now. All you knew how to do was shoot dope and go to prison.
> You could never take care of your daughter before. You didn't know how to be a mother. It's garbage. All a dope fiend knows how to do is shoot dope. Forget it.

There are two obvious illustrations of the antidrug and anticrime nature of the group's subculture. First, there is a strong taboo against what is called "street talk." Discussion of how it feels to take a fix, who one's connection was, where one took his shot, the crimes one has committed, or who one associated with is severely censured. One's best friend and confidant at Synanon might well be the person that administers a tongue lashing for street talk, and the person who calls your undesirable behavior to the attention of the entire group during a general meeting.

Second, a member must never, in any circumstances, identify with the "code of the streets," which says that a criminal is supposed to keep quiet about the criminal activities of his peers. Even calling an ordinary citizen "square" is likely to stimulate a spontaneous lecture, in heated and colorful terms, on the notion that the people who are *really* square are those that go around as bums sticking needles in their arms. A person who, as a criminal, learned to hate stool pigeons and finks with a passion must now turn even his closest friend over to the authorities, the older members of Synanon, if the friend shows any signs of nonconformity. If he should find that a member is considering "sneaking off to a fix somewhere," has kept pills, drugs, or an "outfit" with him when he joined the organization, or even has violated rules such as that prohibiting walking alone on the beach, he must by Synanon's code relinquish his emotional ties with the violator and expose the matter to another member or even to the total membership at a general meeting. If he does not do so, more pressure is put upon him than upon the violator, for he is expected to have "known better." Thus, for perhaps the first time in his life he will be censured for *not* "squealing" rather than for "squealing."[11] He must identify with the law and not with the criminal intent or act.

The sanctions enforcing this norm are severe, for its violation threatens the very existence of the group. "Guilt by association" is the rule. In several instances, during a general meeting the entire group spontaneously voted to "throw out" both a member who had used drugs and a member who had known of this use but had not informed the group. Banishment from the group is considered the worst possible punishment, for it is stressed over and over again that life in the streets "in your condition" can only mean imprisonment or death.

That the group's purpose is keeping addicts off drugs is given emphasis in formal and informal sessions—called "haircuts" or "pull ups"—as well as in spontaneous denunciations, and in denunciations at general meetings. The "synanon," discussed below, also serves this purpose. A "haircut" is a deliberately contrived device for minimizing the importance of the individual and maximizing the importance of the group, and for defining the group's basic purpose—keeping addicts off drugs and crime. The following is the response of a leader to the questions, "What's a haircut? What's its purpose?"

When you are pointing out what a guy is doing. We do this through mechanisms of exaggeration. We blow up an incident so he can really get a look at it. The Coordinators [a coordinator resembles

11. See Lewis Yablonsky, "The Anti-Criminal Society: Synanon," *Federal Probation,* XXVI (September, 1962), 50–57; and Lewis Yablonsky, *The Violent Gang* (New York: Macmillan, 1962), 252–263.

an officer of the day] and the Board members and sometimes an old timer may sit in on it. We do this when we see a person's attitude becoming negative in some area.

For a *real* haircut, I'll give you myself. I was in a tender trap. My girl split. She called me on the job three days in a row. I made a date with her. We kept the date and I stayed out all night with her. Now, she was loaded [using drugs]. I neglected—or I refused —to call the house. By doing this I ranked everybody. You know doing something like that was no good. They were all concerned. They sent three or four autos looking for me because I didn't come back from work. You see, I was in Stage II.

X found me and he made me feel real lousy, because I knew he worked and was concerned. Here he was out looking for me and he had to get up in the morning.

Well, I called the house the next morning and came back. I got called in for a haircut.

I sat down with three Board members in the office. They stopped everything to give the haircut. That impressed me. Both Y and Z, they pointed out my absurd and ridiculous behavior by saying things like this—though I did not get loaded, I associated with a broad I was emotionally involved with who was using junk. I jeopardized my *own* existence by doing this. So they told me, "Well, you fool, you might as well have shot dope by associating with a using addict." I was given an ultimatum. If I called her again or got in touch with her I would be thrown out.

("Why?")

Because continued correspondence with a using dope fiend is a crime against *me*—it hurts *me*. It was also pointed out how rank I was to people who are concerned with me. I didn't seem to care about people who were trying to help me. I'm inconsiderate to folks who've wiped my nose, fed me, clothed me. I'm like a child, I guess. I bite the hand that feeds me.

To top that off, I had to call a general meeting and I told everybody in the building what a jerk I was and I was sorry for acting like a little punk. I just sort of tore myself down. Told everyone what a phony I had been. And then the ridiculing questions began. Everybody started in. Like, "Where do you get off doing that to us?" That kind of stuff. When I was getting the treatment they asked me what I'd do—whether I would continue the relationship, whether I'd cut it off, or if I really wanted to stay at Synanon and do something about myself and my problem. But I made the decision before I even went in that I'd stay and cut the broad loose. I had enough time under my belt to know enough to make that decision before I even came back to the house. . . .

Group cohesion. The daily program at Synanon is consistent with Cressey's third principle, and appears to be an unwitting attempt to implement that principle:

> The more cohesive the group, the greater the member's readiness to influence others and the more relevant the problem of conformity to group norms. The criminals who are to be reformed and the persons expected to effect the change must, then, have a strong sense of belonging to one group: between them there must be a genuine "we" feeling. The reformers, consequently, should not be identifiable as correctional workers, probation or parole officers, or social workers.

Cohesion is maximized by a "family" analogy and by the fact that all but some "third-stage" members live and work together. The daily program has been deliberately designed to throw members into continuous mutual activity. In addition to the free, unrestricted interaction in small groups called "synanons," the members meet as a group at least twice each day. After breakfast, someone is called upon to read the "Synanon Philosophy," which is a kind of declaration of principles, the day's work schedule is discussed, bits of gossip are publicly shared, the group or individual members are spontaneously praised or scolded by older members. Following a morning of work activities, members meet in the dining room after lunch to discuss some concept or quotation that has been written on a blackboard. Stress is on participation and expression; quotations are selected by Board members to provoke controversy and examination of the meaning, or lack of meaning, of words. Discussion sometimes continues informally during the afternoon work period and in "synanons," which are held after dinner (see below). In addition, lectures and classes, conducted by any member or outside speaker who will take on the responsibility, are held several times a week for all members who feel a need for them. Topics have included "semantics," "group dynamics," "meaning of truth," and "Oedipus complex."

There are weekend recreational activities, and holidays, wedding anniversaries, and birthdays are celebrated. Each member is urged: "Be yourself," "Speak the truth," "Be honest," and this kind of action in an atmosphere that is informal and open quickly gives participants a strong sense of "belonging." Since many of the members have been homeless drifters, it is not surprising to hear frequent repetition of some comment to the effect that, "This is the first home I ever had."

Also of direct relevance to the third principle is the *voluntary* character of Synanon. Any member can walk out at any time; at night the doors are locked against persons who might want to enter, but not against persons who might want to leave. Many do leave.

Holding addicts in the house once they have been allowed to enter is a strong appeal to ideas such as, "We have all been in the shape you are now in," or "Mike was on heroin for twenty years and *he's* off." It is significant, in this connection, that addicts who "kick" (go through withdrawal distress) at Synanon universally report that the sickness is not as severe as it is in involuntary organizations, such as jails and mental hospitals. One important variable here, we believe, is the practice of not giving "kicking dope fiends" special quarters. A newcomer kicks on a davenport in the center of the large living room, not in a special isolation room or quarantine room. Life goes on around him. Although a member will be assigned to watch him, he soon learns that his sickness is not important to men and women who have themselves kicked the habit. In the living room, one or two couples might be dancing, five or six people may be arguing, a man may be practicing the guitar, and a girl may be ironing. The kicking addict learns his lesson: These others have made it. This subtle device is supplemented by explicit comments from various members as they walk by or as they drop in to chat with him. We have heard the following comments, and many similar ones, made to new addicts lying sick from withdrawal. It should be noted that none of the comments could reasonably have been made by a rehabilitation official or a professional therapist.

"It's OK boy. We've all been through it before."
"For once you're with people like us. You've got everything to gain here and nothing to lose."

"You think you're tough. Listen, we've got guys in here who could run circles around you, so quit your bull——."

"You're one of us now, so keep your eyes open, your mouth shut and try to listen for a while. Maybe you'll learn a few things."

"Hang tough, baby. We won't let you die."

Status ascription. Cressey's fourth principle is:

> Both reformers and those to be reformed must achieve status within the group by exhibition of "pro-reform" or anti-criminal values and behavior patterns. As a novitiate . . . he is a therapeutic parasite and not actually a member until he accepts the group's own system for assigning status.

This is the crucial point in Cressey's formula, and it is on this point that Synanon seems most effective. The house has an explicit program for distributing status symbols to members in return for staying off the drug and, later, for actually displaying anti-drug attitudes. The resident, no longer restricted to the status of "inmate" or "patient" as in a prison or hospital, can achieve any staff position in the status hierarchy.

The Synanon experience is organized into a career of roles that represent stages of graded competence, at whose end are roles that might later be used in the broader community. Figure 1 shows the status system in terms of occupational roles, each box signifying a stratum. Such cliques as exist at Synanon tend to be among persons of the same stratum. Significantly, obtaining jobs of increased responsibility and status is almost completely dependent upon one's attitude toward crime and the use of drugs. To obtain a job such as Senior Coordinator, for example, the member must have demonstrated that he can remain free of drugs, crime, and alcohol for at least three to six months. Equally important, he must show that he can function without drugs in situations where he might have used drugs before he came to Synanon. Since he is believed to have avoided positions of responsibility by taking drugs, he must gradually take on positions of responsibility without the use of drugs. Thus, he cannot go up the status ladder unless his "attitudes" are right, no matter what degree of skill he might have as a workman. Evaluation is rather casual, but it is evaluation nevertheless—he will not be given

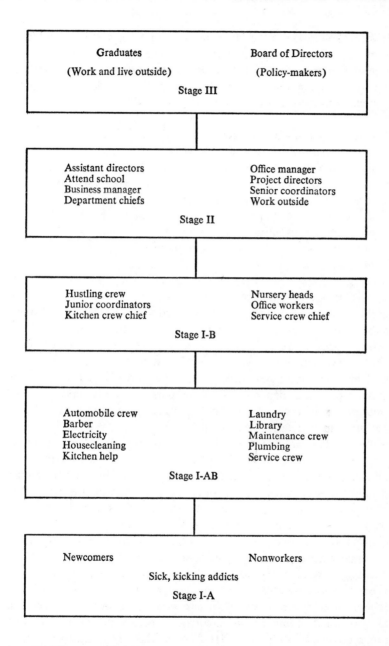

FIGURE 1. Division of labor and stratification system, Synanon, June, 1962.

a decent job in the organization unless he relinquishes the role of the "con artist" and answers questions honestly, expresses emotions freely, cooperates in group activities, and demonstrates leadership. In a letter to a public official in May, 1960, the founder explained the system as follows:

> Continued residence [at Synanon], which we feel to be necessary to work out the problem of interpersonal relationships which underlie the addiction symptom is based on adherence by the individual to standards of behavior, thinking, and feeling acceptable to our culture. There is much work to be done here, as we have no paid help, and each person must assume his share of the burden. Increased levels of responsibility are sought and the experience of self-satisfaction comes with seeking and assuming these higher levels and seems to be an extremely important part of emotional growth.[12]

An analogy with a family and the development of a child also is used. Officially, every member is expected to go through three "stages of growth," indicated by Roman numerals in Figure 1. Stage I has two phases, "infancy" and "adolescence." In the "infancy" phase (I-A) the member behaves like an infant and is treated as one; as he kicks the habit "cold turkey" (without the aid of drugs) in the living room, he is dependent on the others, and he is supervised and watched at all times. When he is physically and mentally able, he performs menial tasks such as dishwashing and sweeping in a kind of "preadolescent" stage (I-AB) and then takes on more responsible positions (I-B). In this "adolescence" phase he takes on responsibility for maintenance work, participates actively in group meetings, demonstrates a concern for "emotional growth," mingles with newcomers and visitors, and accepts responsibilities for dealing with them. In work activities, for example, he might drive the group's delivery truck alone, watch over a sick addict, supervise the dishwashing or cleanup crews, or meet strangers at the door.

Stage II is called the "young adult stage." Here, the member is in a position to choose between making Synanon a "career," attending school, or going to work at least part time. If he works for Synanon, his position is complex and involves enforcing policy over a wide range of members. In Stage III, "adult," he moves up to a policy-

12. See Volkman, *op cit.,* 90–96.

making position in the Board of Directors or moves out of Synanon but returns with his friends and family for occasional visits. He can apparently resist the urge to resort to drugs in times of crisis without the direct help of Synanon members. One man described this stage by saying, "They go out, get jobs, lose jobs, get married, get divorced, get married again, just like everyone else." However, the group does maintain a degree of control. Graduates are never supposed to cut off their ties with their Synanon "family," and they are expected to return frequently to display themselves as "a dope fiend made good."

From Table 5 it is apparent that seniority in the form of length of residence (equivalent to the number of "clean" days) is an important determinant of status. As time of residence increases, responsibilities to the group, in the forms of work and leadership, tend to increase, In June, 1962, twenty-seven of the 105 members of Synanon were in Stage III. It should be noted that while stage is associated with length of residence, advancement through the stages is not automatic. The longer one lives at Synanon, the "cleaner" he is, the more diffuse the roles he performs, and the higher his status.

It is also important to note that high status does not depend entirely upon one's conduct within the house. Before he graduates to Stage III a member must in some way be accorded an increase in status by the legitimate outside community. This is further insurance that status will be conferred for activities that are anti-drug in character. In early 1960, the members began to take an active part in legitimate community activities, mostly in the form of lectures and discussion groups. Since Synanon's inception, more than 350 service groups,

Table 5. Length of Residence and "Stage"
of Members, June, 1962

Length of Residence (In Months)	Stages			No.	Percent
	I	II	III		
1– 3	20	0	0	20	19
4– 6	15	0	0	15	14
7– 9	7	3	0	10	9
10–12	2	0	0	2	2
13–15	3	4	0	7	7
16–18	3	0	2	5	5
19–21	4	1	0	5	5
22–24	0	4	1	5	5
25 and over	0	12	24	36	34
Total	54	24	27	105	100

church groups, political groups, school and college classes, etc., have been addressed by speakers from Synanon. Such speeches and discussions gain community support for the organization, but they further function to give members a feeling of being important enough to be honored by an invitation to speak before community groups. Similarly, members are proud of those indivduals who have "made good" in the outside community by becoming board members of the P.T.A., Sunday-school teachers, college students, and members of civic and service organizations. Over thirty-five Synanon members are now working full or part time in the community, holding a wide range of unskilled (janitor, parking attendant), skilled (truck driver, carpenter, electrician), white-collar (secretary, photographer), and executive (purchasing agent) posts.

Further, the legitimate status of the *group* has increasingly risen during the last two years. Since the summer of 1960, an average of 100–150 guests have attended open-house meetings, and the guests have included distinguished persons from all walks of legitimate life. Well-known psychiatrists, correctional workers, businessmen, newspapermen, and politicians have publicly praised the work of the group. There have been requests for Synanon houses and for Synanon groups from several communities, and Synanon projects are now being conducted at Terminal Island Federal Prison and the Nevada State Prison. Recently, the group has been featured in films, on television and radio shows, and in national magazines. At least two books and a movie are being written about it. Over five hundred citizens have formed an organization called "Sponsors of Synanon." Even strong attacks from some members of the local community and complicated legal battles about zoning ordinances have served principally to unite the group and maximize the *esprit de corps*.

The "synanon." Synanon got its name from an addict who was trying to say "seminar." The term "Synanon" is used to refer to the entire organization, but when it is spelled with a lower-case *s* it refers only to the meetings occurring in the evenings among small groups of six to ten members. Each evening, all members are assigned to such groups, and membership in the groups is rotated so that one does not regularly interact with the same six or ten persons. The announced aim of these meetings is to "trigger feelings" and to allow what some members refer to as "a catharsis." The sessions are not "group therapy" in the usual sense, for no trained therapist is present.

Moreover, the emphasis is on enforcing anti-criminal and anti-drug norms, as well as upon emotional adjustment.[13] These sessions, like the entire program, constitute a system for implementing Cressey's fifth principle, although they were not designed to do so.

> The most effective mechanisms for exerting group pressure on members will be found in groups so organized that criminals are induced to join with noncriminals for the purpose of changing other criminals. A group in which criminal A joins with some noncriminals to change criminal B is probably most effective in changing criminal A, not B; in order to change criminal B, criminal A must necessarily share the values of the anti-criminal members.

In the house, the behavior of all members is visible to all others. What a member is seen to do at the breakfast table, for example, might well be scrutinized and discussed at his synanon that evening. The synanon sessions differ from everyday honesty by virtue of the fact that in these discussions one is expected to *insist on* the truth as well as to tell the truth. Any weapon, such as ridicule, cross-examination, or hostile attack, is both permissible and expected. The sessions seem to provide an atmosphere of truth-seeking that is reflected in the rest of the social life within the household so that a simple question like, "How are you?" is likely to be answered by a five-minute discourse in which the respondent searches for the truth. The following discussion is from a tape recording of a synanon session held in June, 1961. It should be noted that an "innocent" question about appearance, asked by an older member who has become a noncriminal and a non-addict, led to an opportunity to emphasize the importance of loyalty to the anti-drug, anti-crime group.

> "What are you doing about losing weight?"
> "Why? Is that your business?"
> "I asked you a question."
> "I don't intend to answer it. It's not your business."
> "Why do you want to lose weight?"
> "I don't intend to answer it."

13. See Cressey, "Contradictory Theories in Correctional Group Therapy Programs," *op. cit.*

"Why?"

"Because it's an irrelevant and meaningless question. You know I had a baby only three weeks ago, and you've been attacking me about my weight. It's none of your business."

"Why did you call your doctor?"

"Why? Because I'm on a diet."

"What did he prescribe for you?"

"I don't know. I didn't ask him."

"What did you ask for?"

"I didn't. I don't know what he gave me."

"Come on now. What kind of pills are they?"

"I don't know. I'm not a chemist. Look, the doctor knows I'm an addict. He knows I live at Synanon. He knows a whole lot about me."

"Yeah, well, I heard you also talking to him on the phone, and you sounded just like any other addict trying to cop a doctor out of pills."

"You're a goddamned liar!"

"Yeah, well X was sitting right there. Look, does the doctor know and does the Board know?"

"I spoke to Y [Board member]. It's all been verified."

"What did Y say?"

"I was talking to . . ."

"What did Y say?"

"Well, will you wait just a minute?"

"What did Y say?"

"Well, let her talk."

"I don't want to hear no stories."

"I'm not telling stories."

"What did Y say?"

"That it was harmless. The doctor said he'd give me nothing that would affect me. There's nothing in it. He knows it all. I told Y."

"Oh, you're all like a pack of wolves. You don't need to yell and scream at her."

"Look, I heard her on the phone and the way she talked she was trying to manipulate the doctor."

"Do you resent the fact that she's still acting like a dope fiend and she still sounds like she's conning the doctor out of something? She's a dope fiend. Maybe she can't talk to a doctor any differently."

"Look, I called the doctor today. He said I should call him if I need him. He gave me vitamins and lots of other things."

"Now wait a minute. You called to find out if you could get some more pills.

"Besides, it's the attitude they heard over the phone. That's the main thing."

"Yeah, well they probably projected it onto me."

"Then how come you don't like anyone listening to your phone calls?"

"Are you feeling guilty?"

"Who said?"

"Me. That's who. You even got sore when you found out X and me heard you on the phone, didn't you? You didn't like that at all, did you?"

"Is that so?"

(*Silence.*)

"I don't think her old man wants her back."

"Well, who would? An old fat slob like that."

"Sure, that's probably why she's thinking of leaving all the time and ordering pills."

"Sure."

(*Silence.*)

"My appearance is none of your business."

"Everything here is our business."

"Look, when a woman has a baby you can't understand she can't go back to normal weight in a day."

"Now *you* look. We're really not interested in your weight problem now. Not really. We just want to know why you've got to have pills to solve the problem. We're going to talk about that if we want to. That's what we're here for."

"Look, something's bugging you. We all know that. I even noticed it in your attitude toward me."

"Yeah, I don't care about those pills. I want to know how you're feeling. What's behind all this? Something's wrong. What is it?"

(*Silence.*)

"Have you asked your old man if you could come home yet?"

(*Softly.*) "Yes."

"What did he say?"

(*Softly.*) "He asked me how I felt. Wanted to know why I felt I was ready to come home. . . ."

(*Silence.*)

(*Softly.*) "I did it out of anger. I wasn't very happy. (*Pause.*) A day before I tried [telephoning him] and he wasn't there. *(Pause.)* Just this funny feeling about my husband being there and me here. My other kid's there and this one's here. (*Pause.*) A mixed-up family."

"Why do you want to stay then? Do you want to be here?"

"No. I don't want to be here. That's exactly why I'm staying. I need to stay till I'm ready."

"Look, you've got to cut them loose for a while. You may not be ready for the rest of your life. You may not ever be able to be with those people."

(*Tears.*)

"I know. . . ."

After the synanon sessions, the house is always noisy and lively. We have seen members sulk, cry, shout, and threaten to leave the group as a result of conversation in the synanon. The following comments, every one of which represents the expression of a pro-reform attitude by the speaker, were heard after one session. It is our hypothesis that such expressions are the important ones, for they indicate that the speaker has become a reformer and, thus, is reinforcing his own pro-reform attitudes every time he tries to comfort or reform another.

"Were they hard on you?"

"I really let him have it tonight."

"I couldn't get to her. She's so damned blocked she couldn't even hear what I was trying to tell her."

"Hang tough, man; it gets easier."

"One of these days he'll drop those defenses of his and start getting honest."

"Don't leave. We all love you and want you to get well."

At Synanon, disassociating with former friends, avoiding street talk, and becoming disloyal to criminals are emphasized at the same time that loyalty to noncriminals, telling the truth to authority figures, and legitimate work are stressed. We have no direct evidence that hair-cuts, synanons, and both formal and spontaneous denunciations of street talk and the code of the streets have important rehabilitative effects on the actor, as well as (or, perhaps even "rather than") on the victim. It seems rather apparent, however, that an individual's own behavior must be dramatically influenced when he acts in the role of a moral policeman and "takes apart" another member. It is significant that older members of Synanon like to point out that the "real Synanon" began on "the night of the big cop out" (confession). In its earliest days, Synanon had neither the group cohesiveness nor the degree of control it now has. Some participants remained as addicts while proclaiming their loyalty to the principle of anti-addiction, and other participants knew of this condition. One evening in a general meeting a man spontaneously stood up and confessed ("copped out") that he had sneaked out for a shot. One by one, with no prompting, the others present rose to confess either their own violations or their knowledge of the violations of their friends. From that moment, the Board of Directors believe, the organization became a truly anti-drug group; there has been no problem of drug use since.

The Results

Of the fifty-two residents described earlier, four are "graduates" of Synanon, are living in the community, and are not using alcohol or drugs. Twenty-three (44.2 percent) are still in residence and are not using alcohol or drugs. Two of these are on the Board of Directors and eleven are working part or full time. The remaining twenty-five left Synanon against the advice of the Board and the older members.

Information regarding the longest period of voluntary abstinence from drugs after the onset of addiction but prior to entering Synanon was obtained on forty-eight of the fifty-two persons. Eleven reported that they were "never" clean, six said they were continuously clean for less than one week, ten were continuously clean for less than one month. Thirty-nine (81 percent) said they had been continuously clean for less than six months, and only two had been clean for as long as a one-year period. Twenty-seven (52 percent) of the fifty-two residents have now abstained for at least six months; twelve of these have been clean for at least two years and two have been off drugs continually for over three years.

Between May, 1958 (when Synanon started), and May, 1961, 263 persons were admitted or readmitted to Synanon. Of these, 190 (72 percent) left Synanon against the advice of the Board of Directors and older members. Significantly, 59 percent of all dropouts occurred within the first month of residence, 90 percent within the first three months. Synanon is not adverse to giving a person a second chance, or even a third or fourth chance: of the 190 persons dropping out, eighty-three (44 percent) were persons who had been readmitted. The dropout behavior of persons who were readmitted was, in general, similar to first admissions; 64 percent of their dropouts occurred within the first month, 93 percent within the first three months after readmission.

Of all the Synanon enrollees up to August, 1962, 108 out of 372 (29 percent) are known to be off drugs. More significantly, of the 215 persons who have remained at Synanon for at least one month, 103 (48 percent) are still off drugs; of the 143 who have remained for at least three months, 95 (66 percent) are still non-users; of the 87 who have remained at least seven months, 75 (86 percent) are non-users. These statistics seem to us to be most relevant, for they indicate that once an addict actually becomes a member of the anti-drug community (as indicated by three-to-six months of participation), the probability that he will leave and revert to the use of drugs is low.

Conclusions

Synanon's leaders do not claim to "cure" drug addicts. They are prone to measure success by pointing to the fact that the organization now includes the membership of forty-five persons who were heroin addicts for at least ten years. Two of these were addicted for more than thirty years and spent those thirty years going in and out of prisons, jails, the United States Public Service Hospital, and similar institutions. The leaders have rather inadvertently used a theory of rehabilitation that implies that it is as ridiculous to try to "cure" a man of drug addiction as it is to try to "cure" him of sexual intercourse. A man can be helped to stay away from drugs, however, and this seems to be the contribution Synanon is making. In this regard, its "success" rate is higher than that of those institutions officially designated by society as places for the confinement and "reform" of drug addicts. Such a comparison is not fair, however, both because it is not known whether the subjects in Synanon are comparable to those confined in institutions, and because many official institutions do not concentrate on trying to keep addicts off drugs, being content to withdraw the drug, build up the addicts physically, strengthen vocational skills, and eliminate gaps in educational backgrounds.[14]

We cannot be certain that it is the group relationships at Synanon, rather than something else, that is keeping addicts away from crime and drugs. However, both the times at which dropouts occur and the increasing anti-drug attitudes displayed with increasing length of residence tend to substantiate Sutherland's theory of differential association and Cressey's notion that modifying social relationships is an effective supplement to the clinical handling of convicted criminals. Drug addiction is, in fact, a severe test of Sutherland's sociological theory and Cressey's sociological principles, for addicts have the double problem of criminality and the drug habit. The statistics on dropouts suggest that the group relations method of rehabilitation does not begin to have its effects until newcomers are truly integrated into the anti-drug, anti-crime group that is Synanon.

14. Cf. Harrison M. Trice, "Alcholism: Group Factors in Etiology and Therapy," *Human Organization,* XV (Summer, 1956), 33–40. See also Donald R. Cressey, "The Nature and Effectiveness of Correctional Techniques," *Law and Contemporary Problems,* XXIII (Fall, 1958), 754–771.

15
The Inmate Group in Custodial and Treatment Settings
David Street

Prisons are more than ordinary organizations because of the
way they totally encompass inmates' lives. Still the effects
of prison life on inmates' character occur largely through the
familiar mechanism of interaction with other inmates
and with prison staff. Thus the general principles of
socialization should serve as a foundation for evaluating
prisons as correctional institutions and for explaining why
sometimes prisons may do more harm than good. This

chapter shows some of the ways that orientations of a prison's custodial staff get translated into specific attitudes among the inmates.

Goals and Institutions

Goals may usefully be regarded as the conception of the organization's tasks held by the members whose positions make their definitions of events authoritative. Their conception of task is expressed in their views of the organization's desired end product, the "materials" it must work with, the ideal and practical requirements of the task, and the organization's distinctive competencies for it. The goals imply and set limits upon the organizational technologies seen as appropriate. Thus, goals define as required, or preferred, alternative sets of social relations between staff and inmates.

Analysis of the goals of correctional institutions provides a basis for classifying these organizations along a rough custodial-treatment continuum. This classification reflects the relative emphasis on containing the inmates as against rehabilitating them. More analytically, the continuum incorporates two dimensions of the staff conception of the organization's task: the staff members' view of the actual rehabilitational potential of the inmates, and their concept of the "materials" they have to work with and the implicit "theory of human nature" they apply to these materials.[1] At the custodial extreme,

Abridged from David Street, "The Inmate Group in Custodial and Treatment Settings," in *American Sociological Review,* 30 (1965), 40–55. Reprinted by permission of the American Sociological Association and the author. Footnotes have been renumbered.

An earlier version of this paper was read at the meetings of the Midwest Sociological Society, Milwaukee, Wis., April, 1963. This research was carried out in part under a pre-doctoral fellowship from the National Institute of Mental Health, Public Health Service, and was done in close association with a comprehensive study of juvenile correctional institutions directed by Robert D. Vinter and Morris Janowitz and supported by NIMH Grant M-2104. Not only the data from this project but also the ideas and criticisms of the participants were of great help.

1.   On the theory of human nature, see Erving Goffman, "On the Characteristics of Total Institutions: Staff-Inmate Relations," in Donald Cressey, ed., *The Prison: Studies in Institutional Organization and Change* (New York: Holt, Rinehart, 1961), 78.

major emphasis is placed on the need to protect the community by containing the inmates within the institution. The inmates are seen as simple, similar, and relatively unchangeable creatures who require simple, routine, conventional handling. To succeed here, the inmate must conform. At the treatment extreme, community and containment are comparatively unimportant, and stress is put on changing the inmate's attitudes and values by increasing his insight or otherwise altering his psychological condition. The inmate's social identity is viewed as problematic, and the inmates are seen as relatively complex beings who need complex, individualized, flexible handling—an attitude that sometimes requires such departures from conventional morality as tolerance of "acting out." To succeed here, the inmate must indicate intra-psychic change. These variations in organizational goals are accompanied by variations in the distribution of power in the organization: as institutions become more treatment-oriented, power to define events flows into the hands of a highly educated and professionalized "clinic staff."

These characterizations of the custodial and treatment types of institution are supported by a wide variety of data from the institutions we studied. The institutions were selected nonrandomly to insure variation in goals and other dimensions. Each was studied intensively through observation, interviewing, analysis of documents and file data, and administration of questionnaires to virtually all staff members and inmates.[2] Two of the institutions stressed custody; the other two, treatment. Ranked from more custodial to more treatment-oriented and identified by mnemonic labels they were:

Dick (Discipline)—a large (200–250 inmates) public institution which had no treatment program, whose staff felt no lack because of this, and which concentrated on custody, hard work, and discipline.

Mixter (Mixed Goals)—a very large (375–420 inmates) public institution with poorly integrated "mixed goals" of custody and treat-

2. Here I shall report findings principally on the four "closed" institutions studied intensively in the juvenile corrections project. Near the end of this paper I shall refer to findings on three additional institutions, not as directly comparable for the problems discussed here. For details of questionnaire administration and other research techniques, see David Street, "Inmate Social Organization: A Comparative Study of Juvenile Correctional Institutions," unpublished Ph.D. dissertation, University of Michigan, 1962, 198–202.

ment. Some treatment was attempted, but this was segregated from the rest of the activities, and for most boys the environment was characterized by surveillance, frequent use of negative sanctions, and other corollaries of an emphasis on custody.

Milton (Milieu Therapy)—a fairly large (160–190 inmates) public institution using not only individual therapy but a range of other treatment techniques. This institution resembled Mixter in its bifurcation between treatment and containment staffs and activities, but by and large the clinicians were in control, used treatment criteria, and influenced the nonprofessional staff to allow the inmates considerable freedom.

Inland (Individual Therapy)—a small (60–75 inmates) private "residential treatment center" in which the clinicians were virtually in complete control, allowing much freedom to the inmates while stressing the use of psychotherapeutic techniques in an attempt to bring about major personality change.

Limitations of space preclude full analysis and documentation of these differences between organizations, which in any case are presented elsewhere,[3] but some indication of their nature may be conveyed by [mention of] staff-inmate ratios and contacts . . . and by data from the staff questionnaire. . . . Higher ratios of staff, especially social service staff, to inmates, and higher inmate-social service contacts characterize the treatment institutions. The questionnaire results show that in the more treatment-oriented institutions staff members are more likely (1) to see the organization's goal as producing change in attitudes, values, and insights; (2) to value treatment programs more highly than custodial considerations; (3) to believe that inmates can be rehabilitated; and (4) to believe that adults can have trusting, close, and understanding relations with inmates, the development of such relationships being part of the staff's task. In contrast, staff members in the more custodial organizations are more likely (5) to stress order, discipline, and the use of powerful negative sanctions; (6) to insist on inmate conformity to institutional rules, including immediate response to staff members' demands; (7) to believe in universalistic application of rules; and (8) to have negative attitudes

---

3. See especially Juvenile Correctional Institutions Project, *Research Report* (Ann Arbor: University of Michigan, 1961).

toward informal relations among the inmates, believing that the inmates should keep to themselves. Such attitudinal differences between institutions hold up among cottage parents and in other groups when the respondent's staff position and his education are controlled,[4] and, further, the implied differences in behavior toward the inmates are confirmed by observations made in the institutions of the use of physical punishment, for example. To see how these different institutional environments affect the inmates, let us consider the inmate social system.

The Inmate Group

Informal group structure grows out of primary relations among inmates in all institutions, and it can be assumed to have a significant role in socializing and relating the inmate to the institution, in defining informal norms of inmate behavior and approved sets of values and beliefs, and in defining and allocating valued objects (e.g., contraband) among the inmates. Given the inmate group as a system potentially oriented toward ameliorating its members' deprivation, two major environmental factors could condition its response: (1) variations in the balance of gratifications and deprivations, and (2) variations in the conditions under which the group must attempt to solve its problem—that is, in the patterns of control and authority that the staff exercise over inmate action and behavior.

1. Variations in the balance of gratifications and deprivations. By limiting the available supply of rewards and thus creating a high ratio of deprivation to gratification the institution sets the stage for the development of a system for obtaining and distributing scarce values, both licit (e.g., choice job assignments) and illicit (contraband). Development of such a system presupposes that some inmates have access to values in short supply, and that inmates are sufficiently interdependent to set up a system of allocation and stabilize it in role expectations. Continuing access to the valued objects, and various forms of mutual aid, require a division of labor, which in turn is likely to produce a leadership structure reflecting differential power with regard to values within the system. Norms of reciprocity are likely to develop, to limit the advantages of those

4. *Ibid.*, Chapters 7 and 9.

powerful enough to monopolize scarce values, but the latter nevertheless form a leadership cadre in which power is relatively highly centralized. To the extent that the system is deeply involved in the secretive and illicit transactions of contraband allocation, these leaders may have, at least covertly, very negative attitudes toward the staff and institution. Such leadership cadres might influence the group and make it more hostile to the official system than it otherwise would be.

2. Variations in staff patterns of control and authority. Rigid and categorical practices of control and authority are likely to facilitate the inmates' recognition of a common fate and their potentialities for collective problem solving. Differences in authority, general status, age, and often social class, between staff and inmates, generally lead inmates to see each other as members of the same category in all institutions, but the authority structure and its impact vary among institutions. Frequent scheduling of mass activities in the company of other inmates, group punishment before groups of inmates enhance the probability that inmates identify strongly with one another against staff. When, in addition, staff maintain domineering authority relationships and considerable social distance, inmates further perceive themselves as members of a group opposed to staff, and divergent interests between these groups are more fully recognized.

Staff patterns of control and authority also limit inmate association and group elaboration. Thus at the same time that rigorous practice of control and authority stimulate recognition of a common problem and the use of group solutions, they also make such solutions more difficult to achieve. Although only extreme techniques, such as keeping the inmates locked in separate rooms, effectively prevent the emergence of social relations among the inmates,[5] rigorous control could severely limit and structure opportunities for interaction and group formation—particularly the formation of groups covering the entire institution. In this situation, group activities must be conducted on a covert level, involving norms of secrecy and mutual defense against the staff.

5. Even this technique is not necessarily effective. See Richard McCleery's account of an adult maximum security unit, "Authoritarianism and the Belief Systems of Incorrigibles," in Donald Cressey, ed., *The Prison: Studies in Institutional Organization and Change, op. cit.,* 260–306.

Hypotheses

These two dimensions, gratification-deprivation and patterns of control and authority, link the institutional goals with the responses of the inmate group; both vary between the custodial and treatment settings. On the first of these dimensions, treatment institutions place much less emphasis on degradation ceremonies, the use of powerful sanctions, and denial of impulse gratification, and much greater emphasis on providing incentives, objectives, and experiences that the inmates consider desirable. On patterns of control and authority, treatment institutions place much less stress on surveillance, control over inmate association, restrictions of freedom, rigid conformity to rules, and domination and high social distance in authority relations. The simultaneous effects of these dimensions on informal groups in each type of setting should be as follows:

The Custodial Setting. Because of the high level of deprivation, the group is organized to allocate legitimate and illicit values and provide mutual aid. These functions reflect and generate relatively negative and "prisonized" orientations toward the situation and staff. Although staff control and authority practices increase the need for inmate group solutions, they also handicap interaction and group formation, so that integration and solidarity are relatively underdeveloped. The leaders, highly involved in illicit and secret activities, tend to have a negative orientation toward the institution.

The Treatment Setting. The inmate group is organized more voluntaristically, around friendship patterns. Since the level of deprivation is lower, mutual aid is less necessary, and any ameliorative system tends to lose its market. The group is involved in the allocation of values among its members, but these are positive rewards, more consonant with staff definitions of merit. Staff gives much freer rein to inmate association, so that primary group integration and norms of group solidarity are at a higher level than in the custodial setting. This cohesiveness does not necessarily imply opposition to staff, however, for the inmate group emphasizes more positive norms and perspectives and greater commitment to the institution and staff. Leaders' orientation is also more positive.

Finally, the more positive character of staff behavior toward inmates and the positive orientation of the inmate group generates more positive attitudes toward self among the inmates of treatment institutions than among those in custodial organizations.

Data are not available to test all features of the foregoing contrasts, but a reasonably satisfactory test can be made of the following specific hypotheses:

1. In the custodial institutions, the dominant tone of the inmate group will be that of opposition and negative, "prisonized" norms and perspectives with regard to institution, staff, and self; in the treatment institutions, positive, cooperative norms and perspectives will dominate.

2. Inmate groups in the custodial institutions will display somewhat lower levels of primary relations and weaker orientations of solidarity than will groups in the treatment institutions.

3. Relatively uncooperative and negative leaders will emerge in the inmate groups of the custodial institutions; relatively cooperative and positive leaders will emerge in the treatment institutions.

Findings

The hypotheses will be tested here by analyzing results of the inmate questionnaire. The inmates' responses, shown by institution in Table 1, convey the dominant tone of inmate group norms and perspectives.[6]

Findings on all but one of these items support the hypotheses.[7] Inmates in the treatment-oriented institutions more often expressed positive attitudes toward the institution and staff, non-prisonized views of adaption to the institution, and postive images of self-change. The

6. Indices were derived partly from the results of a factor analysis of inmate responses. For details of this analysis and of the construction of indices, see Street, *op. cit.*, 213–224.

7. I have used statistical tests of difference between groups of respondents heuristically, to help decide whether to deny predicted differences between the custodial and treatment types of organization. Although the nonrandom selection of institutions, the clustering of all respondents in four organizations, and the sampling of entire institutonal populations make use of the word "test" in its strict sense illegitimate, no more appropriate bases for decision-making are available. Note, too, that because the tests (as well as the measures of association presented below) combine the data for each of the pairs of institutions, to highlight the differences between the custodial and treatment types, the results may obscure differences within pairs. Important within-type variation will be discussed in the text.

Table 1. Inmate Perspectives, by Institution

Percentage of Inmates Who:	Custodial		Treatment		Statistical Significance[a]
	Dick	Mixter	Milton	Inland	
Score high positive on summary index of perspectives on the institution and staff.[b]	42 (209)	44 (364)	58 (155)	85 (65)	p < .01
Score high on cooperation with staff on summary index of "ratting."[c]	54 (209)	46 (364)	49 (155)	54 (65)	N.S.
Gave a "prisonized" response to question about the best way to get along.[d]	74 (202)	73 (348)	55 (151)	45 (60)	p < .01
Gave a "prisonized" response to question about ways to receive a discharge or parole.[e]	59 (187)	47 (352)	27 (140)	13 (65)	p < .01
Score positive on self-image index.[f]	38 (188)	42 (327)	51 (143)	79 (60)	p < .01

[a] Significance refers to the difference between the inmates of the two custodial institutions combined and those of the two treatment institutions.

[b] The specific items summarized by this index were (paraphrased): (1) Is this a place to help, send, or punish boys? (2) Rather be here or in some other institution? (3) Summary: Did you think this would be a good or bad place, and what do you think about it now? (4) Agree that the adults here don't really care what happens to us. (5) Agree that the adults are pretty fair. (6) Agree that adults here can help me. (7) How much has your stay here helped you?

[c] The specific items summarized in this index followed a presentation of hypothetical situations, and were (paraphrased): (1) Should a boy warn an adult that boys plan to rough up his friend? (2) Should he warn an adult that inmates plan to beat up a staff member? (3) Would you tell an adult which boys were stealing from the kitchen, when group punishment was being used? (4) Would you try to talk a boy out of running?

[d] The question was, "Regardless of what the adults here say, the best way to get along here is to . . ." ("stay out of the way of the adults but get away with what you can" and "don't break any rules and keep out of trouble" were classified as "prisonized" responses, and "show that you are really sorry for what you did" and "try to get an understanding of yourself," as "non-prisonized").

[e] The question was "*In your own words*, write what you think a boy has to do to get a parole or discharge from here" (responses of conformity, avoidance of misbehavior, "doing time," and overt compliance were coded as "prisonized").

[f] Those classified as "positive" on the index of self-image said that they had been helped by their stay a great deal or quite a bit and that the way they have been helped was by having "learned something about myself and why I get into trouble," rather than having "learned my lesson."

exception is that on the index of "ratting to staff" no difference between custodial and treatment institutions appeared.

Background Attributes and Length of Stay. Question immediately arises as to whether these differences in perspectives on the institution and staff, adaptation, and self might not reflect variations in inmates' predispositions rather than variations in the institutional setting. A careful analysis of the impact, by institution, of delinquency history, past institutional record, age, race, IQ, family situation, urban-rural background, and social class indicates a negative answer to this question.[8]

. . . The direction of the effect of each of the background variables on perspectives varies from institution to institution, and the custodial-treatment differences in perspectives hold up when background attributes are controlled. In nearly every instance, the inmates of both treatment institutions were more likely to have positive perspectives on staff and institution than the inmates of either custodial institution. The three exceptions to this predicted pattern were: (1) among those with fewer offenses, Mixter inmates (51 percent positive) did not differ from those in Milton (50 percent positive); (2) disproportionately few (29 percent) of the Milton inmates classified as returnees had positive perspectives; and (3) a disproportionately large number of positive responses came from Mixter inmates with white-collar backgrounds.

The first of these exceptions suggests that a portion of the relatively negative overall response at Mixter may be a result of its heavy recruitment of inmates with many offenses. But this would not explain why those with three or more offenses are so negative compared with similar inmates at Milton and Inland. The second exception is probably a result of the fact that the Milton returnees, as indicated in the note to the table, are not directly comparable with the others, apparently constituting an especially "hard core." The last exception may simply reflect the small number of "white-collar" inmates at both Mixter and Milton. Altogether, these exceptions do not challenge the conclusion that these background attributes cannot explain the observed differences between types of institution.

Similarly, inter-institutional variations were not simply a reflection of the fact that the treatment institutions usually keep their inmates

8. Street, *op. cit.*, 75–83.

longer. Data on this point may also be used to assess the degree to which the prisonization model or one of its variants "fits" these institutions.[9] Figure 1, graphing positive perspectives on the institution and staff against length of stay, indicates that differences between types of institution cannot be accounted for by differences in average length of stay. Inmates of the treatment institutions are more likely to express positive perspectives at almost every point in time. Within the custodial institutions, the overall trend is for the proportion negative to increase with length of stay. Although this tendency toward increasing negativism in the custodial institutions is akin to what one would predict under the prisonization model, attitude changes in the treatment institutions are in the opposite, positive direction. In these institutions, the proportion expressing positive perspectives increases rapidly over time in the early months and, after a downturn, increases further in the later months.[10]

Effects of Primary Group Integration on Perspectives. Data on integration into the inmate group provide a more adequate test of the hypothesis about the dominant tone of the inmate group if one assumes that when those who are better integrated express more positive perspectives, it is because their group exerts a positive influence, and when the better-integrated are more negative, it is because their group exerts a negative influence. Operationally, the better-integrated inmates are those who said they had two or more friends in the institution.[11]

9. Donald Clemmer, *The Prison Community* (New York: Holt, Rinehart, 1958); Stanton Wheeler, "Socialization in Correctional Communities," *American Sociological Review,* 26 (October, 1961); and Peter C. Garabedian, "Social Role and Processes of Socialization in the Prison Community," *Social Problems,* 11 (Fall, 1963).

10. Institutional records show that average stay before release is: Dick, 10 to 11 months; Mixter, 7.5 months; Milton, 15 months; and Inland, 11.5 months, with an average of 18 months for those who complete the institution's program.

11. The question was: "How about *close* friends? Some boys have close friendships with other boys here and some boys don't. How many of the other boys here are close friends of yours?" We assumed that a respondent who reported one or no friends was not really integrated into the group, having at best only a single "buddy." While this definition of integration is subject to questions regarding the probable reporting error and the relation of this "primary relations" interpretation to other meanings of the concept, it provides an empirically profitable starting point for analyzing the consequences of integration.

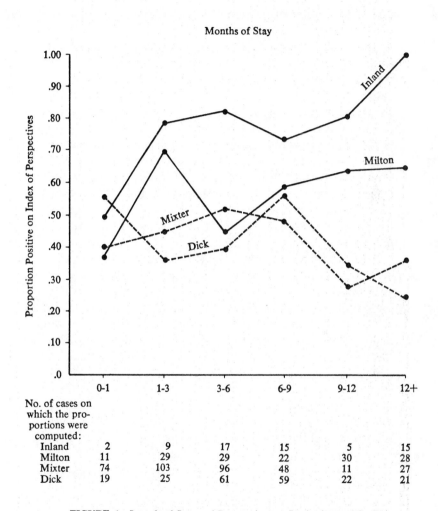

FIGURE 1. Length of Stay and Perspectives on Institution and Staff.

The findings clearly indicate that positive attitudes are more closely associated with primary group integration in the treatment institutions than in the custodial institutions. . . . Results on the four indices significantly related to integration consistently display the predicted pattern. Thus integration into the inmate group was more strongly associated with positive perspectives on the institution and staff in the treatment setting than in the custodial environment. Further, despite the fact that custodial and treatment settings did not differ with respect to scores on the "ratting" index. . . integration and co-operation with staff are postively associated in the treatment but not in the custodial setting. (This finding principally reflects the strong positive association in Milton; in Inland and in both custodial institutions, it was relatively weak.) Finally, in the treatment institutions integration was inversely associated with the prisonized view of adaption and positively related to a positive self-image, while in the custodial institutions there was little or no association with these indices.

An analysis of the joint impact of integration and length of stay on these attitudinal measures indicated that variations in length of stay did not account for these variations in the relation between integration and attitudes.

Levels of Inmate Primary Relations and Solidarity. A variety of findings consistently support the second hypothesis, that inmates in the treatment setting have more highly developed primary relations and stronger orientations of solidarity. . . . Inmates of the treatment institutions more frequently reported "hanging around" with other inmates, having several friends, and (reflecting the difference between Mixter and Milton) wanting to see other inmates again after release. In addition, the treatment inmates more frequently indicated a willingness to talk with other boys about a personal problem and more often rejected the view that you "have to be pretty careful what you say or do" around other inmates.

Finally, scores on an index of solidarity orientation, here defined as emphasis on general loyalty to the group beyond primary ties with particular others, show a similar pattern. In the treatment settings, especially Inland, inmates were more likely to express such an orientation than were those in the custodial institutions. In neither setting was solidary orientation related to a statistically significant degree to perspectives toward the institution and staff or to scores on the "ratting" index.[12]

Leadership. Data bearing on the third hypothesis, that the attitudes of inmate leaders would be relatively positive in the treatment setting and relatively negative in the custodial environment, also tend to follow the predicted pattern. Boys who were nominated four or more times as having the most "influence" in the institution were classified as leaders.[13] On three attitudinal indices, statistically significant differences between leaders and non-leaders were found in either the custodial or treatment setting. . . . Leadership is more strongly associated with positive perspectives on staff and institution in the treatment environment than in the custodial setting, reflecting the strongly positive association at Milton. The same finding emerges on the self-image index—again the Milton leaders are highly positive. On the index of "ratting," leadership and cooperation with staff tend to be negatively associated in all institutions, but the association is stronger in the custodial than in the treatment institutions. Thus, findings on all three indices support the hypothesis that leaders have more positive perspectives in the treatment environment.

A separate analysis indicates that these differences among leaders characterize both "integrated" and "nonintegrated" leaders. And other data, on inmate perceptions of leadership in general, support the characterization of leaders in the treatment settings as having more positive attitudes.[14]

These and the other findings reported here indicate a difference between the two treatment institutions, Milton and Inland. On the

12. That these differences in social relations actually follow from organizational control practices is suggested by responses to a question asking for agreement or disagreement with the statement that "You have to be careful about the boys you get friendly with around here. To stay out of trouble with the adults you have to keep to yourself." Considerably higher proportions of inmates rejected this statement in the treatment setting (79 percent in Inland and 52 percent in Milton) than in the custodial institutions (30 percent in both Mixter and Dick).

13. The specific question was: "What three boys are best at getting other boys to do what they want them to do—that is, which three have the most influence among the boys? Think of the boys that you know in your cottage, in school, and in the work program, or recreation."

14. Street, *op. cit.,* 116–119.

one hand, data on inmate perspectives, effects of length of stay, and social relations clearly indicates that inmates have more positive attitudes and more highly developed primary relations at Inland. On the other hand, group involvement, as measured by integration and leadership, was more closely associated with positive perspectives at Milton than at Inland. Milton is a "milieu" institution; perhaps this finding reflects its conscious attempt to manipulate the inmate group.

Data from Additional Institutions. Data on inmate groups in three other institutions for juvenile offenders, studied less thoroughly than the four organizations just analyzed, shed additional light on the custodial-treatment differences I have reported. The first of these units, *Maxwell* (Maximum Security) was a geographically and administratively separate part of Mixter, established to handle the "most difficult" inmates of the parent institution shortly before the end of our field work. The other units, *Regis* (Religious) and *Bennett* (Benign), were small private institutions that were "open," sending their charges away from the institution every day for ordinary public or parochial schooling. In their goals and in the staff's behavior toward the inmates, these two open institutions seemed to fall between the custodial and treatment types; their goal might be characterized as "training." The inmate is viewed as changeable, but such simple techniques as altering skills and habits are considered appropriate. Within this training model, Regis stressed constant work and recreation activities along with indoctrination and enforcement of obedience and religiosity, while Bennett emphasized the creation of a homelike environment with staff serving as parental surrogates.

Results from these three units are represented by findings on the association between integration into the inmate group and responses to four attitudinal items. . . . These data, together with those from the major institutions . . . show, first, that integration is negatively associated with positive perspectives on the institution and staff, cooperativeness with staff in "ratting," and self-image in Maxwell but not in the custodial or treatment institutions, and that a direct association between integration and "prisonized" response to the ["getting along" item, Table 1, third item and footnoted] occurs only at Maxwell. Second, patterns in the two open institutions are generally inconsistent: Regis resembles Maxwell on the first two items, Bennett resembles the treatment institutions on all items, and in both institutions the association between integration and self-image is positive, as it is in the treatment institutions.

These findings and other results suggest that in Maxwell—which, with its stringent security regulations, resembles the traditional adult prison more than any of the other institutions—the "solidary opposition" model fits the inmate group reasonably well. Only in this institution was the relation between scoring high on the index of solidary orientations and strong opposition to staff on the "ratting" index statistically significant ($p < .05$ and $Q = .75$). Our data collection took place only three months after the unit was opened, however, and after several crises of organizational birth, when the inmates may have had a special *esprit de corps* because they were the first group considered incorrigible enough to be sent there. We have no evidence, therefore, that the "solidary opposition" model will continue to fit inmate groups in this type of setting.

Despite the fact that Regis and Bennett were open, allowing their inmates considerable freedom away from the institution, this milieu did not consistently generate as positive a response as did the closed treatment setting. On the other hand, the fact that on some dimensions, e.g., self-image, the association with integration is positive, and as strong as in Milton and Inland, suggests that a relatively benign, open environment might make it possible to achieve some of the benefits of treatment without the expense of a treatment program.

Part IV
Cultures and Subcultures

Humans partition themselves into groups on the basis of territory, on the basis of differences in privilege and power, and on the basis of various other distinctions that people sometimes deem important. The segregated populations that result tend to develop idiosyncratic cultures and social systems partly because of their isolation from one another and partly because of their varying ecological and economic situations. In turn, the sociocultural systems work in diverse ways on individual psychological development. While it turns out that global distinctions as the "Southern Mind," "the German character," or "middle-class mentality" are difficult to substantiate, it nevertheless is true that people in different regions, nations, and social classes do show reliable average differences on a large number of specific characteristics. These are demonstrated in Chapters 16 through 20 in this section.

One of the most studied of all sociocultural variables is social class. Two of the chapters in this section (17 and 18) present materials demonstrating some psychological differences between social classes (these chapters also present information concerning nationality differences). Many of the other chapters in this book also allude to social class differences, and detailed discussions appear especially in Chapter 12 concerning the relations between social class and values; Chapter 26, concerning the relation between social class and mental illness; and Chapter 8, concerning class differences in friendship patterns and their consequences for individual adjustment.

To a large extent, sociocultural systems have their impact on individuals by affecting family patterns and family structure, by exerting a selective pressure on choices of peers and intimates, and by generating particular kinds of organizations and channels of recruitment into organizations. So, the sections of this book concerned with the family, with peers, and with organizations can be read as defining the mechanisms by which sociocultural systems affect people. This two-step process from sociocultural systems, to specific institutions, to individual personality, is the focus in Chapter 20 in this section. Chapter 13 suggests another mechanism by which some rural-urban differences in personality might be generated.

The readings in this section suggest some ways that sociocultural change can affect individual psychology; Chapter 24 also should be consulted in this regard.

16
A Comparison of Political Attitude and Activity Patterns in Central Cities and Suburbs
Joseph Zikmund

It seems to be widely accepted that attitudes in central cities differ from attitudes in the suburbs. This study suggests that there is no uniform urban-suburban effect on attitudes and political behavior: the differences that exist tend to vary from one central city to another. On the other hand, Zikmund finds substantial variation by metropolitan region documenting the fact that cultural differences develop on a geographic basis even within the same nation.

It is now common practice in social science research to use the convient, three-way urban-suburban-rural classification to distinguish among the several geographic areas and kinds of people in the United States.[1] These three categories seem to describe roughly our intuitive understanding of the political and social forces in this country. Certainly, urban-rural (or urban-frontier) differences go back to the earliest colonial years and have been emphasized continuously in historical and social science literature since that time. The urban-suburban division, by contrast, is new, and it undoubtedly reflects the desire on the part of social scientists to bring the twentieth-century suburban phenomenon into an established urban-rural frame of reference.

Despite the wide acceptance of this theoretical distinction between central cities and suburbs as geographic entities and between urban and suburban residents as individuals, very little empircal research has been done to test the validity of this idea. In actual fact, we do not know how different or how similar urbanites and suburbanites really are. The purpose of this study is to begin to explore this problem with regard to urban and suburban patterns of political attitudes and political action.

The Study

The data for this study come from a pyramided sample of urban and suburban interviews taken in seven, self-representing, major metropolitan areas as part of the Survey Research Center's 1952, 1958,

Reprinted from Joseph Zikmund, "A Comparison of Political Attitude and Activity Patterns in Central Cities and Suburbs," in *Public Opinion Quarterly,* 31 (1967), 69–75. Reprinted by permission of the *Quarterly* and the author. Some footnotes have been renumbered.

The author wishes to express his appreciation to the Inter-University Consortium for Political Research, Survey Research Center, Ann Arbor, Michigan, which provided the data and financial support for the project, and to Miss Caroline Wolf and Mrs. Milda Hedblom of the University of Minnesota, who helped with the research for this study.

1. Bernard Lazerwitz, "Suburban Voting Trends: 1948 to 1956," *Social Forces,* 39, No. 1 (1960), 29–36.

1962, and 1964 national election polls. In total, 729 urban interviews and 731 suburban interviews are included.[2]

Four kinds of political data are used for each respondent: first, the person's general attitudes toward government and politicians; second, his (or her) party identification; third, his level of political interest; and fourth, his level of political activity, his party loyalty in past presidential elections, and his record of split-ticket voting.[3]

Two distinct types of statistical procedure are used to analyze these data. First, the proportions of interviewees giving similar responses to particular questions are compared between the total, nationwide (seven metropolitan areas) central-city sample and the total, nation-wide suburban sample. . . . [Reported] are the results from difference-of-proportions tests run on each of the comparisons to determine its level of statistical significance.[4] From this we can begin to deter-

2. The interviews are distributed into fourteen city and suburban sub-samples, as follows:

Metropolitan Area	Central-City Interviews	Suburban Interviews
Boston	31	73
Chicago	123	106
Detroit	60	82
Los Angeles	108	152
New York	280	186
Philadelphia	69	65
San Francisco	58	67

The metropolitan area samples taken by the Survey Research Center are sub-divided into three categories—central city, suburban, and rural fringe. The "suburban" portion of these samples is designed to represent the full range of "suburbs" in each particular metropolitan area. The author has checked the places used by the Center for its "suburban" samples in the metropolitan areas involved in this study and is confident that they meet his own standards for differentiating suburbs from central cities, satellite cities, and rural fringe. Readers who wish to make a similar check for themselves may consult the Center's Codebooks for each of the elections used in this study. These are readily available on request through the Inter-University Consortium for Political Research.

3. Because the questions related to the respondent's general attitude toward government and politicians were included in only two of the four polls, the samples for these questions are about half the size of the samples for the other questions.

4. Hubert M. Blalock, *Social Statistics* (New York: McGraw-Hill, 1960), 176–178.

mine, generally, just how different or similar urbanites and suburban-ites across the nation really are.

Second, the results from an analysis-of-variance test are presented to show the relative importance of three distinct kinds of forces that affect urban-suburban attitude and activity patterns. These forces are (1) the nationwide urban-suburban division implied in the urban-suburban-rural classification scheme; (2) the *inter*-metropolitan-area differences appearing when we disregard the urban-suburban division within each particular metropolitan area and treat the entire metro-politan area (central city and suburbs together) as a single analytical unit; and (3) the urban-suburban differences within each of the seven individual metropolitan areas. By working with each of the fourteen urban and suburban sub-samples as if it were an independent, co-equal unit, it is possible to break down the total variance of these fourteen sub-samples around their group mean into its component parts—that is, the part attributable to a nationwide city-suburb divi-sion, the part attributable to differences among metropolitan areas, and the part attributable to city-suburb differences within each indi-vidual metropolitan area.[5] In this way we can measure the relative importance of a nationwide urban-suburban division as compared with other relevant forces that may affect political attitude and activity patterns among urban and suburban residents.

Data and Analysis

. . . Clear-cut, average differences do not always exist between urban and suburban respondents. Statistically significant differences appear, as expected, with regard to party identification, party loyalty in past presidential elections, split-ticket voting, and one of the basic attitude questions. All of the other comparisons [of proportions] show no significant difference between urban and suburban attitude and activity patterns.

Table 1 indicates the proportion of variance among the fourteen sub-samples attributable to nationwide urban-suburban differences,

5. For more technical explanations, see Donald E. Stokes, "A Variance Com-ponents Model of Political Effects," in J. M. Claunch, ed., *Mathematical Appli-cations in Political Science:Arnold Foundation Monograph XII* (Dallas: Arnold Foundation of Southern Methodist University, 1965); E. A. Haggard, *Intraclass Correlation and the Analysis of Variance* (New York: Dryden, 1958); and Bla-lock, *op. cit.*, 242–271.

Table 1. Proportion of Total Variance among Fourteen Urban and Suburban Sub-Samples Attributable to Nationwide Urban-Suburban, Inter-Metropolitan-Area, and Intra-Metropolitan-Area (Urban-Suburban) Differences[a]

Political Attitude or Activity	Percent of Total Variance Attributed to		
	Nationwide Urban-Suburban Difference	Inter-Metropolitan Area Differences	Intra-Metropolitan Area Difference[b]
Attitude:			
Believe "hardly any" people running the government are crooked	0	65	35
Believe "quite a lot" of people running the government are crooked	0	37	63
Believe that people in government waste "not very much" tax money	4	62	34
Believe that people in government waste "a lot" of tax money	12	57	31
Believe one can "always" trust the government in Washington	6	37	57
Believe one can trust the government in Washington "only some of the time"	6	82	12
Party identification:			
Generally identify as "independents"	54	16	30
Generally identify as "Democrats"	46	7	47
Generally identify as "Republicans"	14	26	60
Interest:			
Have "high" interest in election campaign	3	84	13
Party loyalty:			
Talked to people during recent campaign in partisan way	4	82	14
Voted for candidates of "different" parties in past presidential elections	4	65	31
Voted a split ticket at state or local level in most recent general election	31	60	9
Mean average for columns	14	52	34

[a] The figure in each cell is the percent of the total variance among the 14 sub-samples with regard to the particular response that can be attributed to the urban-suburban or metropolitan-area factor in question. Each row adds to 100 percent.

[b] The figures in this column are the combined influence of intra-metropolitan area differences and of a small residue of other factors not included in the three major kinds of differences being studied.

to inter-metropolitan area differences, and to intra-metropolitan city-suburban differences. Once again, the data are somewhat irregular; however, a few general patterns are discernible. First, the nationwide city-suburban division is the *least* influential of the three kinds of forces studied. In only 1 of the 13 comparisons presented does the national city-suburban distinction account for more than 50 percent of the total variance among the fourteen sub-samples, and in 10 instances out of 13 it accounts for less than 20 percent of the total variance. By contrast, inter-metropolitan area differences account for more than 50 percent of the variance in 8 of the 13 cases. Averaging together the data for all 13 comparisons, 51 percent of the total variance is attributable to inter-metropolitan differences, 35 percent to intra-metropolitan urban-suburban differences, and only 14 percent to a nationwide urban-suburban division.

Conclusions

The idea that one can make a meaningful city-suburban distinction at the national level involves a number of empirically testable assumptions. Among the most important of these is that, on the average, there are meaningful differences between the political attitude and political activity patterns of a nationwide sample of urban residents and the political attitude and political activity patterns of a nationwide sample of suburban residents. In addition, this idea assumes that the importance of other forces (other than a nationwide urban-suburban difference) influencing urban and suburban attitude and activity patterns is small and that the effects of these other forces are random or unidentifiable by current research techniques. The data presented above cast serious doubts on the validity of both these assumptions, for we find that there is little or no difference between some urban and suburban attitude and activity patterns and that the nationwide urban-suburban division is the *least* rather than the most influential of the forces used to explain these urban and suburban data patterns.

If some kind of nationwide urban-suburban distinction does not prove to be very useful in explaining the attitude and activity patterns of urban and suburban residents in the United States, then what tack should social scientists take to try to solve this problem? The analysis of variance presented above clearly points to the individual metropolitan area as the most fruitful focus of attention for this kind of research.

Recent evidence indicates that the rapid growth of suburbia during the 1940s and 1950s can best be explained as a somewhat haphazard overflow of urban people into the surrounding suburbs and rural areas.[6] In addition, we are coming to realize that all parts of a particular metropolitan area share common problems and a common political, social, and economic environment. The political experiences and attitudes of all the people in a metropolitan area are necessarily different from those of people outside the vague metropolitan boundaries. The metropolis has its own newspapers and its own radio and television stations. Economic integration brings together similar people from all parts of the metropolitan area. The urban stockbroker and the suburban stockbroker are likely to differ politically only on intra-metropolitan issues, and the same holds for the urban blue-collar worker and his suburban counterpart. From this perspective, the key to an accurate understanding of the suburban phenomenon rests with theories and research that concentrate on each particular metropolitan area and on the unique environment it provides for suburbs and suburban residents.

---

6. Fred W. Wirt, "The Political Sociology of American Suburbia," *The Journal of Politics,* 27, No. 3 (1965), 664–666.

17
Role Relations, Sociocultural Environments, and Autocratic Family Ideology

Glen H. Elder, Jr.

A correlation between education and democratic ideology has been noted in Chapter 12. Here that relation is documented again, showing that it exists within a wide variety of nations. However, Elder's analysis adds another dimension to the issue by showing that national differences in democratic ideology are correlated with a nation's overall level of industrialization and modernization, in addition to the educational level within the nation.

Adherence to autocratic ideology in adult life results in part from childhood socialization and supportive cultural patterns.[1] Parental domination is a prevalent antecedent of autocratic ideology among adults concerning the degree of autonomy considered appropriate for youth.[2] Education during the adolescent years also influences ideological orientations; autocratic views in child rearing are inversely related to level of education.[3] Among adults, changes in residence and conditions in the work setting may either modify or reinforce autocratic ideas acquired during years of dependency.[4]

The relation of these experiences to an autocratic position on the participation of youth in family decision making is assessed in this paper in five nations which differ markedly in cultural support for autocratic ideology in the family: the United States, Great Britain, West Germany, Italy, and Mexico.[5] The analysis uses data which were

Reprinted from Glen H. Elder, Jr., "Role Relations, Sociocultural Environments, and Autocratic Family Ideology," in *Sociometry*, 28 (1965), 173–196. Reprinted by permission of the American Sociological Association and the author.

I am indebted to John Clausen and M. Brewster Smith for comments and suggestions on aspects of the manuscript and the analysis, and gratefully acknowledge research support from the Institute of International Studies and the Computer Center at Berkeley.

1. Daniel J. Levinson, "Idea Systems in the Individual and in Society," in George K. Zollschan and Walter Hirsch, eds., *Explorations in Social Change* (Boston: Houghton, 1964).

2. Hazel L. Ingersoll, "A Study of the Transmission of Authority Patterns in the Family," *Genetic Psychology Monographs,* 38 (1948), 225–302; E. Bjorklund and J. Israel, *The Authoritarian Ideology of Upbringing* (Uppsala, Sweden: 1957); Richard H. Willis, "Political and Child-Rearing Attitudes in Sweden," *Journal of Abnormal and Social Psychology,* 53 (July, 1956), 74–77; Leone Kell and Joan Aldous, "Trends in Child Care Over Three Generations," *Marriage and Family Living,* 22 (May, 1960), 176–177; and Gerald R. Leslie and Kathryn P. Johnsen, "Changed Perceptions of the Maternal Role," *American Sociological Review,* 28 (December, 1963), 919–928.

3. For an extensive list of sources see Leslie and Johnsen, *op. cit.*

4. On the relation of occupational role and work setting to the attitudes, values, and behavior of fathers in the family see Donald G. McKinley, *Social Class and Family Life* (New York: Free Press of Glencoe, 1964); and Martin Gold, *Status Forces in Delinquent Boys* (Ann Arbor, Mich.: Institute for Social Research, 1963).

5. Family ideology, constitutes "a *rationale* that serves to justify, interpret, and integrate" norms, social patterns, and processes in the family; see Levinson, *op. cit.,* 306. Child rearing and family ideology have been conceptualized along a variety of dimensions: traditional-modern, strict-permissive, and democratic-

originally collected from approximately 1,000 persons in each nation for a study of political behavior.[6] We shall also investigate the extent to which an autocratic orientation in this area of family life is related to similar orientations in other content domains among respondents in each nation. Available evidence indicates that a person who is autocratic in family ideology is likely to be similarly inclined in inter-group relations and in politics.[7]

Autocratic ideology refers in this analysis to the belief that youth of 16 should not participate in family decision making.[8] The index used

---

autocratic. Each of these conceptual dimensions indicates a continuum running from large power and status differences and a unilateral flow of communication between parent and child, at one extreme, to minimal power and statue differences at the other. A general ideological orientation in the family, whether autocratic or democratic, tends to be a composite of ideas regarding different behavioral areas. And these ideas may not be consistently autocratic or democratic. Leslie and Johnsen, *op. cit.*, found considerable variation in American maternal role concepts and performance across three behavioral areas: aggression toward mother, self-direction, and sex behavior.

6. These samples were obtained in 1959 and 1960 by Gabriel Almond and Sydney Verba for a study of political behavior in these five countries. See, *The Civic Culture* (Princeton: Princeton University Press, 1963). I am indebted to the Data Library of the Survey Research Center at Berkeley for the opportunity to conduct this secondary analysis. The United States sample used in the present study does not include Negroes. Though the samples in each of the five countries are stratified, multistage, probability samples, the institutes that designed and executed the surveys differed in the techniques employed and in field experiences. Each sample was originally intended to be a representative cross section of the national population, yet this objective was not achieved in Mexico. In the other four nations, only a rough approximation was obtained. Due to cost and technical difficulties, the Mexican sample was drawn from an urban population of persons living in urban places of 10,000 or more in size. Furthermore, it was necessary to weigh the interviews obtained in Mexico City by a factor of 2.5 in order to make this urban stratum of the sample equivalent to its proportion in the national population. These conditions, as well as the high mortality rate in obtaining interviews at assigned addresses (40 percent), seriously weaken any cross-national comparison between Mexico and the other four nations. Exclusion of the rural population tends to yield, in effect, an underestimation of the actual differences between Mexico and the other nations. One indication of the quality of the other four samples is shown by the non-completion rate in interviewing: Germany, 26 percent; Italy, 28 percent; Great Britain, 41 percent; and the United States, 17 percent.

7. See Levinson, *op. cit.,* 301.

8. Ideally, a composite index of the amount of involvement and responsibility of youth in making decisions in a set of areas would have been desirable to measure ideology regarding the participation of youth in family decision

reflects autocratic and democratic orientations toward the position of youth in the family based on conceptions of age and status differences between youth and parents. One aspect of the democratic family which distinguishes it from an autocratic family is the greater inclusion of children in family decision making and consideration of their ideas and opinions. An autocratic orientation is illustrated in Herbert Gans's description of an adult-centered ideology among second-generation Italian parents in the West End of Boston. Children "are raised in a household that is run to satisfy adult wishes first."[9] The distance between the parents' and child's world in these families appears in clear detail in patterns of age segregation and in the passivity of children when in the presence of adults. Similarly, in the Mexican village of Tepoztlan, "children are brought up to obey their elders and to submit to the will of their mother and father as long as they live under the parents' roof. From infancy on, they are encouraged to be passive and unobtrusive; older children are expected to be self-controlled and helpful."[10]

The five nations represent a wide range of sociocultural contexts and of ideological variation. Over the past three decades, democratic family ideology seems most widespread in the United States and Great Britain, and is least prevalent in Italy and Mexico. The spread of this ideology is possibly linked with changes in family patterns. Goode notes that "the modern doctrine that members of the nuclear family

---

making. In the absence of such specific indicators, a general index of the amount of responsibility and involvement in decision making which is viewed as appropriate for 16 year olds is used. The item used is, "In general, how much voice do you think children of 16 should have in family decisions"?— *Democratic ideology,* "Great deal" and "Some"; *Autocratic ideology,* "Little" and "None"; "Other" and "Don't know" responses were not scored. Though one item may be highly unstable, the association of this item with other items measuring democratic and autocratic orientations and with background variables yield consistent relations and results which parallel findings reported in other studies. Internal analysis of the data constitutes a critical test of the validity and usefulness of any indicator. A cross-national analysis based on a single item index of adolescent independence in job choice is reported in Robert J. Smith, Charles E. Ramsey, and Gelia Castillo, "Parental Authority and Job Choice: Sex Differences in Three Cultures," *The American Journal of Sociology,* 69 (September, 1963), 143–149.

9. Herbert J. Gans, *The Urban Villagers* (New York: Free Press, 1962), 56.

10. Oscar Lewis, *Tepoztlan: Village in Mexico* (N   York: Holt, Rinehart, 1960), 59.

should love one another, that permissive love is 'psychologically healthful' for the child, has given ideological support to the normal pressures of children toward greater choice in all matters and to the greater opportunity to be free economically at an early age."[11]

Four interrelated factors, we suggest, account in large measure for a decline in, and the relative prevalence of, autocratic family ideology in the five nations: (1) a decline or absence of cultural and institutional support, (2) increasing urbanization and industrialization, (3) an elevation in median educational attainment, and (4) the exposure of the national population to democratizing child-rearing literature.[12] Rural residence and low education are particularly related to intolerance and to acceptance of traditional authority patterns.[13] If a numerical index of each of these factors were constructed, it would show conditions in the United States to be most favorable to both a low prevalence and a decline in this ideology with Britain and West Germany next in order. Italy and Mexico, on the other hand, would rank lowest.[14]

Data on the attitudes, ideology, and practices of American parents suggest that permissive and democratic ideology have become more widespread most noticeably in the middle class over the last 30 years.[15] A recent comparison of 265 college-educated American mothers and grandmothers on desirability of self-direction on the part of children indicated a trend toward greater tolerance for the child in

11. William J. Goode, *World Revolution and Family Patterns* (New York: Free Press of Glencoe, 1963), 77.

12. See Goode, *ibid.,* and Urie Bronfenbrenner, "Socialization and Social Class Through Time and Space," in Eleanor E. Maccoby, Theodore M. Newcomb, and Eugene L. Hartley, eds., *Readings in Social Psychology* (New York: Henry Holt, 1958).

13. On tolerance towards others, see Samuel G. Stouffer, *Communism, Conformity, and Civil Liberties* (Garden City, N. Y.: Doubleday, 1955); Robin M. Williams, Jr., *Strangers Next Door* (New York: Prentice-Hall, 1964); James G. Martin, *The Tolerant Personality* (Detroit: Wayne State University Press, 1964); and Seymour M. Lipset, "Working-Class Authoritarianism," in *Political Man* (New York: Doubleday, 1960), Chapter 4.

14. On national variations in education and in economic development, see Frederick Harbison and Charles A. Myers, *Education, Manpower, and Economic Growth: Strategies of Human Resource Development* (New York: McGraw-Hill, 1964).

15. See Martha Wolfenstein, "The Emergence of Fun Morality," *The Journal of Social Issues,* 7 (1951), 15–25, and Leslie and Johnsen, *op. cit.*

making his own decisions.[16] Also, in a study of Vassar alumnae, about one-third of the class of 1904 disagreed with the statement, "obedience and respect for authority are the most important virtues that children should learn" in contrast to 77 percent of women in classes 1940–1943.[17] Similar downward trends across age groups were obtained by Stouffer in a national sample of Americans.[18]

In a sample of German adults, nearly two-thirds agreed that children should have their own views, suitable for their own world, which should be respected and not corrected by the person who rears them.[19] This statement does not refer to the inclusion of youth in family decision making. Yet the data suggest that autocratic family ideology is less common among post- than prewar generations of German parents.

In Italy and Mexico, the father-centered authoritarian family and male-oriented, traditional cultural patterns generally persist. Wives are subservient to their husbands, and children are subordinate to both.[20] The Mexican-American male, Madsen observes, "is entitled to unquestioning obedience from his wife and children. He is above criticism due to his 'superior' male strength and intelligence."[21]

The effects of these national variations on hypothesized relations within nations are most likely to be evident in Italy and Mexico, the two nations in which autocratic family ideology seems most prevalent. Due to supportive cultural and institutional patterns, differences in role relations and in status changes are apt to account for appreciably less variation in autocratic ideology in these two countries. Specific hypotheses on the formation and support of autocratic ideology and on the relation of this perspective to similar views in other domains within these contexts are presented below.

16. Leslie and Johnsen, *op. cit.*
17. Mervin B. Freedman, "Changes in Six Decades of Some Attitudes in Values Held by Educated Women," *Journal of Social Issues,* 17, No. 1 (1961), 19–28.
18. Stouffer, *op. cit.*
19. Cited in Goode, *op. cit.,* 78. See also Rene König, "Family and Authority: The German Father in 1955," *Sociological Review,* 5 (July, 1957), 107–127.
20. See, for instance, Oscar Lewis, *op. cit.;* Charles J. Erasmus, *Man Takes Control* (Minneapolis: University of Minnesota Press, 1961); Edward C. Banfield, *The Moral Basis of a Backward Society* (New York: Free Press of Glencoe, 1958); and Luigi Barzini, *The Italians* (New York: Atheneum, 1964).
21. William Madsen, *The Mexican-Americans of South Texas* (New York: Holt, Rinehart, 1964), 48.

Hypotheses

1. *The Acquisition and Reinforcement of Autocratic Ideology.* We hypothesize that parent-youth relations, educational attainment, residential change, and occupational role and work setting are related to adherence to autocratic ideology. Research and theory relevant to the effects of each of these independent variables are discussed briefly in relation to the following hypotheses.

    a. *Parent-Youth Relations.* In the family, children learn how to relate to others through interaction with their parents, and orientations acquired during these years are frequently carried over into adult life. Thus, we find that the child-rearing practices of mothers who are themselves from strict homes are more likely to be autocratic than those of mothers from any other type of home.[22] Aggressive tendencies may also result from authoritarian upbringing since autocratic parents are frequently punitive and coercive.[23] Later in life these tendencies may find expression in relations with subordinates such as children. Data presented in *The Authoritarian Personality* and in subsequent studies also show a moderate relationship between dominant parents and an autocratic view toward children in adulthood.[24] According to these data, *adults who report authoritarian parents should be most inclined to advocate the exclusion of youth from family decision making.*[25]

    b. *Educational Attainment.* In accordance with a large number of studies which have found autocratic family ideology and child-rearing

---

22. Leslie and Johnsen, *op. cit.,* 928.

23. Martin Gold, "Suicide, Homicide, and the Socialization of Aggression," *The American Journal of Sociology,* 56 (May, 1958), 651–661.

24. See Theodore W. Adorno et al., *The Authoritarian Personality* (New York: Harper, 1950); Willis, *op. cit.;* and Ingersoll, *op. cit.*

25. An index of parent-youth relations was constructed from the following two items, with scores ranging from 0 to 4. "As you were growing up, let's say when you were around 16, how much influence do you remember having in family decisions affecting yourself?" (*2,* much influence; *1,* some; *0,* none at all; other and don't know responses not scored); "At around the same time, if a decision were made that you didn't like, did you feel *free* to complain, did you feel a little *uneasy* about complaining, or was it *better* not to complain?" (*2,* felt *free; 1,* felt a little *uneasy; 0* it was *better not* to complain; other and don't know responses were not scored). Gamma coefficients based on total samples in each nation show these items to be highly related: United States, 6.1; Italy, 6.3; West Germany, 6.5; Great Britain, 5.6; and Mexico, 4.6. For the purposes of the analysis, we shall consider scores 3 and 4 as an indication of *democratic* parent-child relations, and 0 and 2 as indicating an *authoritarian* pattern.

practices to be inversely related to parental education, we hypothesize that *persons in each nation will be most likely to be autocratic in ideology if they have not attended secondary school.*[26] This relation may be modified substantially by the degree to which autocratic ideology receives cultural and institutional support—i.e., Italy versus the United States.[27]

c. *Place of Residence and Migration.* Adults who have remained in rural areas and those rural-born persons who now live in urban communities should be . . . inclined to adhere to an autocratic perspective since father-centered, authoritarian families are generally more common in rural than urban areas.[28] Data which partially support this expectation are provided by Bronfenbrenner in a reanalysis of Miller and Swanson's Detroit data: mothers with a rural background were likely to adhere to more restrictive techniques of socialization than mothers of urban background who were comparable in social class status.[29]

A rural-born adult who moves to an urban community is likely to be confronted with a set of child-rearing and family practices which are foreign to his past experiences and acquired perspectives. For some newcomers the experience may create confusion and be unsettling as shown in the feelings and responses of European immi-

26. For a listing of studies, see Leslie and Johnsen, *op. cit.;* see also, Marvin Zuckerman and Mary Oltean, "Some Relationships Between Maternal Attitude Factors and Authoritarianism Personality Needs, Psychopathology, and Self-Acceptance," *Child Development,* 30 (March, 1959), 27–36; and Melvin L. Kohn, "Social Class and the Exercise of Parental Authority," *American Sociological Review,* 24 (June, 1959), 352–366.

27. Educational attainment is measured by the question, "How far did you get with your education?" The responses ranged from no education to various types of higher education. For an index of high attainment (a level which is achieved by appreciable members of persons in each of five countries), it was decided to use the proportion who said they reached secondary school. The phrasing of the question does not necessarily imply completion of this level of education. The item measuring the education of Italian respondents distinguished between junior and senior high school within the secondary level. For these respondents, the percentage reaching junior high school was used as the index of achievement with the result that the percentage of Italian respondents reaching secondary school is slightly inflated. The proportion who reached twelve years of education was used as the index in the United States, since it seems to be similar in level of achievement to reaching secondary school in the other four nations.

28. See Glen H. Elder, Jr., "Achievement Orientations and Career Patterns of Rural Youth," *Sociology of Education,* 37 (Fall, 1963), 30–58.

29. Bronfenbrenner, *op. cit.,* 441.

grants in New York City.[30] Seeing children question parents and assert independence might support the rationale for autocratic policy in child rearing. On the other hand, newcomers might adopt the more democratic views prevalent in the community. Both of these responses are plausible alternatives, yet it seems most probable that adoption of a democratic perspective would be more common among second-generation, urban residents. Newcomers to urban areas, on the other hand, *should be more inclined to rely upon self-other orientations acquired through socialization in rural areas.* Of the rural born living in urban places, this should be most true of those who experienced authoritarian control in their families of orientation and who did not reach secondary school.

d. *Occupational Role and Work Setting.* The work experiences of men significantly affect their behavior in the family and their attitudes toward children. Dissatisfaction on the job is associated with conflict in the home,[31] and a low, subordinate occupational status has been found to be linked with paternal coerciveness in rearing sons.[32] *Thus, autocratic family ideology is most likely among men who occupy low-status work roles, and among those who experience coercion by superiors in the work setting.*

Moving from the unskilled to professional workers, many of the conditions which support democratic, humanistic values increase in frequency and strength. High-status occupations require more years of formal education, are more rewarding from a monetary standpoint, and require ambition, self-reliance, judgment, and drive. Advocacy of the exclusion of youth from the decision-making process in the family seems neither compatible with the greater potential satisfactions derivable from professional and white collar work, nor with personal qualities stressed in these work settings. A partial test of these observations was made by Inkeles in a secondary analysis of child-rearing values in eleven nations.[33] Inkeles assumed that "traditional, restrictive, cautious, conventional values are much stronger among manual

30. Oscar Handlin, *The Uprooted* (New York: Little Brown), 1951.

31. O. A. Oeser and S. A. Hammond, *Social Structure and Personality in a City* (London: Routledge & Kegan Paul, 1954), 248.

32. McKinley, *op. cit.,* and Gold, *op. cit.*

33. Alex Inkeles, "Industrial Man: The Relation of Status to Experience, Perception, and Value," *American Journal of Sociology,* 66 (July, 1960), 22, Table 9.

workers, whereas the belief in effort, striving, energetic mastery, and the sacrifice necessary to those ends is much stronger among the middle class."[34] Of the values presented, manual workers were least likely to choose ambition in six of the countries and most likely to indicate obedience in eight nations. The consistency of these results is encouraging, although percentage differences were relatively small.

Two types of worker-supervisor relationships, benevolent and coercive, should produce quite different attitudes and ideas about controlling youth. In benevolent relationships, the worker can express his views and make complaints, while workers under coercive management are not allowed to discuss problems and air complaints. Hostility and resentment stirred by coercive management may heighten the receptivity of workers to autocratic dogma regarding subordinates.[35] Under such conditions, differences in age and wisdom may be emphasized in adult-youth relations.

2. *Autocratic and Democratic Family Ideology in Relation to Orientations in Other Ideological Domains.* Data indicate that individuals who are autocratic in one ideological domain are inclined to hold autocratic orientations in other areas.[36] These domains include the family, polity, education, intergroup relations, religion, and the economy. Willis, in a Swedish sample of 73 men and 71 women, ages 18 and over, obtained a correlation of .43 between a scale measuring acceptance of authoritarian political policies and a thirteen-item index measuring demands for obedience from children.[37] Both of these ideological orientations were moderately related to authoritarian upbringing (.25 for political and .28 for child-rearing ideology). Ethnocentrism has been shown in numerous studies to be related to autocratic family and child-rearing ideology.[38] In the domain of economic life, pessimism regarding social advancement and the future is moderately associated with autocratic, intolerant beliefs.[39]

---

34. *Ibid.,* p. 21.
35. Hamblin found punitive supervision to be related to high turnover, tension, and aggressive feelings among workers in a concrete-products company; see Robert L. Hamblin, "Punitive and Non-punitive Supervision," *Social Problems,* 11 (Spring, 1964), 345–359.
36. Levinson, *op. cit.,* 301.
37. Willis, *op. cit.*
38. Adorno et al., *The Authoritarian Personality, op. cit.,* and Williams, *op. cit.*
39. Martin, *op. cit.*

Correlations across ideological domains obtained in a number of studies are not particularly strong, ranging from .3 to .8.[40] Both personality and environmental factors may account for this variation. Levinson suggests that it is partly "a reflection of deeper-lying contradictions of personality," and partly an indication of "contradictory ideological demands and opportunities in the social milieu."[41] It seems probable that ideological consistency is apt to be greatest under conditions which minimize the influence of relevant environmental factors on the expression of personal orientations. Middle-class status seems likely to index such a condition for individuals who adhere to an autocratic family ideology. Structural support for autocratic thinking is least likely to be experienced in the middle class, yet when this orientation does occur, it should be largely a function of personality, and thus should be more likely to be expressed in a variety of social and political areas. [Elder's test of the hypothesis is not reprinted here.—EDITOR]

Prevalence and Change in Autocratic Ideology

Secular change in the prevalence of autocratic ideology is shown in Table 1 across seven age groups ranging from respondents (18–25 years of age) who were born just prior to or during the early part of World War II to those (61 years of age and older) who were born before 1900.

National differences in the spread and decline of autocratic ideology are generally similar to those we have described. Moving from older to younger respondents, the percentage against adolescent involvement in family decision making declines appreciably for the United States, Great Britain, and West Germany. Little consistent change is evident in Italy and Mexico. Autocratic ideology is least extensive in the United States and is most prevalent in Italy. Great Britain and West Germany are in between these two extremes, although percentage differences between the two are not sufficiently consistent to indicate meaningful national differences. No appreciable variations by sex were obtained.

In the United States and Great Britain, the greatest percentage decrease occurs among those who were adolescents during the late

40. Levinson, *op. cit.*
41. *Ibid.*, 306.

Table 1. Percentage Autocratic in Family Ideology by Age and Nation

Nation	Age (and Year of Birth)						
	18–25 (1934–41)	26–30 1929–34	31–35 (1924–29)	36–40 (1919–24)	41–50 (1909–19)	51–60 (1900–09)	61+ (Before 1900)
United States	10(100)	10(72)	14(79)	13(86)	16(153)	25(138)	31(208)
Great Britain	31(81)	29(93)	35(111)	32(136)	25(188)	52(169)	58(159)
West Germany	24(107)	40(76)	45(91)	39(102)	44(158)	44(171)	58(165)
Italy	58(156)	69(107)	70(100)	64(106)	71(178)	83(156)	74(113)
Mexico	53(229)	44(208)	43(170)	45(167)	44(209)	54(165)	66(97)

Note: Total N's per cell are given in parentheses.

1920s and early 1930s; thereafter, little consistent change is evident. Technological and mass communication innovations following World War I may have contributed to this decline. The sharpest declines in Germany and Italy appear among persons who were adolescents during the two world wars. Among Germans and Italians whose adolescence postdates World War II, the results seem to reflect the impetus given democratization in all sectors of national life since the war. These changes have been most noted in the German family.[42] In Mexico, an autocratic perspective is least common among those born between the Revolution of 1910 and 1935; this curvilinear pattern appears to parallel the high rate of social and economic change which occurred in rural areas as part of agrarian reform.[43] Equalitarianism, as part of the revolutionary spirit of these reform years, may have inculcated generations born in this period with a more democratic ideology regarding parent-youth relations. It is also likely that social change resulted in an entrenchment of traditional beliefs for some. For instance, the distribution of land to peasants and collectivization during the years of agrarian reform in Mexico may have had quite different effects on the rural family system and on traditional beliefs. These possibilities merely suggest that the relation between social-structural change and ideological change is complex, and requires a more detailed empirical assessment.

National differences in the pervasiveness of autocratic ideology (shown in Table 1) correspond to differences inferred from area studies and other materials. Secular trends in ideology in each nation also parallel known differences among these nations and vary meaningfully in relation to their social, economic, and demographic histories. Yet these results are subject to a number of methodological problems. Since we do not have measurements on adult-child pairs, we lack a base from which to assess degree of change. Furthermore, we compared the prevalence of autocratic ideology across age groups at a point in time rather than across time periods among persons of the same age: as a result, the findings obtained may be a function of age differences rather than of social, economic, and ideological conditions during periods of this century. Several aspects of the data suggest

42. König, *op. cit.*
43. Oscar Lewis, *Five Families* (New York: Basic Books, 1958), 17.

that the trends obtained are a result, to a significant extent, of conditions during the childhood and adolescence of the respondents. First, the trends vary in expected fashion in relation to events such as world wars and social upheavals. In addition, the percentage urban-born and reaching secondary school—factors which we have suggested partially account for change toward more liberal ideology—tend to increase from the oldest to the youngest age groups in the three nations which show substantial change. Finally, if age is the main factor, a decline in ideology should be fairly similar in each nation. This pattern, of course, does not hold for Mexico and Italy. Yet, even with this supporting evidence, weaknesses in the data require that these results be considered as tentative.

The Formation and Support of Autocratic Ideology

Parent-Youth Relations. Data from other studies indicate that the strictest adults in both ideology and in practices are those who were themselves reared by domineering parents. Since the spread of equalitarianism resulting from other changes in society tends to enhance the probability of movement away from an extreme ideological position, the most pronounced decline in autocratic ideology across age groups should be evident among authoritarian-reared respondents.

Table 2 supports our expectations. Autocratic ideology is more widespread among persons within each age group who described relations with their own parents during adolescence as authoritarian. All fifteen comparisons produce differences in the expected direction (an average difference of 22 percent). A decline in this perspective is primarily evident among those who described their parents as authoritarian. Of the persons with authoritarian parents in each nation, we find that autocratic ideology occurs most frequently among those born before 1910 and least among those born after 1929. Much less change is shown for democratically reared persons in the three birth cohorts. If national comparisons are made among persons reporting similar adolescent role patterns, differences between nations remain large and of the same order as those shown in Table 1.

Although measures of permissive ideology and parent-youth relations were not available in the data, it seems likely that a number of adults who were reared in this manner by their parents would be in-

Table 2. Percentage Autocratic in Family Ideology by Type of Parent-Youth Relation, Age and Nation

Nation	Type of Parent-Youth Relations	Age and Birth Group Cohorts		
		18–30 (1929–41)	31–50 (1909–41)	51 + (Before 1909)
United States	Authoritarian	13[45]	24[131]	40[194]
	Democratic	9[128]	16[169]	14[152]
Great Britain	Authoritarian	48[54]	45[164]	75[227]
	Democratic	22[120]	21[261]	35[141]
West Germany	Authoritarian	44[75]	56[212]	67[243]
	Democratic	26[114]	23[154]	23[105]
Italy	Authoritarian	67[146]	71[246]	86[184]
	Democratic	57[110]	65[188]	65[85]
Mexico	Authoritarian	53[309]	54[372]	63[184]
	Democratic	39[129]	22[174]	40[78]

clined to move away from this extreme position in family ideology. Leslie and Johnsen found that a number of the American mothers who were permissively reared with respect to self-direction moved toward a more moderate position in their own ideas and practices.[44] Movement away from parental patterns thus appears most likely among adults who experienced extremes in power relations in their families of orientation. In such cases change can occur in only one direction.

Educational Attainment. It was hypothesized that autocratic ideology would be most common among persons who had not attended secondary school. The paucity of rural-born British respondents and Mexicans with a secondary education required exclusion of these two nations from the analyses on educational attainment and residential patterns.

Persons who have attained secondary school are less likely to adhere to autocratic ideology than those with a primary education in each of the three age groups (Table 3). Absolute percentage differences between the old and young age groups indicate that the decline in autocratic ideology is greatest among persons who reached secondary school in West Germany and Italy. The association is relatively weak among Americans. The low prevalence of autocratic ideology in the United States and the index of educational attainment, which is least satisfactory for indicating differences in the United States, may partially account for this result. As indicated earlier, surveys in the United States tend to show greater change toward democratic and permissive ideas in the middle than in the working class.[45] The equally small relation between education and ideology in Italy may be due to the countervailing influence of sociocultural patterns.

In each of the three nations, persons adhering to an autocratic ideology are most likely to have been born early in the twentieth century, to have been reared by authoritarian parents and to have gone no further than primary school in their formal education. Thus, the greatest contrasts in adherence to this normative belief should be indicated by contrasts in age, parent-youth relations, and education.

. . . The highest and lowest prevalence of autocratic ideology in each nation tend to appear in these extreme subgroups (percentage differences of 30 for the United States and Italy, and 47 for West Ger-

44. Leslie and Johnsen, *op. cit.,* p. 927.
45. *Ibid.*

Table 3. Percentage Autocratic in Family Ideology in Relation to Level of Educational Attainment in the United States, Great Britain and Italy with Age Controlled

Nation	Level of Education	Percentage Autocratic by Age Groups			Average Percentage Differences
		18–30	31–50	51+	
United States	Primary	12(41)	21(137)	33(242)	9.7
	Secondary	9(132)	10(180)	18(104)	
West Germany	Primary	39(105)	46(299)	56(305)	20.3
	Secondary	16(43)	27(66)	37(41)	
Italy	Primary	70(150)	71(267)	80(209)	9.3
	Secondary	52(111)	64(117)	77(60)	

many). The new generation of adults who attended secondary school or were reared by democratic parents are least likely to have autocratic views. Yet, even in this subgroup, Italians are nearly seven times as likely as Americans to be autocratic. The greater cultural and institutional support for autocratic family ideology in Italy is the most likely explanation for this pronounced difference. It is also possible that the meaning of the item differs between these nations. Adolescent involvement in family decision making may represent a substantially different type of behavior in an extended family than in an urban nuclear family unit. Nevertheless, the national differences obtained do appear to correspond to inferences based on ethnographic reports.

Another indication of the socialization orientation of the home and its effect on the formation of ideology is provided by religious affiliation. Comparison of Protestant and Catholic respondents in the United States with education controlled, shows that Catholics are more likely to be autocratic, both on the primary (24 versus 18 percent) and secondary level (15 versus 8 percent). Among West Germans, a similar difference was obtained for persons who failed to enter secondary school. The number of Catholics in the British sample were too few to permit analysis.

Residential Patterns. Autocratic ideology, we reasoned, should be most widespread in the rural-to-urban group among authoritarian-reared persons with a primary education.[46] The lowest prevalence over all migration patterns should be characteristic of democratically reared persons in the urban-urban subgroup who reached secondary school.

The above expectations are only partially realized in the above analysis (depletion of cases made an analysis of German cases impractical). Overall, autocratic ideology is most widespread among authoritarian-reared persons with a primary education who moved from a rural to an urban community. These respondents stand out from all other persons in the rural-urban subgroup. On the other hand, the lowest prevalence of this belief is not clearly specified by any of the migration patterns.

---

46. Rural residence is indicated by communities of 5,000 or less, and urban places are those larger in size. Rural-urban is thus a residential move to communities above 5,000 in size. The relatively small size of the rural to urban flow in West Germany and Italy necessitated a crude breakdown of this kind.

With age, adult status, and parent-youth relations statistically controlled[47] similar results were obtained. . . . In three nations (the Mexican sample did not include persons living in rural areas), autocratic ideology appears to occur most frequently among migrants from rural areas. This orientation is least common to respondents with a stable urban pattern in the United States and West Germany. . . . Variations by residential patterns are negligible for Great Britain, the most urbanized of the five countries.

Occupational Status and Work Setting. The rewards, stresses, and values which characterize work settings and have relevance for the way males view family relations are indexed by the status of the work role and by the nature of autonomy and control in the work setting. We hypothesized that an intolerant and domineering approach toward youth would be inversely related to occupational status. Self-reliance, initiative and independent judgment are more valued in high status jobs, and rewards from work, both intrinsic and extrinsic, are greater. Secondly, we hypothesized that coercive supervision on the job should induce a more intolerant and controlling approach toward others, and in particular toward youth.

Table 4 shows the percentage of autocratic males by six occupational levels with all other variables except education controlled.[48] The degree of overlap between education and occupation prevented statistical control of the former. In most nations, an autocratic ideology is least common among professionals. Differences in ideology among professionals in the five nations are small in relation to cross-national comparisons in other occupational groups. If Italy is excluded, the percentage variation is about 18 percent. Manual workers, farmers, and small businessmen are generally more likely to be autocratic than

47. In Tables 4 and 5, a technique of multivariate analysis which permits the use of test factors with categorical response classes is used to control statistically for extraneous variables such as age. This technique enables the simultaneous control of all test factors in the analysis by statistically adjusting subclass percentages simultaneously for the effects of all other variables and the interrelations. No assumption concerning the linearity of the effects of each factor are required. It provides estimates of the main effects of each factor. See Alan B. Wilson, "Analysis of Multiple Cross-Classifications in Cross-Sectional Designs," a revision of a paper presented to the American Association for Public Opinion Research, Excelsior Springs, Missouri, May 9, 1964.

48. *Ibid.*

Glen H. Elder, Jr.

Table 4. Percentage of Males Autocratic in Family Ideology by Sociocultural Factors in Five Nations: Adjusted Percentages for Subclasses in a Multiple Classification Analysis

Sociocultural Factors	United States	Great Britain	West Germany	Italy	Mexico
1. Age					
a. 18–30	16(89)	37(96)	36(104)	59(133)	50(155)
b. 31–50	20(141)	37(206)	40(173)	59(197)	42(200)
c. 51+	26(175)	53(158)	45(172)	72(140)	56(109)
2. Residential Pattern					
a. Rural-rural	22(100)	43(63)	42(143)	55(123)	*
b. Rural-urban	25(120)	42(32)	48(63)	68(79)	—
c. Urban-urban	20(155)	43(300)	39(202)	62(194)	—
3. Religion					
a. Protestant	20(261)	44(324)	41(226)	—	—
b. Catholic	31(92)	44(52)	40(187)	—	—
4. Parent-Youth Relations					
a. Authoritarian	28(167)	55(178)	53(209)	69(238)	56(265)
b. Democratic	16(201)	34(237)	26(171)	56(158)	34(138)
5. Occupation					
a. Professional	20(53)	26(40)	34(47)	47(29)	38(18)
b. White Collar	14(85)	46(58)	28(49)	65(71)	45(78)
c. Small Business	24(33)	54(33)	40(36)	65(42)	59(61)
d. Farmer or farm worker	32(33)	*	46(41)	68(78)	*
e. Skilled	24(89)	40(151)	46(123)	62(84)	50(196)
f. Unskilled	26(98)	42(92)	46(56)	68(86)	47(36)
Grand Percent	22	43	41	64	48
Total N	405	460	449	470	464

Note: Starred cells have less than 20 cases. Since the Mexican sample was drawn from urban areas, a delineation of residential patterns is not possible. Some of the frequency distributions will not equal the total number of cases due to the exclusion of nonresponses, don't know, and other responses.

white collar workers and professionals. In fact, across the five nations, small businessmen and farmers are virtually as likely to be autocratic as skilled and unskilled workers, a finding which corresponds to results obtained on political ideology. Extremist and intolerant political sentiments tend to be particularly strong among these entrepreneurs.[49]

Self-employment and two types of supervision, benevolent and coercive, were measured by three questions. Workers were described as "under benevolent supervision" if they felt free to complain when they strongly disagreed with a decision, if they believed that their complaining did some good, and if they felt that management considered their needs and interests.[50] The remainder were considered to be under more *coercive* supervision. Farmers and farm workers have been deleted from this analysis. The effects of age, residential pattern, parentyouth relations, and religion are statistically controlled.

Comparison of men by type of supervision indicates that autocratic ideology is likely to occur more widely among middle-class men who work under coercive management. Differences are very inconsistent among manual workers; in three nations, manual workers with benevolent supervision are more apt to be autocratic. In sum, these data provide tentative support for the hypothesized effects of different types of work supervision only among non-manual workers.

Among non-manual workers, the self-employed resemble coercively supervised workers in ideology. Fairly similar proportions espouse an autocratic view regarding participation in family decision making on the part of youth. In addition, the manual and non-manual self-employed tend to differ very little in ideology. This lack of difference is surprising since free professionals and small businessmen have achieved a higher average level of education than the self-employed craftsman.

An Overview. We have examined the effects of age, parent-youth relations, education, residential patterns, religion, occupational status,

49. See Lipset, "Working-Class Authoritarianism," *op. cit.,* and Martin Trow, "Small Businessmen, Political Tolerance, and Support for McCarthy," *American Journal of Sociology,* 64 (November, 1958), 270–281.

50. A clearer test of the consequences of coercive and benevolent supervision would require a more precise specification of coercion which the number of cases does not permit, and an item or two on how the foreman or supervisor reacted to trouble, workers' mistakes, etc. See Hamblin, *op. cit.*

and supervision in work setting on autocratic ideology. Parent-youth relations and formal education are significant factors in the formation of an individual's idea system. Religious affiliation, as an index of the cultural orientation of the home, is also associated with autocratic ideology. With education controlled, Protestants are generally less likely to espouse an autocratic approach in the United States and West Germany than are Catholics. Movement from one sociocultural system to another may lead either to adoption and assimilation of new beliefs, or to retrenchment and a heightening of threatened beliefs. The likelihood of each of these outcomes depends in large part, we hypothesized, on experiences and predispositions acquired in the parent-child relationship. Another stimulus to acceptance of beliefs was explored in the occupational role and in supervision in the work setting. Nonmanual workers with benevolent supervision on the job, and professionals, as well as white collar workers, were least inclined toward autocratic ideology.

These independent variables were assessed more or less serially without an attempt to present a complex multivariate picture. Table 4 shows the main effects of each of the independent variables except education. Since education and occupation overlap to some extent, it was not possible to assess meaningfully the main effects of each factor by using this statistical technique. The main effects of supervision in the work setting were shown in Table 5.

The downward trend in the occurrence of autocratic ideology with decreasing age is still evident in each nation, although the decline shown in Table 1 is substantially reduced. In the three most industrialized nations—United States, Great Britain, and West Germany—the four independent variables markedly reduce the trend by age group: in each nation, the percentage difference between the youngest and oldest age groups is halved or nearly halved. These same factors are much less effective in accounting for age variations in Mexico and Italy, the two nations in which autocratic ideology is most prevalent.[51]

---

51. Level of educational attainment was added to the independent variables in an analysis to determine variation in ideology by age could be more completely explained. The results showed no appreciable reduction in the unexplained variance. In exploratory analysis the crude indexes of educational attainment and occuptional status appear to account for a similiar proportion of the variance in autocratic ideology.

Table 5. Percentage of Males Autocratic in Family Ideology by Supervision in Work Setting with Occupational Status, Parent-Youth Relations, Age and Residence Controlled

Control in the Work Setting	United States		Great Britain		West Germany		Italy		Mexico	
	Non-Manual	Manual	Non-Manual	Manual	Non-Manual	Manual	Non-Manual	Manual	Non-Manual	Manual
Self-employed	12(26)	*	42(52)	*	36(50)	*	56(66)	60(53)	50(67)	47(70)
Benevolent Control	8(34)	20(07)	34(52)	43(107)	28(47)	49(70)	55(28)	76(19)	39(52)	47(84)
Coercive Control	20(35)	32(02)	47(26)	32(117)	31(22)	43(79)	70(34)	70(83)	44(38)	57(77)

Note: Farmers and farm workers are excluded from the analysis. Starred cells contain less than 20 cases.

Religious affiliation and parent-youth relations, as indexes of familial environment, continue to be associated with autocratic ideology when all other factors are controlled. Protestant-Catholic differences are pronounced only in the United States with Catholics more apt to be autocratic than Protestants. As in previous analyses, parent-youth relations are strongly related to ideology in each of the five nations. Variations by this index are greater than by any other factor examined.

18

Continuities and Discontinuities in Childhood Moral Development

L. Kohlberg and R. Kramer

This chapter provides a rich introduction into the ways that moral perspectives develop as a function of age, as a function of sociocultural environments, and as a function of the vicissitudes of life. The differences by social class and by nationality are only one of the matters considered, but these are especially important in indicating that cultures and subcultures differ in more than attitudes and ideology. People from different societies are apt to think differently in the sense of employing different modes of analysis and explanation.

Let us first clarify what child psychology in the Piaget-Werner tradition has meant by "development" and "stage" (Werner, 1948; Piaget, 1964; Kohlberg, 1968). There are three criteria used by the tradition to distinguish psychological development from behavior change in general.

The first criterion is that development involves change in the general shape, pattern, or organization of response, rather than change in the frequency or intensity of emission of an already patterned response. Under reinforcement, bar-pressing increases in frequency; such increase is not development. Under food deprivation, hunger behaviors increase in frequency and intensity; such behavior is not development. With age, sexual impulses wax or wane in intensity. Such changes are not development.

A second criterion, closely related to the first, is that developmental change involves newness, a qualitative difference in response. Developmental change does not have to be sudden or saltatory but it does entail the emergence of a novel structure of response. Novelty involves the quality-quantity distinction, which in turn involves the distinction between form and content. In a sense, any change in content is new. A really new kind of experience, a really new mode of response, however, is one that is different in its form or organization, not simply in the element or the information it contains.

The third criterion implied by the word development is irreversibility. Once a developmental change has occurred, it cannot be reversed by the conditions and experiences which gave rise to it. Learned bar-pressing can be reversed or extinguished by withdrawing the reinforcement which conditioned it. A developmental change cannot. Smedslund (1961) has used this criterion to distinguish cognitive development from associationistic learning. He reports that if a Piaget conservation was taught to a preconserver by instruction and reinforcement, it could be reversed by use of the same mechanisms. Naturally developing conservation could not be reversed by the same procedures. The concept of developmental irreversibility does not rule out the existence of behavior change backward to a previous pattern.

Reprinted from L. Kohlberg and R. Kramer, "Continuities and Discontinuities in Childhood Moral Development," in *Human Development,* 12 (1969), 93–120. Reprinted by permission of the publisher, S. Karger AG Basel/New York, and the authors. Footnotes have been renumbered.

Research supported by NICHD, Grant HD 02469-01.

As an example, seniles and schizophrenics seem to lose the Piaget conservations. Such backward changes are labelled regression; however, it is important to point out that they are rare and their conditions or causes are markedly different from the conditions or causes of forward development.

The three criteria of development just mentioned, plus three others, are involved in the concept of developmental stage. The stage concept not only postulates irreversible qualitative structural change, but in addition postulates a fourth condition that this change occurs in a pattern of universal stepwise invariant sequences. Fifth, the stage concept postulates that the stages form a hierarchy of functioning within the individual. This implies, sixth, that each stage is a differentiation and integration of a set of functional contents present at the prior stage.

Before considering application of the stage concept to adulthood, let me first quickly sketch how the criteria implied by this rigorous conception have been met in child psychology. For obvious reasons, our example will come from our work on stages of moral judgment (Kohlberg, 1958, 1963, 1969). Table I presents a summary characterization of six stages of moral judgment.

Table I. Definition of Moral Stages

I. Preconventional Level

At this level the child is responsive to cultural rules and labels of good and bad, right or wrong, but interprets these labels in terms of either the physical or the hedonistic consequences of action (punishment, reward, exchange of favors) or in terms of the physical power of those who enunciate the rules and labels. The level is divided into the following two stages:

Stage 1: *The punishment and obedience orientation.* The physical consequences of action determine its goodness or badness regardless of the human meaning or value of these consequences. Avoidance of punishment and unquestioning deference to power are valued in their own right, not in terms of respect for an underlying moral order supported by punishment and authority (the latter being Stage 4).

Stage 2: *The instrumental relativist orientation.* Right action consists of that which instrumentally satisfies one's own needs and occasionally the needs of others. Human relations are viewed in terms like those of the market place. Elements of fairness, of reciprocity and equal sharing are present, but they are always interpreted in a physical pragmatic way. Reciprocity is a matter of "you scratch my back and I'll scratch yours," not of loyalty, gratitude, or justice.

II. Conventional Level

At this level, maintaining the expectations of the individual's family, group, or nation is perceived as valuable in its own right, regardless of immediate and obvious consequences. The attitude is not only one of *conformity* to personal expectations and social order, but of loyalty to it, of actively *maintaining,* supporting, and justifying the order and of identifying with the persons or group involved in it. At this level, there are the following two stages:

Stage 3: *The interpersonal concordance or "good boy—nice girl" orientation.* Good behavior is that which pleases or helps others and is approved by them. There is much conformity to stereotypical images of what is majority or "natural" behavior. Behavior is frequently judged by intention—"he means well" becomes important for the first time. One earns approval by being "nice."

Stage 4: *The "law and order" orientation.* There is orientation toward authority, fixed rules, and the maintenance of the social order. Right behavior consists of doing one's duty, showing respect for authority, and maintaining the given social order for its own sake.

III. Post-Conventional, Autonomous, or Principled Level

At this level, there is a clear effort to define moral values and principles which have validity and applications apart from the authority of the groups or persons holding these principles and apart from the individual's own identification with these groups. This level again has two stages:

Stage 5: *The social-contract legalistic orientation* generally with utilitarian overtones. Right action tends to be defined in terms of general individual rights and in terms of standards which have been critically examined and agreed upon by the whole society. There is a clear awareness of the relativism of personal values and opinions and a corresponding emphasis upon procedural rules for reaching consensus. Aside from what is constitutionally and democratically agreed upon, the right is a matter of personal "values" and "opinion." The result is an emphasis upon the "legal point of view," but with an emphasis upon the possibility of changing law in terms of rational considerations of social utility, (rather than freezing it in terms of Stage 4, "law and order"). Outside the legal realm, free agreement, and contract is the binding element of obligation. This is the "official" morality of the American government and Constitution.

Stage 6: *The universal ethical principle orientation.* Right is defined by the decision of conscience in accord with the self-chosen *ethical principles* appealing to logical comprehensiveness, universality, and consistency. These principles are abstract and ethical (the Golden Rule, the categorical imperative); they are not concrete moral rules like the Ten Commandments. At heart, these are universal principles of *justice* of the *reciprocity* and *equality* of the human *rights* and of respect for the dignity of human beings as *individual persons.*

The operational meaning of these stages is suggested by table II with regard to one moral concept, the worth of human life.

Table II. Six Stages in Conceptions of the Moral Worth of Human Life

Stage 1: No differentiation between moral value of life and its physical or social-status value.

Tommy, age ten (Why should the druggist give the drug to the dying woman when her husband couldn't pay for it?): "If someone important is in a plane and is allergic to heights and the stewardess won't give him medicine because she's only got enough for one and she's got a sick one, a friend, in back, they'd probably put the stewardess in a lady's jail because she didn't help the important one."

(Is it better to save the life of one important person or a lot of unimportant people?): "All the people that aren't important because one man just has one house, maybe a lot of furniture, but a whole bunch of people have an awful lot of furniture and some of these poor people might have a lot of money and it doesn't look it."

Stage 2: The value of a human life is seen as instrumental to the satisfaction of the needs of its possessor or of other persons. Decision to save life is relative to, or to be made by, its possessor. (Differentiation of physical and interest value of life, differentiation of its value to self and to other.)

Tommy, age thirteen (Should the doctor "mercy kill" a fatally ill woman requesting death because of her pain?): "Maybe it would be good to put her out of her pain, she'd be better off that way. But the husband wouldn't want it, it's not like an animal. If a pet dies you can get along without it—it isn't something you really need. Well, you can get a new wife, but it's not really the same."

Jim, age thirteen (same question): "If she requests it, it's really up to her. She is in such terrible pain, just the same as people are always putting animals out of their pain."

Stage 3. The value of a human life is based on the empathy and affection of family members and others toward its possessor. (The value of human life, as based on social sharing, community and love, is differentiated from the instrumental and hedonistic value of life applicable also to animals.)

Tommy, age sixteen (same question): "It might be best for her, but her husband—it's a human life—not like an animal, it just doesn't have the same relationship that a human being does to a family. You can become attached to a dog, but nothing like a human you know."

Stage 4: Life is conceived as sacred in terms of its place in a categorical moral or religious order of rights and duties. (The value of human life, as a categorical member of a moral order, is differentiated from its value to specific other people in the family, etc. Value of life is still partly dependent upon serving the group, the state, God, however.)

Jim, age sixteen (same question): "I don't know. In one way, it's murder, it's not a right or privilege of man to decide who shall live and who should die. God put life into everybody on earth and you're taking away something from that person that came directly from God, and you're destroying something that is very sacred, it's in a way part of God and it's almost destroying a part of God when you kill a person. There's something of God in everyone."

Stage 5: Life is valued both in terms of its relation to community welfare and in terms of being a universal human right. (Obligation to respect the basic right to life is differentiated from generalized respect for the socio-moral order. The general value of the independent human life is a primary autonomous value not dependent upon other values.)

Jim, age twenty (same question): "Given the ethics of the doctor who has taken on responsibility to save human life—from that point of view he probably shouldn't but there is another side, there are more and more people in the medical profession who are thinking it is a hardship on everyone, the person, the family, when you know they are going to die. When a person is kept alive by an artificial lung or kidney it's more like being a vegetable than being a human who is alive. If it's her own choice I think there are certain rights and privileges that go along with being a human being. I am a human being and have certain desires for life and I think everybody else does too. You have a world of which you are the center, and everybody else does too and in that sense we're all equal."

Stage 6: Belief in the sacredness of human life as representing a universal human value of respect for the individual. (The moral value of a human being, as an object of moral principle, is differentiated from a formal recognition of his rights.)

Jim, age twenty-four (Should the husband steal the drug to save his wife? How about for someone he just knows?): "Yes. A human life takes precedence over any other moral or legal value, whoever it is. A human life has inherent value whether or not it is valued by a particular individual."

(Why is that?): "The inherent worth of the individual human being is the central value in a set of values where the principles of justice and love are normative for all human relationships."

The concept of human life is valued at each stage. The way in which this value is conceived differs, however, at each stage. In parentheses we indicate the sense in which each higher stage involves a differentiation in thinking about life's values not made at the immediately preceding stage of thought. The sense in which each stage is a new integration is more difficult to define, but will be intuitively evident to you in reading the examples. The table illustrates this one aspect of moral development with responses from two boys in the 10-year longitudinal study. Tommy was first interviewed at 10, and then again at 13, and 16. At 10 he is Stage 1, at 13 Stage 2, at 16 Stage 3. To represent more mature stages we have used Jim.

Jim, when first interviewed at 13, is primarily Stage 2. At 16 he is Stage 4, at 20 Stage 5, at 24 Stage 6 on this aspect. These two boys, then, suggest a sequential pattern holding for each individual. While Tommy is slower in development than Jim and likely will never get as far, both go through the same steps insofar as they move at all. While various statistical qualifications are required in making the generalization, it is true that the pattern of most of our longitudinal data is a pattern of directed irreversible one-step progressions.

We have said that our sequence is invariant for individuals in the United States. Our evidence also suggests that this sequence is culturally universal.

Figure 1a presents age trends for middle-class urban boys in the United States, Taiwan, and Mexico. At age 10 in each country, the order of use of each stage is the same as the order of its difficulty or maturity. In the United States, by age 16 the order is the reverse, from the highest to the lowest, except that Stage 6 is still little used. At age 13, the middle stage (Stage 3) is most used. The results in Mexico and Taiwan are the same, except that development is a little slower. Figure 1b presents similar trends for two isolated villages in Turkey and Yucatan. Here development is slower, but the trends for these far distant villages are very similar to one another.

Let us now turn to the facts of adult development of moral thought (Kramer, 1968, 1969). Some of these are contained in the graphs of Figure 2. Figure 2 shows the percentage usage of each type of thought by our middle class and lower class longitudinal sample at ages 16, 20, and 24. While not all boys were seen at every age, the trends shown fairly represent both longitudinal and cross-sectional trends. The middle-aged group were the fathers of the longitudinal subjects and so comparable to them in all the usual ways.

The first question to be asked is answered by the fact that there is no Stage 7 on the graph. In other words there was no way of thinking about our moral situations found in adulthood and not found in adolescence. While no new modes of moral thought are born in adulthood, there is a not quite significant (p. < 15) increase in Stage 6 thinking from 16 to 24. The figure indicates about twice as much Stage 6 thinking at 24 as at 16. To a certain extent, some of this Stage 6 thinking is new at age 24. Eighty percent of

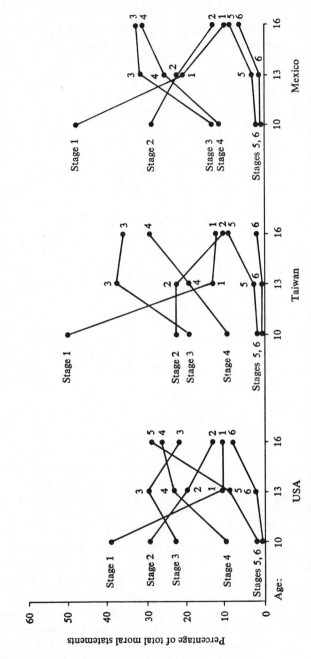

FIGURE 1A. Middle-class urban boys in the U.S., Taiwan and Mexico. At age 10 the stages are used according to difficulty. At age 13, Stage 3 is most used by all three groups. At age 16, U.S. boys have reversed the order of age 10 stages (with the exception of 6). In Taiwan and Mexico, conventional (3-4) stages prevail at age 16, with Stage 5 also little used.

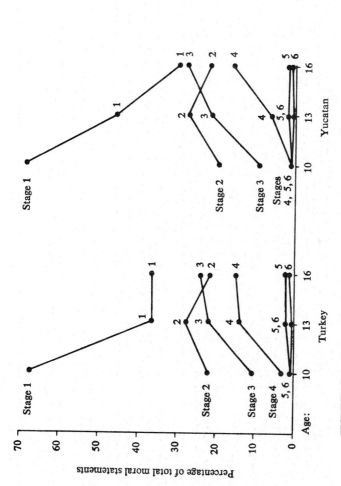

FIGURE 1B. Two isolated villages, one in Turkey, the other in Yucatan show similar patterns in moral thinking. There is no reversal of order, and preconventional (1-2) does not gain a clear ascendancy over conventional stages at age 16.

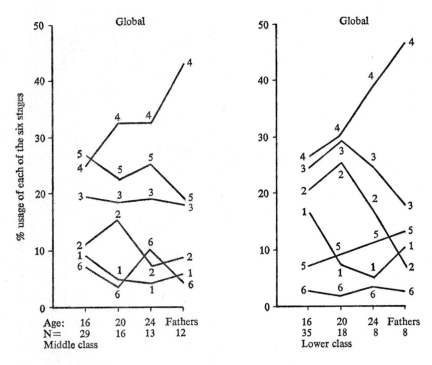

FIGURE 2. Moral judgment profiles (percentage usage of each stage by global rating method) for middle-and lower-class males at four ages. (From Richard Kramer, "Changes in Moral Judgment Response Pattern During Late Adolescence and Young Adulthood," Ph.D. dissertation, University of Chicago, 1968.)

the middle-class high school students who showed no use of Stage 6 thought showed at least a little such thought (5 percent) by age 24. It is difficult to speak very definitely about the development of Stage 6 in our small longitudinal sample because clear Stage 6 types are so rare in every population. Haan, Smith, and Block (1968) found 4 percent of their Bay area college students to be predominantly Stage 6. Holstein (1969) gets about the same percentage in 106 suburban college-educated parents. In our longitudinal sample, we get about the same percentage, amounting to one of our 14 middle-class 24-year-olds. He was predominantly Stage 5 in late high school and early college.

While there is some evidence that Stage 6 thinking can be born or at least stabilized in the post-high school years, principled thought of the Stage 5 variety is pretty completely developed by the end of high school. Figure 2 indicates no clear increase in Stage 5 thinking from high school to age 24. All young adults showing appreciable amounts of Stage 5 thinking (over 15 percent) also showed appreciable (over 15 percent) amounts of Stage 5 thinking in high school. The 25 percent of Stage 5 thinking in our college-educated young adults sample is also about that found in the other studies mentioned. We can summarize our results by saying that principled thought, especially Stage 5, is born in adolescence, but that Stage 6 principled thought tends not to become crystalized until the early 20s. Figure 2 also indicates that little development occurs after the early 20s. Our middle-class college-educated fathers are slightly, but not quite significantly (p. < 20) *lower* on Stage 5 and 6 thought than their sons. Like the young, we put the advantage of the younger generation to social or cultural evolution.[1]

Regardless of the ambiguity of the cross-sectional differences graphed in Figure 2, it is evident that adult development is primarily a matter of dropping out of childish modes of thought rather than the formation of new or higher modes of thought. Figure 2 indicates that the major change in moral thought past high school is a significant increase or stabilization of conventional morality of a Stage 4 variety, at the expenses of preconventional stages of thought. This stabilization of moral thought is not only reflected in the trends of stage usage for the group as a whole, it is also reflected in the trends of variability of stage usage within individuals. . . .

. . . While our data do not present direct evidence for it, there is reason to believe that adult age change is not only toward greater consistency of moral judgment but toward greater consistency between moral judgment and moral action. Hartshorne and May (1928–

---

1. The case for historical or cultural evolution of moral thought, as made by Hobhouse (1906) is well thought through. Its appeal at the moment is enhanced by the relative position of the generations about the universal moral issues of war. The writer finds no reason to find generational increase in moral level more surprising than the documented generational increases in general intelligence. Recent longitudinal findings (Bayley, 1955) indicate historical or cohort increases in intelligence in adulthood masked by cross-sectional estimates. We would not be surprised to find a similar masking in our cross-sectional comparison of our subjects and their fathers.

1930) found that in the period 11 to 14, there was no decline in cheating behavior but there was a decline in the inconsistency of cheating behavior. With age some children became more consistently honest, some more consistently dishonest, leaving a net mean amount of cheating that was constant. Comparison of cheating studies in preadolescence and in college suggests that not only is cheating behavior more consistent in college but it is more consistently related to level of moral judgment in college than in preadolescence (Kohlberg, 1969). These fragments of data on consistency suggest support for the folk wisdom which proclaims that the middle aged are more reliable or trustworthy than the young, even if they seem less given to expressing lofty moral ideals in either words or heroic action.

Adult stabilization is not adult development. We could dignify an increase in the consistency of moral ideology with itself and with moral action under the name of integration, the integration of moral thought with itself and with one's self-concept. One reason we hesitate to do so is because much adult moral stabilization seems to be not development but socialization or internalization of the conventional code. This is suggested by the fact that conventional (Stage 4), as well as post-conventional, moral ideologies stabilize in adulthood. There is no Babbitt like an old Babbitt.

While the Babbitts become even more conventional with age, to some extent so do the deviants and the rebels. One of the best predictors for parole is chronological age. Old criminals get burnt out and learn that you can't beat the system. The interpretation that adult moral stabilization is 'socialization' not 'development' is further suggested by the fact that the breed of conventional morality which stabilizes in adulthood depends upon one's adult social sex role. Only 6 percent of our Stage 3 boys in high school remained Stage 3 in young adulthood, the rest having moved to Stage 4. In contrast, Stage 3 appears to be a stable adult stage for women. At high school there are about the same percentage of Stage 3 boys and girls (Turiel, 1969). In the Bay area college population of Haan, Smith, and Block (1968) there are about twice as large a percentage of Stage 3 girls as boys. Among the parent samples of Holstein (1969), the difference is even more marked, about four times as many Stage 3 women as men. In other words, while girls are moving from high school or college to motherhood, sizeable proportions of them remaining at Stage 3, while their male age mates are dropping Stage 3 in favor of the stages above it. Stage 3 personal concordance morality is a functional morality for housewives and mothers; it is not for businessmen and professionals.

Adult moral stabilization, then, appears to be more a matter of increased congruence between belief and social role than of novel integration of experience. As such, it appears to be more like "socialization" or "social learning" than development. As we have discussed at length elsewhere (Kohlberg, 1968), there is plenty of evidence that while the ordinary mechanisms of social learning (repetition, reinforcement, observational learning) or of attitude change (dissonance reduction) cannot cause or explain structural development, they can cause or explain the strengthening or weakening of "naturally" or "structurally" developing systems of response, a strengthening or weakening that seems to be what we have discussed as "stabilization." [See Chapter 6 in this volume.—EDITOR]

Before dismissing adult functional stabilization as "socialization," however, it will pay to examine the most dramatic finding of the Kramer study. This finding seems to fit neither our generalization that adult change is functional stabilization nor our earlier generalization that developmental change is forward and sequential. These generalizations hold true for our longitudinal subjects at every age and social class with one exception, the college sophomore. That paradigm of the psychological study of the normal, the college sophomore, turns out to be the oddest and most interesting moral fish of all. Between late high school and the second or third year of college, 20 percent of our middle class sample dropped or retrogressed in moral maturity scores. Retrogression was defined as a drop in maturity scores greater than any found in a two-month-test-retest sample. This drop had a definite pattern. In high school 20 percent who dropped were among the most advanced in high school, all having a mixture of conventional (Stage 4) and principled (Stage 5) thought. In their college sophomore phase, they kicked both their conventional and their Stage 5 morality and replaced it with good old Stage 2 hedonistic relativism, jazzed up with some philosophic and sociopolitical jargon. An example of a college Stage 2 response is given in table III along with Stage 2 responses by children and delinquents which are structurally similar to it.

Table III. Examples of Sophisticated and Unsophisticated Stage 2 Responses to One Story

Story III. American

In Europe, a woman was near death from a very bad disease, a special kind of cancer. There was one drug that the doctors thought might save her. It was a form of radium that a druggist in the same town had recently discovered. The drug was expensive to make, but the druggist was charging ten times what the drug cost him to make. He paid $200 for the radium and charged $2,000 for a small dose of the drug. The sick woman's husband, Heinz, went to everyone he knew to borrow the money, but he could only get together about $1,000 which is half of what it cost. He told the druggist that his wife was dying, and asked him to sell it cheaper or let him pay later. But the druggist said, "No, I discovered the drug and I'm going to make money from it." So Heinz got desperate and broke into the man's store to steal the drug for his wife.

Should the husband have done that? Why?

Guide for Scoring Story III at Stage 2—as oriented to instrumental necessity of stealing:

1. *Value.* "The ends justify the means." Says has to, is best to, or is right to steal, to prevent wife from dying. (Without implication that saving the wife is a good deed.)

2. *Choice.* Little conflict in *decision to steal.* Implies decision is based on instrumental reasoning or impulse.

3. *Sanction.* Little concern about punishment, or punishment may be avoided by repayment, etc.

4. *Rule.* Little concern about stealing in this situation. May see stealing in this situation as not hurting the druggist.

5. *Husband role.* Orientation to a family member or a relative whom one needs and is identified with. May be an act of exchange, but not of sacrifice or duty.

6. *Injustice.* Druggist's "cheating" makes it natural to steal. However, not actually indignant at the druggist, who may be seen as within his rights to charge whatever he wants.

Roger (age 20, a Berkeley Free Speech Movement student)

He was a victim of circumstances and can only be judged by other men whose varying value and interest frameworks produce subjective decisions which are neither permanent nor absolute. The same is true of the druggist. I'd do it. As far as duty, a husband's duty is up to the husband to decide, and anybody can judge him, and he can judge anybody's judgment. If he values her life over the consequences of theft, he should do it.

(Did the druggist have a right?) One can talk about rights until doomsday and never say anything. Does the lion have a right to the zebra's life when he starves? When he wants sport? Or when he will take it at will? Does he consider rights? Is man so different?

(Should he be punished by the judge?) All this could be avoided if the people would organize a planned economy. I think the judge should let him go, but if he does, it will provide less incentive for the poorer people to organize.

John (age 17, reform school inmate)

Should the husband steal the drug for his wife? I would eliminate that into whether he wanted to or not. If he wants to marry someone else, someone young and good-looking, he may not want to keep her alive.

(How about the law, he is asked): He replies, The laws are made by the rich, by cowards to protect themselves. Here we have a law against killing people but we think it's all right to kill animals. In India you can't. Why should it be right to kill people but not animals? You can make anything right or wrong. To me what is right is to follow your own natural instincts.

Hamza (Turkish village, age 12)

Yes, because nobody would give him the drug and he had no money, because his wife was dying it was right.

(Is it a husband's duty to steal the drug?) Yes—when his wife is dying and he cannot do anything he is obliged to steal. If he doesn't steal his wife will die.

(Does the druggist have the right to charge that much for the drug?) Yes, because he is the only store in the village it is right to sell.

(Should he steal the drug if he doesn't love his wife?) If he doesn't love his wife he should not steal because he doesn't care for her, doesn't care for what she says.

(How about if it is a good friend?) Yes—because he loves his friend and one day when he is hungry his friend will help him.

(Should the judge punish him?) They should put him in jail because he stole.

Jimmy (American city, age 10)

It depends on how much he loved his wife. He should if he does.

(If he doesn't love her much?) If he wanted her to die, I don't think he should.

(Would it be right to steal it?) In a way it's right because he knew his wife would die if he didn't and it would be right to save her.

(Does the druggist have the right to charge that much, if no law?) Yes, it's his drug, look at all he's got invested in it.

(Should the judge punish?) He should put him in jail for stealing and he should put the druggist in because he charged so much and the drug didn't work.

The college response is that of a new left Bay area student, from the Haan, Smith, and Block (1968) study. Very similar statements are made by new right Ayn Rand objectivist students. Our Stage 2 longitudinal college subjects had similar ideologies but without extremist sociopolitical affiliations, except for one self-defined Nietzschean racist, a Chicagoan who went to a Southern all-white college.

In terms of behavior, every one of our retrogressed subjects had high moral character ratings in high school, as defined by both teachers and peers. In college at least half had engaged in anti-conventional acts of a more or less delinquent sort. As an example, our Nietzschean racist had been the most respected high school student council president in years. In his college sophomore interview, however, he told how two days before he had stolen a gold watch from a friend at work. He had done so, he said, because his friend was just too good, too Christ-like, too trusting, and he wanted to teach him what the world was like. He felt no guilt about the stealing, he said, but he did feel frustrated. His act had failed, he said, because his trusting friend insisted he lost or mislaid the watch and simply refused to believe it had been stolen. This personal moral rebellion in the behavior of college Stage 2 men must be added to the picture of political protest behavior of Stage 2 college men provided by the Haan, Smith, and Block (1968) study.

Now if the mysterious forces of development have led our 20 percent from upstanding conventional morality to Raskolnikov moral defiance, these same mysterious forces set them all to right. Every single one of our retrogressors had returned to a mixed Stage 4 and 5 morality by age 24, with a little more 5 or social contract principle, a little less 4 or convention, than at high school. All, too, are conventionally conforming in behavior, at least as far as we can observe them. In sum, this 20 percent was among the highest group at high school, was the lowest in college and again among the highest at 24. The correlation of moral maturity from age 16 to age 24 is .89, the correlations from high school to college and of college to 24 are only .41.[2]

In what sense is the story just told, the story of rebellious use of lower stages followed by a return to the suburbs of conventional-principled moral stabilization, a story of development? Our interpretation of this story allows us to consider the sense in which the universal stabilization of morality in adulthood may be a form of adult development, even if it is not the structural transformation of moral thought itself. By focussing upon the dramatic cases of stabilization involving retrogression, rather than the placid cases of stabilization which look like ordinary socialization and social learning, we may perhaps arrive at an answer to the question. The first point in our argument is that the retrogression of our subjects is more like a functional regression than it is like a structural regression. While our retrogressors choose to use Stage 2 relativistic egoism, they have not lost their earlier capacity to Stage 4 and Stage 5 thinking. This is evidenced by three facts. First, the retrogressors continue to use a little Stage 4 and 5 thinking. Second, when asked to give what the world would consider a high moral response to our stories, the retrogressors tend to give straight Stage 4 responses. Third, the fact that the retrogressors eventually return to Stage 4 and 5 strongly suggests that these stages were never lost. In contrast to this group there do appear to be some groups in which cases of genuine structural regression in adulthood can be found. We have found adults who were pure Stage 1, pure Stage 2, or combinations of Stage 1 and 2 among schizophrenics, among people over 65, and among incarcerated criminals. The schizophrenics were college educated, currently functioning well on psychometric tests of intelligence and preparing to leave the hospital. The criminals were in our longitudinal sample and had shown some Stage 3 and 4 thinking earlier. The elderly were college

2. The pattern of correlations I have just discussed is pointed to in Marjorie Honzik's paper in this symposium as the adolescent sleeper effect, an effect not unique to the moral area.

educated, and intact in intelligence according to norms for their age. While interviews of these cases did not use the methods of testing the limits for structural capacity or understanding of higher stages we have recently developed (Rest, 1968) they give an overwhelming impression of unawareness of alternative or higher points of view which contrast with our college retrogressors.

If the regression of our college sophomores is functional, not structural, does it fit formulations of ego-psychology about "regression in the service (function) of the ego"? One way of stating this question is provided by a graduate student, who proclaimed in a seminar that Stage 7 is reached when you can use all six stages for whatever you want. This student formulates regression in the service of the ego "as a way of life," and ends up advocating plain old regression to Stage 2. Surely, when we cut through the cloudy lofty aura of such words as "identity," "self-realization," "authenticity" which hover around the ego, we must recognize that an ego which uses moral values for whatever it pleases is just our good old instrumentally egoistic, manipulating Stage 2 ego.[3] Moral "regression in the service of the ego" is not the usual law of life. It is true that everyone seems to share our retrogressors' capacity to fall back upon lower stages. Rest (1968) has demonstrated that the capacity to comprehend and (less clearly) to use lower stages of thinking remains, even where these lower stages are never used spontaneously in response to moral problems. He has also demonstrated, however, that the polymorphous-perverse flexibility of stage usage called Stage 7 by the graduate student, the use of various stages for whatever you want, is extremely uncharacteristic of adolescents. In spontaneous usage, people are quite consistent from situation to situation in use of a modal stage and the stages immediately adjacent to them (Kohlberg, 1969). In confronting the moral judgments of others, people prefer the highest level they can comprehend (Rest, 1968;

3. There is a sense in which there is morally "legitimate" regression of moral thought in the service of the ego. The hierarchy of moral stages is only hierarchy in moral situations. No one uses Stage 6 thinking in bargaining in an Oriental marketplace, anymore than does anyone use Piaget formal operations to drive a car or paint a picture. The capacity to write a compelling novel or to tell a good off-color joke depends upon using lower stages of moral thinking; the inability to think lowerstage thoughts is the mark of the prig.

Rest, Turiel, and Kohlberg, 1968). In a sense, the kind of adult change we called stabilization is exactly a further increase in consistency of response, a further decline in moral regression in the service of the ego.

In summary, while there is nothing unusual in our retrogressors' capacity to use lower stages of thought, their actual usage of such thinking is not evidence of a general human tendency toward regression in the service of the ego. It is not an adaptive bending to particular social situational presses in the service of some general ego needs.

The fact that awareness of relativism constitutes a universal developmental challenge or task for men attending a college with some claims to intellectual standing is clearly documented by the work of Perry (1968). In the case of our retrogressors, there is considerable use of relativism and of anti-moral protest to free themselves from familiarly induced guilt. At least half of our regressors gave conscious and clear statements of strong sensitivity to and preoccupation with guilt feelings in preadolescence and adolescence. In this pre-regression period, the guilt was completely accepted as the voice of higher morality, as something self-accepted and internal. At the same time, the capacity of the boy's parents to inflict this sense of guilt was also noted by the boys. After they left home, they started to test out their capacity to be guilt-free. The most striking example was the Nietzschean who stole the watch from his friend. We labelled him "Raskolnikov" with good reason. Like Raskolnikov's crime, his crime was an effort to prove that the strong need not be moral, and that the good were good only out of stupidity and weakness. Like Raskolnikov's crime, his crime too was an effort to prove that he need never feel (or fear) guilt (Kohlberg, 1963). After the theft he kept remarking that it was strange, but he felt no guilt. Four years later, after his return to the fold, he spontaneously announced that he had later felt guilt about it. The use of relativism by young men, then, is similar to that noted by Perry (1968, p. 137). "The reactive students, in becoming aware of intellectual and moral relativism, see authorities as imperialistically extending their prejudices over the underdog's rightful freedom, and engage in a fight against the constraint of (unwarranted) guilt. Consider the conventional misuse of cultural relativism, 'Since it's all right for the Trobriand islanders to do thus and so, you have no right to make me feel guilty about it. It's purely a matter of individual decision.' Far from being amoral, such pronouncements are made in a tone of moralistic absolutism, which reveals its emotional continuity with the earlier absolutistic structures" (which we term Stage 4).

While using relativism to free themselves from guilt, our retro-gressors are equally upset at relativism and deviance, i.e. at the disappearance of the moral world they believed in childhood. Our regressors are acutely aware of the breakdown of their expectations of a conventional moral world in the college environment. When they left high school, they thought that people lived by conven-tional morality and that their rewards in life depended on living that way, too. In college, they tell us, they learned that people did not live in terms of morality, and that if they did, they weren't re-warded for it. As one college Stage 2 said in explaining his "re-gressive" shift: "College accounts for the change. You see what a dog-eat-dog world it is. Everyone seems to be out for himself. When you live at home you're always trying to please your parents. You don't notice it, but in some way you are. Now I hang around with guys I don't try to please."

Related to this theme is the theme that morality doesn't get you ahead. This boy says, "I'd try to get as far as I can without becoming totally dishonest."

The "oppositional" quality of our regressor's moral ideology is, then, as much to be understood as being a protest against the im-morality of the world as it is a protest against the authoritarian morality of parental figures.

There are, then, two developmental challenges to conventional morality to which our regressors are unhappily responding. The first is the relativity of moral expectations and opinion; the second is the gap between conventional moral expectations and actual moral be-havior. Now it is clear that these developmental challenges are uni-versal general challenges. The integration of one's moral ideology with the facts of moral diversity and inconsistency is a general "developmental task" of youth in an open society. So, too, are the more "psychodynamic" problems faced by our regressors—the prob-lems of freeing themselves from childhood moral expectations and childhood moral guilt. While "psychodynamic," these conflicts are neither unusual nor pathological. Who has not desired to free him-self from parentally induced guilt, who has not faced the shocks of finding there are no rewards for being a good boy or girl? The conflicts of our regressors differ only in quantity, not in quality, from our own.

If the challenges which our retrogressors face are universal, in what sense can their responses to them be said to be "development"? We shall contend that our retrogressors are in a sense taking a developmental step forward, even though this step is reflected in a lower stage. We shall further contend that in "returning" to their high school pattern of Stage 4 and Stage 5 thought, they are not simply reverting to an earlier pattern, retreating to the suburbs after the failure of rebellion, but are taking a still further developmental step forward.

In discussing these changes as development, we shall first cast them in Erikson's (1950) familiar terms. In such terms, our retrogressors are living in a late adolescent psycho-social moratorium, in which new and nonconforming patterns of thought and behavior are tried out. Their return to the high school pattern of moral thought is the eventual confirmation of an earlier identification as one's own "identity." To find a socio-moral identity requires a rebellious moratorium, because it requires liberation of intiative from the guilt which our retrogressors suffer from. At the "stage" of identity the adult conforms to his standards because he wants to, not because he anticipates crippling guilt if he does not.

In introducing such terminology, we are indicating that late adolescent or adult moral changes reflect ego development rather than representing the development of morality or moral stage structures itself. Our moral stages are hierarchical structures for fulfilling the the function of moral judgment. Ego development in the moral sphere is learning how to use the moral structures one has for one's personal integration. From this point of view, modes of moral thought are structures developed in childhood, but the uses of these modes of thought, their significance for the individual self are matters for late adolescent development. Until late adolescence, the child lives within a world he did not make and in which the choices he must make are circumscribed. His moral ideology is not a direct reflection of his home-school-class-nation environment; it is his own construction designed to make sense of it. However, use of his moral ideology in childhood is primarily to fit and make sense of his given world, not to guide him in autonomous choice. It gives him a rationale for accepting and conforming to the bulk of the patterns of his home, his peer group, his school. This rationale also allows him to reject some patterns in his environment, his world. It does not lead him to question or reject his entire world, however.

The early adolescent's characteristic pattern is either to protest or to secretly deviate from the particular rejected pattern, but to place it in the context of a world he must accept. Sometimes in the back of the conventionally moral high school boy's mind is the notion that he is "putting in time" in the family and the high school until he can live a free life in terms of his own values and desires. While the adolescent may see a free life as a living out of hedonistic values, he may at the same time look forward to the opportunity to live or act in terms of sacrifice to higher moral principles, to give a moral meaning to his life in a way he cannot within the conventional structures of family and school.

Erikson has made us familiar with the fact that Western society provides the post-high-school student with a psycho-social moratorium which allows him to live out either hedonistic or morally idealistic impulses (reflected in anything from life in protest groups to life in the Peace Corps) with a freedom he has neither earlier nor later in life. This moratorium comes to an end when inner establishment of an identity or outer pressure to take responsibility in a role of work and parenthood leads the individual to a commitment to a pattern of values which "works" within a definite social world. The restraint which results from adult role commitment differs vastly from the childhood restraint which comes from a dependent acceptance of such a world. They share in common, however, the acceptance of a core set of rules required to keep a social group or system going.

Neither the egoism of Stage 2 relativism of our retrogressors, nor its pretentious world-changing "idealism" will keep a social world of responsibility for other people going. It is not, of course, that our retrogressors' moral code does not work at all—it can work to the extent of creating social movements—but it does not work if these movements are to become worlds of life-long responsibility and commitment. When the communist movement became an enduring one, it lost its orientation toward the pursuit of happiness and human equality and hardened into a Stage 4 morality of party loyalty as an absolute value. Our retrogressors' "return to the suburbs" of contractual (Stage 5) and conventional (Stage 4) rules is not, then, a defeat. It is not so much that Stage 2 Yippie or Hippie or objectivism is tried and found not to work as it is that our late adolescent retrogressors were in a moratorium in which they didn't care about having an ideology that "worked," that formed a foundation for life-long responsibility or commitment.

Not only is the retrogressor's return not a defeat, but it clearly brings something to conventional contractual morality which is in some sense a developmental advance. When the retrogressors return to a morality of contract and rules, they do so with less distortive idealization of their own group and authority system, and with greater tolerance and realism about those who deviate from it or are outside of it.

The formulation we have just made is inadequate. We have superimposed developmental task "stages" of ego function in adulthood upon childhood stages of moral structure and claimed structural regression was functional advance. Obviously, such an attempt to have one's cake and eat it too is inadequate. A sequel to the paper attempts to correct this inadequacy by defining ego "stages" in terms of metaethical theories and world views, in contrast to moral stages which are normative ethical theories for making moral judgments in specific moral conflict situations. For the moment, however, our formulation allows us to approproximate some conclusions about the relations between childhood and adult moral development.

Moral development involves a continual process of matching a moral view to one's experience of life in a social world. Experiences of conflict in this process generate movement from structural stage to structural stage. Even after attainment of the highest stage an individual will reach, there is continued experience of conflict. The developmental product of such conflict is stabilization, i.e. a greater consistency of structure with itself (greater stage "purity") and a greater consistency between thought structure and action. The evidence that adult stabilization is the integration of conflict rather than "social learning" or socialization, is indicated by our finding one pattern of adult stabilization that involves temporary retrogression. The integration of conflict in adult development may be conceived in terms of functional "stages" of ego development which are quite different from structural stages. While we have discussed only moral change at the "ego stage" of late adolescent identity, the moral changes in late adulthood of the Tolstoys or the Saint Pauls presumably could be discussed in the same general terms.

There is, then, a sense in which there is adult moral development. There is an adult movement toward integration of moral thought in its application to life. There may even be typical phases in this integrative process. There are, however, no adult stages in the structural sense, and accordingly no clear solution to the two problems of adult development which we initially posed. We cannot integrate childhood and adult moral development into a single theoretical series or sequence of stages. Nor can we claim that adulthood has a moral wisdom denied to the youth. While structural stages involve a logic of responsiveness to the next stage up, this is not true of ego functional stages. . . .

References

Bayley, N. "On the growth of intelligence," *American Psychologist,* 10 (1955), 805–818.

Erikson, E. *Childhood and Society.* New York: Norton, 1950.

Haan, Norma, M. Brewster Smith, and Jeanne Block. "Moral reasoning of young adults: political-social behavior, family background, and personality correlates, *J. Person. Soc. Psychol.,* 10 (1968), 183–201.

Hartshorne, H., and M. A. May. *Studies in the Nature of Character,* 3 vols. New York: Macmillan, 1928–1930.

Hobhouse, L. T. *Morals in Evolution.* London: Chapman and Hall, 1906.

Holstein, C.: "The relation of children's moral judgment to that of their parents and to communication patterns in the family." Unpublished dissertation, University of California, Berkeley, 1969.

Kohlberg, L. "Psychological analysis and literary forms. A study of the doubles in Dostoevsky," *Daedalus,* 92 (1963), 345–363.

Kohlberg, L. "Stage and sequence: the cognitive-developmental approach to socialization," in David A. Goslin, ed., *Handbook of Socialization Theory and Research.* Chicago: Rand McNally, 1968.

Kohlberg, L. *Stages in the Development of Moral Thought and Action.* New York: Holt, Rinehart, 1969.

Kramer, R. "Moral development in young adulthood." Unpublished doctoral dissertation, University of Chicago, 1968.

Kramer, R. "Progression and regression in adolescent moral development," *Soc. Res. Child Development,* Santa Monica, March 26, 1969.

Perry, W. "Forms of intellectual and ethical development in the college years," mimeographed monograph, Bureau at Study Counsel, Harvard University, 1968.

Piaget, J. "Cognitive development in children," in R. Ripple and V. Rockcastle, *Piaget Rediscovered: A Report on Cognitive Studies in Curriculum Development*. Ithaca, N. Y.: Cornell University School of Education, 1964.

Rest, J. "Developmental hierarchy in preference and comprehension of moral judgment." Unpublished doctoral dissertation, University of Chicago, 1968.

Rest, J., E. Turiel, and L. Kohlberg. "Level of moral development as a determinant of preference and comprehension of moral judgments made by others," *J. Pers.*, 37 (1969), 225–252.

Smedslund, J. "The acquisition of conservation of substance and weight in children," *Scandinavian J. Psychol.*, 2 (1961), 85–87, 156–160, 203–210.

Turiel, E. "Developmental processes in the child's moral thinking," in P. H. Mussen, J. Langer, and M. Covington, eds., *New Directions in Developmental Psychology*. New York: Holt, Rinehart, 1969.

Werner, H. *The Comparative Psychology of Mental Development*. Chicago: Wilcox and Follett, 1948.

19

A Cognitive-Style Approach to Cross-Cultural Research

Herman A. Witkin

Cultural differences extend far beyond our usual levels of awareness. This chapter is concerned with field independence and field dependence, a variable that relates literally to the way we see things. Witkin discusses a variety of issues relevant to this trait, but in particular, he shows that people from different cultures do exhibit substantially different levels of field independence.

Perception may be conceived as articulated, in contrast to global, if the person is able to preceive item as discrete from organized ground when the field is structured (analysis), and to impose structure on a field, and so perceive it as organized, when the field has little inherent organization (structuring). . . .

Extensive research (Witkin, Lewis, Hertzman, Machover, Meissner, and Wapner, 1954; Witkin et al., 1962) has shown that a tendency toward more global or more articulated functioning is a consistent feature of a given individual's manner of dealing with a wide array of perceptual and intellectual tasks. Because it represents the characteristic approach which the person brings to situations with him, we consider more global or more articulated functioning to be an individual's cognitive *style*. Research has shown that persons with an articulated cognitive style are also likely to give evidence of an articulated body concept and a developed sense of separate identity. Another way of casting these findings is to say that the person who experiences the field around him in relatively articulated fashion is also likely to show an articulated quality in experience which has body or self as its source. An articulated cognitive style, an articulated body concept and a sense of separate identity are all taken as indicators of developed differentiation. It has been demonstrated in many studies that persons who show these indicators of developed differentiation also show greater differentiation in their tendency to use structured, specialized defenses and controls, as intellectualization and isolation, for channeling of impulse and expenditure of energy. In contrast, persons with a global cognitive style, and with it a global body concept and a limited sense of separate identity, are likely to use such defenses as massive repression and primitive denial; because these defenses involve a relatively indiscriminate turning away from perception of stimuli and memory for past experiences, they represent rela-

Abridged from Herman A. Witkin, "A Cognitive-Style Approach to Cross-Cultural Research," in *International Journal of Psychology*, 2 (1967), 233–250. Reprinted by permission of the International Union of Psychological Science, DUNOD, Publisher, France, and the author. Footnotes have been renumbered.

Expanded from a paper presented at a symposium on Intercultural Studies of Mental Development, at the International Congress of Psychology, Moscow, August, 1966. Portions of the work described in this paper were supported by a grant (M-628) from the United States Public Health Service, National Institutes of Health.

tively nonspecific, and hence relatively less differentiated ways of functioning.

Assessment of Cognitive Style

From the extensive research done on the global-articulated dimension, specific tests are available which evaluate this dimension in both perception and intellectual activity and which consider both the analytical and structuring aspects of articulation. Most widely used are the tests which assess the analytical aspect of the dimension in perception. These are tests of perceptual *field dependence-independence,* described in detail in Witkin et al., 1962. In a field dependent mode of perception, the organization of the field as a whole dominates perception of its parts; an item within a field is experienced as fused with organized ground. In a field independent mode of perception, the person is able to perceive items as discrete from the organized field of which they are a part. The field dependence-independence dimension is a continuous one, most persons falling between these two extremes. One test of field dependence is the rod-and-frame test. The subject is seated in a completely darkened room and adjusts a luminous rod, contained within a tilted luminous square frame, to a position he perceives as upright, while the frame remains at its initial position of tilt. In a relatively field dependent performance the rod is adjusted close to the axes of the tilted frame. In a relatively field independent performance the rod is adjusted independently of the frame, and brought close to the true upright through reference to body position. A second test of field dependence is the embedded-figure test. Here the subject must locate a previously seen simple geometric figure within a complex figure designed to embed it. Some subjects quickly break up the complex figure in order to find the simple figure within it; this is a field independent performance. For other subjects, at the opposite extreme, the simple figure seems to remain "fused" with the complex organized design; they take a good deal of time to "tease out" the simple figure. Finally, in the body-adjustment test, the subject, seated in a tilted room, must adjust his own body to the upright while the room remains tilted. Some subjects require that the body be more or less aligned with the room, tilted at 35°, in order for the body to be perceived as straight. In this field dependent way of performing perception of body position is dominated in an extreme degree by the axes of the surrounding field. Other subjects, whose perception is field independent, seem able to keep body separate from field in experience and to adjust the body close to the upright independently of room position.

Individuals show a high degree of consistency in performance across these three tests (Wilkin et al., 1954, 1962). A tendency to perform in a relatively field dependent or field independent fashion is also a highly stable feature of an individual's cognitive functioning over time, in one study (Witkin, Goodenough, and Karp, 1967) over a 14-year span (10 to 24 years of age) covering a period of considerable psychological growth. In pinpointing further the nature of the field dependence-independence dimension, it is important to comment on its relation to intelligence. Performance in tests of field dependence has been found to show only a low level of relation to scores on a verbal-comprehension cluster (Vocabulary, Information, and Comprehension) and an attention-concentration cluster (Digit Span, Arithmetic, and Coding) of Wechsler sub-tests. Field dependence measures relate very highly to scores on a triumvirate of Weschsler intelligence scale sub-tests (Block Design, Object Assembly, and Picture Completion) which tap the same kind of analytical ability as do the tests of field dependence. Thus, the field dependence dimension is represented by performance on portions of standard intelligence tests. The Block Design in fact provides an excellent measure of field dependence, and it has been used for this purpose in several of the cross-cultural studies to be considered.

Another technique, the figure-drawing test, which should be mentioned here because of its potential value in cross-cultural work, does not assess perception but articulation of body concept, which, as suggested, is another important indicator of differentiation. Ratings of articulation of figure drawing according to a five-point "sophistication-of-body-concept scale" (described in Witkin et al., 1962) have repeatedly been shown to relate quite highly to measures of field dependence. Because it is easy to obtain figure drawings and to score them reliably for articulation, the figure-drawing technique has often been used to evaluate the same broad differentiation dimension which tests of field dependence seek to assess. Drawings rated most articulated on the sophistication-of-body-concept scale show such characteristics as high form level, representation of appendages and details in realistic relation to body outline, representation of role and sex. Drawings rated as least articulated show such characteristics as very low form level (body in form of ovals, rectangles, sticks) and lack of evidence of role or sex identity.

Studies of the Relation Between Cognitive Style and Family Experiences in Western Settings

The initial investigations of family experiences (Witkin et al., 1962; Dyk and Witkin, 1965) were done with children growing up in a large urban center (New York City), and focused particularly on mother-child interactions. In the first of a progression of studies we used as subjects a group of 10-year-old boys and their mothers. The boys were assessed for cognitive style and for extent of differentiation in other areas of functioning; and the nature of these boys' relations to their mothers was explored through interviews with the mothers. Overall ratings were made of the mother-child interactions in terms of whether, *in toto,* they appeared to have fostered the development of differentiation or to have interfered with its development. These ratings were anchored to a number of specific indicators or clues, which fall into three categories, together covering the "socialization" cluster described earlier: (1) Indicators concerned with separation from mother. Included here were five indicators which, stated in terms of hampering of separation, were: *a.* Mother's physical care is not appropriate to child's age; *b.* Mother limits child's activity and his movement into the community because of her own fears and anxieties for the child or ties to him; *c.* Mother regards her child as delicate, in need of special attention or protection, or as irresponsible; *d.* Mother does not accept a masculine role for her child; *e.* Mother limits the child's curiosity and stresses conformity. (2) Indicator concerned with nature of control over aggressive, assertive behavior in the child. This indicator was: Mother's control is not in the direction of the child's achieving mature goals and becoming responsible, or is consistently directed against the child asserting himself. Specific patterns illustrative of this mode of control are: administration of discipline arbitrarily and impulsively, with the use of irrational threats to control aggression; submissive, indulgent maternal behavior; wavering by the mother between indulgent and coercive behavior. The child's development of controls is likely to be hampered when the mother is unable to set limits for her child or to help him identify and internalize a set of values and standards. (3) Indicators concerned with personal characteristics of the mother which may influence her role in the separation process and in the impulse-regulation process. The two indicators were: *a.* Mother does not have assurance in herself in raising her child. Lack of self-assurance hampers a mother's ability to define her role as a mother, and, accordingly, her ability to help her child identify himself as a separate person. It is also likely to make it difficult for the mother to set and maintain limits, thereby interfering with the child's achievement of self-regulation; *b.* Mother does not have a feeling of self-realization in her own life. A mother who lacks a sense of self-realization is less able to allow her child to separate from her and to develop as an individual in his own right.

Ratings made of mother-child interactions, guided by these indicators, showed a picture of significant correlations with measures of differentiation for the child. Thus, boys who were field independent and gave evidence of an articulated body concept, a developed sense of separate identity, and a tendency to use specialized, structured defenses tended to have mothers who were judged to have interacted with them in ways that had fostered differentiation. The impression gained from the interviews that mothers of more differentiated and less differentiated boys differed in particular personal characteristics was in general supported when the mothers themselves were assessed by some of the techniques used to assess differentiation in their children. Less differentiated boys were found likely to have mothers who were also less differentiated. It is plausible that mothers who have some of the personal qualities implied by limited differentiation should be handicapped in helping their children separate from them. The finding that relatively more differentiated boys are likely to have relatively more differentiated mothers has been confirmed by Seder (1957) and by Corah (1965).

Cross-Cultural Studies

The initial studies in which patterns of mother-child interactions associated with cognitive style and level of differentiation were first identified were done with families from a large urban setting, predominately Jewish and middle class. The relations observed do not seem limited to this particular kind of social group, however. For example, in the study by Seder (1957) the families were from a small suburb of Boston, in the United States, middle class, and of diversified religious backgrounds. The studies to be considered now suggest that the patterns of parent-child interactions we originally found to be associated with a more global or more articulated cognitive style, and with greater or more limited differentiation, in fact hold under a very wide range of social conditions; and they provide additional validation of our original findings.

A Study of Temne and Mende, by Dawson

Dawson (1963, 1967) carried out a study with adult male subjects in Sierra Leone, Africa. He examined individual cognitive functioning in relation to family experiences and compared cognitive style in tribal groups differing in child-rearing practices. From the American investigations, specific hypotheses were available as guides to the study. To assess field dependence, Dawson used the embedded-figures test, abbreviated and adapted in its administration to the Sierra Leone group, as well as the Kohs Block Design test. The first hypothesis tested by Dawson was that relatively field dependent men would more likely have mothers who exercised strict dominant control in rearing them, as compared to field independent men. Ratings made by the subjects themselves of degree of maternal strictness to which they had been subject showed a significant relation to measures of field dependence, confirming the hypothesis. A similar check on paternal role yielded a non-significant trend in the same direction. This difference in outcome for maternal role and paternal role may be related to the finding of Corah (1965) that children's level of differentiation tends to be related to level of differentiation of opposite-sex parent but not of same-sex parent.

In another part of his study Dawson made a comparison of cognitive style in two tribal groups in Sierra Leone, the Temne and Mende. These groups differ in socialization emphases in ways which, on the basis of our American studies, led to the expectation of relatively greater field dependence in the Temne. Information about child-rearing practices was obtained both from the social anthropological literature as well as from responses to questionnaires administered for the sake of this study. As described by Dawson (1963, 1967), the Temne child, after weaning, is subjected to severe discipline. Great stress is placed on conformity to adult authority, and extreme forms of physical punishment are commonly used to enforce conformity. Children are not encouraged to adopt an adult role. Altogether the mother plays an extremely dominant part in raising the child, whereas the father is a background figure; in fact, children very rarely have close contact with their fathers.[1] Consistent with the nature of their interpersonal relations, among the Temne the chief is powerful, and in their responses to a specially devised questionnaire they showed themselves to be strongly tradition-oriented. The Mende present a contrasting picture in a number of these characteristics. They tend not to punish their children to the same extent as the Temne, and their punishment is likely to take the form of deprivation rather than physical punishment. Great emphasis is placed on giving the child responsibility at a very early age. Further, Mende parents tend to be more consistent than Temne parents in their child-rearing behavior. Particularly important, the Mende family is less dominated by the mother than the Temne family; and the Mende are less tradition-oriented. Reflecting these differences in socialization between the Temne and Mende, overall ratings of parental strictness made by members of the two tribes showed the Temne subjects more prone to perceive themselves as strictly raised. Temne ratings of both maternal and paternal strictness were significantly higher than Mende ratings.

This account of socialization practices among the Temne and Mende indicates a marked contrast between them in quite specific features of the "socialization cluster" found in our American studies to be related to the development of a relatively more global or more articulated cognitive style. Considering the components of the cluster (handling of separation, regulation of impulse expression, and personal characteristics of parents affecting their part in these processes), it may reasonably be expected, as Dawson hypothesized, that Temne children would be relatively more field dependent than Mende children. This hypothesis was essentially confirmed when perceptual test

---

1. It is relevant here that Barclay and Cusumano (1967) found a tendency for boys from fatherless homes to be field dependent. Seder (1957) observed that among field independent boys, fathers are more the mediators of discipline than mothers. In our own studies, mothers judged to have interfered with differentiation in their sons complained that their husbands did not participate in the sons' raising.

performances were compared for Temne and Mende males matched for age, occupation, sex, education, and intelligence.

A Study of Temne and Eskimo, by Berry

Berry (1966a, 1966b) selected for study two societies presenting a striking contrast in the socialization practices found important in our studies and in Dawson's for development of the field dependence-independence dimension. These societies differed as well in particular ecological characteristics conceived to play a role in the development of this dimension. The two societies were the Temne of Sierra Leone, studied by Dawson, and the Eskimo of Baffin Island. Child-rearing practices among the Temne were described in detail in the preceding section. The summary given by Berry of the available social anthropological literature reveals that among the Eskimo punishment of children is generally avoided; blows or even scolding or harsh words are rarely used, and extreme freedom is allowed the individual child. There is strong encouragement of personal self-reliance, individualism, skill and ingenuity, and discouragement of dependence and incompetence. The personal qualities emphasized in child rearing are of importance for the kinds of solitary activities in which the Eskimo engage (hunting, kayaking). It is not surprising that the emphasis on individualism evident in both child rearing and economic activities should be found in the social system as well. Class distinction and social and political stratification are nonexistent. The impressive differences in child rearing emphases between the Temne and Eskimo were reflected in differences in perception by members of the two societies of the severity of the discipline to which they had been subjected while growing up. Berry's Temne subjects rated their parents as significantly stricter than his Eskimo subjects. Berry predicted that the Eskimo would be much more field independent than the Temne, a prediction which is entirely appropriate in light of the socialization cluster found in the American studies, to be relevant to development of the field dependence-independence dimension.

Differences in the ecological requirements of the two groups contributed further to Berry's expectation of greater field independence among the Eskimo. Whereas the environment of the Temne, with its bush and colorful vegetation, is highly variegated, the environment of the Eskimo with its endless, uniform snowfields is extremely homogeneous. Articulation is thus a built-in feature of the visual field of the Temne world but essentially lacking in the Eskimo world. Against this starting difference in their visual worlds there is a marked difference between the two groups in the kind of engagement with the environment which their economies demand. The hunting life of the Eskimo requires that they travel widely. The necessity of finding their way around in a highly uniform terrain must place a great premium during development upon investment in the articulation of space. The fostering of articulation, we may speculate, is likely to be stronger than in a society where the same need to travel widely is met by an environment which is inherently articulated. The Temne, in contrast, endowed with a highly articulated world, do not need to invest in articulation even to the degree of "taking over" what is available to them as a "given," for as farmers they tend to "stay put." Berry identified in the complex system of geometrical-spatial terms of the Eskimo language a very useful device for helping the growing child achieve an articulated concept of space.

Berry's subjects were two matched groups of Eskimo and Temne, each containing a subgroup drawn from a traditional and transitional society. To permit comparison with Western society, Berry also tested a matched group of Scottish subjects, similarly divided. Field dependence was assessed by the embedded-figures and Kohs Block Design tests. In keeping with expectations, the Eskimo traditional and transitional groups were strikingly more field independent than the corresponding Temne groups. In fact, the Eskimo were not significantly different from the Scots in level of field independence. Berry's finding that the Eskimo are markedly field independent is consistent with results reported by Vernon (1965) and MacArthur (personal communication). Examination of the relation between self-ratings of parental discipline and extent of field dependence within each sample showed the anticipated tendency for greater parental strictness to be associated with more field-dependent perception. Thus, in within-culture comparisons as well as in cross-cultural comparisons, a relation is evident between extent of field dependence and particular child-rearing practices. To add to this picture, in all three societies the transitional sample was more field independent than the traditional sample.

There is some evidence that it is not in the cognitive sphere alone that the Eskimo are more differentiated than the Temne. For example, Berry found that in an Asch-type of situation, Eskimo subjects in judging line lengths were significantly less influenced by the standard attributed to an authoritative group than were Temne subjects. This tendency of the Eskimo to establish their own standards independently of the prevailing social context is indicative of what we earlier called a developed sense of separate identity, signifying developed self-differentiation. In fact, in some of the American studies which showed a relation between field dependence and sense of separate identity, situations of the Asch type were used to assess sense of separate identity. (See, for example, Linton, 1955; Rosner, 1956.) Considering the area of body concept, there is some evidence that the Eskimo tend to be highly differentiated here as well. Harris (1963) found figure drawings made by Eskimo children to be even more articulated than drawings made by a comparison group of American children. The high degree of articulation of the world-renowned Eskimo soapstone carvings of human figures is in line with Harris' observation. It is relevant here that Witkin, Birnbaum, Lomonaco, Lehr, and Herman (1970) found extent of field dependence to be related to degree of articulation of clay representations of the human body.

It thus appears that the Eskimo may show a generally high level of differentiation across psychological areas. In seeking to understand the process involved, one possibility to be considered is that investment in articulation of experience of the outer field, compelled by ecological requirements, may result in a generalization of interest in articulation to other areas where the source of experience is body and self. It is equally possible that the socialization and ecological factors operative in the Eskimo child's world may act directly on development of differentiation in each of the areas considered.[2]

2. In still another cross-cultural study, Wober (1966) studied field dependence among Nigerians with the interesting hypothesis that specialized experience in a particular sense modality, without an equal degree of experience in other modalities alone, with the result that the individual consistency in extent of field dependence across modalities repeatedly observed among Western subjects will not be found. The absence of significant correlations in one group of Nigerian subjects between the rod-and-frame test, on the one hand, and the embedded-figures and Kohs Block tests, on the other, was taken to support the hypothesis. However, in a sub-sample of Nigerian manual workers (Wober, 1966) the correlations tended to be higher and one of the two obtained was significant. In view of this, and in the absence of a validation study, it seems appropriate to consider that Wober's hypothesis remains to be confirmed. It is a hypothesis which clearly merits further inquiry.

A Subcultural Comparison, by Dershowitz

Like the Dawson and Berry studies, a study by Dershowitz (1966) also selected for investigation two social groups which present a contrast in child-rearing practices conceived to be important for development of the global-articulated cognitive style and related characteristics of differentiation. Dershowitz's groups, however, were drawn from subcultures within the same country (the United States). Though as Frijda and Jahoda (1966) have pointed out, research with subcultural groups is not cross cultural, this study in a sense meets the cross-cultural rubric since one of the groups was taken as a conveniently available representative of a cultural group ordinarily found outside the United States.

The subjects in Dershowitz's study were 10-year-old boys. One group, on which the study focused, consisted of Jewish boys attending a Hebrew all-day school located in a neighborhood of Brooklyn, New York, with a large orthodox Jewish population of Eastern European origin. The school was judged to provide a particularly intense program of Jewish acculturation. The families from which the boys came were all of Eastern European origin; religious observance in these families, and among the boys of the study as well, was strict. The boys used in the study were thus strongly affected by Jewish acculturation. Moreover, the group from which the Jewish boys were drawn is a quite cohesive one, in its shared values, beliefs and patterns of behavior, though located in as diversified a cultural setting as New York. The characteristics of this cultural group have been described as typical of the *shtetl,* the Jewish community in the small town or village of Eastern Europe. Several dominant characteristics of socialization emphases in this group led Dershowitz to predict that its members would be field dependent and show other characteristics of limited differentiation. First is the difference in typical role of father and mother. The ideal Jewish man is a scholar, "a man of thought." His concern with his children, particularly his sons, is for their spiritual and religious development. It is to the woman that responsibility falls for the everyday conduct of family living, including the physical and emotional care of the children. Not only does such a family structure place the mother in a primary role vis-à-vis the "personal" being of her son, but there is also evidence that her role is a dominating one, exercised in a fashion to inhibit her son's development of autonomous functioning. The combination of the dominant, separation-inhibiting role of the mother, on the one hand, and the essential psychological absenteeism of the father in relation to the son's physical and emotional being, on the other, was one ground on which Dershowitz predicted a tendency toward field dependence and other characteristics of limited differentiation in this group.

A second ground for making this same prediction is the denigration of the body in this culture. This is reflected not only in attitudes held toward the body (outside the head and its functions), but also in the emphasis on "knowing" rather than "doing." Such a combination of forces in the life of the growing boy works against finding out "what the body is like," which comes both through exploration motivated by positive interest in the body and through feed-back resulting from body activity. A limitedly articulated body concept was, therefore, predicted for these Jewish boys. For comparison with this group, Dershowitz used white Protestant boys of Anglo-Saxon derivation, also living in Brooklyn, New York. This group is more difficult to characterize than the relatively homogeneous Jewish group. However, the roles of parents, particularly the mother, in areas that matter for the development of cognitive style are sufficiently different from what is typical of the Jewish group, and the emphasis on "doing" as compared to "knowing," with its consequences for development of body concept, sufficiently greater to justify the prediction that the Jewish boys would both be more field dependent and have a more global body concept than the white Protestant boys. The test results for the two groups clearly supported this prediction. It is also noteworthy that when the traditional orthodox Jewish boys and the Protestant boys were in turn compared to a third group of boys from more assimilated Jewish families, this third group occupied an intermediate position in performance on the various cognitive tests of differentiation.

Sex Differences in Cognitive Style

Sex differences in cognitive style have been observed in a wide variety of groups by now. Their existence raises a number of significant questions about the role of socialization in cognitive development and suggests further lines of cross-cultural inquiry. Boys and men tend to be more field independent than girls and women. The difference between the sexes is small in magnitude, compared to the range of individual differences within each sex, but it is clear-cut and pervasive. Moreover these sex differences are evident over a large segment of the life span, although they may not exist in children below the age of 8 (Crudden, 1941; Goodenough and Eagle, 1963) or in geriatric groups (Schwartz and Karp, 1967). Greater field dependence in females has been observed in numerous groups of varied educational and social backgrounds in the United States. It has also been observed in a number of Western European countries, including England, Holland, France, and Italy (see Witkin et al., 1962) as well as in Israel (Rothman, personal communication), Japan (Kato, 1965), Hong Kong (Goodnow, personal communication) and in Sierra Leone, Africa (Dawson, 1963, 1967), although, interestingly enough, not among the Eskimo (Berry, 1966a, 1966b; MacArthur, 1967). Moreover, within each sex, extent of field dependence has been related to scores on masculinity-femininity inventories, which in effect assess the extent to which an individual does what men or women typically do in our culture, in other words, their social roles; greater masculinity within each sex was associated with greater field independence (Miller, 1953; Crutchfield, Woodworth, and Albrecht, 1958; Fink, 1959). Finally, congruent with their greater field independence, men have been found to show more articulated functioning in intellectual activities as well. (See, for example, Guetzkow, 1951; Sweeney, 1953; Milton, 1957.) There is some evidence in the literature that sex differences in differentiation may exist in other psychological areas as well as in cognitive functioning. A number of studies have identified sex differences in behavior suggestive of differences in sense of separate identity. For example, it has been found repeatedly that women as a group are more likely than men to use external standards for definition of their attitudes and judgments (for example, Feinberg, 1951; Crutchfield, 1955; Nakamura, 1955; Patel and Gordon, 1961). (See Witkin et al., 1962, for a review of the evidence on sex differences in behavior indicative of developed sense of separate identity.) Whether sex differences in differentiation do in fact exist across many areas of psychological functioning remains to be checked in further research.

Sex differences in cognitive style, which have now been clearly established for a wide variety of social groups, have to this point not been specifically studied in relation to the socialization process. Some observations that have been made do, however, provide a basis for speculating about the possible source of these sex differences. In our own studies, which focused on mother-son interactions, we formed the impression in those cases where the mothers had daughters, in addition to the sons, taking part in our studies, that the mothers were more encouraging of achievement and accepting of assertiveness for their sons but placed more stress on social training for their daughters. This observation seems consistent with the overall impression that our society places greater value for boys than for girls on characteristics associated with developed differentiation. Thus, in Tyler (1965) we find evidence that in America there is a commonly held view that women are dependent and men are independent. Already among children, boys held in esteem by their peers are likely to be independent, whereas esteemed girls tend to be dependent (Tuddenham, 1951, 1952). There is evidence from studies by Carden (1958) and Iscoe and Carden (1961) connecting these social emphases directly to cognitive style. These studies showed that boys prefer other boys who are field independent, whereas girls prefer girls who are field dependent. Our sex-role stereotypes, which even young children learn to value, thus include characteristics subsumed under differentiation. Pressure on growing children to comply with these stereotypes may well contribute to the sex differences in field dependence observed pervasively in the United States, and perhaps to broader overall differences in differentiation.

It is possible that non-Western societies may show some of these characteristics of American culture. Barry, Bacon, and Child (1957) have observed that in a large number of cultures, mainly illiterate, men typically engage in activities, such as work and combat, which stress self-reliance and achievement; women in contrast have the nurturant role of homemaking and child rearing. These differences, in turn, are consistent with differences in training goals for the two sexes, independence being more often stressed for boys. Thus it seems that the emphases in socialization repeatedly found in association with development of a global cognitive style, are, in a wide array of cultural settings, more evident in the raising of girls than of boys. From the data now available the Eskimo seem to be an exception to the consistent picture of sex differences in field dependence (Berry, 1966a, 1966b; MacArthur, 1967).[3] The absence of sex differences in this

---

3. Davila, Diaz-Guerrero, and Tapia (1966) in a recent study found no sex differences among 8- and 12-year-old Mexican school children. Since the report of the study does not describe socialization practices in the samples tested, it is not possible to determine whether the absence of sex differences is specifically attributable to the socialization practices followed.

group, if confirmed in further studies, would not contradict the observations made about socialization factors important in the development of cognitive style. As Berry points out, despite different economic and social role assignments, women are not treated as dependent among the Eskimo and very loose controls are exercised over them. The Eskimo findings raise the possibility that changes in ways of raising boys and girls from those now commonly practiced, even if these common ways are derived from originally compelling biological and economic forces, may reduce or even eliminate sex differences in cognitive style and, perhaps with it, sex differences in at least some of the other related characteristics of personal functioning.

For a deeper understanding of the role of socialization factors in the production of sex differences in cognitive style, studies are needed which specifically direct themselves to this issue. Of particular value would be a comparison of extent of sex differences in field dependence in a series of cultures varying in the degree to which male and female roles are similar or different.

Discussion

On a variety of grounds the global-articulated cognitive style is of considerable value in cross-cultural studies, particularly in studies of the role of socialization processes in psychological development. Extensive research has shown this style to be a salient dimension of individual differences in cognitive functioning (Smith, 1964; Vernon, 1965; Witkin et al., 1954, 1962). Vernon (1965), in fact, came to the following conclusion from a review of the factor-analytic literature on cognitive functioning: "After removing the general factor (whether by group-factor technique or by rotation of centroid factors), the positive residual correlations always fall into two main groups: the verbal-educational (v:ed) group and the spatial-practical mechanical group" (p. 725). The global-articulated dimension is clearly subsumed by the second of these two basic cognitive factors. (See Witkin et al., 1962, for a review of the evidence relating field dependence to spatial ability.) The global-articulated cognitive style is also basic in the additional sense that the function involved is undoubtedly a universally occurring one in individual human development. Further, past evidence, now added to by the findings reviewed here, indicates that individual differences in the global-articulated dimension reflect differences in socialization experiences, and so may serve to compare groups with regard to their socialization practices. Finally, an individual's standing on this dimension, particularly its perceptual component, field dependence-independence, may be assessed by controlled laboratory tests which are objective and essentially nonverbal.

The occurrence of a sex difference in field dependence in the very wide range of social groups in which it has been observed makes it tempting to think of this difference as rooted in constitutional and/or genetic differences between men and women. While this is certainly a possibility, it is equally plausible that the sex difference is so pervasive because the same differences between the socialization practices followed in raising boys and girls, particularly those important for the development of differentiation, exist in a great many cultures. Moreover, even if biological differences between the sexes are a source of sex differences in cognitive style, it is quite likely that these biological differences exert their influence through strongly fostering both different methods of raising the two sexes and different social roles for them, even in widely different cultural contexts, and it is these differences in child rearing and social role which in turn influence the development of cognitive style and related characteristics of differentiation. Biological differences may also contribute to sex differences in differentiation through the role they play in individual psychological development, but again their influence is complex and indirect. As one example, psychoanalytic writers have commented on the fact that the presence of a vagina rather than a penis (of "hidden" genitals rather than apparent ones) makes for greater confusion in the growing girl as to the nature of her sexual parts and their functioning. Since the genital area is in a way a "center of gravity" of the body, both because of the libidinal investment made in it and the significance attached to it by society, confusion about this area may make achievement of an articulated concept of the body altogether more difficult. In still another way may biological differences between the sexes contribute more or less universally to sex differences in differentiation of the body concept, but again by a very indirect route. The body with which the growing boy has greatest early contact, his mother's, is, of course, different from his own. Confrontation with differences may be a particularly effective route for sharpening the child's awareness of his own bodily characteristics, thereby aiding development of an articulated body concept. Girls have less of this experience of contrast, since an infant's bodily contact with the father is not as great as with the mother.

Still in the biological domain, the possibility must be raised that group differences in cognitive style may be based, in part at least, on genetic differences. Adaptive selection is particularly apt to play a role in groups that have lived in the same environment over a very long period, and have remained in relative sexual isolation from other groups. The Eskimo have both these characteristics; it is conceivable that the highly adaptive value of analytical competence in coping with the world in which they live may have caused selection for this attribute, leading in time to marked field independence in this quite homogeneous group. As Berry points out, in arguing against this possibility, his transitional Eskimo group was significantly more field independent than his traditional group. In rejoinder, it cannot be ruled out that this difference reflects the selective migration of relatively field-independent persons to cities. The problem of adaptive selection for particular cognitive characteristics within human populations is an intriguing one for further research.

References

Barclay, A., and D. R. Cusumano. "Father absence, cross-sex identity, and field-dependent behavior in male adolescents," *Child-Development,* 38 (1967), 243–250.

Barry, H., M. Bacon, and I. A. Child. "A cross-cultural survey of sex differences and socialization," *J. Abnormal Soc. Psychol.,* 3 (1957), 55.

Berry, J. W. "Cultural determinants of perception." Unpublished thesis, University of Edinburgh, 1966 (a).

Berry, J. W. "Temne and Eskimo perceptual skills," *International J. Psychol.,* 1 (1966), 207–229 (b).

Carden, J. A. "Field dependence, anxiety, and sociometric status in children." Unpublished master's thesis, University of Texas, 1958.

Corah, N. L. "Differentiation in children and their parents," *J. Pers.,* 33 (1965), 300–308.

Crudden, C. H. "Form abstraction by children," *J. Genet. Psychol.,* 58 (1941), 113–129.

Crutchfield, R. S. "Conformity and character," *American Psychologist,* 10 (1955), 191–198.

Crutchfield, R. S., D. G. Woodworth, and R. E. Albrecht. "Perceptual performance and the effective person." Lackland AFB, Texas, USAF, WADC Technical Note, No. 58–60, 1958.

Davila, De la Luz F., R. Diaz-Guerrero, and L. L. Tapia. "Primera fase en la investigacion de la prueba de figuras ocultas de Witkin en escolares Mexicanos." Paper presented at Xth Inter-American Congress of Psychology, Lima, Peru, 1966.

Dawson, J. L. M. "Cultural and physiological influences upon spatial-perceptual processes in West Africa," Parts I and II, *International J. of Psychol.*, 2 (1967), 115–128, 171–185.

Dawson, J. L. M. "Psychological effects of social change in a West African community." Unpublished doctoral thesis, University of Oxford, 1963.

Dershowitz, Z. "Influences of cultural patterns on the thinking of children in certain ethnic groups: a study of the effect of Jewish subcultures on the field-dependence-independence dimension of cognition." Unpublished doctoral dissertation, New York University, 1966.

Dyk, R. B., and H. A. Witkin. "Family experiences related to the development of differentiation in children," *Child Development,* 30 (1965), 21–55.

Feinberg, I. R. "Sex differences in resistance to group pressure." Unpublished master's thesis, Swarthmore College, 1951.

Fink, D. M. "Sex differences in perceptual tasks in relation to selected personality variables." Unpublished doctoral dissertation, Rutgers University, 1959.

Frijda, N., and G. Jahoda. "On the scope and methods of cross-cultural research," *International J. Psychol.,* 1 (1966), 109–127.

Goodenough, D. R., and C. J. Eagle. "A modification of the embedded-figures text for use with young children," *J. Genet. Psychol.,* 103 (1963), 67–74.

Goodnow, R. Personal communication.

Guetzkow, H. "An analysis of the operation of set in problem-solving behavior," *J. General Psychol.,* 45 (1951), 219–244.

Harris, D. B. *Children's Drawings as Measures of Intellectual Maturity.* New York: Harcourt, 1963.

Iscoe, I., and J. A. Carden. "Field dependence, manifest anxiety, and sociometric status in children," *J. Consult. Psychol.,* 25 (1961), 184.

Kato, N. "The validity and reliability of new rod-frame test," *Japanese Psychol. Res.,* 7 (1965), 120–125.

Linton, H. B. "Dependence on external influence: correlates in perception, attitudes, and judgment," *J. Abnormal Soc. Psychol.,* 51 (1955), 502–507.

MacArthur, R. S. Personal communication.

MacArthur, R. S. "Sex differences in field dependence for the Eskimo," *International J. Psychol.,* 2 (1967), 139–140.

Miller, A. S. "An investigation of some hypothetical relationships of rigidity and strength and speed of perceptual closure." Unpublished doctoral dissertation, University of California, 1953.

Milton, G. A. "The effects of sex-role identification upon problem-solving skill," *J. Abnormal Soc. Psychol.,* 55 (1957), 208–212.

Nakamura, C. Y. "The relation between conformity and problem solving." *Technical Report,* No. 11, Stanford University, 1955.

Patel, A. S., and J. E. Gordon. "Some personal and situational determinants of yielding to influence," *J. Abnormal Soc. Psychol.,* 61 (1961), 411–418.

Rosner, S. "Studies of group pressure." Unpublished doctoral dissertation, New School for Social Research, 1956.

Rothman, M. Personal communication.

Schwartz, D., and S. A. Karp. "Field dependence in a geriatric population," *Perceptual and Motor Skills,* 24 (1967), 495–504.

Seder, J. A. "The origin of differences in extent of independence in children: developmental factors in perceptual field dependence." Unpublished bachelor's thesis, Radcliffe College, 1957.

Smith, J. M. *Spatial Ability.* London: University of London Press, 1946.

Sweeney, E. J. "Sex differences in problem solving." *Technical Report,* No. 1, Stanford University, 1953.

Tuddenham, R. D. "Studies in reputation: I. Sex and grade differences in school children's evaluations of their peers," *Psychol. Monographs,* 66 (1952), Whole No. 333.

Tuddenham, R. D. "Studies in reputation: III. Correlates of popularity among elementary school children," *J. Educ. Psychol.,* 42 (1951), 257–276.

Tyler, L. E. *The Psychology of Human Differences,* 3rd ed. New York: Appleton-Century, 1965.

Vernon, P. E. "Ability factors and environmental influences," *American Psychologist,* 20 (1965), 723–733.

Witkin, H. A., J. Birnbaum, S. Lomonaco, S. Lehr, and J. L. Herman. "Cognitive patterning in congenitally totally blind children, in Lester R. Aronson, et al., eds., *Development and Evolution of Behavior, Essays in Memory of T. C. Schneirla.* San Francisco: W. H. Freeman, 1970.

Witkin, H. A., R. B. Dyk, H. F. Faterson, D. R. Goodenough, and S. A. Karp. *Psychological Differentiation.* New York: Wiley, 1962.

Witkin, H. A., D. R. Goodenough, and S. A. Karp. "Stability of cognitive style from childhood to young adulthood," *Jr. of Person. Soc. Psychol.,* 7 (1967), 291–300.

Witkin, H. A., H. B. Lewis, M. Hertzman, K. Machover, P. B. Messner, and S. Wapner. *Personality Through Perception.* New York: Harper, 1954.

Wober, J. M. "Psychological factors in the adjustment to industrial life among employees of a firm in South Nigeria." Unpublished doctoral dissertation, University of Edinburgh, 1966.

20

Male Models
and Sexual Identification:
A Case from the Out Island Bahamas

William B. Rodgers and John M. Long

A series of early studies demonstrated that initiation
ceremonies in adolescence are especially likely in societies
where boys have been over-feminized in childhood, the
interpretation being that the initiation serves to strengthen
boys' identification with males and increases their motivation
to engage in male adult roles. This field study suggests that
such initiations might take a variety of forms, including
apprenticeships, and it also provides evidence that

psychological changes relevant to masculinity/femininity really do occur at the time of such initiations. The comparison of two societies provides insights into the multiple ways sociocultural systems can influence psychological development, since in both societies the end products are the same, but the ways of getting there are quite different.

On Great Abaco, one of the larger and northernmost of the Out Island Bahamas, economic factors determine to a great degree the spatial distribution of Negro males. The people of underdeveloped communities such as Crossing Rocks (population 119) rely on subsistence farming and fishing for part of their living, and on commercial smack fishing and crawfishing for the rest of it. The men plant the fields and the women thereafter are, to a great extent, responsible for the weeding, maintenance, and harvesting. The men, through their fishing trips, provide the money necessary for purchasing necessities that cannot be produced in the home environment. These fishing trips take the men away from the community for long periods of time, but the pattern of absence varies slightly according to the type of fishing. In Crossing Rocks, approximately half of the men go out on commercial smacks, and the other half go crawfishing. The crawfishing season lasts about six months, during which the men go to the Little Bahama Bank in small dinghies to catch the crawfish and sell them to passing traders.

Abridged from William B. Rodgers and John M. Long, "Male Models and Sexual Identification: A Case from the Out Island Bahamas," in *Human Organization,* 27 (1968), 326–331. Reprinted by permission of The Society for Applied Anthropology and the authors. Notes have been renumbered.

The research and writing of this paper was supported by fellowships and grants from the National Institute of Mental Health, for which the authors express their gratitude. The one-year period of field work which yielded the data presented herein was conducted in 1964 by Rodgers, who completed a preliminary analysis of the material in 1965. The material was reworked by Rodgers and Long in 1966–1967.

Typically, they are out for about three weeks at a time, and return to their homes between traps for only a day or two, in order to renew provisions, see their families, and turn over their profits to their wives. The smack fishermen, on the other hand, are at sea from four to six weeks at a time; about seven or eight trips are made in a year's time.

As a result of these fishing trips, Crossing Rocks for a large part of the year is essentially a community of women and children. The men are of the community, but are frequently not in it. Almost every household in Crossing Rock is, temporarily, a mother/child household.

This same situation would have been true of Murphy Town (population 315) no longer than ten years ago. Now, however, with exposure to economic development and the advent of wage labor, the majority of the Murphy Town men are home at least in the evenings. Further, many of the Murphy Town men are often home all day, for employment is sporadic and at any one time many of them are unemployed. It is true that some of the men in Murphy Town continue to crawfish, but by and large it is a community of wage laborers and the unemployed, in which the men are generally present throughout the year, both in the community and in the home (1).

Research Design and Methodology

We thus have for comparison two communities, one (Crossing Rocks) where the adult males are often absent, and another (Murphy Town) where they are most often present. This situation allows the testing of an hypothesis which asserts that *if male adult models are absent during the crucial periods in a boy's maturation, the boy tends to manifest evidence of cross-sex identification.* On the operational level, *the young males in Crossing Rocks should manifest more cross-sex identification, as measured by operationalized indices of such identification, than the young males of Murphy Town. . . .*

This design is obviously far from perfect for testing the effects of household composition on an aspect of personality, such as cross-sex identification. There is, of course, some overlapping in the types of household present in the two communities. In Murphy Town, for example, there are permanent mother/child households as well as those temporary mother/child households which are created by the minority of the population still involved in crawfishing. However, only 9.7 percent of the households are permanently matrifocal; and male models are far more prevalent in Murphy Town throughout the year than they are in Crossing Rocks. In a gross manner, then, this research design can determine whether the developments that have affected Murphy Town's pattern of household composition have also affected the personality structure of its younger males. Development is considered to be the independent variable, which, acting through the intervening variable of household composition, determines the presence or absence of cross-sex identification in young males; cross-sex identification is, then, the dependent variable.

The independent and intervening variables are provided by the natural setting in such a way that we can compare Crossing Rocks, a community with no exposure to economic development and with few adult males present much of the time, to Murphy Town, a community which has been exposed to economic development and in which most adult males were usually present. Selection and operationalization of the dependent variables is more difficult. Cross-sex identification is not itself observable, although its presence can be deduced from the observation of behavior. Determination of the specific behavior to be measured in order to deduce the presence of cross-sex identification is an empirical problem. It involves, briefly, locating a behavior or a behavioral response (2) which will differentiate "normal" males from "normal" females. The specific behavior selected for measurement matters very little, so long as it discriminates at a level of statistical significance between normal males and normal females. With reference to our study in Abaco, a behavior had to be found which would differentiate between the young males and young females of Murphy Town, where both male and female adult models were present. If such behavior could be located, it could then be used to compare the responses of Murphy Town boys to those of Crossing Rocks boys. Since the absence of adult male models in Crossing Rocks should have a feminizing effect on the boys there, it could be predicted that the boys of Crossing Rocks would respond in a manner significantly different from that of the boys of Murphy Town and more like that of the Murphy Town girls. Our interest centered on the boys of Crossing Rocks, as there was nothing in the typical household structure or in observed behavior to suggest that girls of the community differed from those in Murphy Town. Although the number of Crossing Rocks girls tested was small, the results indicate that our impressions were correct.

Initially, we attempted to measure observed natural behaviors in order to determine differences in sex-typed behavior. We found, for example, that Murphy Town boys seemed more aggressive than either Murphy Town girls or Crossing Rocks boys (3). However, the task of observation was too time-consuming to permit quantification of this finding with large enough representative samples. We, therefore, constructed a test which could be administered to the children individually. Familiar with the work of McElroy, who had demonstrated sex differences for Scottish school children, we designed a preference-for-shapes test. We did not employ the same shapes as McElroy, but we followed his procedure in providing twelve choice-sets of paired line drawings, each pair of which offered a choice between a predominantly *curved* shape and a predominantly *angular* shape (4).

The entire test was administered by native helpers to 49 boys and 36 girls in Murphy Town and to 20 boys in Crossing Rocks, all of whom were between six and fifteen years of age. This sample included all of the Murphy Town boys and the overwhelming majority of the Murphy Town girls and Crossing Rocks boys in this age-group (36 of 39 and 20 of 25, respectively). Nine of the 13 Crossing Rocks girls between six and fifteen were also tested. Time considerations alone prevented testing of all the children, for the tests were conducted near the end of the period of our field work there.

The native helpers who administered the tests were two married women, each in her early forties, one living in Murphy Town and the other in Crossing Rocks. Each worked in her own locale. The women were trained to follow exactly the same routine and to avoid imposing their own choices on their subjects. The training included actual administration of the tests under our observation. (The subjects of these observed tests were not included in the test sample presented here.) Each helper was also tested, prior to being trained, and they scored identically on the test. Differences in the responses obtained from the two communities cannot, therefore, be attributed to the test administration.

The twelve pairs of shapes were dittoed on sheets of paper, and the native helper asked each child which shape of each pair he "liked best." This frame had been found in the period of training to be perfectly reliable. As the child responded the helper marked the shape chosen and the scores were later cross-tabulated for analysis. The scores were tabulated in various ways, but as an operating principle, we selected for analytic purposes the *one* choice-set (of the twelve pairs of shapes offered) *that showed the most difference* in response between Murphy Town boys and Murphy Town girls (5). This was choice-set number 11, reproduced here as Figure 1.

Findings

Table 1 presents the choice distributions for the choice-set number 11 for boys and girls in Murphy Town. It clearly indicates that there is a significant difference in response between boys and girls in our control community, where economic development has occurred and where there is a high frequency of adult male models regularly present. Sixty-seven percent of the girls in Murphy Town selected the curved shape, while only 39 percent of the boys did so; the boys instead preferred the angular shape 61 percent of the time. Such results would be expected by chance only once in a hundred times.

Having located a behavioral response which discriminated between boys and girls where both male and female adult models were present, we were in a position to test our hypothesis. The assumption that the

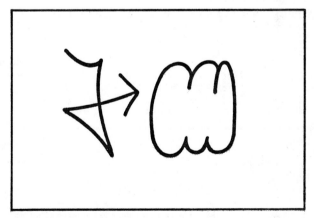

FIGURE 1. Shapes in Choice–Set #11

Table 1. Murphy Town Shape Preferences*

	Curved Shape	Angular Shape	Totals
Children under 15 Years			
Boys	19 (39%)	30 (61%)	49
Girls	24 (67%)	12 (33%)	36
Total	43	42	85
	$x^2 = 7.0$	$p = < .01$	

*Frequencies within the table indicate the number of boys and girls who selected each shape.

absence of adult male models in Crossing Rocks, the undeveloped community, would have a feminizing effect on the young males in that community, could be checked by comparing the latter's scores (on choice-set 11) with the scores of boys in Murphy Town. If the theory of the effects of adult models' presence on children's sex-identification were predictive, the comparison should show a statistically significant difference between the two sets of scores, and the boys of Crossing Rocks should respond in a pattern more like that of the girls of Murphy Town, than did the Murphy Town boys. The cross-tabulated scores are presented in Table 2 with the statistical test.

The results indicate that there is an extreme difference in responses between the boys of the two communities which strongly suggests affirmation of our hypothesis. Where only 31 percent of the Murphy

Table 2. Shape Preferences of Murphy Town and Crossing Rocks Boys Under Fifteen Years of Age*

	Curved Shape	Angular Shape	Totals
Murphy Town Boys	19 (39%)	30 (61%)	49
Crossing Rocks Boys	15 (75%)	5 (25%)	20
Total	34	35	69
	$x^2 = 6.04$	$p = < .01$	

*Frequencies in the table indicate the number of individuals who selected each shape.

Town boys chose the curved shape, 75 percent of the Crossing Rocks boys did so. Furthermore, there is no significant difference in the response of the Crossing Rocks boys and the Murphy Town girls, and the response of the girls of Crossing Rocks were identical to those of the girls of Murphy Town: 67 percent of each group selected the curved shape (6). These results allow the conclusion that, in this instance, the absence of adult male models has led to cross-sex identification in young males. Furthermore, we may safely conclude that economic development in Murphy Town, by providing opportunities for wage labor locally and by thus allowing the men of the community to be regularly present in their households, has indirectly led to this specific personality change in the young males of that community.

. . . Despite the apparent cross-sex identification of the Crossing Rocks boys, no sex-inappropriate behavior among the adult males was observed. Because of this, we hypothesized that the Crossing Rocks men had changed from a cross-sex identification in boyhood to a more masculine identification, and that their responses on the test would indicate such a change. We, therefore, tested, in addition to our sample of children, twenty-five adult males (16 years of age or older) in Crossing Rocks. The results, which are presented in Table 3, suggest the accuracy of our hypothesis; twenty of the twenty-five men tested selected the angular shape in choice-set 11.

This difference between the young males and adult males of Crossing Rocks can be explained . . . partly by the tendency of social deviates to migrate from such communities, and, more importantly, by the sudden transition from boyhood role to that of apprentice fisherman, a transition which functions as an informal initiation rite in

Table 3. Shape Preferences of Crossing Rocks Men
(16 and Older) and Boys (Ages 6–15)*

	Curved Shape	Angular Shape	Totals
Boys (ages 6–15)	15 (75%)	5 (25%)	20
Men (16 and older)	5 (20%)	20 (80%)	25
Total	20	25	45
	$x^2 = 13.56$	$p = \, < .001$	

*Frequencies in the table indicate the number of individuals who selected each shape.

Crossing Rocks. At about age 14, Crossing Rocks boys are taken on their first fishing trip by their fathers, who are expressly anxious about the childish irresponsibility of their sons. The boys are quickly and roughly taught the skills necessary to fishing. For a period of about a year thereafter, they go through what natives describe as a "mooning" stage, during which they appear apathetic most of the time and seem passively hostile toward the older men. Beaten when they disobey, the boys at this stage generally acquiesce to the men's authority, but as often as possible sneak off from them to rejoin younger companions in play. By the end of the first year of fishing, however, most have completely severed their ties with younger boys and spend their free time in the company of older men. The significance of this apprenticeship period in shifting the sex identification of Crossing Rocks males is further indicated by the fact that there is no suggestion of a progressive patterning in the distribution, by age, of shape selections on choice-set 11; rather, boys 15 years old and younger show consistently a strong tendency toward selecting the curved shape while men sixteen and older tend strongly to the angular shape.

Conclusion

By employing a natural laboratory, we have been able to explore the relationship between the absence of adult male models and the presence of indices of cross-sex identification (7). Our conclusion, in this instance, is that the absence of such models is significantly correlated with these indices. Moreover, our study reinforces the concept that the initiation rite (whether formal or, as in this instance, informal) functions as a harsh but apparently necessary and effective corrective for cross-sex identification of young boys raised in the absence of adult male models. We have in addition ordered the data in a conceptual time perspective. From the results of this ordering, we have concluded that economic development in Murphy Town, by promoting the spatial stability of adult males in the community, has indirectly brought about a personality change in the Murphy Town children. It is suggested that these findings may be useful in planning development programs, for the success or failure of a development project may be partially determined by such indirect effects of economic changes. We do not argue that the specific personality change described above is desirable or undesirable; we suggest only that preconsideration of such factors can aid in the evaluation of the potential success and desirability of the total effects of a specific program.

Notes and References

1. For a more thorough description of the economic changes involved in the comparison of these communities see William B. Rodgers, "Development and specialization: A case from the Bahamas," *Ethnology*, 5 (1966), 409–414.

2. Such behavioral responses have been noted cross-culturally; for Americans, math-verbal distinctions reported in Lyn Carlsmith, "Effect of early father absence on scholastic aptitude," *Harvard Educ. Rev.*, 34 (1964), 3–21; and the Franck Test as reported by R. G. D'Andrade, "Father-absence and cross-sex identification," unpublished doctoral dissertation, Harvard University, 1962; for Scottish schoolchildren, a preference-for-shapes test reported in W. A. McElroy, "A sex difference in preference for shapes," *British J. Psychol.*, 45 (1954), 209–216.

3. Aggressive behavior has been shown cross-culturally to be more likely among males than females; see R. G. D'Andrade, "Sex differences and cultural institutions," in Eleanor E. Maccoby, ed., *The Development of Sex Differences,* Stanford University Press, 1966, 191. This is not, of course, an infallible test of sex-typed behavior as will be demonstrated in a reading of Margaret Mead, *Sex and Temperament in Three Primitive Societies,* New York: William Morrow, 1935.

4. The measure is somewhat similar to the Franck Test, a measure of "sex-role orientation," as discussed in Chapter 22 of this volume. [EDITOR]

5. The authors report that appreciably the same results were achieved using all 12 shape choices as were achieved by employing choice-set number 11 alone. [EDITOR]

6. Similar results from testing of middle-class American children are reported in R. R. Sears, M. H. Pintler, and P. S. Sears, "Effect of father separation on preschool children's doll play aggression," *Child Development,* 17 (1946), 219–243. Boys raised in households in which the father was away (in military service) manifested significantly less aggression in doll play than boys raised in father-present households, while girls from the two groups showed no significant difference in this regard. However, unlike the children of Crossing Rocks, the boys and girls in the American father-absent group did differ significantly (although, of course, much less than those in the father-present group).

7. This idea comes originally from Freudian theory and was first substantiated by J. W. M. Whiting, R. Kluckhohn, and A. S. Anthony, "The function of male initiation ceremonies at puberty." in E. Maccoby, T. Newcomb, and E. Hartley, eds., *Readings in Social Psychology,* New York: Henry Holt, 1958.

Part V
Disorganization and Stress

Given the range of societies that have existed on earth, it is difficult to decide which social patterns are normal for humans and which are not. Still, within a given society, there are conditions that deprive some individuals of customary experiences and other conditions that generate experiences that some individuals may be unprepared to assimilate. Psychological research has explored extensively the disturbing properties of deprivations and of change, and the chapters in this section (21 to 26) leave no doubt that pathology—both psychological and physiological—is often a consequence of atypical social conditions.

Retardation due to maternal deprivation or the schizophrenia associated with lower-class urban life, are purely negative consequences that we would like to eliminate. Yet, one should be cautious in generalizing the findings in this section into condemnation of anything that is not normal by middle-class standards in our own society. One reason is that some abnormal conditions might be disturbing only because they appear abnormal, but were they made into a modal pattern they would no longer be pathogenic. Second, some of the things we are inclined to label pathological may actually be desirable traits viewed from a broader perspective; for example, overfeminized boys from father-absent families might grow up to be more sensitive and less bellicose than their peers—desirable traits perhaps in a complex, over-armed world. Finally, there is evidence that distress can stimulate people to transcend their present selves and develop deeper character. For example, Chapter 25 notes some relationships between crisis and religious experience, and Chapter 18 discusses how moral development is affected by the stress involved in the transition from adolescence to adulthood. The initiation into work life discussed in Chapter 20 may also be relevant in this respect.

Chapter 13 also deals with a kind of stress—that special form arising from an anomic absence of social demands. Chapter 9 discusses the relation between marriage and stress. Chapter 3 mentions a number of ways that parents can create stress and act as pathogenic agents through their modes of discipline. Some factors that affect a person's response to stress are noted in Chapter 8 (on friendships) and 19 (on cognitive styles).

21

The Effects of Maternal Deprivation: A Review of Findings and Controversy in the Context of Research Strategy

Mary D. Ainsworth

Studies conducted with animals have indicated that if infants mature without social contacts their "personalities" are severely deformed and they do not act normally as adults. Similar effects also occur with human children deprived of maternal contact, and this chapter provides an overview of the research on this topic. Principles of maternal deprivation perhaps can be used to interpret some kinds of deficiencies among children raised in subcultures where families are so large or so disorganized that contact with mothers is below optimal levels.

During the fifteen years preceding the appearance of Bowlby's *Maternal Care and Mental Health* (5), studies by Levy (27), Skeels (29–33) and his associates, Burlingham and Freud (9–10), Bowlby (3, 4), Bender (21), Goldfarb (17–25), Spitz (34–36), and many others bore witness to the adverse effects of early deprivation of maternal care. Bowlby, in 1951, introduced his timely review of the research evidence by saying:

> The extent to which these studies, undertaken by people of many nations, varied training and, as often as not, ignorant of each others' conclusions, confirm and support each other is impressive. What each individual piece of work lacks in thoroughness, scientific reliability, or precision is largely made good by the concordance of the whole (5, p. 15).

An examination of the evidence should leave no doubt that maternal deprivation in infancy and early childhood indeed has an adverse effect on development both during the deprivation experience and for a longer or shorter time after deprivation is relieved, and that severe deprivation experiences *can* lead in some cases to grave effects that resist reversal. This conclusion is essentially the same as Bowlby's in 1951. Research both during the last ten years and previously, however, makes clear that these adverse effects differ in nature, severity, and duration, and that these differences are themselves related to qualitative and quantitative differences in the deprivation experience. The nature and severity of the deprivation experience are now known to be determined by an interacting and complex set of variables, although much further research is required before the relationship between antecedent depriving conditions and their effects can be specified in detail. In the meantime, certain interim conclusions can be drawn, which, in turn, point towards new directions for research.

Abridged from Mary D. Ainsworth, "The Effects of Maternal Deprivation: A Review of Findings and Controversy in the Context of Research Strategy," in *Deprivation of Maternal Care: A Reassessment of its Effects,* Public Health Paper No. 14 (Geneva: World Health Organization, 1962). Reprinted by permission of the World Health Organization and the author.

Appreciation is due to Florence Howe of Goucher College for her invaluable editorial assistance, without which this complex review would have been considerably less comprehensible to the reader.

Diversity of Early Experiences Subsumed Under the Term "Maternal Deprivation"

Deprivation conditions differing in kind may be equivalent in severity, and may lead to effects that appear to be similar in nature and severity. Severe maternal deprivation is now known to occur under the following diverse conditions: (*a*) when an infant or young child is separated from his mother or permanent mother-substitute and cared for in an institution where he receives insufficient maternal care; (*b*) when a young child undergoes a series of separations from his mother and/or substitute mother-figures to whom he had formed attachments; (*c*) when an infant or young child is given grossly insufficient maternal care by his own mother or permanent substitute mother and has no adequate mothering from other figures to mitigate the insufficiency of mother-child interaction. Although this much is known, more remains to be discovered about the severity of the effects that can be expected to follow from variations in severity of these three main sets of conditions and combinations thereof.

Specific Processes Affected by Deprivation

Maternal deprivation has a differential effect on different processes; most vulnerable seem to be certain intellectual processes, especially language and abstraction, and certain aspects of personality, most especially the ability to establish and maintain deep and meaningful interpersonal relations, but also the ability to control impulse in the interest of long-range goals. There is some reason to believe that the age of the child—more accurately, the state of development of the child—has an influence upon the processes affected; thus, for example, it seems reasonable to conclude from present evidence that deprivation during the first year of life affects language and abstract functioning (and indirectly the IQ or the developmental quotient) more than does deprivation later on. It seems likely that discontinuity of relations has its chief effect on the capacity for affectional ties, especially in instances where separation from mother-figures is repeated.

There are important points here for future research. First, research which purports to assess the effects of separation or deprivation experiences cannot afford to neglect assessment of these special processes known to be most vulnerable to damage. Only by establishing minimal impairment of these processes can it be demonstrated that any cluster of conditions is minimally depriving. Secondly, longitudinal research into the development of these processes seems highly desirable; only when it is known how it is that mother-child interaction facilitates development of these processes can it be understood fully how it is that insufficient interaction hinders development. Furthermore, attention needs to be given to the ways in which discontinuity of relationships affects the development of attachments.

The Diverse Effects of "Maternal Deprivation"

Diverse effects have been found to follow early childhood experiences subsumed under the term "maternal deprivation." Some of this diversity is attributable to the fact that insufficiency, discontinuity, and distortion of interactions have all been loosely classed as depriving. Even when the term "deprivation" is narrowed to cover only insufficiency of interpersonal interaction, there is still, diversity of effects. Both the nature and the degree of the consequent disturbance seem to be related to the degree of severity of the antecedent deprivation experience itself. Some of the diversity may be accounted for by the fact that, although the same process or processes are affected by deprivations of varying severity, the overt manifestations of the effects may be diverse. Of the variables that influence the severity of a deprivation experience, one of the most important seems to be the child's age at the onset of deprivation, for this variable seems even to determine which processes are affected. Since deprived children share with non-deprived children a great diversity of experiences, apart from and including interpersonal ones—and, to be sure, come into the world with different genetic structures—all of which make for diverse personality patterns, diversity cannot always be explained by the variables that influence the nature and severity of the deprivation experience itself. Finally, seemingly diverse effects may be due to different investigators having observed different processes with varying methods of appraisal, some of which may have been more sensitive than others.

Despite all these sources of diversity the patterns of effects seem roughly but meaningfully related to the patterns of antecedent variables, and these interrelationships deserve further intensive exploration. In this task current longitudinal studies are the most promising strategy for studying not only how the variables operative before and during the deprivation experience contribute to the responses to deprivation, but also how later experiences after deprivation has been relieved serve to reinforce, modify, or reverse the processes set up during deprivation.

Some Are Damaged; Some Escape Damage

That some children may emerge from a deprivation experience with grave and permanent adverse effects and others may seem to escape any severe or lasting damage is, in part, covered by the above discussion of the diversity of effects of deprivation; it is assumed that some of the puzzling differences in vulnerability to deprivation experiences will be explained by future research. If, however, future research cannot wholly account for the fact that some children are more gravely affected than others, this will constitute no valid reason for discarding the hypothesis that early deprivation experiences are pathogenic. Inexplicable differential vulnerability has been found in nearly all etiological research; it exists in instances where the chief pathogenic agent has been identified beyond any doubt and even where many of the supplementary factors making for vulnerability or resistance to the agent are known. The fact that some are exposed to the pathogenic agent and escape apparently unscathed does not constitute a valid basis for arguing against preventive efforts.

Are the Effects of Deprivation Reversible or Irreversible?

Related to the question of differential vulnerability to a deprivation experience is the question of differential recovery from its effects. The question "Are the effects of maternal deprivation reversible or irreversible?" surely must be restated. *How readily reversible?* Spontaneously, without relief from deprivation, as Dennis and Najarian (15) believe possible? Or after the ordinary relief from deprivation provided by removal from the depriving situation—through reunion with parents, or placement in an adoptive or foster-home? Or after very careful placement to meet the particular needs of the particular child, as attempted by the reception center of which Lewis (28) writes? Or with once-a-week psychotherapy? Or with intensive psychotherapy such as that reported by David and Appell (1, 14)? *How completely reversible?* Obviously an improvement of IQ from a defective level of, say, 55 to one of 75 implies some reversibility, but it is presumably not complete. *With respect to what functions?* A single measure of intellectual functioning, such as the IQ, may be normal, but the individual may show impairment in specific intellectual processes such as language and abstraction. The individual may perform competently in earning a living and in ordinary social interaction with friends and colleagues and still betray impairment through failure in meeting the more intimate interpersonal demands of marriage or parenthood. *Are there hidden impairments?* The findings both that children who have apparently recovered from a separation experience are particularly vulnerable to subsequent threats of separation, and that there is an empirical association between childhood bereavement and adult depressive illness suggest that early experiences may set up processes which may remain covert for a long time but, when subsequently reactivated by some stressful experience (which might well be minor and relatively undisturbing to other people), cause a pathological reaction. When the question of reversibility is rephrased, therefore— "How readily and completely reversible, both overtly and covertly, are the effects of deprivation and with respect to what specific processes?" —the evidence is considerable.

The question of reversibility itself raises some further important theoretical questions about the nature of development. Three major theoretical positions seem possible.

1. Learning theory implies that development is entirely or almost entirely a matter of environmental stimulation. When the appropriate environmental conditions are provided, learning will take place, and what has not been learned earlier can be learned later after the appropriate conditions have been introduced. According to this position, the child, initially retarded because of a deprivation in environmental stimulation, can eventually catch up, provided that deprivation is relieved and enough time is allowed for the learning to take place. This seems to be the position taken by Clarke and Clarke (11–13).

2. The psychoanalytic position implies that an early experience can set up certain dynamic processes that become entrenched or ingrained, and that tend to continue despite the subsequent alteration of the reality situation. Thus early maternal deprivation can be

viewed as requiring the establishment of defensive operations, which serve to insulate the child against the painful frustration of seeking an interaction with an environment that is unstimulating and unresponsive. Once entrenched, this defensive operation tends to maintain itself, insulating the child against interaction with an environment that could prove supportive, responsive, and helpful if he could only be receptive. According to this position, reversibility depends upon the effect of efforts to break down the defensive processes. Some of Bowlby's publications imply this position.

The defensive processes described by the psychoanalyst seem similar to certain phenomena observed in the psychology of learning; certain sequences of behaviour once well learned may be very resistant to change, and may constitute a serious block to learning a new sequence of behavior. This interference by old habits with the learning of new habits is poignantly familiar to the golfer who first learned to slice his drive and now cannot learn to hit it straight.

3. The "sensitive phase" or "critical period" position in psychology has been influenced by ethology, but has also emerged independently as in Hebb's (26) emphasis on early learning as an essential basis for later learning and in the work of some psychoanalysts such as Erikson (16). This position suggests that there may be phases in the course of development during which certain processes develop normally if adequate environmental conditions are present, but if not present, development of a particular process may be arrested and subsequent stimulation may not or may only with great difficulty activate the development. This position has been given recent emphasis by Bowlby's proposal (6, 8) that the development of the human infant be viewed in an ethological frame of reference.

These three positions are not mutually incompatible. It seems entirely likely that some impairment can be overcome through learning after deprivation has been relieved, while some impairment resists reversal to a greater or lesser degree because of more or less deep-seated defensive operations or habit-patterns, while still other impairment may persist because the sensitive phase of the normal development of the processes in question has been passed. (Indeed, as currently formulated, the "sensitive phase" hypothesis is not essentially different from the psychoanalytic or "interfering-habit" position, for it is now believed that the difficulty in instituting responses not acquired in the sensitive phase is due to the emergence of other responses which interfere with them.)

The findings will be summarized in the light of this discussion:

1. Recovery from a single, brief, depriving separation experience seems fairly prompt and complete with respect to overt behaviour under ordinary conditions; there is evidence, however, of vulnerability to future threats of separation—i.e., there is at least one "hidden" impairment that prevents the reversibility from being described as complete.

2. Relief from deprivation after even fairly prolonged deprivation experiences in early infancy can result in rapid and dramatic improvement in overt behaviour and in generalized intellectual functioning; vocalization, however, may be retarded, even though the relief occurs before twelve months of age, and effects on other specific aspects of intellectual and personality functioning cannot be ruled out until these aspects have been explored in research.

3. Prolonged and severe deprivation beginning early in the first year of life and continuing for as long as three years usually leads to severely adverse effects on both intellectual and personality functioning that do resist reversal.

4. Prolonged and severe deprivation beginning in the second year of life leads to some grave effects on personality that do resist reversal, although the effects on general intelligence seem to be fairly completely reversible; specific impairment of intellectual functions has not yet been studied.

5. The effects of age at the onset and relief of the deprivation experience are undoubtedly important factors in influencing reversibility, but these are not understood in enough detail to set precise limits for a "sensitive phase" of development of special processes.

6. In general, in the first year of life, the younger the infant when deprivation is relieved (and hence the less prolonged the depriva-

tion experience), the more normal is the subsequent development; yet after the first year of life has passed, the older the child at the onset of deprivation the more readily and completely reversible seem to be the effects of a deprivation of a given duration.

7. Certain impairments seem to be less readily and less completely reversible than others—impairments in language, in abstraction and in the capacity for strong and lasting interpersonal attachments.

8. Especially if undertaken when the child is still very young, intensive therapeutic efforts may result in marked improvement of some very severe effects that resist reversal through ordinary relief from deprivation.

9. Subsequent experiences of insufficiency, distortion, or discontinuity in interpersonal interaction may be important in reinforcing impairments that otherwise might have been reversed more or less completely.

Prompt and dramatic reversals may be interpreted in the light of relief from distress or grief or to the sudden giving way of defensive operations that had not been well entrenched. More gradual steady improvements are probably attributable for the most part to catching up through learning. A prolonged resistance to improvement may be attributable either to deep-seated defensive processes or habit patterns that interfere with the acquisition of new responses, or to the difficulty in activating development that ought to have taken place in an earlier sensitive phase. To date, the empirical evidence for the existence of a sensitive phase is clearest for language, abstraction, and other symbolic functions. The sensitive phase seems to be the first year of life, most probably the second half of the first year, with the absolute upper limit of the sensitive phase still uncertain; unfortunately space does not permit a review of the evidence for this particular hypothesis.

The generalizations presented above leave many gaps to be filled through future research. In particular, more needs to be known about the normal course of development of those processes most specifically vulnerable to deprivation; indeed it is deplorable to consider how little is known about the normal course of development, in the early years, of interpersonal attachment and of those processes which later blossom into language and other symbolic processes. During the last twenty-five years child development research has focused on the child of nursery-school age and older; recently the neonate has been studied intensively. The very period which seems the most vulnerable to deprivation—the first three years of life—is largely unexplored, especially with respect to social development. Since the normal course of development is in any detail unknown, the difficulty in being precise about the effects of deprivation experiences in arresting, retarding, or distorting that development is not surprising.

Even at the level of development represented by the older child and the adult, the methods of personality appraisal now available are relatively clumsy and imprecise. Conceptualization of the processes and variables to be explored is still blurred, and perhaps will remain so until there is a better understanding of the underlying developmental processes. Quantitative appraisal of personality processes seems likely to be premature, until there is clear conceptualization of the relevant variables to be quantified. For these reasons, judgments about the reversibility of impairments attributable to early interference with development by deprivation, separation, or distortion in parent-child interaction seem to be very much dependent upon the level of assessment. The more superficial the assessment—and premature quantification makes for superficiality—the more evidence there is of reversibility; the more intensive, clinical, and descriptive the assessment the more evidence there is of lasting damage.

None of these considerations encourages a sanguine view of the reversibility of impairment attributable to severe, early maternal deprivation experiences. Even though the effects of deprivation may be reversible somewhat more readily, more completely, and more frequently than was believed possible in 1951, there are distinct limits to the readiness and extent of improvement in cases of severe impairment of long standing. Moreover, the evidence of covert and subtle effects of even a relatively mild separation experience raises doubt about the completeness of the reversibility possible in cases where early deprivation has been severe. Perhaps "complete reversibility" is an illusory product of crude methods of appraisal.

More research is obviously needed further to delimit the conditions that facilitate reversibility and to identify the types of experience in which deprivation, if unavoidable, can be minimally harmful. Meanwhile the costs of attempting to reverse the effects of early deprivation are of great magnitude—so great that every effort should be bent towards prevention.

References

1. Appell, G., and M. David. "Case notes on Monique," in B. M. Foss, ed., *Determinants of Infant Behavior*. London: Methuen, 1961.

2. Bender, L. "Psychopathic behavior disorders in children," in R. M. Lindner and R. V. Seliger, eds., *Handbook of Correctional Psychology*. New York: Philosophical Library, 1947, 360.

3. Bowlby, J. "The influence of early environment in the development of neurosis and neurotic character," *International J. Psycho-Anal.*, 21 (1940), 154.

4. Bowlby, J. *Fourty-four Juvenile Thieves, Their Characters and Home Life*. London: Baillière, Tyndall and Cox, 1946.

5. Bowlby, J. *Maternal Care and Mental Health*, 2nd ed. Geneva: World Health Organization, Monograph Series, No. 2, 1952.

6. Bowlby, J. "An ethological approach to research in child development," *Brit. J. Med. Psychol.*, 30 (1957), 230.

* 7. Bowlby, J. "The nature of the child's tie to his mother," *International J. Psycho-Anal.*, 39 (1958), 350.

8. Bowlby, J. "Symposium on 'psycho-analysis and ethology,' II. Ethology and the development of object relations," *International J. Psycho-Anal.*, 41 (1960), 313.

9. Burlingham, D., and A. Freud. *Young Children in Wartime*. London: Allen and Unwin, 1942.

10. Burlingham, D., and A. Freud. *Infants Without Families.* London: Allen and Unwin, 1944.

11. Clarke, A. D. B., and A. M. Clarke. "Recovery from the effects of deprivation," *Acta Psychol.*, 16 (1959), 137.

12. Clarke, A. D. B., and A. M. Clarke. "Some recent advances in the study of early deprivation," *J. Child Psychol. Psychiat.*, 1 (1960), 26.

13. Clarke, A. D. B., A. M. Clarke, and S. Reiman. "Cognitive and social changes in the feebleminded: three further studies," *Brit. J. Psychol.*, 49 (1958), 144.

14. David, M., and G. Appell. "Observation et traitement d'un cas d'arriération psychogène," *J. Psychiat. Infant*, 1 (1951), 205.

15. Dennis, W., and P. Najarian. "Infant development under environmental handicap," *Psychol. Monographs*, 71 (1957), No. 436.

16. Erikson, E. H. "Identity and the life cycle," *Psychol. Issues*, 1 (1959), 1.

---

* Additional reference.

17. Goldfarb, W. "Infant rearing and problem behavior," *Amer. J. Orthopsychiat.*, 13 (1943), 249.

18. Goldfarb, W. "Effects of early institutional care on adolescent personality," *J. Exp. Educ.*, 12 (1943), 106.

19. Goldfarb, W. "The effects of early institutional care on adolescent personality," (graphic Rorschach data), *Child Development*, 14 (1943), 213.

20. Goldfarb, W. "Infant rearing as a factor in foster home replacement," *Amer. J. Orthopsychiat.*, 14 (1944), 162.

21. Goldfarb, W. "Effects of early institutional care on adolescent personality: Rorschach data," *Amer. J. Orthopsychiat.*, 14 (1944), 441.

22. Goldfarb, W. "Psychological privation in infancy and subsequent adjustment," *Amer. J. Orthopsychiat.*, 15 (1945), 247.

23. Goldfarb, W. "Effects of psychological deprivation in infancy and subsequent stimulation," *Amer. J. Psychiat.*, 102 (1945), 18.

24. Goldfarb, W. "Variations in adolescent adjustment of institutionally reared children," *Amer. J. Orthopsychiat.*, 17 (1947), 449.

25. Goldfarb, W. "Rorschach test differences between family reared, institution-reared, and schizophrenic children," *Amer. J. Orthopsychiat.*, 19 (1949), 624.

26. Hebb, D. O. *The Organization of Behavior*. New York: Wiley, 1949.

27. Levy, D. M. "Primary affect hunger," *Amer. J. Psychiat.*, 94 (1937), 643.

28. Lewis, M. *Deprived Children (the Mershal Experiment): A Social and Clinical Study*. London: Oxford University Press, 1954.

29. Skeels, H. M., and H. B. Dye. "A study of the effects of differential simulation on mentally retarded children," *Proc. and Addr. Amer. Ass. Ment. Defec.*, 44 (1939), 114.

30. Skeels, H. M., and E. A. Fillmore. "The mental development of children from underprivileged homes," *J. Genet. Psychol.*, 50 (1937), 427.

31. Skeels, H. M., and I. Harms. "Children with inferior social histories: their mental development in adoptive homes," *J. Genet. Psychol.*, 72 (1948), 283.

32. Skeels, H. M., R. Updegraff, B. Wellman, and H. M. Williams. "A study of environment stimulation: an orphanage preschool project," *Iowa Stud. Child Welf.*, 15 (1938), No. 4.

33. Skodak, M., and H. M. Skeels. "A final follow-up study of one hundred adopted children," *J. Genet. Psychol.*, 75 (1949), 85.

34. Spitz, R. A. "Hospitalism," in Ruth S. Eissler et al., eds., *Psychoanalytic Study of the Child*, vol. 1. New York: International Universities Press, 1945, 53.

35. Spitz, R. A. "Hospitalism: a follow-up report," in Ruth S. Eissler et al., eds., *Psychoanalytic Study of the Child*, vol. 2. New York: International Universities Press, 1946, 113.

36. Spitz, R. A. "The role of ecological factors in emotional development in infancy," *Child Development*, 20 (1949), 145.

22

Father Absence and the Personality Development of the Male Child

Henry B. Biller

In some societies it is normal for a father to be absent or rarely present, and this may be a norm in some of the dormitory suburbs of modern cities. Nevertheless, Western cultures usually treat father-absent families as abnormal —a product of social disorganization, implying that they are less than ideal environments for maturing children. This essay reviews the effects of father absence on the psychological development of boys and, whether it is normal or abnormal, father absence is seen to have certain psychological effects. Unfortunately, little research has been done on the psychological development of girls without fathers.

More than one-tenth of the children in the United States live in households where no father is present (Clausen, 1966; Pettigrew, 1964; Schlesinger, 1966). The incidence of fatherless families is especially high among the lower class (Miller, 1958) and particularly among lower-class Negro families, approaching 50 percent in some areas (King, 1945; Moynihan, 1965; Pettigrew, 1964). This article is an attempt to review pertinent data and to stimulate further research concerning the impact of father absence on the personality development of the male child.

Sex-Role Development

Many writers have speculated that the primary effects of father absence are manifested in terms of deficits and/or abnormalities in the boy's sex-role development (Biller and Borstelmann, 1967; Burton and Whiting, 1961; Nash, 1965; Winch, 1962; Yarrow, 1964). Theories of identification have contributed the major hypotheses pertaining to the boy's sex-role development. A primary assumption of these theories is that the father's presence is of crucial importance in the boy's sex-role development. According to these theories, the boy

Abridged from Henry B. Biller, "Father Absence and the Personality Development of the Male Child," in *Developmental Psychology,* 2 (1970), 181–201. Reprinted by permission of the American Psychological Association and the author.

The preparation of this article was supported in part by a Faculty Growth grant from the Faculty Research Council of the University of Massachusetts and in part by Public Health Service Research Grant 1-R03-MH-15728-01 from the National Institute of Mental Health.

408

learns to be masculine by identifying with the father and imitating his behavior (Bandura and Walters, 1963; Biller and Borstelmann, 1967; Bronfenbrenner, 1960).

There is a wealth of evidence pointing to the importance of the father-son relationship in masculine development (reviewed by Biller and Borstelmann, 1967). In general, a warm relationship with a father who is himself masculine seems to be a very significant factor in the boy's sex-role development. Boys who have passive, ineffectual fathers generally appear to be less masculine than boys who have interested fathers who play a decisive role in family interactions. It could be expected from such evidence that father-absent boys will be less masculine than father-present boys.

In a pioneering investigation of the effects of father absence, the doll-play activity of 3-to-5-year-old father-absent and father-present children was analyzed (Sears, 1951; Sears, Pintler, and Sears, 1946). Father-absent boys generally manifested less doll-play aggression than did father-present boys; their doll-play behavior also seemed to be less influenced by the common sex factor of the father and boy dolls. ' Using a similar procedure to study 6-to-10-year-old children, Bach (1946) also found that father-absent boys were less aggressive than father-present boys and noted that, "The father-separated children produced an idealistic and feminine fantasy picture of the father when compared to the control children who elaborated the father's aggressive tendencies [p. 79]."

Stolz et al. (1954) reported that 4-to-8-year-old boys, who for approximately the first 2 years of their lives had been separated from their fathers, were generally regarded by their fathers as "sissies." Their study also revealed that these boys were less assertively aggressive and independent in their peer relations than boys who had not been separated from their fathers; they were more often observed to be overly submissive or to react with immature hostility. In apparent contrast to the studies cited in the preceding paragraph, they were actually more aggressive in doll play than boys who had not been separated from their fathers. However, the fact that the fathers were present in the home at the time of this study, and that the father-child relationships were stressful, makes for difficulty in speculating about the specific effects of father absence on personality development.

Other studies also suggest that boys who have had fathers absent in their preschool years, even after their fathers return, are less masculine than boys whose fathers have been consistently present. Carlsmith (1964) found that, among middle-class and upper-middle-class high school males, early father absence up to and before age 5 was related to the patterning of College Board Aptitude Scores. In contrast to the usual male patterns of math score higher than verbal score, the pattern of the father-absent subjects was more frequently the same as the female pattern; verbal score higher than math score. In addition, Carlsmith (1964) stated that "the relative superiority of verbal to math aptitude increases steadily the longer the father is absent and the younger the child is when the father left [p. 10]."

Leichty (1960) studied male college students who were father absent between the ages of 3–5 and a matched not-father-absent group. On the Blacky Pictures, fewer of the father-absent students said "Blacky" would like to pattern himself after his father, more often choosing "Mother" or "Tippy," a sibling. This item can be conceived of as a projective indication of underlying sex-role orientation, the father-absent males being less masculine. Unfortunately, one does not know from the data Leichty presents how many of the father-absent group chose Tippy, an identification which may also indicate a masculine sex-role orientation. Interestingly, on this same item, Rabin (1958) found that fewer 9-to-11-year-old kibbutz boys compared to non-kibbutz boys said Blacky would like to pattern himself after his father. This can be predicted since the kibbutz boys had less contact with their fathers than did the non-kibbutz boys. But again it is not evident in data presentation how many of the boys chose Tippy.

Tiller (1958) and Lynn and Sawrey (1959) studied Norwegian children aged 8-to-9½, whose fathers were sailors absent at least 9 months a year, and a matched group of children who had not been separated from their fathers. Interviews with mothers and responses to projective tests indicated that the father-absent boys, compared with the father-present boys, displayed more compensatory masculinity (at times behaving in an exaggerated masculine manner, at other times behaving in a highly feminine manner). Similar to the Sears (Sears, 1951; Sears, Pintler, and Sears, 1946) and Bach (1946) studies, Tiller found the father-absent boys less aggressive in doll play. One problem in interpreting the results of the Tiller and Lynn and Sawrey studies is the difference in sociocultural background between the father-absent and father-present families (families headed by sailor officers in contrast to those headed by businessmen and white collar workers).

A number of studies have compared father-absent and father-present boys in terms of their human figure drawings. Phelan (1964) speculated that boys who draw a female when asked to draw a person have failed to make a shift from an initial identification with the mother to an identification with the father, because of a lack of relative paternal influence in the home. She found a higher rate of father absence among elementary school-age boys who drew a female first as compared to those who drew a male first. A further analysis of Biller's (1968a) results with kindergarten-age children revealed that father-absent as compared to father-present boys were significantly less likely to draw a male first or to clearly differentiate their male and female drawings. However, studies with older children have generally not found predicted relationships between father absence and figure drawings (Domini, 1967; Lawton and Sechrest, 1962; Tiller, 1958). Unfortunately, most of these studies concerned with figure drawings do not present specific information regarding length and age of onset of father absence.

Developmental Stages and Aspects of Sex Role

There is some evidence that suggests that father absence before the age of 4 or 5 has a particularly profound effect on masculine development. Hetherington (1966) reported that 9-to-12-year-old father-absent boys manifested less masculine projective sex-role behavior (It Scale for Children, ITSC) and were rated as more dependent, less aggressive, and as engaging in fewer physical contact games by male recreation directors than father-present boys, but only if the father's absence began in the boy's first 4 years of life. Biller (1969a) found that father-absent 5-year-old boys had significantly less masculine sex-role orientations (fantasy game measure) and sex-role preferences (game choice) than did father-present boys. However, the boys who became father absent before the age of 4 had significantly less masculine sex-role orientations than those who became father absent in their fifth year.

The work of Money (1965) and Hampson (1965) has also pointed to the first 2-to-3 years of life as being of crucial importance in the

411

formation of an individual's basic sex-role orientation. These investigators have studied individuals with physical-sexual incongruencies and have concluded that self-conceptions relating to sex role appear particularly hard to change after the second and third years of life. Their conclusions need to be bolstered by more objective and complex assessment of their subjects' sex-role development but such observational findings are nevertheless very provocative. Such data point to the possibility of critical periods in sex-role development; it may be that father absence at different age periods affects different dimensions of personality development.

Using a cross-cultural perspective, Burton and Whiting (1961) discussed the possible differential impact of father absence on different levels of sex-role development. Many societies have what Burton and Whiting refer to as a "discontinuous identification process." There are long periods of exclusive mother-child interaction during which the father is virtually excluded from contact with his children. In such societies, according to Whiting's status envy hypothesis, children of both sexes identify with the mother because, in terms of the child's awareness, the mother is the primary controller of both material and nonmaterial resources. However, in most such societies the boy is pushed into masculine behavior sometime in preadolescence or adolescence,* particularly through his experiences during initiation rites. Suddenly he is under direct control of adult males and feminine behavior is negatively reinforced. A "sexual identification conflict" is assumed to be established because the boy has to learn to repress his earlier feminine identification. Whiting, Kluckhohn, and Anthony (1958) found that societies with exclusive mother-son sleeping arrangements and long postpartum sex taboos were likely to have elaborate male initiation rites; Burton and Whiting (1961) speculated "that the initiation rites serve psychologically to brainwash the primary feminine identity and to establish firmly the secondary male identity [p. 90]."

Burton and Whiting (1961) presented some other rather dramatic cross-cultural evidence in support of their "sex-role identification conflict" hypothesis. They found that in societies where rules of residence were matrilocal and where the infant sleeps and interacts al-

* See Chapter 20 in this volume for a related study.—[EDITOR]

most exclusively with the mother and other females during the first few years of his life, a custom called the couvade is particularly likely to occur. The couvade is a custom which calls for the husband to retire to his bed on the birth of his offspring and act as though he had gone through childbirth. Burton and Whiting interpreted this custom as symbolic of an underlying feminine identification.

Different aspects of sex role may not be affected in the same way by father absence. Hodges, McCandless, and Spicker (McCandless, 1967) found that young children who suffer from father deprivation intensely seek attention from older males. Because of deprivation effects, father-absent boys often have a strong motivation for a father figure and similarly a desire to act masculine (Freud and Burlingham, 1944; Lynn and Sawrey, 1959). They may act masculine in some facets of their behavior and unmasculine and/or feminine in others. Biller and Borstelmann (1967) described three general aspects of sex role based, in part, on earlier conceptualizations (Brown, 1956; Colley, 1959; Fenichel, 1945; Kagan, 1964; Lynn, 1959). Sex-role orientation (or sex-role identification) is considered to be one dimension of an individual's self-concept. It refers to the individual's conscious and/or unconscious perception and evaluation of his maleness and/or femaleness. Sex-role preference relates to the individual's preferential set toward culturally defined representations of sex role. Sex-role adoption pertains to the masculinity and/or femininity of the individual's behavior in social and environmental interactions. Sex-role orientation might be measured through responses to projective tests and fantasy play; sex-role preference through directly expressed likes and dislikes for various toys, games, and activities; sex-role adoption through observer ratings of an individual's behavior (Biller, 1968a; Biller and Borstelmann, 1967).

D'Andrade (1962) compared the effects of several kinds of family patterns on the sex-role development of 5-to-14-year-old children. Using what may be considered a brief sex-role preference measure (asking the child whether he preferred to pretend to be the father, mother, brother, or sister if he were playing a game, and recording the order of his choices), he generally found that boys whose fathers had been continually absent made masculine preferences to the same degree as boys whose fathers had been continually present. Although the number of subjects at different age levels in this study was very

413

small, responses to a projective drawing completion test (Franck Test) suggested that the boys who were without fathers during their first few years of life had unmasculine and/or feminine sex-role orientations even though they were quite masculine in their sex-role preferences.

Barclay and Cusumano (1967) failed to find any differences between father-present and father-absent adolescent males on a measure of sex-role preference (Gough Femininity Scale). However, they did find that the father-absent males, as compared to the father-present males, were more field dependent in terms of Witkin's rod-and-frame test. They conceptualized the field dependence-field independence dimension as reflecting underlying sex-role orientation.

Biller (1968b), studying lower-class 6-year-old boys, found that the father-absent boys were significantly less masculine than father-present boys on a measure of projective sex-role behavior (ITSC). However, no differences were revealed in terms of direct sex-role preferences (asking the boys to name the toys and games they liked) or teachers' ratings of sex-role adoption on a multidimensional scale. Biller's (1969a) results with 5-year-old boys also indicated that sex-role orientation is more affected by father absence than are sex-role preference or sex-role adoption. It is interesting to note that among father-present boys the degree of both perceived father dominance and father dominance in father-mother interactions appears more related to measures of sex-role orientation than to measures of sex-role preference or sex-role adoption (Biller, 1969b).

Data from some studies (Greenstein, 1966; McCord, McCord, and Thurber, 1962; Miller, 1961; Mitchell and Wilson, 1967; Terman and Miles, 1936) suggest the hypothesis that there is relatively little difference among lower-class adolescent father-present and father-absent boys with respect to many facets of sex-role awareness, preference, and adoption.

Greenstein (1966) failed to find any differences, using a masculinity-femininity interest inventory and other sex-role measures, between father-absent and father-present boys referred to a juvenile court affiliated diagnostic center. The major criterion for father absence was that, at least 3 years prior to age 12, no adult male was living in the home. But, at the time of the study, 10 of the 25 father-absent boys were residing in homes in which an adult male was present.

Miller's (1961) findings were consistent with Greenstein's, and Miller's subjects seemed more representative. She found no differences between father-absent lower-class junior high school boys, predominantly Negro and Puerto Rican, and a matched group of father-present boys, on either a masculinity-femininity interest inventory or in teachers' ratings of aggression and dependency. The criterion for father absence was that no male lived in the home for at least 2 years prior to the study.

Unfortunately in both the Greenstein (1966) and Miller (1961) studies, one does not know in how many cases the father (or a father surrogate) was available in the preschool years and if so, for how long. For instance, father presence in the pre-school years for both groups could explain the lack of differences between the "father-absent" and "father-present" boys.

An analysis by McCord, McCord, and Thurber (1962) of social workers' observations of predominantly lower-class 10-to-15-year-old boys revealed no differences in the sex-appropriate behavior of boys separated from their fathers before the age of 6 and father-present boys, although many boys separated from their fathers between the ages of 6 and 12 exhibited a feminine-aggressive pattern of behavior. This feminine-aggressive pattern of behavior seems similar to the behavior of Norwegian father-separated boys (Lynn and Sawrey, 1959; Tiller, 1958), and to reflect sex-role conflict. Nevertheless, the McCord, McCord, and Thurber data are consistent with the proposition that imitation of other models such as peers mitigates the retarding effects of father absence on masculine development.

Assuming that attending college is more typical of middle-class adolescents than of lower-class adolescents, a study by Altus (1958), involving college students, suggests that father-absent middle-class boys, in contrast to father-absent lower-class boys, remain relatively low in masculinity of sex-role preference throughout adolescence. Altus compared father-absent and father-present male freshman at the University of California. The reason for father absence was stated as divorce of parents but no data about the age of onset of father absence were reported. The father-absent group scored significantly higher than the father-present group on the *Mf* scale of the Minnesota Multiphasic Personality Inventory (MMPI), indicating less masculinity of interests and attitudes.

415

Impulsive and Aggressive Behavior

Mischel (1961b) reported data relating father absence and impulse control. He studied 8-and-9-year-old West Indian children in terms of their preferences for delayed or immediate gratification. The criterion of father absence was simply whether or not the father was living at home. Father-absent children showed a stronger preference for immediate gratification than did father-present children. For instance, they significantly more often chose a small piece of candy for immediate consumption rather than waiting a week for a large candy bar.

Using similar procedures in an earlier study, Mischel (1958) found that 7-to-9-year-old Negro West Indian children chose immediate gratification significantly more frequently than did white West Indian children. Especially relevant for the present discussion is the fact that Mischel believed that these differences were due to the greater degree of father absence among the Negro children. Mischel conjectured that young father-absent children often have not learned to trust other people. A related possibility is that many young father-absent children may trust adult females but have not learned to trust adult males; an adult male offered them the choice between immediate and delayed gratification. To put it another way, young father-absent children may learn to be secure in the presence of their mother and generalize to other females, but a basis for trust in adult males is likely to be lacking. Mothers of father-absent children may also be overindulgent with them, satisfying their children's impulses immediately. It is noteworthy that some recent findings suggest that, among lower-class mothers, those without husbands are more concerned with day-to-day activities and less frequently consider future goals for themselves and for their children (Heckscher, 1967; Parker and Kleiner, 1966).

Mischel (1961b) did not find differences in comparisons involving 11-to-14-year-old father-absent and father-present children. He mentioned that among the older subjects in his study, father absence may have occurred relatively recently. (In his study, as in many other studies comparing father-absent and father-present children, there is no measure of duration of father absence, a seemingly important variable.) Mischel also suggested that the child's wider experience as he grows older allows him to develop expectations of promise keeping and trust of others beyond his immediate family. Perhaps with added experience most father-absent children learn they can trust adult males as well as females.

Meerloo (1956) postulated that a lack of accurate time perception is common in father-absent children. According to Meerloo (1956) the father represents social order and social functioning, particularly as manifested in his adherence to time schedules. It is interesting to note that antisocial acts are often impulsive as well as aggressive. Mischel (1961a, 1961c) found that inability to delay gratification is associated with inaccurate time perception, lack of social responsibility, low achievement motivation, and juvenile delinquency.

Miller (1958) concluded that lower-class boys from female-based homes, in their constant effort to prove their masculinity, are more often involved in antisocial acts (at least by middle-class standards) than are father-present boys. Delinquency can have many different etiologies. What may be postulated is that some cases of delinquency are a result of masculine overcompensation, particularly among father-absent boys. In a cross-cultural study Bacon, Child, and Barry (1963) found that degree of father absence as defined by family structure was related to the existence of theft and personal crime in particular societies. Those societies with a predominantly monogamous nuclear family structure tended to be rated low in the amount of theft and personal crime, societies with a polygamous mother-child family structure tended to be rated high in both theft and personal crime. Bacon, Child, and Barry suggested that such antisocial behavior was a reaction against a female-based household and an attempted assertion of masculinity.

Glueck and Glueck (1950) found that more than two-fifths of the adolescent delinquent boys they studied were father absent as compared with less than one-fourth of a matched nondelinquent group; Gregory (1965a) noted a number of investigations linking father absence with delinquent behavior and also detected a strong association between these variables in his study of high school students. McCord, McCord, and Thurber (1962) reported that the lower-class father-absent boys in their study participated in more felonies than the father-present group, although the rates of gang delinquency were not different. Siegman (1966) collected medical students' responses to a questionnaire; those who had been without a father for at least 1 year during their first 4 years of life, compared to those who had been continuously father present, admitted to a greater degree of anti-social behavior in childhood. It seems relevant that father-present juvenile delinquents appear to have very poor relationships with their fathers (e.g., Andry, 1962; Bach and Bremer, 1947).

Cognitive Deficits

There have been several investigations which have revealed that the father-absent child often suffers from intellectual deficits (Bronfenbrenner, 1967; Deutsch, 1960; Deutsch and Brown, 1964; Landy, Rosenberg, and Sutton-Smith, 1967; Maxwell, 1961; Sutherland, 1930; Sutton-Smith, Rosenberg, and Landy, 1968). Deutsch's (1960; Deutsch and Brown, 1964) studies are particularly interesting and indicate that the father-absent Negro child, compared to the father-present Negro child, scores significantly lower on intelligence and academic achievement tests. Father absence seems to be an important factor in the complex and debilitating effects of cultural deprivation.

Kohlberg (1966) has suggested that differences in the sex-role development of father-absent and father-present boys are related to father-absent boys' lower intelligence. He hypothesized that if father-absent and father-present boys are matched in intelligence, differences in sex-role development are not found or are very small. He described the data of one of his students (Smith, 1966) which suggest that differences between father-absent and father-present boys' sex-role preferences are considerably lessened if IQ is controlled. Kohlberg argued compellingly that the learning of socially defined concepts of sex role is the primary ingredient of the sex-role-development process and speculated that many young father-absent boys lack certain types of cognitive experience which retard both their intellectual and sex-role development.

Consistent with Kohlberg's (1966) formulation, recent studies suggest that father-absent children, at least after they reach school age, are not particularly deficient in their general knowledge of social norms concerning sex typing (Biller, 1968b; Thomes, 1968). However, Biller (1969a) found significant differences between IQ matched father-present and father-absent 5-year-old boys with respect to measures of sex-role orientation and sex-role preference: There seems to be much more to sex-role development than the learning of social norms.

Carlsmith's (1964) findings, indicating that middle-class boys who were father absent in their early childhood are more likely than boys who were father present to have a feminine patterning of aptitude test scores, have already been mentioned. Citing evidence from other studies, Carlsmith reasoned that such a score pattern was a reflection of a feminine-global conceptual style. Other evidence (Witkin, 1960) mentioned by Carlsmith indicates that boys who have neglecting or passive fathers adopt a global rather than an analytical conceptual style. The inference is that when the father is absent or not salient, the boy will model himself after his mother in cognitive style. In an intriguing investigation emphasizing the complexity of the familial correlates of cognitive development, Nelsen and Maccoby (1966) also found early father absence related to the feminine patterning of aptitude test scores.

Although Carlsmith (1964) did not specifically analyze her data to see how the father-absent and father-present males' verbal and mathematical aptitudes compared in absolute terms, it appears that the father-absent group was equal or superior in verbal aptitude though inferior in mathematical aptitude. Since academic achievement in most fields is so heavily dependent on verbal ability, father-absent *middle-class* males may not be very handicapped. Hilgard, Neuman, and Fisk's (1960) findings appear relevant: In their interview study in a university town, they found that men who lost their fathers during childhood were highly successful in their academic pursuits despite, or maybe because of, a conspicuous overdependence on their mothers. A study by Gregory (1965b) suggests that many upper-middle-class college students who have been father absent do well in their academic pursuits and data reviewed by Nelsen and Maccoby (1966) indicate that high verbal ability in boys is often associated with a close and restrictive mother-son relationship. The middle-class maternally overprotected boys in Levy's (1943) study also did superior work in school, particularly in subjects requiring verbal facility, but their performance in mathematics was not at such a high level. This seems consistent with Carlsmith's (1964) findings.

If a relationship does hold between father absence and certain types of cognitive functioning, it must be remembered that father absence per se is only one of many variables responsible for such a relationship. The values of the mother and the peer group are extremely important. Among children in the lower class, father absence usually intensifies lack of exposure to certain cognitive experiences. In addition, many boys in their masculine overcompensation perceive intellectual tasks and school in general as "feminine." The school situation which presents women as authority figures, and makes strong demands for obedience and conformity, is particularly antithetical to such boys' conscious values and desperate attempts to feel masculine. Many such boys develop an almost phobic reaction concerning intellectual matters.

Difficulties in Interpersonal Relationships

A number of studies suggest that father-absent boys have more difficulty in forming peer relationships than do father-present boys (Leiderman, 1953; Lynn and Sawrey, 1959; Miller, 1961; Mitchell and Wilson, 1967; Stolz et al., 1954; Tiller, 1958). Father-absent boys may be less popular with their peers than father-present boys because they more often lack a secure masculine sex-role orientation.

Tuddenham's (1951, 1952) extensive studies have demonstrated how important sex-appropriate behavior is in the formation of friendships among elementary school children. For instance, the most popular boys in the first grade were those who were considered by their peers to be good sports, good at games, daring, not bashful, and "real boys." Gray (1957, 1959) found similar results for fifth- to eighth-grade boys. In addition, boys who were rated high in popularity perceived themselves as significantly more like their fathers in terms of an adjective checklist than did boys who were rated low in popularity (Gray, 1959). Payne and Mussen (1956) reported that adolescent boys who were similar to their fathers in terms of responses to the California Personality Inventory were rated as significantly more friendly by their teachers than boys who had responses markedly different from their fathers. Leiderman (1953) found that fourth-grade boys who had high acceptance among their peers had warmer relationships with their fathers than those with low-peer acceptance. Hoffman (1961) reported similar results and also found that elementary school-age boys from mother-dominant homes had much more difficulty in their peer relationships than did boys from father-dominant homes. There is also considerable evidence that boys' masculine development is impeded in mother-dominant homes (e.g., Biller, 1969b; Hetherington, 1965; Moulton, Burnstein, Liberty, and

Altucher, 1966). Taking the findings from these studies together, it appears that, for boys, the presence of a masculine father, a positive father-son relationship, generally sex-appropriate behavior, and popularity with peers are strongly related.

There is some evidence indicating that mothers in father-absent homes are more likely than are mothers in father-present homes to overprotect their children and encourage over-dependency (Biller, 1969a; Neubauer, 1960; Stendler, 1954; Stephens, 1962; Stolz et al., 1954; Tiller, 1958). In homes where the father plays a very submissive or ineffectual role, maternal overprotection and over-dependent behavior on the part of children also appear common (Levy, 1943; Sears, 1953; Stoller, 1968). There are additional data suggesting that mothers in father-absent homes, as compared to those in father-present homes, are less likely to treat their sons and daughters differently, and are less likely to encourage their sons to behave in a masculine manner or enter into masculine peer group activities (Romney, 1965; Stolz et al., 1954; Tiller, 1958).

Although no systematic studies have been made concerning the rates of homosexuality among father-absent males, some investigators have suggested that father-absent males are more likely than father-present males to become homosexual. Both West (1959) and O'Connor (1964) reported that homosexual males more often than neurotic males had histories of long periods of father absence during childhood. West (1967) presented an excellent review of available data pertaining to the antecedents of male homosexuality: Males who as children are father absent or have ineffectual fathers, together with being involved in an intense close-binding relationship with their mothers, seem particularly likely to develop a homosexual pattern of behavior. A close-binding sexualized mother-son relationship seems more common in father-absent homes than in father-present homes and may, along with related factors, lessen the probability of the boy entering into meaningful heterosexual relationships (Freud, 1947; Grønseth, 1957; Neubauer, 1960; Stoller, 1968; Wylie and Delgado, 1959). There is also evidence that a significant proportion of homosexuals as children were discouraged by their mothers from participating in masculine activities and were often reinforced for feminine behavior (Bieber et al., 1962; West, 1967).

Males who have been father absent often appear to have difficulty in forming lasting heterosexual relationships. Winch (1949), in a questionnaire study with college students, found that father absence was negatively related to degree of courtship behavior (defined as closeness to marriage). Hilgard, Neuman, and Fisk (1960) described continued mother dependency of males whose fathers died when they were children, if their mothers did not remarry: Only 1 of the 10 men who fit this category reportedly showed a fair degree of independence in a marital relationship. Pettigrew's (1964) study with working-class Negroes also suggests that father-absent males have difficulty in their heterosexual relationships. He found that father-absent males compared to father-present males were "more likely to be single or divorced—another manifestation of their disturbed sexual identification [p. 420]."

Indirect evidence suggesting that Negro males are less masculine in certain facets of their sex-role behavior than are white males is cited by Pettigrew (1964, pp. 18–24). Two recent studies indicated that lower-class father-absent Negro males, although they appear quite masculine in many manifest facets of their behavior, suffer in terms of their sex-role orientations (Barclay and Cusumano, 1967; Biller, 1968b). In both studies, father availability and sociocultural background were found to be significantly related to what could be considered a projective measure of sex-role orientation. For example, Biller (1968b) found in terms of projective sex-role orientation (ITSC) that among 6-year-old lower-class boys Negro father-absent boys were the least masculine; there was no significant difference between white father-absent and Negro father-present boys; and white father-present boys were the most masculine. Descriptions of the low value put on males in lower-class matriarchal families point to one process by which boys may develop sex-role conflicts (Beller, 1967; Dai, 1953; Frazier, 1939; Kardiner and Ovesey, 1951; Rainwater, 1966; Rohrer and Edmonson, 1960).

Much of the difficulty that some manifestly masculine father-absent lower-class males have in forming meaningful heterosexual relationships may also be associated with a compulsive rejection of anything they perceive as related to femininity (Miller, 1958). Many lower-class males seem intent on constantly proving they are not homosexual and/or effeminate. In their efforts to prove themselves masculine, they frequently engage in a "Don Juan" pattern of behavior, making one conquest after another. In such cases a stable emotional relationship with a female may not be formed even during marriage;

masculinity must be continually proved by new conquests. Such a pattern of behavior seems particularly prevalent among Negro father-absent lower-class males (Rohrer and Edmonson, 1960).

Anxiety and General Personality Dysfunctioning

Psychoanalytic theorists such as Freud and Fenichel viewed anxiety as a primary outcome of father absence. Their emphasis was on anxiety springing from the unresolved Oedipal situation (Fenichel, 1945), but the frequent economic and social insecurity of the father-absent family cannot be ignored. Koch (1961) found that father-absent nursery-school children (eight boys and three girls) were more anxious as measured on a projective test of anxiety than a matched group from intact families; the father-absent children more often selected unhappy faces for the central child depicted in various situations than did the matched group.

Stolz et al. (1954) reported that 4-to-8-year-old children, father absent the first few years of life while their fathers were away in military service, were more anxious than children whose fathers had been continually present. They were observed to be more anxious with peers and adults, in story completion sessions when the situation involved the fathers, and according to mothers' reports of seriousness and number of fears. Again, the Stolz et al. results are difficult to interpret because fathers were not absent at the time of the study and were having stressful relationships with their children.

Using social workers' observations, McCord, McCord, and Thurber (1962) reported that 10-to15-year-old father-absent boys showed more anxiety about sex than a matched group of father-present boys although the difference between the groups in terms of amount of general fearfulness was insignificant. In another study, when asked retrospectively about their experiences with father-absent boys, a group of social workers described them as more effeminate and anxious about sex than father-present boys (Stephens, 1961). However, Leichty (1960), in her study with college students, did not find any evidence that father absence during the Oedipal period was associated with castration anxiety.

There are some studies that suggest that individuals who have been father absent are likely to exhibit, to a pathological degree, feelings of loss and depressed behavior (Beck, Sehti, and Tuthill, 1963; Haworth, 1964; Keeler, 1954; Travis, 1933). It may be that loss of father due to death is more strongly related to chronically depressed behavior than is loss of father due to other factors. However, the available studies concerning father absence and depressed behavior, though of heuristic value, have not been carefully controlled. For instance, many of the subjects suffering from paternal loss in these studies have frequently also had a history of institutionalization.

The general indication from these studies is that the rates of paternal absence are higher for children with emotional problems than for children in the general population. There is a growing amount of literature suggesting that father-present males having inadequate fathering, compared to those with adequate fathering, are much more likely to develop severe behavior disturbances and/or schizophrenia (e.g., Farina, 1960; Johnson and Meadow, 1966; Lidz, Parker, and Cornelison, 1956). There is also accumulating evidence indicating that severely disturbed and/or schizophrenic behavior is associated with difficulties and/or abnormalities in sex-role development (e.g., Cheek, 1964; Gardner, 1967; McClelland and Watt, 1968). Furthermore, a look at files of any child guidance center suggests that among disturbed children, ineffective or psychologically absent fathers, and sex-role conflicts, are much more common than they are among children in the general population; however, more methodologically sound studies must be done.

Rates of childhood father absence among adult patients classified as neurotic (Ingham, 1949; Madow and Hardy, 1947; Norton, 1952) and as schizophrenic (Da Silva, 1963; Oltman, McGarry, and Friedman, 1952; Wahl, 1954) are higher than among the general population. Gregory (1956) critically reviewed many of the relevant studies and emphasized some of the methodological pitfalls in comparisons involving the relative incidence of mental illness among father-present and father-absent individuals; lack of consideration of the possible effects of socioeconomic status is a major shortcoming of most of the studies. Cobliner (1963) presented some provocative findings suggesting that father absence is more likely to be related to serious psychological disturbance in lower-class as compared to middle-class individuals; middle-class families, particularly with respect to the mother-child relationships, may have more psychological as well as economic resources with which to cope with father absence.

Both Bach (1946), in his analysis of "father typing" (the way the mother describes the father to her son), and Colley (1959), in his conceptualization of the sex-role-identity process, suggested that the mother-child relationships can have either a positive or negative effect on the father-absent child's personality development. A number of studies have revealed findings which are consistent with such a proposition (Biller, 1969a; Hilgard, Neuman, and Fisk, 1960; McCord, McCord, and Thurber, 1962; Pedersen, 1966).

Hilgard, Neuman, and Fisk (1960) in an interesting but retrospective study, interviewed adults whose fathers had died when they were children. The mother's ability to use her own and outside resources and assume some of the dual functions of mother and father with little conflict seemed strongly related to her child's adjustment as an adult; the mother's ego strength rather than her warmth and tenderness appeared the essential variable in her child's adjustment.

McCord, McCord, and Thurber (1962) in their analysis of social workers' observations of 10-to-15-year-old boys, discovered that the presence of a rejecting and/or disturbed mother was associated with various behavior problems (sexual anxiety, regressive behavior, and criminal acts) in father-absent boys, but father-absent boys who had seemingly well-adjusted mothers were much less likely to exhibit such behavior problems.

Pedersen's (1966) study of military families also suggests that psychologically healthy mothers may be able to counteract the effects of father absence. Both the emotionally disturbed and non-disturbed 11-to-15-year-old boys in this study had experienced relatively long periods of father absence; however, the mothers of the disturbed group exhibited significantly more psychopathology (in terms of the MMPI) than the mothers of non-disturbed boys and it was only in the disturbed group of boys that degree of father absence was related to level of maladjustment (measured by the Rogers Test of Personality Adjustment).

It would seem that a mother can help a father-absent son by having a positive attitude toward the absent father and other males and by generally expecting and encouraging masculine behavior. Biller (1969a) found that for kindergarten-age father-absent boys, degree of maternal encouragement for masculine behavior (inferred from a multiple-choice questionnaire) was positively related to masculinity of sex-role preference (assessed by game choice) and masculinity of sex-role adoption (measured by a multidimensional teachers' rating scale). Exploring the effects of the mother-child relationship on the father-absent boy appears an especially promising area of personality investigation.

Effects on Girls

Findings reviewed by Biller and Weiss (1970) indicate that a girl's, as well as a boy's, personality development may be adversely affected by father absence (Heckel, 1963; Landy, Rosenberg, and Sutton-Smith, 1967; Lynn and Sawrey, 1959; Neubauer, 1960; Ostrovsky, 1959; Sears, Pintler, and Sears, 1946). Some studies suggest that girls are less affected by father absence than are boys (Bach, 1946; Lynn and Sawrey, 1959; Stolz et al., 1954; Sutton-Smith, Rosenberg, and Landy, 1968; Winch, 1949). It seems probable that both boys and girls can be affected by father absence and that the extent and direction of sex differences is likely to vary with respect to which dimensions of personality development are considered. However, there is a great need for much more systematic research if one is to come to any firm conclusions regarding the differential impact of father absence as a function of sex of child.

References

Altus, W. D. "The broken home and factors of adjustment," *Psychol. Rep.,* 4 (1958), 477.

Andry, R. G. "Paternal and maternal roles in delinquency," in *Deprivation of Maternal Care* (Public Health Paper No. 14). Geneva: World Health Organization, 1962.

Bach, G. R. "Father fantasies and father typing in father-separated children," *Child Development,* 17 (1946), 63–80.

Bach, G. R., and G. Bremer. "Projective father fantasies of preadolescent delinquent children," *J. Psychol.,* 24 (1947), 3–17.

Bacon, M. K., I. L. Child, and H. Barry, III. "A cross-cultural study of correlates of crime, *J. Abnormal Soc. Psychol.,* 66 (1963), 291–300.

Bandura, A., and R. H. Walters. *Social Learning and Personality Development.* New York: Holt, Rinehart, 1963.

* Additional reference.

Barclay, A. G., and D. Cusumano. "Father absence, cross-sex identity, and field-dependent behavior in male adolescents," *Child Development,* 38 (1967), 243–250.

Beck, A. T., B. B. Sehti, and R. W. Tuthill. "Childhood bereavement and adult depression," *Arch. Gen. Psychiat.,* 9 (1963), 295–302.

* Bell, R. Q. "A reinterpretation of the direction of effects of studies of socialization," *Psychol. Rev.,* 75 (1968), 81–95.

Beller, E. K. "Maternal behaviors in lower-class Negro mothers." Paper presented at the meeting of the Eastern Psychological Association, Boston, April, 1967.

Bieber, I. et al. *Homosexuality: A Psychoanalytic Study.* New York: Basic Books, 1962.

Biller, H. B. "A multi-aspect investigation of masculine development in kindergarten-age boys," *Genet. Psychol. Monographs,* 76 (1968), 89–139 (a).

Biller, H. B. "A note on father absence and masculine development in young lower-class Negro and white boys," *Child Development,* 39 (1968), 1003–1006 (b).

Biller, H. B. "Father absence, maternal encouragement, and sex-role development in kindergarten-age boys," *Child Development,* 40 (1969), 539–546 (a).

Biller, H. B. "Father dominance and sex-role development in kindergarten-age boys," *Development Psychol.,* 1 (1969), 87–94 (b).

Biller, H. B., and L. J. Borstelmann. "Masculine development: an integrative review," *Merrill-Palmer Quart.,* 13 (1967), 253–294.

Biller, H. B., and Stephan D. Weiss. "The father-daughter relationship and the personality development of the female," *J. Genet. Psychol.,* 116 (1970), 79–93.

* Brim, O. G. "Family structure and sex-role learning by children: a further analysis of Helen Koch's data," *Sociometry,* 21 (1958), 1–16.

Bronfenbrenner, U. "Freudian theories of identification and their derivatives," *Child Development,* 31 (1960), 15–40.

Bronfenbrenner, U. "The psychological costs of quality and equality in education," *Child Development,* 38 (1967), 909–925.

Brown, D. G. "Sex-role preference in young children," *Psychol. Monographs,* 70 (1956), 14, Whole No. 421.

Burton, R. V., and J. W. M. Whiting. "The absent father and cross-sex identity," *Merrill-Palmer Quart.,* 7 (1961), 85–95.

Carlsmith, L. "Effect of early father-absence on scholastic aptitude," *Harvard Educational Rev.,* 34 (1964), 3–21.

Cheek, F. E. "A serendipitous finding: sex roles and schizophrenia," *J. Abnormal Soc. Psychol.,* 69 (1964), 392–400.

Clausen, J. A. "Family structure, socialization, and personality," in L. W. Hoffman and M. L. Hoffman, eds., *Review of Child Development Research,* vol. 2. New York: Russell Sage Foundation, 1966.

Cobliner, W. G. "Social factors in mental disorders: a contribution to the etiology of mental illness," *Genet. Psychol. Monographs,* 67 (1963), 151–215.

Colley, T. "The nature and origin of psychological sexual identity," *Psychol. Rev.,* 66 (1959), 165–177.

Dai, B. "Some problems of personality development among Negro children," in C. Kluckhohn, H. A. Murray, and D. M. Schneider, eds., *Personality in Nature, Society, and Culture.* New York: Knopf, 1953.

D'Andrade, R. G. "Father absence and cross-sex identification." Unpublished doctoral dissertation, Harvard University, 1962.

Da Silva, G. "The role of the father with chronic schizophrenic patients," *J. Canadian Psychiatric Assn.,* 8 (1963), 190–203.

Deutsch, M. "Minority group and class status as related to social and personality factors in scholastic achievement," *Society of Applied Anthropology Monographs,* (1960), No. 2.

Deutsch, M., and B. Brown. "Social influences in Negro-white intelligence differences," *J. Soc. Issues,* 20 (1964), 24–35.

Domini, G. P. "An evaluation of sex-role identification among father-absent and father-present boys," *Psychology,* 4 (1967), 13–16.

* Fagen, S. A., E. J. Janda, S. L. Baker, E. G. Fischer, and L. A. Cove. "Impact of father absence in military families: II. Factors relating to success of coping with crisis." Paper presented at the meeting of the American Psychological Association, Washington, D. C., September, 1967.

Farina, A. "Patterns of role dominance and conflict in parents of schizophrenic patients," *J. Abnormal Soc. Psychol.,* 61 (1960), 31–38.

Fenichel, O. *The Psychoanalytic Theory of Neurosis.* New York: Norton, 1945.

* Forrest, T. "The paternal roots of male character development," *Psychoanalytic Rev.,* 54 (1967), 81–99.

Frazier, E. F. *The Negro Family in the United States.* Chicago: University of Chicago Press, 1939.

Freud, A., and O. T. Burlingham. *Infants Without Families.* New York: International Universities Press, 1944.

Freud, S. *Leonardo Da Vinci: A Study in Psychosexuality.* New York: Random House, 1947.

Gardner, G. G. "The relationship between childhood neurotic symptomatology and later schizophrenia in males and females," *J. Nervous and Mental Disease,* 144 (1967), 97–100.

Glueck, S., and E. Glueck. *Unraveling Juvenile Delinquency.* New York: Commonwealth Fund, 1950.

Gray, S. W. "Masculinity-feminity in relation to anxiety and social acceptance," *Child Development,* 28 (1957), 203–214.

Gray, S. W. "Perceived similarity to parents and adjustment," *Child Development,* 30 (1959), 91–107.

* Green, A. W. "The middle-class child and neurosis," *Amer. Soc. Rev.,* 11 (1946), 31–41.

Greenstein, J. M. "Father characteristics and sex typing," *J. Person. Soc. Psychol.,* 3 (1966), 271–277.

Gregory, I. "Anterospective data following childhood loss of a parent: I. Delinquency and high school dropout," *Arch. Gen. Psychiat.,* 13 (1965), 110–120 (a).

Gregory, I. "Anterospective data following childhood loss of a parent: II. Pathology, performance, and potential among college students," *Arch. Gen. Psychiat.,* 13 (1965), 110–120 (b).

Grønseth, E. "The impact of father absence in sailor families upon the personality structure and social adjustment of adult sailor sons," Part I, in N. Anderson, ed., *Studies of the Family,* vol. 2. Gottingen: Vandenhoeck and Ruprecht, 1957.

Hampson, J. L. "Determinants of psychosexual orientation," in F. A. Beach, ed., *Sex and Behavior.* New York: Wiley, 1965.

Haworth, M. R. "Parental loss in children as reflected in projective responses," *J. Projective Techniques,* 28 (1964), 31–35.

Heckel, R. V. "The effects of fatherlessness on the preadolescent female," *Ment. Hyg.,* 47 (1963), 69–73.

Heckscher, B. T. "Household structure and achievement orientation in lower-class Barbadian families," *J. Marriage and the Family,* 29 (1967), 521–526.

Hetherington, E. M. "A development study of the effects of sex of the dominant parent on sex role preference, identification, and imitation in children," *J. Person. Soc. Psychol.,* 2 (1965), 188–194.

Hetherington, E. M. "Effects of paternal absence on sex-typed behaviors in Negro and white preadolescent males," *J. Person. Soc. Psychol.,* 4 (1966), 87–91.

Hilgard, J. R., M. F. Neuman, and F. Fisk, "Strength of adult ego following bereavement," *Amer. J. Orthopsychiat.,* 30 (1960), 788–798.

Hoffman, L. W. "The father's role in the family and the child's peer-group adjustment," *Merrill-Palmer Quart.,* 7 (1961), 97–105.

Ingham, H. V. "A statistical study of family relationships in psychoneurosis," *Amer. J. Orthopsychiat.,* 106 (1949), 91–98.

Johnson, M. A., and A. Meadow. "Parental identification among male schizophrenics," *J. Pers.,* 34 (1966), 300–309.

Kagan, J. "Acquisition and significance of sex typing and sex-role identity," in M. L. Hoffman and L. W. Hoffman, eds., *Review of Child Development Research,* vol. 1. New York: Russell Sage Foundation, 1964.

Kardiner, A., and L. Ovesey. *The Mark of Oppression.* New York: Norton, 1951.

Keeler, W. R. "Children's reaction to the death of a parent," in P. H. Hoch and J. Zubin, eds., *Depression.* New York: Grune, 1954.

King, C. E. "The Negro maternal family: a product of an economic and culture system," *Social Forces,* 24 (1945), 100–104.

* Koch, H. L. "Sissiness and tomboyishness in relation to sibling characteristics," *J. Genet.Psychol.,* 88 (1956), 231–244.

Koch, M. B. "Anxiety in preschool children from broken homes," *Merrill-Palmer Quart.,* 1 (1961), 225–231.

Kohlberg, L. "A cognitive-development analysis of children's sex-role concepts and attitudes," in E. E. Maccoby, ed., *The Development of Sex Differences.* Stanford: Stanford University Press, 1966.

Landy, F., B. G. Rosenberg, and B. Sutton-Smith. "The effect of limited father absence on the cognitive and emotional development of children." Paper presented at the meeting of the Midwestern Psychological Association, Chicago, May, 1967.

Lawton, M. J., and L. Sechrest. "Figure drawings by young boys from father-present and father-absent homes," *J. Clin. Psychol.,* 18 (1962), 304–305.

Leichty, M. M. "The effect of father absence during early childhood upon the Oedipal situation as reflected in young adults," *Merrill-Palmer Quart.,* 6 (1960), 212–217.

Leiderman, G. F. "Effect of family experiences on boys' peer relationships." Unpublished doctoral dissertation, Harvard University, 1953.

Levy, D. M. *Maternal Overprotection.* New York: Columbia University Press, 1943.

Lidz, T., N. Parker, and A. R. Cornelison. "The role of the father in the family environment of the schizophrenic patient," *Amer. J. Psychiat.,* 13 (1956), 126–132.

Lynn, D. B. "A note on sex differences in the development of masculine and feminine identification," *Psychol. Rev.,* 66 (1959), 126–135.

Lynn, D. B., and W. L. Sawrey. "The effects of father absence on Norwegian boys and girls," *J. Abnormal Soc. Psychol.,* 59 (1959), 258–262.

McCandless, B. W. *Children: Behavior and Development.* New York: Holt, Rinehart, 1967.

McClelland, D. C., and N. F. Watt. "Sex-role alienation in schizophrenia," *J. Abnormal Psychol.,* 73 (1968), 226–239.

McCord, J., W. McCord, and E. Thurber. "Some effects of paternal absence on male children," *J. Abnormal Soc. Psychol.,* 64 (1962), 361–369.

Madow, L., and S. E. Hardy. "Incidence and analysis of the broken family in the background of neurosis," *Amer. J. Orthopsychiat.,* 17 (1947), 521–528.

Maxwell, A. E. "Discrepancies between the pattern of abilities for normal and neurotic children," *J. Ment. Science,* 107 (1961), 300–307.

Meerloo, J. A. M. "The father cuts the cord: the role of the father as initial transference figure," *Amer. J. Psychotherapy,* 10 (1956), 471–480.

Miller, B. "Effects of father absence and mother's evaluation of father on the socialization of adolescent boys." Unpublished doctoral dissertation, Columbia University, 1961.

Miller, W. B. "Lower-class culture as a generating milieu of gang delinquency," *J. Social Issues,* 14 (1958), 5–19.

Mischel, W. "Preference for delayed reinforcement: an experimental study of a cultural observation," *J. Abnormal and Soc. Psychol.,* 56 (1958), 57–61.

Mischel, W. "Delay of gratification, need for achievement, and acquiescence in another culture," *J. Abnormal Soc. Psychol.,* 62 (1961), 543–552 (a).

Mischel, W. "Father absence and delay of gratification," *J. Abnormal Soc. Psychol.,* 63 (1961), 116–124 (b).

Mischel, W. "Preference for delayed reward and social responsibility," *J. Abnormal Soc. Psychol.,* 62 (1961), 1–7 (c).

Mitchell, D., and W. Wilson. "Relationship of father absence to masculinity and popularity of delinquent boys," *Psychol. Rep.,* 20 (1967), 1173–1174.

Money, J. "Psychosexual differentiation," in J. Money, ed., *Sex Research: New Developments.* New York: Holt, Rinehart, 1965.

Moulton, P. W., E. Burnstein, P. Liberty, and N. Altucher. "The patterning of parental affection and dominance as a determinant of guilt and sex typing," *J. Person. Soc. Psychol.,* 4 (1966), 356–363.

Moynihan, D. P. *The Negro Family: The Case for National Action.* Washington, D. C.: United States Department of Labor, 1965.

Nash, J. "The father in contemporary culture and current psychological literature," *Child Development,* 36 (1965), 261–297.

Nelsen, E. A., and E. E. Maccoby. "The relationship between social development and differential abilities on the scholastic aptitude test," *Merrill-Palmer Quart.,* 12 (1966), 269–289.

Neubauer, P. B. "The one-parent child and his Oedipal development," *Psychoanalytic Stud. of the Child,* 15 (1960), 286–309.

Norton, A. "Incidence of neurosis related to maternal age and birth order," *Brit. J. Soc. Medicine,* 6 (1952), 253–258.

O'Connor, P. J. "Aetiological factors in homosexuality as seen in R.A.F. psychiatric practice," *Brit. J. Psychiat.,* 110 (1964), 381–391.

Oltman, J. E., J. J. McGarry, and S. Friedman. "Parental deprivation and the 'broken home' in dementia praecox and other mental disorders," *Amer. J. Psychiat.,* 108 (1952), 685–694.

Ostrovsky, E. S. *Father to the Child: Case Studies of the Experiences of a Male Teacher.* New York: Putnam, 1959.

Parker, S., and R. J. Kleiner. "Characteristics of Negro mothers in single-headed households," *J. Marriage and the Family,* 28 (1966), 507–513.

Payne, D. E., and P. H. Mussen. "Parent-child relations and father identification among adolescent boys," *J. Abnormal Soc. Psychol.,* 52 (1956) 358–362.

Pedersen, F. A. "Relationships between father absence and emotional disturbance in male military dependents," *Merrill-Palmer Quart.,* 12 (1966), 321–331.

Pettigrew, T. F. *A Profile of the Negro American.* Princeton: Van Nostrand, 1964.

Phelan, H. M. "The incidence and possible significance of the drawing of female figures by sixth-grade boys in response to the Draw-A-Person Test," *Psychiat. Quart.,* 38 (1964), 1–16.

* Phillips, J. "Performance of father-present and father-absent southern Negro boys on a simple operant task as a function of race and sex of the experimenter and the type of social reinforcement." Unpublished doctoral dissertation, University of Minnesota, 1966.

* Rabban, M. "Sex-role identification in young children in two diverse social groups," *Genet. Psychol. Monographs,* 42 (1950), 81–158.

Rabin, A. I. "Some psychosexual differences between kibbutz and non-kibbutz Israeli boys," *J. Projective Techniques,* 22 (1958), 328–332.

Rainwater, L. "Crucible of identity," *Daedalus,* 95 (1966), 172–216.

Rohrer, J. H., and M. S. Edmonson. *The Eighth Generation.* New York: Harper, 1960.

Romney, A. K. "Variations in household structure as determinants of sex-typed behavior," in F. Beach, ed., *Sex and Behavior.* New York: Wiley, 1965.

Schlesinger, B. "The one-parent family: an overview," *Family Life Coordinator,* 15 (1966), 133–137.

Sears, P. S. "Child-rearing factors related to playing of sex-typed roles," *American Psychologist,* 8 (1953), 431 (Abstract).

Sears, P. S. "Doll-play aggression in normal young children: influence of sex-age, sibling status, father's absence," *Psychol. Monographs,* 65 (1951), 6, Whole No. 323.

Sears, R. R., M. H. Pintler, and P. S. Sears. "Effect of father separation on preschool children's doll-play aggression," *Child Development,* 17 (1946), 219–243.

Siegman, A. W. "Father absence during childhood and antisocial behavior," *J. Abnormal Psychol.,* 71 (1966), 71–74.

Smith, C. "The development of sex-role concepts and attitudes in father-absent boys." Unpublished master's thesis, University of Chicago, 1966.

Steimel, R. J. "Childhood experiences and masculinity-femininity scores," *J. Counsel. Psychol.,* 7 (1960), 212–217.

Stendler, C. B. "Possible causes of over-dependency in young children," *Child Development,* 25 (1954), 125–146.

Stephens, W. N. "Judgments by social workers on boys and mothers in fatherless families," *J. Genet. Psychol.,* 99 (1961), 59–64.

Stephens, W. N. *The Oedipus Complex: Cross-cultural Evidence.* Glencoe, Ill.: Free Press, 1962.

Stoller, R. J. *Sex and Gender.* New York: Science House, 1968.

Stolz, L. M. et al. *Father Relations of War Born Children.* Stanford: Stanford University Press, 1954.

Sutherland, H. E. G. "The relationship between IQ and size of family in the case of fatherless children," *J. Genet. Psychol.,* 38 (1930), 161–170.

Sutton-Smith, B., J. M. Roberts, and B. G. Rosenberg. "Sibling associations and role involvement," *Merrill-Palmer Quart.,* 10 (1964), 25–38.

* Sutton-Smith, B., B. G. Rosenberg, and F. Landy. "Father-absence effects in families of different sibling compositions," *Child Development,* 39 (1968), 1213–1221.

Terman, L. M., and C. C. Miles. *Sex and Personality.* New York: McGraw-Hill, 1936.

* Thomas, A., S. Chess, H. G. Birch, M. E. Hertzig, S. Korn. *Behavioral Individuality in Early Childhood.* New York: New York University Press, 1963.

Thomes, M. M. "Children with absent fathers," *J. Marriage and the Family,* 30 (1968), 89–96.

Tiller, P. O. "Father-absence and personality development of children in sailor families," *Nordisk Psykologi's Monograph Series,* 9 (1958), 1–48.

Travis, J. "Precipitating factors in manic-depressive psychoses," *Pyschiat. Quart.,* 8 (1933), 411–418.

Tuddenham, R. D. "Studies in reputation: I. Sex and grade differences in school children's evaluations of their peers. II. The diagnosis of social adjustment," *Psychol. Monographs,* 66 (1952), 1, Whole No. 333.

Tuddenham, R. D. "Studies in reputation: III. Correlates of popularity among elementary school children," *J. Educ. Psychol.,* 42 (1951), 257–276.

Wahl, C. W. "Antecedent factors in family histories of 392 schizophrenics," *Amer. J. Psychiat.,* 110 (1954), 668–676.

West, D. J. *Homosexuality.* Chicago: Aldine, 1967.

West, D. J. "Parental relationships in male homosexuality," *International J. Soc. Psychiat.,* 5 (1959), 85–97.

Whiting, J. W. M., R. Kluckhohn, and A. Anthony. "The function of male initiation ceremonies at puberty," in E. E. Maccoby, T. M. Newcomb, and E. L. Hartley, eds., *Readings in Social Psychology.* New York: Holt, Rinehart, 1958.

Winch, R. F. *Identification and its Familial Determinants.* New York: Bobbs-Merrill, 1962.

Winch, R. F. "The relation between loss of a parent and progress in courtship," *J. Soc. Psychol.,* 29 (1949), 51–56.

Witkin, H. A. "The problem of individuality in development," in B. Kaplan and S. Wapner, eds., *Perspectives in Psychological Theory.* New York: International Universities Press, 1960.

Wylie, H. L., and R. A. Delgado. "A pattern of mother-son relationship involving the absence of the father," *Amer. J. Orthopsychiat.,* 29 (1959), 644–649.

Yarrow, L. J. "Separation from parents during early childhood," in M. L. Hoffman and L. W. Hoffman, eds., *Review of Child Development Research,* vol. 1. New York: Russell Sage Foundation, 1964.

23

Life Change
and Illness Susceptibility
Thomas H. Holmes and Minoru Masuda

Anybody's life can be disorganized at times whether as a
function of growing older, moving into new statuses,
or being subjected to the vicissitudes of fate. This chapter
provides evidence that change, even if it is pleasant or
"upward," is pathogenic to a certain degree in that it can
lower resistance to physical and mental illness. Humans
naturally seek some amount of change and novelty, but the
findings here accent the idea that humans also depend on
society and cultural organization to keep change within
tolerable bounds.

Life Change and Illness Susceptibility

This report documents the development and pilot application of the Social Readjustment Rating Scale (SRRS) as a means investigating the relationship of life change to the occurrence of disease. Here "disease" applies to change in health status and includes a broad spectrum of medical, surgical, and psychiatric disorders.

Development of the SRRS

Since 1949 the life chart device (4) has been used systematically in over 5,000 patients to study the quality and quantity of life events empirically observed to cluster at the time of disease onset. Evolving mostly from ordinary, but some from extraordinary, social and interpersonal transactions, such events relate to changes in family constellation, marriage, occupation, economics, residence, group and peer relationships, education, religion, recreation, and health (Table 1). Studies by Rahe et al. (11) have established that such social events are significantly associated with the time of illness onset. Similarly the relationship of what has been called "life stress," "emotional stress," "object loss," etc., with illness onset has been demonstrated by other investigations (12–23).

During the developmental phase of this research the interview technique was used to assess the meaning of the events for the individual. As expected, the psychological significance and emotions varied widely with the patient. Also from Table 1 it will be noted that only some of the events are negative or "stressful" in the conventional sense, i.e., are socially undesirable. Many are socially desirable and consonant with the American values of achievement,

"Life Change and Illness Susceptibility," by Thomas H. Holmes and Minoru Masuda was excerpted from a paper presented as part of a "Symposium on Separation and Depression: Clinical and Research Aspects," at the annual meeting of the American Association for the Advancement of Science, Chicago, Illinois, December 26–30, 1970. Reprinted by permission of the authors.

This research was supported in part by Public Health Service Undergraduate Training in Human Behavior Grant No. 5-T2-MH-7871-03, Undergraduate Training in Psychiatry Grant No. 5-T2-MH-5939-13, and Graduate Training in Psychiatry Grant No. 5-T1-MH-5557-14 from the Institute of Mental Health; Public Health Service General Research Support Grant No. 1-SO1-FR-5432-04; O'Donnell Psychiatric Research Fund; Scottish Rite Committee for Research in Schizophrenia; and Stuht Psychiatric Research Fund.

success, materialism, practicality, efficiency, future orientation, conformism, and self-reliance.

There was identified, however, one theme common to all these life events. The occurrence of each event usually evoked or was associated with some adaptive or coping behavior on the part of the involved individual. Thus each item has been constructed to contain life events whose advent is either indicative of or requires a significant change in the ongoing life pattern of the individual. The emphasis is on change from the existing steady state and not on psychological meaning, emotion, or social desirability.

The interview or questionnaire technique used in these early studies yielded only the number and types of events making up the cluster. Some estimate of the magnitude of these events was now required to bring greater precision to this area of research and to provide a quantitative basis for new epidemiological studies of diseases. Accordingly, the life event items were scaled using the following procedure.

A sample of convenience composed of 394 subjects completed the paper and pencil test (the items are given in Table 1). The items were the 43 life events empirically derived from clinical experience. The following written instructions were given to each subject who completed the Social Readjustment Rating Questionnaire (SRRQ).

A. Social readjustment includes the amount and duration of change in one's accustomed pattern of life resulting from various life events. As defined, social readjustment measures the intensity and length of time necessary to accommodate to a life event, *regardless of the desirability of this event.*

Table 1. Social Readjustment Rating Scale

Rank	Life Event	Mean Value
1	Death of spouse	100
2	Divorce	73
3	Marital separation from mate	65
4	Detention in jail or other institution	63
5	Death of a close family member	63
6	Major personal injury or illness	53
7	Marriage	50
8	Being fired from work	47

Table 1. (continued)

Rank	Life Event	Mean Value
9	Marital reconciliation with mate	45
10	Retirement from work	45
11	Major change in the health or behavior of a family member	44
12	Pregnancy	40
13	Sexual difficulties	39
14	Gaining a new family member (e.g., through birth, adoption, oldster moving in, etc.)	39
15	Business readjustment	39
16	Major change in financial state (e.g., a lot worse off or a lot better off than usual)	38
17	Death of a close friend	37
18	Changing to a different line of work	36
19	Major change in the number of arguments with spouse (e.g., either a lot more or a lot less than usual regarding childrearing, personal habits, etc.)	35
20	Taking on a mortgage greater than $10,000 (e.g., purchasing a home, business, etc.)	31
21	Foreclosure on a mortgage or loan	30
22	Major change in responsibilities at work (e.g., promotion, demotion, lateral transfer)	29
23	Son or daughter leaving home (e.g., marriage, attending college, etc.)	29
24	In-law troubles	29
25	Outstanding personal achievement	28
26	Wife beginning or ceasing work outside the home	26
27	Beginning or ceasing formal schooling	26
28	Major change in living conditions	25
29	Revision of personal habits (dress, manners, associations, etc.)	24
30	Troubles with the boss	23
31	Major change in working hours or conditions	20
32	Change in residence	20
33	Changing to a new school	20
34	Major change in usual type and/or amount of recreation	19
35	Major change in church activities (e.g., a lot more or a lot less than usual)	19
36	Major change in social activities (e.g., clubs, dancing, movies, visiting, etc.)	18
37	Taking on a mortgage or loan less than $10,000 (e.g., purchasing a car, TV, freezer, etc.)	17
38	Major change in sleeping habits (a lot more or a lot less sleep, or change in part of day when asleep)	16
39	Major change in number of family get-togethers (e.g., a lot more or a lot less than usual)	15
40	Major change in eating habits (a lot more or a lot less food intake, or very different meal hours or surroundings)	15
41	Vacation	13
42	Christmas	12
43	Minor violations of the law (e.g., traffic tickets, jaywalking, disturbing the peace, etc.)	11

Reprinted from Holmes, T. H., and Rahe, R. H., "The Social Readjustment Rating Scale," *Journal of Psychosomatic Research*, 11 (1967), Table 2, p. 215, with permission of Microfilms International Marketing Corporation and the authors. Table number has been changed.

B. You are asked to rate a series of life events as to their relative degrees of necessary readjustment. In scoring, *use all of your experience* in arriving at your answer. This means personal experience where it applies as well as what you have learned to be the case for others. Some persons accommodate to change more readily than others; some persons adjust with particular ease or difficulty to only certain events. Therefore, strive to give your opinion of the average degree of readjustment necessary for each event rather than the extreme.

C. The mechanics of rating are these: Event 1, Marriage, has been given an arbitrary value of 500. As you complete each of the remaining events think to yourself, "Is this event indicative of more or less readjustment than marriage?" "Would the readjustment take longer or shorter to accomplish?" If you decide the readjustment is more intense and protracted, then choose a *proportionately larger* number and place it in the blank directly opposite the event in the column marked, VALUES. If you decide the event represents less and shorter readjustment than marriage then indicate how much less by placing a proportionately smaller number in the opposite blank. (If an event requires intense readjustment over a short time span, it may approximate in value an event requiring less intense readjustment over a long period of time.) If the event is equal in social readjustment to marriage, record the number 500 opposite the event.

The Social Readjustment Rating Scale (SRRS) from the scaling analysis is shown in Table 1. This table contains the magnitude of the life events which is derived when the mean score, divided by 10, of each item for the entire sample is calculated and arranged in rank order. That consensus is high concerning the relative order and magnitude of the means of items is demonstrated by the high coefficients of correlation (Pearson's r) between the discrete groups contained in the sample. Table 2 reveals that all the coefficients of correlation are above 0.90 with the exception of that between whites and Negroes (0.82). . . .

In the development of the SRRS, the high correlations between minority groups and the white population (Table 2) (24) suggested

Table 2. Pearson's Coefficient of Correlation Between Mean Ratings
Made By Discrete Groups in the Sample

Group	No. in Group		Group	No. in Group	Coefficient of Correlation
Male	179	vs.	Female	215	0.965
Single	171	vs.	Married	223	0.960
Age < 30	206	vs.	Age 30–60	137	0.958
Age < 30	206	vs.	Age > 60	51	0.923
Age 30–60	137	vs.	Age > 60	51	0.965
1st Generation	19	vs.	2nd Generation	69	0.908
1st Generation	19	vs.	3rd Generation	306	0.929
2nd Generation	69	vs.	3rd Generation	306	0.975
< College	182	vs.	4 Years of College	212	0.967
Lower Class	71	vs.	Middle Class	323	0.928
White	363	vs.	Negro	19	0.820
White	363	vs.	Oriental	12	0.940
Protestant	241	vs.	Catholic	42	0.913
Protestant	241	vs.	Jewish	19	0.971
Protestant	241	vs.	Other Religion	45	0.948
Protestant	241	vs.	No Religious Preference	47	0.926

Reprinted from Holmes, T. H., and Rahe, R. H., "The Social Readjustment Scale," *Journal of Psychosomatic Research*, 11 (1967), Table 3, p. 216, with permission of Microfilms International Marketing Corporation and the authors. Table number has been changed.

the desirability of extending the investigation further into the cross-cultural area. The mean ratings obtained in six different groups (Americans, Japanese, Western European, Spanish, Negro Americans, and Mexican Americans) all correlate .72 or more (40–43). More recently, Seppa (44) has compared a sample from El Salvador, a Spanish-speaking Central American country, with the Spanish sample studied by Celdrán (42) and found the consensus high. Rahe (45), in addition to summarizing some of the above studies, cited data on literate populations from Denmark and Sweden and on a semi-literate sample from Hawaii. Again, the consensus was high, with Spearman's rank order correlation coefficients ranging from 0.629 to 0.943.

Studies of Illness Onset Using the SRRS

The life event items contained in the SRRS were originally used to construct a Schedule of Recent Experience (SRE) (11, 20). This instrument, a self-administered questionnaire, allowed the respondent to document over a 10-year period the year of occurrence of the life event items. In retrospective studies carried out before the development of the SRRS, the SRE had been used to adduce data that the life events cluster significantly in the 2-year period preceding onset of tuberculosis, heart disease, skin disease, hernia, and pregnancy (11). Now the development of the scale of magnitudes for the life event items (SRRS) provides a unique method for reexamining the early findings using a quantitative definition of a life crisis. In a pilot study done by Rahe (47), the SRE was mailed to 200 resident physicians in the University of Washington integrated hospital system. The cover letter requested the participation of residents in a research project but did not disclose the project's purpose. The subjects were asked to list all "major health changes" by year of occurrence for the past 10 years. In this pilot study it was assumed that the subjects were sophisticated in matters of health and disease, and no systematic attempt was made to verify the report of health changes. The 88 subjects (86 males, 2 females; ages 22 to 33 years) who completed and returned the questionnaire provided retrospective data which were analyzed for the relationship of health changes to life changes. The items subscribed to in the SRE by the subjects were assigned their values from the Social Readjustment Rating Scale (Table 1). The values were summed for each year and the total life change units (LCU) derived were plotted for each subject for the decade under study. Upon this profile were superimposed the reported health change data.

A total of 96 diseases or changes in health status were reported by the 88 subjects for the previous 10 years. The 34 varieties reported were classified into 7 categories: infectious and parasitic, allergic, musculoskeletal, psychosomatic, psychiatric, physical trauma, and miscellaneous. Infectious (45 percent), allergic (13 percent), musculoskeletal (11 percent), and psychosomatic (7 percent) composed the majority of reported health changes.

Based on the previous studies (11), an arbitrary criterion was established for the temporal association of an illness or health change with life change events: a reported change in health must occur within the 2-year period following the occurrence of a cluster of life changes. This 2-year period was the time when the subject was "at risk" following the life change clustering. Eighty-nine of the 96 major health changes reported (93 percent) were associated temporally with a clustering of life changes whose values summed to at least 150 LCU per year. A life crisis was thus defined as any clustering of life change events whose individual values summed to 150 LCU or more in one year. The health change itself was not counted as one of the life changes making up the LCU total for the year. In some instances the life crisis peaks mounted to over 500 LCU. The magnitude of most of the reported life changes was between 18 and 25 LCU. While the number of life changes making up a peak of 150–500 LCU ranged between 7 and 25, the duration of a life crisis was occasionally observed to persist longer than 2 years. The relationship of the magnitude of the life crises to the proportion of life crises associated with major health changes is shown in Table 3 (47). The 93 percent association of reported health changes with a life crisis was significantly greater than chance association.

Further analysis of the data in Table 3 indicated a direct relationship between the magnitude of the life crisis and the risk of health change. As the life change units increased, so did the percentage of illness associated with the life crisis. Of the life crises between 150 and 190 LCU, 37 percent had an associated health change. This association rose to 51 percent for crises with scores between 200 and 299 LCU, and to 79 percent for crises with scores of 300 or greater LCU. These three ranges of scores have been used to define a *mild*

Table 3. Relationship of Life Crisis Magnitude to Percentage
of Life Crises Associated with Health Changes*

	Number of Life Crises			
	Associated with Health Changes	Not associated with Health Changes	Total Number of Life Crises	% of Life Crises Associated with Health Changes
Mild Life Crisis 150–199 LCU	13	22	35	37%
Moderate Life Crisis 200–299 LCU	29	28	57	51%
Major Life Crisis 300+ LCU	30	8	38	79%
Totals	72**	58	130	55%

*Rahe (47).
**Some life crises were associated with more than one health change.

(150–199 LCU), *moderate* (200–299 LCU), and *major* (300+ LCU) life crisis. In some subjects, two or more major health changes occurred during the time at risk. This accounts for the fact that in Table 3, the 89 health changes were associated with 72 life crises.

Figure 1 is an example of one subject's LCU profile over a 10-year period, and it illustrates graphically the relation between life crises and major health changes. The solid line connects points that indicate yearly total LCU. Reported health changes are indicated over their year of occurrence. The subject's depressive episodes in 1956 coincided with the appearance of a life crisis, whereas his episodes of prostatitis in 1960 and of tonsillitis in 1964 occurred about one year after the appearance of the life crisis with which they were associated. On the average, associated health changes followed a life crisis by about a year.

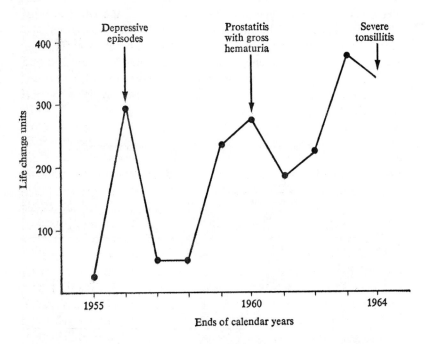

FIGURE 1. Temporal relationship of life crisis and disease occurrence for one patient (47).

Profiles of Life Change Prior to Hospitalization

Holmes (48) used the Schedule of Recent Experience and the Social Readjustment Rating Scale to define a qualitative and quantitative psychosocial history and to characterize certain aspects of the life style of 199 hospitalized patients on the medical wards of University Hospital and Veterans Administration Hospital in Seattle.

The most frequent items over the 10 years prior to hospitalization were vacation, personal injury or illness, and change in residence. Together these items accounted for 28 percent of all the reports. The least frequent were foreclosure of mortgage or loan, fired at work, and death of spouse. These accounted for only 0.5 percent of all the items reported. The three most frequent items were reported over 50 times for each report of the three least frequent items.

Men and women displayed no significant difference in the average number of life changes per person. Single, married, and divorced-separated patients displayed an average of 50 percent more life changes per person than widowed patients. Patients between 20 and 30 years of age displayed about 50 percent more life changes per person than those between 45 to 60, and twice as many as those over 60 years of age.

Prospective Studies

Rahe followed up 84 of the 88 resident physicians described above (47) as subjects for a prospective study (49). In this study the life changes for the previous 18 months were used as the quantitative base for predicting illness onset for the near future. When data about the disease occurrence were obtained 8 months later, 49 percent of the high risk group (300+LCU) reported illness; 25 percent of the medium risk group (200–299 LCU) reported illness; and 9 percent of the low risk group (150–199 LCU) reported illness.

Holmes (48), using a somewhat different method, followed 54 medical students from the beginning of their freshman year to the end of their sophomore year. Again, using the SRE to collect data, the life change magnitude of the year before entering medical school was used to predict disease occurrence for a full 2-year period at risk. At the end of that time, the SRE was administered a second time so that retrospective data could be compared with the prospective data. Allowing for a few percentage points of difference, the outcome of both approaches was essentially the same. Thus, in both the prospective and retrospective surveys, 52 percent of the subjects experienced major health changes during the 2-year period at risk. Of these, 86 percent with high life change scores, 48 percent with moderate life change scores, and 33 percent with low life change scores experienced major health changes. Thus individuals who remained in good health for the first year of the period at risk had the same chance of experiencing major health changes during the remainder of the period as they did at its beginning, depending on the magnitude of their life change scores. The data also revealed that subjects with major health changes experienced more minor health changes than subjects without major health changes.

Rahe et al. (50, 51) expanded their studies to Naval personnel. Using the previous 6-month period as the time base for establishing the predictive life change score, approximately 2,500 officers and enlisted men aboard three United States Navy cruisers provided health change data after 6 months at sea. The upper 30 percent of the rank ordering of the LCU provided subjects for the high risk group, and the lower 30 percent provided the subjects for the low risk group. In the first month of the cruise, the high risk group had nearly 90 percent more *first* illnesses than the low risk group. The high risk group consistently reported more illnesses each month for the 6-month cruise period, and had a third more illnesses over the follow-up period than did the low risk group. Although the high risk group, relatively speaking, had more serious illnesses than the low risk group, the health changes reported in this study were considerably *less* serious than those reported when the risk period was 1 or 2 years, as in the prospective studies reported above by Holmes (48) and Rahe (49).

Rubin et al. (52) improved the ability of the SRE scores as predictors of illness among Naval personnel by employing stepwise multiple regression analysis. It was their judgment that empirical regression weights derived specifically for a military population predicted future illness better than the prior weights derived from the civilian population.

Holmes and Holmes (53) adduced data about the association of life change and minor health change defined as those signs and symptoms of everyday life (cuts, bruises, headaches, stomach aches, backaches, and colds, etc.) which do not cause time lost from work or require a visit to the doctor. The findings indicated that subjects were much more likely to experience the signs and symptoms of everyday life on days of greater than average life changes. Life changes tended to cluster significantly around health changes. The opposite was also confirmed: subjects were much less likely to experience signs and symptoms on days of less than average life change; and low amounts of life change tended to cluster significantly around symptom-free days.

Another experimental approach has been taken by Holmes (54). Holding age, sex, and risk injury as relative constants, the magnitude of life changes for the year prior to the season was used as the base to evaluate the association with injury in college football players. In the first study, the 100 subjects were divided by thirds, according to the rank order of their life change scores, into a high, medium, and low risk group. When evaluated at the end of their athletic season, approximately 3 months later, 50 percent of the high risk group had been injured, 25 percent of the medium risk group, and 9 percent of the low risk group. Of the 10 players who sustained multiple injuries during the season, 7 were in the high risk group. Using a specially constructed Athletic Schedule of Recent Experience, whose items were derived from the Social and Athletic Readjustment Rating Scale described above (33), Holmes (54), in subsequent studies, found the association of injury in the high risk group had risen from 50 percent to 70 percent.

Association of Magnitude of Life Change to Seriousness of Illness

During the course of these investigations, inspection of the data suggested a positive relationship between the seriousness of illness judged intuitively and life change magnitude for the year prior to the onset of disease. Since there was no satisfactory scale of the seriousness of individual illnesses (50, 55), Wyler et al. set themselves the task of constructing one (56, 57). Using a method similar to that employed in developing the Social Readjustment Scale, 500 units were assigned to the "seriousness" of peptic ulcer. Using this as the modulus item, 125 diseases were rated by two separate samples of physicians. The rank order correlation (Spearman's rho) was 0.98. When physicians were compared to a sample of laymen, the correlation of 0.94 was almost as high. Also, the fact that comparison of Spanish, Irish, and American laymen yielded correlations of 0.90 or greater suggested a broad, cross-cultural consensus about the seriousness of illness (42, 58).

Using the Seriousness of Illness Rating Scale, Wyler et al. assigned appropriate values to 42 diseases experienced by 232 patients (59). These values were compared with the life change magnitude occurring in the 2-year period of time preceding onset of disease. The correlation was highly significant (Spearman's rho 0.648) for chronic diseases. No significant relationship was found with infectious diseases of acute onset.

These data suggest that the greater the life change or adaptive requirement the greater the vulnerability or lowering of resistance to disease, and the more serious the disease that does develop. The concept of a variable threshold of resistance and the necessity of having a special pathogen present may help account for the differences observed in the acute infectious diseases. Thus the concept of life change appears to have relevance to the areas of causation of disease, time of onset of disease, and severity of disease. It does not seem to contribute much to an understanding of specificity of disease type (12).

References

* 1.   Stevens, S. S. "A metric for the social consensus," *Science,* 151 (1966), 530.

* 2.   Stevens, S. S., and E. H. Galanter, "Ratio scales and category scales for a dozen perceptual continua," *J. Exp. Psychol.,* 54 (1957), 377.

* 3.   Lief, A., ed. *The Commonsense Psychiatry of Dr. Adolf Meyer.* New York: McGraw-Hill, 1948.

4.   Wolff, H. G., S. Wolf, C. C. Hare, eds. *Life Stress and Bodily Disease.* Res. Publs. Ass. Res. Nerv. Ment. Dis., vol. 29. Baltimore: Williams and Wilkins, 1950.

* 5.   Holmes, T. H., H. Goodell, S. Wolf, and H. G. Wolff. *The Nose: An Experimental Study of Reactions Within the Nose in Human Subjects During Varying Life Experiences.* Springfield, Ill.: Charles C Thomas, 1950.

* 6.   Wolf, S. *The Stomach.* New York: Oxford University Press, 1965.

* 7.   Wolf, S., P. V. Cardon, E. M. Shepard, and H. G. Wolff. *Life Stress and Essential Hypertension.* Baltimore: Williams and Wilkins, 1955.

* Additional reference.

* 8.   Grace, W. J., S. Wolf, and H. G. Wolff, *The Human Colon*. New York: Paul B. Hoeber, 1951.

* 9.   Sellin, T., and M. E. Wolfgang. *The Measurement of Delinquency*. New York: Wiley, 1964.

* 10.   Rashevsky, N. *Some Medical Aspects of Mathematical Biology*. Springfield, Ill.: Charles C Thomas, 1964.

11.   Rahe, R. H., M. Meyer, M. Smith, G. Kjaer, and T. H. Holmes. "Social stress and illness onset," *J. Psychosom. Res.*, 8 (1964), 35.

12.   Graham, D. T., and I. Stevenson. "Disease as response to life stress," in H. I. Lief, V. F. Lief, and N. R. Lief, eds., *The Psychological Basis of Medical Practice*. New York: Harper, 1963.

13.   Greene, W. A., Jr. "Psychological factors and reticuloendothelial disease: I. Preliminary observations on a group of males with lymphomas and leukemias," *Psychosom. Med.*, 16 (1954), 220.

14.   Greene, W. A., Jr., L. E. Young, and S. N. Swisher. "Psychological factors and reticuloendothelial disease: II. Observations on a group of women with lymphomas and leukemias," *Psychosom. Med.*, 18 (1956), 284.

15.   Greene, W. A., Jr., and G. Miller. "Psychological factors and reticuloendothelial disease: IV. Observations on a group of children and adolescents with leukemia: an interpretation of disease development in terms of the mother-child unit," *Psychosom. Med.*, 20 (1958), 124.

16.   Weiss, E., B. Dlin, H. R. Rollin, H. K. Fischer, and C. R. Bepler. "Emotional factors in coronary occlusion," *AMA Arch. Internal. Med.*, 99 (1957), 628.

17.   Fischer, H. K., B. M. Dlin, W. L. Winters, S. B. Hagner, G. W. Russell, and E. Weiss. "Emotional factors in coronary occlusion. II. Time patterns and factors related to onset," *Psychosomatics,* 5 (1964), 280.

18.   Kissen, D. M. "Specific psychological factors in pulmonary tuberculosis," *Health Bull. Edinburgh,* 14 (1956), 44.

19.   Kissen, D. M. "Some psychosocial aspects of pulmonary tuberculosis," *International J. Soc. Psychiat.*, 3 (1958), 252.

20.   Hawkins, N. G., R. Davies, and T. H. Holmes. "Evidence of psychosocial factors in the development of pulmonary tuberculosis," *Amer. Rev. Tuberc. Pulmon. Dis.*, 75 (1957), 5.

21.   Smith, M. "Psychogenic factors in skin disease." Medical thesis, University of Washington, Seattle, 1962.

22.   Rahe, R. H., and T. H. Holmes. "Social, psychologic, and psychophysiologic aspects of inguinal hernia," *J. Psychosom. Res.*, 8 (1965), 487.

23.   Kjaer, G. "Some psychosomatic aspects of pregnancy with particular reference to nausea and vomiting." Medical thesis, University of Washington, Seattle, 1959.

24.   Holmes, T. H., and R. H. Rahe. "The Social Readjustment Rating Scale," *J. Psychosom. Res.*, 11 (1967), 213.

* 25.   Masuda, M., and T. H. Holmes. "Magnitude estimations of social readjustments," *J. Psychosom. Res.*, 11 (1967), 219.

* 26. Arkin, H., and R. R. Colton. *Statistical Methods,* 4th ed. New York: Barnes and Noble, 1959, 26.

* 27. Edwards, A. E. *Statistical Analysis.* New York: Holt, Rinehart, 1958, 44.

* 28. Siegel, S. *Nonparametric Statistics for the Behavioral Sciences.* New York: McGraw-Hill, 1956.

* 29. Ruch, L. O., and T. H. Holmes. "Scaling of life change: comparison of direct and indirect methods," *J. Psychosom. Res.,* 15 (1971), 221.

* 30. Pasley, S. "The social readjustment rating scale: a study of the significance of life events in age groups ranging from college freshman to seventh grade." Part of tutorial in psychology, Chatham College, Pittsburgh, Pa., 1969.

* 31. Torgerson, W. S. *Theory and Methods of Scaling.* New York: Wiley, 1958.

32. Thurstone, L. L. *The Measurement of Values.* Chicago: University of Chicago Press, 1959.

33. Bramwell, S. T. "Personality and psychosocial variables in college athletes." Medical thesis, University of Washington, Seattle, 1971.

* 34. Casey, R. L., M. Masuda, and T. H. Holmes. "Quantitative study of recall of life events," *J. Psychosom. Res.,* 11 (1967), 239.

* 35. Haggard, E. A., A. Brekstad, and A. G. Skard. "On the reliability of the anamnestic interview," *J. Abnormal Soc. Psychol.,* 61 (1960), 311.

* 36. Wenar, C., and J. B. Coulter. "A reliability study of developmental histories," *Child Development,* 33 (1962), 453.

* 37. Mechanic, D., and M. Newton. "Some problems in the analysis of morbidity data," *J. Chron. Dis.,* 18 (1965), 569.

* 38. United States National Health Survey. "Health interview responses compared with medical records," Series D-5. Washington, D. C.: Public Health Service, June, 1961.

* 39. United States National Health Survey. "Comparison of hospitalization reporting in three survey procedures," Series D-8. Washington, D. C.: Public Health Service, January, 1963.

40. Komaroff, A. L., M. Masuda, and T. H. Holmes. "The social readjustment rating scale: a comparative study of Negro, Mexican, and white Americans," *J. Psychosom. Res.,* 12 (1968), 121.

41. Harmon, D. K., M. Masuda, and T. H. Holmes. "The social readjustment rating scale: a cross-cultural study of Western Europeans and Americans," *J. Psychosom. Res.,* 14 (1970), 391.

42. Celdrán, H. H. "The cross-cultural consistency of two social consensus scales: the seriousness of illness rating scale and the social readjustment rating scale in Spain." Medical thesis, University of Washington, Seattle, 1970.

43. Masuda, M., and T. H. Holmes. "The social readjustment rating scale: a cross-cultural study of Japanese and Americans," *J. Psychosom. Res.,* 11 (1967), 227.

44. Seppa, M. T. "The social readjustment rating scale and the seriousness of illness rating scale: a comparison of Salvadorans, Spanish, and Americans." Medical thesis, University of Washington, Seattle, 1972.

45. Rahe, R. H. "Multi-cultural correlations of life change scaling: America, Japan, Denmark, and Sweden," *J. Psychosom. Res.,* 13 (1969), 191.

* 46.   DeVos, G. "The relation of guilt towards parents to achievement and arranged marriage among the Japanese," *Psychiatry*, 23 (1960), 287.

47.   Rahe, R. H. "Life crisis and health change," in P. R. A. May and J. R. Wittenborn, eds., *Psychotropic Drug Response: Advances in Prediction*. Springfield, Ill.: Charles C Thomas, 1969, 92–125.

48.   Holmes, T. S. "Adaptive behavior and health change." Medical thesis, University of Washington, Seattle, 1970.

49.   Rahe, R. H. (1969) *op. cit.*

50.   Rahe, R. H. "Life-change measurement as a predictor of illness," *Proc. Royal Society of Med.*, 61 (1968), 1124 (Section of Psychiatry, 44–46).

51.   Rahe, R. H., J. L. Mahan, and R. J. Arthur. "Prediction of near-future health change from subjects' preceding life changes," *J. Psychosom. Res.*, 14 (1970), 401.

52.   Rubin, R. T., E. K. E. Gunderson, and R. J. Arthur. "Life stress and illness patterns in the United States Navy: III. Prior life change and illness onset in an attack carrier's crew," *AMA Arch. Environ. Health*, 19 (1969), 753.

53.   Holmes, T. S., and T. H. Holmes. "Short-term intrusions into the life style routine," *J. Psychosom. Res.*, 14 (1970), 121.

54.   Holmes, T. H. "Psychologic screening," in *Football Injuries. Papers Presented at a Workshop*. Sponsored by Subcommittee on Athletic Injuries, Committee on the Skeletal System, Division of Medical Sciences, National Research Council, February, 1969. National Academy of Sciences, Washington, D. C., 1970, 211–214.

55.   Hinkle, L. E., Jr., R. Redmont, N. Plummer, and H. G. Wolff. "An examination of the relation between symptoms, disability, and serious illness in two homogeneous groups of men and women," *Amer. J. Public Health*, 50 (1960), 1327.

56.   Wyler, A. R., M. Masuda, and T. H. Holmes. "Seriousness of illness rating scale," *J. Psychosom. Res.*, 11 (1968), 363.

57.   Wyler, A. R., M. Masuda, and T. H. Holmes. "The seriousness of illness rating scale: reproducibility," *J. Psychosom. Res.*, 14 (1970), 59.

58.   McMahon, B. J. "Seriousness of illness rating scale: a comparative study of Irish and Americans." Medical thesis, University of Washington, Seattle, 1971.

59.   Wyler, A. R., M. Masuda, and T. H. Holmes. "Magnitude of life events and seriousness of illness," *Psychosom. Med.*, 33 (1971), 115.

24
Effects of Social Change on Mental Health
Marc Fried

Many large scale processes like migration, war, and technological modernization would seem to imply life changes for massive numbers of persons. Here Fried reconsiders the evidence that such processes lead to widespread psychopathology. There seems to be less evidence of disturbance than one might expect, and it appears that an important intervening variable is the degree to which individuals' expectations are disrupted. One of the implications of Fried's conclusion is that much of the pathological effect of change might be mollified by proper education and socialization before the change occurs.

Long-Term Trends in Social Change. There are only a few epidemiological studies that deal directly with the effects of societal change on mental illness. One important group of studies investigates the changes over periods of time in rates of psychiatric hospitalization. Goldhamer and Marshall's (22) brilliant study of these rates between 1840 and 1940 shows that, with appropriate adjustments, "age-specific first admission rates for ages under 50 are just as high during the last half of the nineteenth century as they are today." They do find short-term fluctuations associated with wars and depressions but the long-term trend reveals no marked increase that might correspond to this century of urbanization and industralization in Massachusetts. Dunham (10) has corroborated the Goldhamer and Marshall findings for the 1910–1950 period and shows that an apparent increase during these years can be accounted for by the increased rate of hospitalization of patients "without psychosis." Other studies of relatively long-term time trends draw a similar conclusion (36, 50).

Thus, although *patterns* of hospitalization have changed markedly during the past century, the relative *frequency* of hospitalization for psychosis has remained strikingly constant. Rates of psychiatric hos-

Excerpted from Marc Fried, "Effects of Social Change on Mental Health," in the *American Journal of Orthopsychiatry,* 34 (1964), 3–28. Reprinted by permission of the American Orthopsychiatric Association, Inc., and the author. Footnotes have been numbered.

The Editorial Board and the Program Committee of the Association, to stimulate thought on the 1964 annual meeting theme, "Orthopsychiatric Responsibility in Social Change," invited Dr. Fried to prepare this paper for the *Journal.* The opportunity to investigate these materials was offered by our study, "Relocation and Mental Health: Adaptation Under Stress," NIMH Study No. 3M 9137-C3. I am extremely grateful to Drs. Erich Lindemann and Leonard Duhl for stimulating many of my ideas on this subject. Dr. Hilda Perlitsh, Miss Joan Levin, Mrs. Elaine Frieden, and my wife, Dr. Joan Zilbach, have read the manuscript and provided helpful criticism. Mrs. Gay Rosenwald and Miss Patricia McKenney bore with typing the manuscript in a spirit of valor.

pitalization cannot be used as unambiguous evidence of the incidence of mental illness in the community but they point up the fairly stable flow of individuals extruded from the community for disturbed and "nonfunctional" behavior. The trend toward increasing rates of psychiatric hospitalization for less severely disturbed people, however, represents a significant form of social change within both the community and the mental health field that may, in turn, be related to other changes in society. It suggests that *professional mental health services have become a more integral component of the social resources our society provides and accepts in dealing with problems of adaptation and adjustment.* It remains unclear whether this signifies a greater appreciation of the therapeutic potential of psychiatric services, a decrease in such nonprofessional social resources as extended interpersonal networks, which can cope with milder levels of disturbance, an "adaptive" change in psychiatric criteria or the luxurious orientation of an affluent society that can afford to or, perhaps, must dispense with the economic and social contribution of a relatively large proportion of the population.

The acculturation of preliterate groups under the impact of Western civilization is another form of social change involving the impact of urbanization and industrialization. Ideally it should be possible to study the effects of acculturation on mental illness and even of different types of acculturation in a few of the developing countries of Asia, Africa, or South America, which have had fairly extensive mental hospital services for some time. Since no such studies have appeared, we must consider the more extreme instances of transition; these may also be due to marked difference in mental hospital facilities and conceptions of mental illness before and after acculturation.

There seems to be little doubt that preliterate societies now undergoing rapid acculturation are subject to considerable stress (25, 40, 55, 62). Several comprehensive reviews of the literature on mental illness in preliterate and preindustrial societies support the view that acculturation to Western patterns leads to increased rates of psychopathology (3, 49). However, contrary evidence abounds, evidence that stresses the association of rates of hospitalization for mental illness with available facilities for care and treatment (4, 5, 7, 56, 64). A comparison of three different ethnic groups in Singapore reveals marked differences in rates and patterns of psychiatric hospitalization that are quite unrelated to rates of acculturation (47). And an analysis of projective data from a group of Arabs living in an oasis with others from the same oasis who had migrated to Algiers reveals no marked differences between them in levels of maladjustment although both are quite different from an American comparison group (8). Nonetheless, we cannot dismiss the possibility that acculturation experiences, particularly those entailing a very rapid and uncoordinated change only for some members of a society, may lead to increased impairments in functioning.

In the well-known study of mental disorder among the "preindustrial" Hutterites, Eaton and Weil (14) speak of *controlled acculturation* as a characteristic of this group that permits them to maintain low rates of mental disorder. Controlled acculturation refers to the acceptance of change with the framework of familiar values, traditional patterns of social relationship, and a continuing sense of group identity. This coherence, continuity, and integration is the antithesis of those forms of disruptive conflict and social disorganization Durkheim (13) found to be the core of high suicide rates. The degree of social disorganization entailed by acculturation, as Leighton (39) points out, is the necessary intervening factor in considering effects on mental illness.

Despite the evidence that rates of psychiatric hospitalization have not risen substantially in our society over long periods of time, there are suggestions of increased rates of other forms of emotional disturbances. Although the data leave much to be desired, Halliday (24) does make an excellent case for both the rise in psychosomatic disorders and changing distributions of physical illness according to age and sex, which suggest the increasing importance of stress in impaired functioning. Unfortunately rates of change, even those that distinguish the data by categories such as age and sex, provide only a primitive source of information. A rise in rates for any one sign of disturbed reactions to the stress of social change may be, hypothetically, offset or compensated by a decline in other disordered reactions (even if we assume that our criteria for malfunctioning remain constant). Without a complete census, not merely of mental hospitalization and of psychiatric clinic visits, but of suicide, homicide, alcoholism, narcotics use, and a host of other indicators of impaired performance, it is difficult to feel confident in any judgments of changes in the patterns of mental health and illness.

Migration: The Impact of Industrial Society. Epidemiological analysis of the relationship between migration and mental hospitalization is more extensive than any other body of work on social change and mental illness. The early literature was quite clear about the relationship between "nativity" and mental illness; the foreign-born showed higher rates of hospitalization for mental illness than the native-born; and the native-born of foreign parents showed higher rates than the native-born of native parents (17, 26, 54, 60). Further confirmation was obtained from Ødegaard's famous comparison of Norwegians who had migrated to Minnesota and showed higher rates of hospitalization for mental illness than Norwegians who remained at home. This study was particularly important in suggesting that racial-ethnic factors were not the critical source of these differences in rates since two groups of the same racial-ethnic background were compared.

The progress of studies on migration and mental illness has led to the increasing use of controls to determine the precise factors involved in these rate differentials. With improved sources of data and greater appreciation of the variables that might have led to spurious results, efforts were made to adjust for some of these group differences in rates of disorder and to examine that data within specific categories of sex, age, origin, and status. The effect of these finer studies was to reduce the differences in rates of mental hospitalization between the native-born and the foreign-born (38, 41, 42-44, 48, 49).

However, all the United States data and most of the studies done in other countries continue to reveal some residual rate differential in mental illness between individuals who have migrated into a country and those who have been born there. Thus, it appears that some aspect of that transition from one society to another or one type of society to another is a hazardous situation leading to increased frequency of functional impairment.[1]

A number of considerations support the view that the forms of social structure characterizing the urban-industrial complex are pri-

---

1. The most recent and thorough analysis of this issue is Lee's paper (38). It is noteworthy that, with education adjusted, the rates for the foreign-born remain higher than for native-born. But this is due mostly to the 20–29-year-old group. Among the 30–49– and 40–59-year-old groups, with education controlled, the foreign-born have *lower* rates than the *native-born*. This distinction also reveals a difficulty in interpreting epidemiological results based on adjustments for education, age, and the like, instead of education-specific or age-specific data. Such adjustments eliminate the potentially "contaminating" effects of intercorrelated variables but do not permit an analysis of the contribution these factors make to the total difference in rates.

mary sources of adaptive difficulty for migrants. Although most of the epidemiological data point to higher rates of mental hospitalization for immigrants, a few studies reverse these findings. In Israel, in Singapore, and in Canada, the rates for the native-born appear to be higher than those for the foreign-born (48, 49). By an astute and imaginative analysis of these differences, Murphy (48) has shown that there are *lower* rates for the foreign-born compared to the native-born: (1) in those countries in which there is less pressure for rapid acculturation, and (2) in those countries in which the immigrant group represents a larger proportion of the total population. Both these factors imply that *either the absence of strong pressures for immediate acculturation or a relatively large number of similar immigrants allows for a more gradual, more coherent and less conflictful process of adaptation to a new society.* This may result from the development of ethnic communities that serve as *transitional areas,* or it may be due to the availability of *social resources* and interpersonal networks that can provide external support in the face of intrapsychic, interpersonal, role or cultural conflict.

The importance of conflicted status and the significance of opportunities to maintain a period of transitional status, a psychosocial moratorium (16) is further suggested by a number of other results from epidemiological inquiry. The available data indicate that differential rates of hospitalization for mental disorders can be traced, not to nativity as such or to a foreign cultural background, but to the fact of migration itself (37, 41). In fact, interstate migrants, both Negro and white, have *higher* rates of mental disorder than do foreign-born migrants (37, 44). Moreover, these differences cannot be accounted for wholly by education or occupational status (38). It is striking that interstate migrants from the same country should manifest such disproportionately high rates of hospitalization. However, a similarly surprising disproportion in rates of mental hospitalization occurs for the native-born with one or both parents of foreign birth (43).[2] A plausible interpretation devolves again on the conflicted status and the relative absence of meaningful transitional opportunities for both the interstate migrant and the second generation.

2. The same finding concerning the second-generation group is given in some unpublished data for psychiatric hospitalization in the City of Boston for 1950–1951, which Ralph Notman has kindly shown me.

The sources of interstate migration are, of course, manifold. Two factors stand out as critical elements: They most frequently involve movement from less developed areas to large, industrial cities, and while greater opportunities are generally the ostensible reason for moving, a large proportion of these moves are impelled by desires to leave a situation of conflict and disruption.[3] In either case, interstate migrants have neither communal nor other social supports for transitional status, despite the fact that they are often as unprepared to deal with the demands and opportunities of an urban, industrial environment as are the foreign migrants. As does the foreign-born migrant, individuals who have moved from rural areas in the United States also experience a sharp disjunction between personal patterns of adaptation and the demands and expectations of an unfamiliar and ambiguous situation. The fact that the highest rates among the interstate migrants occur during the earliest years after migration (44) is perhaps related to the crisislike nature of this transition period. The conflicted situation of the second generation is even more evident. Their parents were able to settle most frequently in the familiar and protected world of the stable, working-class ethnic community. While the second generation often retains this resource and often accepts this means of achieving a slow rate of assimilation, both the demands and opportunities of the urban, industrial environment are necessarily greater for them then they were for their parents (18). In essence, they are frequently caught in a conflict between familiar patterns of *adaptation to stability* and the challenge of *adaptation to change*.

The Impact of Crisis on Mental Health. Migration is an individual phenomenon and, most frequently, selective factors operate in the decision to migrate. Societal changes in urbanization and industrialization are widespread but very gradual processes. Some transition states, however, are quite sudden and have an effect on the entire population. One such major crisis is war. Yet, except under conditions of dire war stress, there appears to be little effect of this crisis on population rates for mental illness. During war, rates of mental hospitalization for civilian populations show either no marked change or a decline (49,

---

3. These observations derive from a recent study of migrants into and out of Aberdeen, Scotland (32), and are also related to more general propositions concerning migratory movements (1, 15, 27, 28, 61). The study by Illsley et al. (32), stresses the important differences in reasons for migration depending on social class status, and the points above apply particularly to the lower status migrants.

53). Moreover, there is no evidence of a delayed reaction with a disproportionate increase of hospitalizations after a war.[4] And there is only scattered evidence of an increase in the less severe manifestations of emotional problems, particularly as a function of specific stress experiences associated with a war (53). Even among children, increases in emotional disturbance associated with war appear to be directly connected with other forms of separation, particularly from the family (49). This does not mean that certain kinds of individuals may not be adversely affected as civilians in wartime but this does not show up as an increase in the relative numbers with mental disorder. In passing we may note that war is a crisis of social change that provides specific and relatively organized channels for responding to the crisis. That these channels are effectively motivated even beyond their legitimate bounds is suggested by the increased homicide rates during war (30).

Among the armed forces, the picture is more complex but several facts stand out. Neuropsychiatric admissions in the United States Army were higher than civilian rates for a comparable age group (49). In combat zones, as the intensity of combat increases, composite rates for all neuropsychiatric referrals also increase in precise correlation with one another (20, 53, 54). However, variations in rates for psychosis are minimally associated with combat intensity and almost all differences are due to variations among non-psychotic conditions in response to combat stress (20, 21, 53).

Evidence of wartime stress other than *severity* of combat (duration of combat, flying time) are not clearly associated with increased neuropsychiatric rates. On the other hand, high morale is a distinctive factor that modifies the impact of stresses other than severe combat and is, in fact, associated with decreased neuropsychiatric rates (20, 21, 53, 54).

There is relatively little data on predispositional factors related to incidence of neuropsychiatric disorders. Glass (20) found age and ex-

---

4. In a recent, analytic examination of this issue, Pugh and MacMahon have challenged this view (50). These authors raise doubts concerning the data previously reported and indicate that examination of both prevalence and incidence data show that, for young adult males in the United States, World War II produced "an appreciable increase in mental hospital use." They also suggest that a similar phenomenon occurred for World War I. If these interpretations are substantiated by subsequent analysis, it would lend further support to the importance of *crises* of social change as determinants of increased rates of psychiatric hospitalization.

tremely low educational level to be the only factors consistently associated with higher incidence of psychiatric difficulties. However, there is evidence that prewar neurotic traits and neuroses are correlated with psychiatric disorder under combat conditions (54). Although the statistical and interview studies point up the complex of factors involved in psychiatric reactions to combat, clinical studies introduce a much broader array of considerations (19, 23). An observation of particular interest is that of Futterman and Pumpian-Mindlin (19), who indicate that a combination of intense stimuli and inability to respond directly to these stimuli is particularly frequent in traumatic neuroses. This combination is manifested, for example, among noncombat troops in combat zones and among soldiers with injuries that required immobilization. This observation also suggests that the epidemiological correlation of psychiatric disorders and combat intensity need not be due primarily to stress on the combatants themselves.

Another form of large-scale crisis that has impact on the entire society is economic depression. Data from the depression of the 1930s, comparing rates of psychiatric hospitalization before, during, and after the depression, are uniform in showing that there was no marked increase or decrease in rates for this period (11, 53). In fact, Dunham (11) shows that if the cases diagnosed as "without psychosis" are deducted from the totals for each age group, there was a *decrease in rates of hospitalization for psychosis* during the depression for all age groups except those over 70.[5] Thus, increased rates during this period, which continue, except for the interruption of the war years, after that time, seem to be related to increased proportions of less severely disturbed patients (11, 50).

Effects of the depression on rates of disturbance do show up in forms other than psychosis. There is a marked increase in suicide rates during economic depressions (9, 30, 59) as well as an increase in psychosomatic disease and in other symptomatic manifestations of disturbance (20, 24, 53, 66). The available reports do not allow any subtle analysis of the personal or social selective factors. However,

---

5. The relationship between the depression and increased rates of psychiatric hospitalization requires further scrutiny. There is some indication that, as with suicide, rates of psychiatric hospitalization increased during the onset of the great depression (1928 to 1930) at the point of initial decline in employment rates and then leveled off during the years immediately following 1930.

the initial disruptions of family life and the adaptive reorganization of the family around new conditions of livelihood and often around new breadwinners have been described (2, 35). And it seems quite clear that increased suicide rates occurred most frequently among those for whom the depression was most likely to signify a serious loss of status: among the well-do-to, among men, among younger and middle-aged groups (30).

The results of systematic studies are thus quite various. The limitation of most of them to psychiatric hospitalization and the relative absence of corresponding data to reveal whether stability of *rates* can be interpreted as signifying *no difference* in the mental health status of the population necessitates a tentative view of these results. With this in mind, the data can be summarized succinctly.

No marked change in rates of psychiatric hospitalization for psychosis has been found (a) for large-scale continuous changes in "modernization" in industrial countries, (b) among civilian populations during war, and (c) during periods of severe economic depression. This conclusion, however, must be modified by the fact that there has been a change, particularly during the past 30 years, in increased rates of psychiatric hospitalization for less severe conditions, a pattern apparently initiated during the depression. Moreover, in all three situations, which reveal no marked change, there is some data suggesting (and clearly demonstrated for the great depression) that emotional disturbances do increase in spheres other than the major mental disorders.

With varying degrees of certainty, there seem to be *increased rates* of psychiatric hospitalization (a) among recently acculturated individuals who are also separated from their culture of origin, (b) among foreign migrants in specific conditions (some countries, some age groups), (c) among second-generation offspring of foreign migrants, (d) among migrants from one state to another in the United States, and (c) among the armed forces in combat zones during periods of severe combat.

Integration of Expectations

The results of epidemiological analyses on migration and mental disorder converge on the observations that (a) situations of heightened conflict between individual patterns of adaptation and social expectation increase the rates of mental hospitalization, and (b) this effect is particularly notable in the absence of reliable, external resources for modifying the impact of the transition experience. Other fragments of data also point in the same direction. For example, rates of mental hospitalization for Negroes are extremely high, higher than for any other distinguishable group, and are highest of all for migrants (37). A similar conclusion is suggested by several studies indicating that there are increased rates of emotional disturbance after either voluntary or forced relocation from a stable, working-class slum. Despite manifest housing improvements and an increased range of options, the transition from a solidary and cohesive community most frequently involves too large a demand for individual, internal resources for a great many of the working-class relocatees.[6]

The data on migration and mental illness suggest that meaningful transitional resources, particularly transitional communities, may offset some of the impact of this change.[7] Working-class ethnic communities in the United States seem to have served this purpose well for the lower-status migrants from abroad. But they cannot so effectively and consistently provide a useful resource for their more acculturated, more assimilated, and more easily challenged offspring. The second generation is neither generally adapted to the stability of the ethnic community nor fully prepared to adapt itself to the ambiguity and change of the urban, industrial situation.[8] Some ethnic communities in other countries that have witnessed large-scale immigration also

6. A number of studies indicate the stress involved in this transition experience (18, 31, 46, 65). One of them (45), further, gives data for disproportionate rates of emotional impairment manifest both in psychiatric hospitalization and in other forms of psychological malfunctioning; and preliminary results from the study of forced relocation in the West End of Boston (18) also show an upswing in rates of psychiatric hospital admissions after relocation.

7. Curle and Trist (6) utilized "transitional communities" in England after World War II to allow a gradual reorganization of adaptive patterns to the altered situation after military service.

8. A comparison of the different types of second-generation Italian described so beautifully by Whyte (63) reveals the range of variation in the corner boy and the college boy. Even the college boy must devote much of his energy to establishing his status and his independence from past commitments, but cannot really free himself for the individuality and unpredictability of his desired roles. This is, perhaps, a major source of excessive rigidity in defining the new sets of norms and values, assimilating the conceptions of the urban, industrial environment to the dominance of rules, traditions, and conformity of the peasant community and of its transposed form in the working-class ethnic community.

appear to have provided a protective milieu in which individuals could adapt themselves to transitional patterns of stability and limit their confrontation of the demands and expectations implicit in the way of life of an urban, industrial society. By contrast, migrants from within the United States immediately face the expectations of urban Americans, although they may have moved directly from a rural area without any sense of the structure and meaning of an open society. A different situation obtains for the Negro, who must also make it on his own or resign himself to all the indignities of both lower-class and lower-caste status, since Negro working-class areas have not achieved the cohesiveness required of an effective transitional community.

In discussing problems of acculturation in preliterate societies, I have suggested that *social disorganization* was the critical intervening variable in the relationship between various forms of social change and mental health or illness. The data on migration and mental illness recommend a modification of this view. Individual failures in conflict resolution, marital difficulties, social isolation (6, 34), inconsistencies in social status (33), conflicts in cultural status have all been implicated as sources of emotional disturbance or of major mental disorders. As with Durkheim's (12) concept of anomie, a variety of concrete patterns can manifest the same fundamental structure of disorganization and, provided the pattern fits the general criteria, it is likely to be associated with higher rates of mental disorder.

But what general criteria for disorganization comprehend the various concrete forms? A common feature of definitions of disorganization is the failure to reach a minimal level of goal-attainment or role-fulfillment by an individual, a group, or a population. And *such failures in goal-attainment or role-fulfillment can always be traced to a lack of integration between individual patterns of adaptation and the demands, expectations, and opportunities in the immediate environment.* However, if the ultimate source of difficulty lies in the lack of integration between individual adaptation and social roles or cultural goals, a change in either individual behavior or in socio-cultural pattern could reestablish some degree of "fit," thereby increasing the likelihood of goal-attainment or of role-fulfillment. From this we are led to conclude that pervasive failures in role-fulfillment or goal-attainment for an individual, for many individuals, or for a collectivity, can only result from *simultaneous adaptive failures in personality and in social organization.*

461

There are many examples of this constellation. The situations described by Stanton and Schwartz (57, 58) in which conflict between two or more staff members leads to disturbed behavior on the part of the patient demonstrate this nicely. They show that, if order is introduced between the staff members, they can adapt to the patient (rather than to one another) and can provide an external resource which the patient cannot supply from within. Another type of example is found in the kinds of delinquent patterns described by Redl (52) in which the ego deficit is represented by a lack of inner controls. Ordinarily the delinquent has difficulty with self-initiated role- and goal-pursuits but can rely upon his gang. But, if the gang breaks up or he is separated from it, then only a few alternatives remain. He may provoke the imposition of a higher level control by police, therapist, or rival gang. Or, because of the absence of his usual networks (his variant form of social organization), the delinquent may resort to the only forms of precarious stability and role definition he knows on his own. These are the more restricted, primitive, and embedded patterns of defense. The process may be described as decompensation or regression from an individual point of view. At the same time it is evident that these decompensations represent a retreat from more flexible (although socially disapproved) forms of adaptive relationship between the individual and his social networks under conditions of separation and loss.

These failures of mutual adaptation are by no means limited to situations of individual pathology. Similar integrative disorders may be found in any crisis that carries the threat of potential disorganization. When failures of goal-attainment or role-fulfillment are widespread, as in war, depression, or invasion, a higher order of commitment to common values frequently develops as an alternative to chaos. To the extent that values of a higher order are not shared or the crisis reveals the absence of common values, as occurred during the depression of the 1930s, mass movements develop among citizens in the form of unions, political action groups and, in the extreme, revolution. These movements serve, at each level, to impose a higher level of organization that may facilitate goal-attainments and role-fulfillments which are impeded at the level of individual or small-group behavior. Ultimately, these movements generally stimulate social changes, which also imply a new order of social organization.

In these examples we have tried to show that disorganization implies a simultaneous adaptive failure in several of the systems guiding social action. Failures of individual role-definition and goal-seeking are tolerable, provided there are societal arrangements to fulfill human needs and desires. This points to a *principle of psychosocial complementarity:* Resources or controls provided by the individual from within need not be provided by the immediate social environment and, conversely, the availability of resources or controls within the environment eliminates the need for their activation as functions of the personality. In fact, except for some central areas of overlap with respect to socially intolerable behaviors, the organization of resources and controls in personality and social structure are *mutually exclusive.* The widespread existence of specific ego resources or control mechanisms as typical attributes of personality in a society precludes the effective functioning of social resources or control mechanisms through role relationships or collective rules to guide behavior. Thus, individuals for whom self-control is of the utmost importance cannot tolerate the imposition of external rules and guidance. Similarly, individuals whose lives are oriented to the achievement of long-range personal goals find it difficult to submit to clearly-defined roles even in the service of these same goals, or to accept the realization of the goals unless they have been personally earned.[9] Alternatively, the existence of dominant control mechanisms and social resources in the group or collectivity facilitates the development of personalities that "depend" upon environmental influence and, further, involve forms of social structure that allow no place for the independence and individuality necessarily associated with extensive "inner" personality functions.[10]

A major set of components in expressed ideals of personality and of mental health in our society is the individuality of goal-formulation,

---

9. Often, of course, a subtle shift in adaptive mode may arise in which social status becomes a substitute for self-esteem but not without a gradual reorganization of other adaptive patterns which substitute a new form of stability and security for change and innovation. This, even more than the existence of widespread patterns of adaptation to stability among lower-status groups, is a major impediment to changes in political and social structure that are meaningfully related to the process of industrial and urban development.

10. Durkheim (12), Hartmann (29), and Rapaport (51) have suggested similar relationships.

the independence of decisions and judgment, and the flexibility of role definitions. Within the context of an "open society," these attributes, which require an extensive development of inner resources and controls, are extremely important adaptive assets. Individuals oriented to change and opportunity ordinarily have greater option, greater freedom to define roles and modify goals, to restructure a resourceful world to meet individual wishes. But these patterns of adaptation cannot so readily be reoriented to constricted goal-opportunities and restricted role-conceptions. With a diminution of opportunities and an increase in demands for fairly narrow compliance, there is serious danger that adaptive achievements will give way to adaptive failures except in the relatively small number of leadership roles. Such noncomplementary relationships between personality and social milieu occur in many situations. The change-oriented individual in the lower levels of a highly bureaucratic structure, the inner-directed person in a tradition-bound small town, people directed toward excitement and status in the midst of a severe depression exemplify one type of noncomplementary pattern. And individuals oriented to security and safety in situations of challenge, the other-directed person who must function apart from a group of reliable peers, the passive individual precipitated into a leadership role because of a crisis, all present alternative forms of noncomplementarity. While there may be a general trait of individual adaptive mastery that can be deployed in a wide range of quite different social situations, responses of most individuals to noncomplementary patterns and to changes leading to noncomplementarity are not so highly predictable.

However, conditions of noncomplementarity do not necessarily imply mental illness. They do imply strains for movement out of the previous social context, either in the direction of environmental (alloplastic) changes or of internal (autoplastic) changes. Those changes, which reduce the effective environmental opportunities or the effective personal goals to the minimum, are the forms of adaptation generally defined as maladaptation and as psychopathology. It is also evident that in all noncomplementary situations which lead to pathology, there is a failure in *mutual* adaptation in which neither the individual nor the immediate social environment responds to the disequilibrium and to the increasing disorganization of relationships between the individual and his social milieu.

References

* 1.   Arensberg, C., and S. T. Kimball. *Family and Community in Ireland.* Cambridge: Harvard University Press, 1948.

2.   Bakke, E. W. *Citizens Without Work.* New Haven, Conn.: Yale University Press, 1940.

3.   Benedict, P. R., and I. Jacks. "Mental illness in primitive societies," *Psychiatry,* 17 (1954), 377–389.

4.   Berne, E. "Comparative psychiatry and tropical psychiatry," *Amer. J. Psychiat.,* 113 (1956), 193–200.

5.   Berne, E. "Difficulties of comparative psychiatry: the Fiji Islands," *Amer. J. Psychiat.,* 116 (1959), 104–109.

6.   Curle, C. T. W., and E. L. Trist. "Transitional communities and social reconnection," *Human Relations,* 1 (1947), 42–68, 240–288.

7.   Demerath, N. J. "Schizophrenia among primitives," in A. M. Rose, ed., *Mental Health and Mental Disorder: A Sociological Approach.* New York: Norton, 1955.

8.   DeVos, G., and H. Miner. "Algerian culture and personality in change," *Sociometry,* 21 (1958), 225–268.

9.   Dublin, L. I., and B. Bunzel. *To Be or Not to Be.* New York: Harrison Smith and Robert Haas, 1933.

10.   Dunham, H. W. "Current status of ecological research in mental disorder," in A. M. Rose, ed., *Mental Health and Mental Disorder: A Sociological Approach.* New York: Norton, 1955.

11.   Dunham, H. W. *Sociological Theory and Mental Disorder.* Detroit: Wayne State University Press, 1959.

12.   Durkheim, E. *On the Division of Labor in Society,* trans. G. Simpson. New York: Macmillan, 1933.

13.   Durkheim, E. *Suicide,* trans. G. Simpson. Glencoe, Ill.: Free Press, 1951.

14.   Eaton, J. W., and R. J. Weil. *Culture and Mental Disorders.* Glencoe, Ill.: Free Press, 1955.

15.   Eisenstadt, S. N. *The Absorption of Immigrants.* London, England: Routledge and Kegan Paul, 1954.

16.   Erikson, E. H. "Growth and crises of the healthy personality," *Psychol. Issues,* 1 (1959), 50–100.

17.   Faris, R., and H. W. Dunham. *Mental Disorders in Urban Areas.* Chicago: University of Chicago Press, 1939.

18.   Fried, M. "Grieving for a lost home," in L. J. Duhl, ed., *The Urban Condition.* New York: Basic Books, 1963.

19.   Futterman, S., and E. Pumpian-Mindlin. "Traumatic war neuroses five years later," *Amer. J. Psychiat.,* 108 (1951), 401–408.

* Additional reference.

20. Glass, A. J. "Observations upon the epidemiology of mental illness in troops during warfare," in *Symposium on Preventive Social Psychiatry*. Washington, D. C.: Walter Reed Army Institute of Research, 1957.

21. Glass, A. J., J. J. Gibbs, V. C. Sweeney, and K. L. Artiss. "The current status of army psychiatry," *Amer. J. Psychiat.*, 117 (1961), 673–683.

22. Goldhamer, H., and A. W. Marshall. *Psychosis and Civilization: Two Studies in the Frequency of Mental Disease*. Glencoe, Ill.: Free Press, 1949.

23. Grinker, R. R., and J. P. Spiegel. *Men Under Stress*. Philadelphia: The Blakiston Co., 1945.

24. Halliday, J. L. *Psychosocial Medicine*. New York: Norton, 1948.

25. Hallowell, A. I. "Some sociopsychological aspects of acculturation," in R. Linton, ed., *The Science of Man in the World Crisis*. New York: Columbia University Press, 1945.

26. Hammer, M., and E. Leacock. "Source material on the epidemiology of mental illness," in J. Zubin, ed., *Field Studies in the Mental Disorders*. New York: Grune and Stratton, 1961.

27. Handlin, O. *Boston's Immigrants: A Study in Acculturation,* rev. ed. Cambridge: Harvard University Press, 1959.

28. Handlin, O. *The Uprooted*. Boston: Little, Brown, 1952.

29. Hartmann, H. *Ego Psychology and the Problem of Adaptation*. New York: International Universities Press, 1958.

30. Henry, Andrew F., and J. F. Short, Jr. *Suicide and Homicide*. Glencoe, Ill.: Free Press, 1954.

31. Hole, V. "Social Effect of Planned Rehousing," *Town Planning Rev.*, 30 (1959), 161–173.

32. Illsley, R., A. Finlayson, and B. Thompson. "The motivation and characteristics of internal migrants: a socio-medical study of young migrants in Scotland," *Milbank Mem. Fund Quart.*, 41 (1963), 115–144.

33. Jackson, E. F. "Status consistency and symptoms of stress," *Amer. Soc. Rev.*, 27 (4) (1962), 469–480.

34. Jaco, E. G. "The social isolation hypothesis and schizophrenia," *Amer. Soc. Rev.*, 19 (1954), 567–577.

35. Komarovsky, M. *The Unemployed Man and His Family*. New York: Dryden Press, 1940.

36. Kramer, M., E. S. Pollack, and R. W. Redick. "Studies of the incidence and prevalence of hospitalized mental disorders in the United States: current status and future goals," in P. Hoch and J. Zubin, eds., *Comparative Epidemiology of the Mental Disorders*. New York: Grune and Stratton, 1961.

37. Lazarus, J., B. Z. Locke, and D. S. Thomas. "Migration differentials in mental disease," *Milbank Mem. Fund Quart.*, 41 (1963), 25.

38. Lee, E. S. "Socioeconomic and migration differentials in mental disease," *Milbank Mem. Fund Quart.*, 41 (1963), 249–268.

39. Leighton, A. H. "Mental illness and acculturation," in I. Galdston, ed., *Medicine and Anthropology*. New York: International Universities Press, 1959.

40. Linton, R., ed. *Acculturation in Seven American Indian Tribes,* New York: Appleton-Century, 1940.

41. Locke, B., M. Kramer, and B. Pasamanick. "Immigration and insanity," Public Health Rep., 75 (1960), 301–306.

42. Malzberg, B. "Mental disease among the native and foreign-born white populations of New York State, 1939–1941," Ment. Hyg., 39 (1955), 545–563.

43. Malzberg, B. Social and Biological Aspects of Mental Disease. Utica, N. Y.: State Hospitals Press, 1940.

44. Malzberg, B., and E. Lee. Migration and Mental Disease: A Study of First Admissions to Hospitals for Mental Disease, New York, 1939–1941. New York: Social Science Research Council, 1956.

45. Martin, F. M., J. H. F. Brotherston, and S. P. W. Chave. "Incidence of neurosis in a new housing estate," Brit. J. Prev. Soc. Med., 11 (1957), 196–202.

46. Mogey, J. M. Family and Neighbourhood. London, England: Oxford University Press, 1956.

47. Murphy, H. B. M. "Culture and mental disorder in Singapore," in M. K. Opler, ed., Culture and Mental Health: Cross-Cultural Studies. New York: Macmillan, 1959.

48. Murphy, H. B. M. "Migration and the major mental disorders: a reappraisal," in M. Kantor, ed., Mobility and Mental Health. Princeton, N. J.: Van Nostrand, 1964.

49. Murphy, H. B. M. "Social change and mental health," in Causes of Mental Disorders: A Review of Epidemiological Knowledge, 1959. New York: Milbank Mem. Fund, 1961.

50. Pugh, F., and B. MacMahon. Epidemiological Findings in United States Mental Hospital Data. Boston: Little, Brown, 1962.

51. Rapaport, D. "On the psychoanalytic theory of motivation," in M. R. Jones, ed., Nebraska Symposium on Motivation. Lincoln: University of Nebraska Press, 1960.

52. Redl, F., and D. Wineman. Children Who Hate. Glencoe, Ill.: Free Press, 1951.

53. Reid, D. D. "Precipitating proximal factors in the occurrence of mental disorders: epidemiological evidence," in Causes of Mental Disorders: A Review of Epidemiological Knowledge, 1959. New York: Milbank Mem. Fund, 1961.

54. Rose, A. M., and H. R. Stub. "Summary of studies on the incidence of mental disorders," in A. M. Rose, ed., Mental Health and Mental Disorder: A Sociological Approach. New York: Norton, 1955.

55. Spindler, G. D. Socio-Cultural and Psychological Processes in Menomini Acculturation. Berkeley: University of California Press, 1955.

56. Sreenivasan, U., and J. Hosnig. "Case and mental hospital admissions in Mysore State, India," Amer. J. Psychiat., 117 (1960), 37–43.

57. Stanton, A., and M. Schwartz. "Observations on dissociation as social participation," Psychiatry, 12 (1949), 339–354.

58. Stanton, A., and M. Schwartz. The Mental Hospital. New York: Basic Books, 1954.

59. Swinscow, D. "Some suicide statistics," Brit. Med. J., 1 (1951), 1417–1423.

60. Thomas, D. "Introduction," in B. Malzberg and E. Lee, eds., Migration and Mental Disease. New York: Social Science Research Council, 1956.

61. Thomas, W. I., and F. Znaniecki. *The Polish Peasant in Europe and America.* New York: Dover Publications, 1958.

62. Thurnwald, R. C. "The psychology of acculturation," *Amer. Anthrop.,* 34 (1932), 557–569.

63. Whyte, W. F. *Street Corner Society,* rev. ed. Chicago: University of Chicago Press, 1955.

64. Wittkower, E. D., and J. Fried. "A cross-cultural approach to mental health problems," *Amer. J. Psychiat.,* 116 (1959), 423–428.

65. Young, M., and P. Willmott. *Family and Kinship in East London.* Glencoe, Ill.: Free Press, 1949.

66. Zawadski, B., and P. Lazarsfeld. "The psychological consequences of unemployment," *J. Soc. Psychol.,* 6 (1935), 224–251.

25
Crisis and Religious Conversion
David R. Heise

It might be easy to conclude from previous chapters that social change and crisis are always undesirable. Yet scattered research findings indicate that stress, even if pathogenic in the short run, can yield growth and deepening of character in the long run. Chapters 18 and 20 can be read from such a viewpoint, and this brief selection suggests that profound changes in religious values and orientations can grow out of incidents of crisis and stress.

There is ample evidence[1] that a group which is undergoing rapid enculturation, which is in the wake of a disaster, or which for any reason [may be] in a state of social disorganization characterized, for example, by many unstable marriages, drunkenness, violence, etc., not only lacks resistance to innovations of beliefs and values by religious missionaries but may actually seek out such innovations. A variety of evidence[2] also supports the proposition that anything that increases tension and anxiety ("storm and stress") in the individual and/or anything that tends to isolate him from his group lends that individual greater susceptibility to religious conversion.

Adolescents in Western societies, individuals in foreign circumstances (prisoners, patients, migrants, etc)., persons sorrowing over the death of a relative or friend, and persons subjected to intense emotional stimulation are all noted as excellent subjects for missionary efforts. The materials in this area, therefore, are in substantial agreement with theories postulating either structural strain or psychological

Excerpted from David R. Heise, "Prefatory Findings in the Sociology of Missions," *Journal for the Scientific Study of Religion,* 6 (1967), 49–53. Reprinted by permission of the Society for the Scientific Study of Religion, Inc. The excerpt has been retitled.

This work was done while the author was receiving support from the National Institute of Mental Health in the form of a pre-doctoral fellowship at the University of Chicago and a post-doctoral fellowship at the University of Wisconsin. Elihu Katz encouraged this study and gave much helpful direction for which the author is grateful.

1. M. T. Price, *Christian Missions and Oriental Civilizations: A Study in Culture Contact* (Shanghai: privately printed, 1924), 469; R. N. Rapoport, "Changing Navaho Religious Values: A Study of Christian Missions to the Rimrock Navahos," *Papers of the Peabody Museum of American Archaeology and Ethnology,* 41, No. 2 (1954), 71–73; F. Hawley, "The Kereson Holy Rollers: An Adaptation to American Individualism," *Social Forces,* 26 (1947), 272–280; G. F. Vicedom, "The Growth of the Lutheran Church in New Guinea," *International Review of Missions,* 45 (1956), 297–306; W. D. Reyburn and M. F. Reyburn, "Toba Caciqeship and the Gospel," *International Review of Missions,* 45 (1956), 194–203.

2. Price, *op. cit.,* 40, 469; Rapoport, *op. cit.,* 69, 75–76; E. D. Starbuck, *The Psychology of Religion: An Empirical Study of the Growth of Religious Consciousness,* 4th ed. (New York: Walter Scott, 1914). Emotionality of revivals is noted by Price and by Starbuck and is treated in I. Cunnison, "A Watchtower Assembly in Central Africa," *International Review of Missions,* 40 (1951), 456–469; and J. T. Seamands, "The Hathra," in R. W. Scott, ed., *Ways of Evangelism* (Mysore, India: Christian Literature Society of India, 1953).

tension in the collectivity as precipitating factors of value-oriented social movements.[3]

Conversion as A Special Reaction to Stress

Strain and anxiety precede movements other than religious conversion, e.g., panic, aggression, withdrawal, secular-value conversion, recovery of old organizations, etc. Available theoretical and empirical analyses in sociology[4] provide some propositions concerning what conditions favor one movement rather than another. Recurring traumas, or disasters for which people have been prepared, are unlikely to yield enough disorientation and anxiety to produce a climate for conversion; the most likely adaptation in such cases is recovery. Panic and atomization of the social system are likely when an escape or means of relief is prominent but there is competition for it. Aggression, accompanied by social reorganization on a conflict basis, is likely if a vulnerable person or group can be identified as the cause of tensions (correctly or merely as a scapegoat). Withdrawal, passivity, and perhaps assimilation into other groups may occur if no individual or collective action defined by the old culture is believed capable of restoring stability. Conditions specifically favoring value-oriented movements are difficult to identify, but at least one hypothesis is suggested by the literature. Agents who are relatively tension-free and uninvolved in a disaster often make great gains in status and influence by leading others in coping behavior, and these leaders probably can

3. Neil J. Smelser, *Theory of Collective Behavior* (New York: Free Press, 1963); Kurt Lang and Gladys Engel Lang, "Mass Conversion: Changes in Group Norms," Chapter 6, in *Collective Dynamics* (New York: Crowell, 1961), 153–177.

4. Reviews and summaries of the literature are available in: R. W. Brown, "Mass Phenomena," in G. Lindzey, ed., *Handbook of Social Psychology,* vol. II (Cambridge, Mass.: Addison-Wesley, 1954), 833–876; N. J. Demerath and A. F. C. Wallace, eds., *Human Adaptation to Disaster,* a special issue of *Human Organization,* 16, No. 2 (1957); Lang and Lang, *op. cit.;* R. H. Turner, "Collective Behavior," in R. E. L. Faris, ed., *Handbook of Modern Sociology* (Chicago: Rand McNally, 1964), 485–529; R. H. Turner and L. M. Killian, *Collective Behavior* (Englewood Cliffs, N. J.: Prentice-Hall, 1957); Smelser, *op. cit.* The reaction of passivity is examined by R. E. Forman, "Resignation as a Collective Behavior Response," *American Journal of Sociology,* 69 (1963), 285–290.

facilitate value conversions by presenting interpretations which explain tensions as a failure of old values and by offering ideologies that promise readjustment and future security. Special conditions favoring religious rather than secular conversion cannot be specified with assurance, but perhaps movement in one or the other direction depends largely on whose agents best foster the image of confidence and command and on who best exploits the suggestibility of persons during their personal disorientation.

In summary, value conversions are facilitated when (1) some historical event or series of events creates anxiety; and (2) the old sociocultural system does not operate effectively as a stabilizer, either by providing coping techniques, by suggesting unrestricted routes of escape, or by identifying enemies for retaliation. An additional condition, especially relevant for missionary action in disaster, may be (3) external agents (or deviates in the old culture) organize effective coping operations, and these agents exploit their upsurge in prestige and the suggestibility of the population to degrade old values and promote new ones.

26
Social Class and Schizophrenia: A Critical Review
Melvin L. Kohn

Severe psychopathology usually is not evenly distributed
across all groups in a society, and in particular there is a
general tendency for less privileged groups to suffer more
mental illness. Kohn analyzes this phenomenon in detail and
weighs the most plausible explanation—that less privileged
groups are subject to more disorganization and life stress.

473

My intent in this paper is to review a rather large and all-too-inexact body of research on the relationship of social class to schizophrenia, to see what it adds up to and what implications it has for etiology (1). Instead of reviewing the studies one by one, I shall talk to general issues and bring in whatever studies are most relevant. It hardly need be stressed that my way of selecting these issues and my evaluation of the studies represent only one person's view of the field and would not necessarily be agreed to by others.

Before I get to the main issues, I should like to make five prefatory comments:

1. When I speak of schizophrenia, I shall generally be using that term in the broad sense in which it is usually employed in the United States, rather than the more limited sense used in much of Europe. I follow American rather than European usage, not because I think it superior, but because it is the usage that has been employed in so much of the relevant research. Any comparative discussion must necessarily employ the more inclusive, even if the cruder, term.

2. I shall generally not be able to distinguish among various types of schizophrenia, for the data rarely enable one to do so. This is most unfortunate; one should certainly want to consider "process" and "reactive" types of disturbances separately, to distinguish between paranoid and non-paranoid, and to take account of several other possibly critical distinctions.

Worse yet, I shall at times have to rely on data about an even broader and vaguer category than schizophrenia—severe mental illness in general, excluding only the demonstrably organic. The excuse for this is that since the epidemiological findings for severe mental illness seem to parallel those for schizophrenia alone, it would be a shame to ignore the several important studies that have been addressed to the larger category. I shall, however, rely on these studies as sparingly as possible and stress studies that focus on schizophrenia.

Reprinted from Melvin L. Kohn, "Social Class and Schizophrenia: A Critical Review," in *Psychiatric Research*, 6, Sup. 1 (1968), 155–173. Reprinted by permission of Pergamon Press Limited, Oxford, England, and the author.

3. Social classes will be defined as aggregates of individuals who occupy broadly similar positions in the hierarchy of power, privilege, and prestige (2). In dealing with the research literature, I shall treat occupational position (or occupational position as weighted somewhat by education) as a serviceable index of social class for urban society. I shall not make any distinction, since the data hardly permit my doing so, between the concepts "social class" and "socioeconomic status." And I shall not hesitate to rely on less than fully adequate indices of class when relevant investigations have employed them.

4. I want to mention only in passing the broadly comparative studies designed to examine the idea that mental disorder in general, and schizophrenia in particular, are products of civilization, or of urban life, or of highly complex social structure. There have been a number of important studies of presumably less complex societies that all seem to indicate that the magnitude of mental disorder in these societies is of roughly the same order as that in highly urbanized, Western societies. I refer you, for example, to Lin's study in Taiwan (3), the Leightons' in Nova Scotia (4), Leighton and Lambo's in Nigeria (5), and Eaton and Weil's of the Hutterites (6). For a historical perspective within urban, Western society, Goldhamer and Marshall's study in Massachusetts (7) is the most relevant; it indicates that the increasing urbanization of Massachusetts over a period of 100 years did not result in any increase in rates of functional psychosis, except possibly for the elderly.
These data are hardly precise enough to be definitive, but they lead one to turn his attention away from the general hypothesis that there are sizable differences in rates of mental disorder between simpler and more complex social structures, to look instead at differences within particular social structures, where the evidence is far more intriguing. I do not argue that there are no differences in rates of schizophrenia among societies, only that the data in hand are not sufficient to demonstrate them (8). We have more abundant data on intra-social variations.

5. One final prefatory note. Much of what I shall do in this paper will be to raise doubts and come to highly tentative conclusions from inadequate evidence. This is worth doing because we know

so little and the problem is so pressing. Genetics does not seem to provide a sufficient explanation (9), and, I take it from Kety's critical review, biochemical and physiological hypotheses have thus far failed to stand the test of careful experimentation (10). Of all the social variables that have been studied, those related to social class have yielded the most provocative results. Thus, inadequate as the following data are, they must be taken seriously.

It must be emphasized, however, that there are exceedingly difficult problems in interpreting the data that I am about to review. The indices are suspect, the direction of causality is debatable, the possibility that one or another alternative interpretation makes more sense than the one I should like to draw is very real indeed. These problems will all be taken up shortly; first, though, I should like to lay out the positive evidence for a meaningful relationship between class and schizophrenia.

I. Evidence on the Possible Relationship of Social Class to Rates of Schizophrenia

Most of the important epidemiological studies of schizophrenia can be viewed as attempts to resolve problems of interpretation posed by the pioneer studies, Faris and Dunham's ecological study of rates of schizophrenia for the various areas of Chicago (11) and Clark's study of rates of schizophrenia at various occupational levels in that same city (12). Their findings were essentially as follows:

Faris and Dunham: The highest rates of first hospital admission for schizophrenia are in the central city areas of lowest socioeconomic status, with diminishing rates as one moves toward higher-status peripheral areas (13).

Clark: The highest rates of schizophrenia are for lowest status occupations, with diminishing rates as one goes to higher status occupations.

The concentration of high rates of mental disorder, particularly of schizophrenia, in the central city areas (14) of lowest socioeconomic status has been confirmed in a number of American cities—Providence, Rhode Island (15); Peoria, Illinois (16); Kansas City, Missouri (17); St. Louis, Missouri (18); Milwaukee, Wisconsin (19); Omaha, Nebraska (20); Worcester, Massachusetts (21); Rochester, New York (22); and Baltimore, Maryland (23). The two ecological studies done in European cities—Sundby and Nyhus's study of Oslo, Norway (24) and Hare's of Bristol, England (25)—are in substantial agreement, too.

The concentration of high rates of mental disorder, particularly of schizophrenia, in the lowest status occupations has been confirmed again and again. The studies conducted by Hollingshead and Redlich in New Haven, Connecticut (26), and by Srole and his associates in midtown, New York City (27), are well-known examples; a multitude of other investigations in the United States have come to the same conclusion (28). Moreover, Svalastoga's re-analysis of Strömgren's data for northern Denmark is consistent (29), as are the Leightons' data for "Stirling County," Nova Scotia (30), Ødegaard's for Norway (31), Brooke's for England and Wales (32), Stein's for two sections of London (33), Lin's for Taiwan (34), and Steinbäck and Achté's for Helsinki (35).

But there are some exceptions. Clausen and I happened across the first, when we discovered that for Hagerstown, Maryland, there was no discernible relationship between either occupation or the social status of the area and rates of schizophrenia (36). On a reexamination of past studies, we discovered a curious thing: the larger the city, the stronger the correlation between rates of schizophrenia and these indices of social class. In the metropolis of Chicago, the correlation is large, and the relationship is linear: the lower the social status, the higher the rates. In cities of 100,000 to 500,000 (or perhaps more), the correlation is smaller and not so linear: it is more a matter of a concentration of cases in the lowest socioeconomic strata, with not so much variation among higher strata. When you get down to a city as small as Hagerstown—36,000—the correlation disappears.

Subsequent studies in a number of different places have confirmed our generalization. Sundby and Nyhus, for example, showed that Oslo, Norway, manifests the typical pattern for cities of its half-million size: a high concentration in the lowest social stratum, little variation above (37). Hollingshead and Redlich's data on new admissions for schizophrenia from New Haven, Connecticut, show that pattern, too (38).

There is substantial evidence, too, for our conclusion that socioeconomic differentials disappear in areas of small population. The Leightons found that although rates of mental disorder do correlate with socioeconomic status for "Stirling County," Nova Scotia, as a whole, they do not for the small (population 3,000) community of

477

"Bristol" (39). Similarly, Buck, Wanklin, and Hobbs, in an ecological analysis of Western Ontario, found a high rank correlation between median wage and county first admission rates for mental disorder for counties of 10,000 or more population, but a much smaller correlation for counties of smaller population (40). And Hagnell found no relationship between his admittedly inexact measures of socioeconomic status and rates of mental disorder for the largely rural area of southwestern Sweden that he investigated (41).

I think one must conclude that the relationship of socioeconomic status to schizophrenia has been demonstrated only for urban populations. Even for urban populations, a linear relationship of socioeconomic status to rates of schizophrenia has been demonstrated only for the largest metropolises. The evidence, though, that there is an unusually high rate of schizophrenia in the lowest socioeconomic strata of urban communities seems to me to be nothing less than overwhelming. The proper interpretation why this is so, however, is not so unequivocal.

II. The Direction of Causality

One major issue in interpreting the Faris and Dunham, the Clark, and all subsequent investigations concerns the direction of causality. Rates of schizophrenia in the lowest socioeconomic strata could be disproportionately high either because conditions of life in those strata are somehow conducive to the development of schizophrenia, or because people from higher social strata who become schizophrenic suffer a decline in status. Or, of course, it could be some of both. Discussions of this issue have conventionally gone under the rubric of the "drift hypothesis," although far more is involved.

The drift hypothesis was first raised as an attempt to explain away the Faris and Dunham findings. The argument was that in the course of their developing illness, schizophrenics tend to "drift" into lower status areas of the city. It is not that more cases of schizophrenia are "produced" in these areas, but that schizophrenics who are produced elsewhere end up at the bottom of the heap by the time they are hospitalized, and thus are counted as having come from the bottom of the heap.

When the Clark study appeared, the hypothesis was easily enlarged to include "drift" from higher to lower-status occupations. In its

broadest formulation, the drift hypothesis asserts that high rates of
schizophrenia in the lowest social strata come about because people
from higher classes who become schizophrenic suffer a decline in
social position as a consequence of their illness. In some versions of
the hypothesis, it is further suggested that schizophrenics from smaller
locales tend to migrate to the lowest status areas and occupations of
large metropolises; this would result in an exaggeration of rates there
and a corresponding underestimation of rates for the place and class
from which they come.

Incidentally, the drift hypothesis is but one variant of a more general hypothesis that any differences in rates of schizophrenia are the
result of social selection—that various social categories show high
rates because people already predisposed to schizophrenia gravitate
into those categories. This has long been argued by Ødegaard, but
with data that are equally amenable to social selection and social
causation interpretations (42). Dunham has recently made the same
point, but I think his data argue more convincingly for social causation
than for social selection (43). Intriguing though the issue is, it is presently unresolvable; so it would be better to focus on the more specific
question, whether or not the high concentration of schizophrenia in
the lowest socioeconomic strata is the result of downward drift.

One approach to this problem has been to study the histories of
social mobility of schizophrenics. Unfortunately, the evidence is inconsistent. Three studies indicate that schizophrenics have been downwardly mobile in occupational status (44), three others that they have
not been (45). Some of these studies do not compare the experiences
of the schizophrenics to those of normal persons from comparable
social backgrounds. Those that do are nevertheless inconclusive—
either because the comparison group was not well chosen, or because
the city in which the study was done does not have a concentration of
schizophrenia in the lowest social class. Since no study is definitive,
any assessment must be based on a subjective weighing of the strengths
and weaknesses of them all. My assessment is that the weight of this
evidence clearly indicates either that schizophrenics have been no
more downwardly mobile (in fact, no less upwardly mobile) than
other people from the same social backgrounds, or at minimum, that
the degree of downward mobility is insufficient to explain the high
concentration of schizophrenia in the lowest socioeconomic strata.

There is another and more direct way of looking at the question, however, and from this perspective the question is still unresolved. The reformulated question focuses on the social class origins of schizophrenics; it asks whether the occupations of fathers of schizophrenics are concentrated in the lowest social strata. If they are, that is clear evidence in favor of the hypothesis that lower class status is conducive to schizophrenia. If they are not, class might still matter for schizophrenia—it might be a matter of stress experienced by lower class adults, rather than of the experience of being born and raised in the lower class—but certainly the explanation that would require the fewest assumptions would be the drift hypothesis.

The first major study to evaluate the evidence from this perspective argued strongly in favor of lower class origins being conducive to mental disorder, although perhaps not to schizophrenia in particular. Srole and his associates found, in their study of midtown New York, that rates of mental disorder correlate nearly as well with their parents' socioeconomic status as with the subjects' own socioeconomic status (46). But then Goldberg and Morrison found that although the occupations of male schizophrenic patients admitted to hospitals in England and Wales show the usual concentration of cases in the lowest social class, their fathers' occupations do not (47). Since this study dealt with schizophrenia, the new evidence seemed more directly in point. One might quarrel with some aspects of this study—the index of social class is debatable, for example, and data are lacking for 25 percent of the originally drawn sample—but this is much too good a study to be taken lightly. Nor can one conclude that the situation in England and Wales is different from that in the United States, for Dunham reports that two segments of Detroit show a similar picture (48).

There is yet one more study to be considered, however, and this the most important one of all, for it offers the most complete data about class origins, mobility, and the eventual class position of schizophrenics. Turner and Wagonfeld, in a study of Monroe County (Rochester), New York, discovered a remarkable pattern: rates of first treatment for schizophrenia are disproportionately high, both for patients of lowest occupational status and for patients whose fathers had lowest occupational status, but these are by and large not the same patients (49). Some of those whose fathers were in the lowest occupational class had themselves moved up and some of those ending up in the lowest occupational class had come from higher class origins. Thus, there is evidence both for the proposition that lower class origins are conducive to schizophrenia and for the proposition that most lower-class schizophrenics come from higher socioeconomic origins. No wonder partial studies have been inconsistent!

The next question one would want to ask, of course, is how the schizophrenics' histories of occupational mobility compare to those of normal people of comparable social class origins. Turner and Wagonfeld have not the data to answer this definitively, for they lack an appropriate control group. They are able, however, to compare the mobility experiences of their schizophrenics to those of a cross section of the population, and from this they learn two important things. More schizophrenics than normals have been downwardly mobile. This downward mobility did not come about because of a loss of occupational position that had once been achieved, but reflected their failure ever to have achieved as high an occupational level as do most men of their social class origins.

This argues strongly against a simple drift hypothesis—it is not, as some have argued, that we have erroneously rated men at lower than their usual class status because we have classified them according to their occupations at time of hospitalization, after they have suffered a decline in occupational position. It is more likely that a more sophisticated drift hypothesis applies—that some people genetically or constitutionally or otherwise predisposed to schizophrenia show some effects of developing illness at least as early as the time of their first jobs, for they are never able to achieve the occupational levels that might be expected of them. If so, the possibilities of some interaction between genetic predisposition and early social circumstances are very real indeed.

One direction that further research must take is well pointed out by the Turner and Wagonfeld study. The question now must be the degree to which the correlation of class and schizophrenia results from a higher incidence of schizophrenia among people born into lower-class families, the degree to which it results from schizophrenics of higher class origins never achieving as high an occupational level as might have been expected of them—and why.

For the present, I think it can be tentatively concluded that despite what Goldberg and Morrison found for England and Wales, the weight of evidence lies against the drift hypothesis being a sufficient explanation. In all probability, lower-class families produce a disproportionate number of schizophrenics, although perhaps by not so large a margin as one would conclude from studies that rely on the patients' own occupational attainments.

Parenthetically, there is another important question involved here, the effects of social mobility itself. Ever since Ødegaard's classic study of rates of mental disorder among Norwegian migrants to the United States (50), we have known that geographic mobility is a matter of considerable consequence for mental illness (51), and the same may be true for social mobility (52). But we have not known how and why mobility matters—whether it is a question of what types of people are mobile or of the stresses of mobility—and unfortunately later research has failed to resolve the issue.

III. The Adequacy of Indices

The adequacy of indices is another major issue in interpreting the Faris and Dunham, the Clark, and all subsequent investigations. Most of these studies are based on hospital admission rates, which may not give a valid picture of the true incidence of schizophrenia. Studies that do not rely on hospital rates encounter other and perhaps even more serious difficulties, with which we shall presently deal.

The difficulty with using admission rates as the basis for computing rates of schizophrenia is that lower-class psychotics may be more likely to be hospitalized, and if hospitalized to be diagnosed as schizophrenic, especially in public hospitals. Faris and Dunham tried to solve this problem by including patients admitted to private as well as to public mental hospitals. This was insufficient because, as later studies have shown, some people who suffer serious mental disorder never enter a mental hospital (53).

Subsequent studies have attempted to do better by including more and more social agencies in their search for cases; Hollingshead and Redlich in New Haven (54), and Jaco in Texas (55), for example, have extended their coverage to include everyone who enters any sort of treatment facility—Jaco going so far as to question all the physicians in Texas. This is better, but clearly the same objections hold in principle. Furthermore, Srole and his associates have demonstrated that there are considerable social differences between people who have been treated, somewhere, for mental illness, and severely impaired people, some large proportion of them schizophrenic, who have never been to any sort of treatment facility (56). So we must conclude that using treatment—any sort of treatment—as an index of mental disorder is suspect.

The alternative is to go out into the community and examine everyone—or a representative sample of everyone—yourself. This has been done by a number of investigators, for example Essen-Möller in Sweden (57), Srole and his associates in New York (58), the Leightons in Nova Scotia (59). They have solved one problem, but have run into three others.

1. The first is that most of these investigators have found it impossible to classify schizophrenia reliably, and have had to resort to larger and vaguer categories—severe mental illness, functional psychosis, and such. For some purposes, this may be justified. For our immediate purposes, it is exceedingly unfortunate.

2. Second, even if you settle for such a concept as "mental illness," it is difficult to establish criteria that can be applied reliably and validly in community studies (60). For all its inadequacies, hospitalization is at least an unambiguous index, and you can be fairly certain that the people who are hospitalized are really ill. But how does one interpret the Leightons' estimate that about a third of their population suffer significant psychiatric impairment (61), or Srole's that almost a quarter of his are impaired? (62)

Personal examination by a single psychiatrist using presumably consistent standards is one potential solution, but usable only in relatively small investigations. Another possible solution is the further development of objective rating scales, such as the Neuropsychiatric Screening Adjunct first developed by social scientists in the Research Branch of the United States Army in World War II (63) and later incorporated into both the Leightons' and Srole's investigations, but not developed to anything like its full potential in either study. The limitation here is that such scales may be less relevant to the measurement of psychosis than of neurosis.

To make significant further advances, we shall have to break free of traditional methods of measurement. Epidemiological studies still largely rely on a single, undifferentiated overall assessment. Even when such an assessment can be demonstrated to be reliable within the confines of a single study, it has only limited use for comparative studies and is questionable for repeated application in studies designed to ascertain how many new cases arise in some given period of time. At minimum, we must begin to make use of our developing capacities

483

at multivariate analysis. One obvious approach is to try to differentiate the several judgments that go into clinical diagnoses, develop reliable measures of each, and examine their interrelationship. At the same time, it would be well to develop reliable measures of matters conventionally given only secondary attention in epidemiological research —for example, the degree of disability the individual has sustained in each of several major social roles (64). A third path we might try is the further development of objective measures of dimensions of subjective state (such as anxiety, alienation, and self-abasement) thought to be indicative of pathology. All these and others can be measured as separate dimensions, and then empirically related to each other and to clinical assessments.

Whether or not these particular suggestions have merit, I think the general conclusion that it is time for considerable methodological experimentation is indisputable.

3. The third problem in community studies is that it is so difficult to secure data on the incidence of mental disturbance that most studies settle for prevalence data (65). That is, instead of ascertaining the number of new cases arising in various population groups during some period of time, they count the number of people currently ill at the time of the study. This latter measure—prevalence—is inadequate because it reflects not only incidence but also duration of illness. As Hollingshead and Redlich have shown, duration of illness—insofar as it incapacitates—is highly correlated with social class (66).

Various approximations to incidence have been tried, and various new—and often somewhat fantastic—statistical devices invented to get around this problem, but without any real success. Clearly, what is needed are repeated studies of the population, to pick up new cases as they arise and thus to establish true incidence figures. (This is what Hagnell did, and it was a very brave effort indeed.) The crucial problem, of course, is to develop reliable measures of mental disorder, for without that our repeated surveys will measure nothing but the errors of our instruments. Meantime, we have to recognize that prevalence studies use an inappropriate measure that exaggerates the relationship of socioeconomic status to mental disorder.

So, taken all together, the results of the studies of class and schizophrenia are hardly definitive. They may even all wash out—one more example of inadequate methods leading to premature, false conclusions. I cannot prove otherwise. Yet I think the most reasonable interpretation of all these findings is that they point to something real. Granted that there isn't a single definitive study in the lot, the weaknesses of one are compensated for by the strengths of some other, and the total edifice is probably much stronger than you would conclude from knowing only how frail are its component parts. A large number of complementary studies all seem to point to the same conclusion: that rates of mental disorder, particularly of schizophrenia, are highest at the lowest socioeconomic levels, at least in moderately large cities, and this probably isn't just a matter of drift or inadequate indices or some other artifact of the methods we use. In all probability, more schizophrenia is actually produced at the lowest socioeconomic levels. At any rate, let us take that as a working hypothesis and explore the question further. Assuming that more schizophrenia occurs at lower socioeconomic levels—why?

IV. Alternative Interpretations

Is it really socioeconomic status, or is it some correlated variable that is operative here? Faris and Dunham did not take socioeconomic status very seriously in their interpretation of their data. From among the host of variables characteristic of the high-rate areas of Chicago, they focused on such things as high rates of population turnover and ethnic mixtures and hypothesized that the really critical thing about the high-rate areas was the degree of social isolation they engendered. Two subsequent studies, one by Jaco in Texas (67), the other by Hare in Bristol, England (68), are consistent in that they, too, show a correlation of rates of schizophrenia to various ecological indices of social isolation. The only study that directly examines the role of social isolation in the lives of schizophrenics, however, seems to demonstrate that while social isolation may be symptomatic of developing illness, it does not play an important role in etiology (69).

Several other interpretations of the epidemiological evidence have been suggested, some supported by intriguing, if inconclusive, evidence. One is that it is not socioeconomic status as such that is principally at issue, but social integration. The Leightons have produced plausible evidence for this interpretation (70). The problems of defining and indexing "social integration" make a definitive demonstration exceedingly difficult, however, even for the predominantly rural populations with which they have worked.

Another possiblity is that the high rates of schizophrenia found in lower-class populations are a consequence of especially high rates for lower-class members of some "ethnic" groups who happen to be living in areas where other ethnic groups predominate. In their recent study in Boston, for example, Schwartz and Mintz showed that Italian–Americans living in predominantly non-Italian neighborhoods have very high rates of schizophrenia, while those living in predominantly Italian neighborhoods do not (71). The former group contribute disproportionately to the rates for lower-class neighborhoods. (The authors suggest that this may explain why small cities do not show a concentration of lower-class cases: these cities do not have the ethnic mixtures that produce such a phenomenon.)

Wechsler and Pugh extended this interpretive model to suggest that rates should be higher for any persons living in a community where they and persons of similar social attributes are in a minority (72). Their analysis of Massachusetts towns provides some surprisingly supportive data.

Other possibilities deal more directly with the occupational component of socioeconomic status. Ødegaard long ago showed that rates of schizophrenia are higher for some occupations that are losing members and lower for some that are expanding (73). His observation was correct, but it explains only a small part of the occupational rate differences. Others have focused on alleged discrepancies between schizophrenics' occupational aspirations and achievements (74), arguing that the pivotal fact is not that schizophrenics have achieved so little but that they had wanted so much more. The evidence is limited.

One could argue—and I see no reason to take the argument lightly —that genetics provides a quite sufficient explanation. If there is a moderately strong genetic component in schizophrenia, then one would expect a higher than usual rate of schizophrenia among the fathers and grandfathers of schizophrenics. Since schizophrenia is a debilitating disturbance this would be reflected in grandparents' and parents' occupations and places of residence. In other words, it could be a rather complex version of drift hypothesis. The only argument against this interpretation is that there is no really compelling evidence in favor of it; one can accept it on faith, or one can keep it in mind while continuing to explore alternatives. Prudence suggests the latter course. . . .

There are other possibilities we might examine, but since there is no very strong evidence for any of them, that course does not seem especially profitable. One must allow the possibility that some correlated variable might prove critical for explaining the findings; it might not be social class, after all, that is operative here. Until that is demonstrated, however, the wisest course would seem to be to take the findings at face value and see what there might be about social class that would help us to understand schizophrenia.

V. Class and Etiology

What is there about the dynamics of social class that might affect the probability of people becoming schizophrenic? How does social class operate here; what are the intervening processes?

The possibilities are numerous, almost too numerous. Social class indexes and is correlated with so many phenomena that might be relevant to the etiology of schizophrenia. Since it measures status, it implies a great deal about how the individual is treated by others—with respect or perhaps degradingly; since it is measured by occupational rank, it suggests much about the conditions that make up the individual's daily work, how closely supervised he is, whether he works primarily with things, with data, or with people; since it reflects the individual's educational level, it connotes a great deal about his style of thinking, his use or non-use of abstractions, even his perceptions of physical reality and certainly of social reality; furthermore, the individual's class position influences his social values and colors his evaluations of the world about him; it affects the family experiences he is likely to have had as a child and the ways he is likely to raise his own children; and it certainly matters greatly for the type and amount of stress he is likely to encounter in a lifetime. In short, social class pervades so much of life that it is difficult to guess which of its correlates are most relevant for understanding schizophrenia. Moreover, none of these phenomena is so highly correlated with class (nor class so highly correlated with schizophrenia) that any one of these facets is obviously more promising than the others.

This being the case, investigators have tended to pursue those avenues that have met their theoretical predilections and to ignore the others. In practice, this has meant that the interrelationship of class, family, and schizophrenia has been explored, and more recently the relationship of class, stress, and schizophrenia, but the other possibilities remain largely unexamined. Given the inherent relevance of some of them—class differences in patterns of thinking, for example, have such obvious relevance to schizophrenia—this is a bit surprising.

But let me review what has been done. The hypothesis that stress is what is really at issue in the class-schizophrenia relationship is in some respects especially appealing, in part because it is so direct. We have not only our own observations as human beings with some compassion for less fortunate people, but an increasingly impressive body of scientific evidence (75), to show that life is rougher and rougher the lower one's social class position. The stress explanation seems especially plausible for the very lowest socioeconomic levels, where the rates of schizophrenia are highest.

There have to my knowledge been only two empirical investigations of the relationship of social class to stress to mental disorder. The first was done by Langner and Michael in New York as part of the "Midtown" study (76). This study, as all the others we have been considering, has its methodological defects—it is a prevalence study, and many of the indices it uses are at best questionable—but it tackles the major issues head-on, and with very impressive and very intriguing results. It finds a strong linear relationship between stress and mental disturbance, specifically, the more sources of stress, the higher the probability of mental disturbance. It also finds the expected relationship between social class and stress. So the stress hypothesis has merit. But stress is not all that is involved in the relationship of social class to mental disorder. No matter how high the level of stress, social class continues to be correlated with the probability of mental disturbance; in fact, the more stress, the higher the correlation (77). Thus, it seems that the effect of social class on the rate of mental disorder is not only, or even principally, a function of different amounts of stress at different class levels.

In a more recent study in San Juan, Puerto Rico, Rogler and Hollingshead ascribe a more important role to stress (78). Theirs was an intensive investigation of the life histories of a sample of lower-class schizophrenics, along with comparable studies of a well-matched sample of non-schizophrenics. Rogler and Hollingshead found only insubstantial differences in the early life experiences of lower-class schizophrenics and controls; they did find, however, that in the period of a year or so before the onset of symptoms, the schizophrenics were subjected to an unbearable onslaught of stress. In effect, all lower-class slum dwellers in San Juan suffer continual, dreadful stress; in addition to this "normal" level of stress, however, the schizophrenics were hit with further intolerable stress which incapacitated them in one or another central role, leading to incapacitation in other roles, too.

The picture that Rogler and Hollingshead draw is plausible and impressive. It is not possible, however—at least not yet—to generalize as far from their data as one might like. Their sample is limited to schizophrenics who are married or in stable consensual unions. These one would assume to be predominantly "reactive" type schizophrenics—precisely the group whom one would expect, from past studies, to have had normal childhood social experiences, good social adjustment, and extreme precipitating circumstances. So their findings may apply to "reactive" schizophrenia, but perhaps not to "process" schizophrenia. In addition, for all the impressiveness of the argument, the data are not so unequivocal. Their inquiry was not so exhaustive as to rule out the possibility that the schizophrenics might have had different family experiences from those of the controls. Furthermore, the evidence that the schizophrenics were subjected to significantly greater stress is not so thoroughly compelling as one might want. Thus, the case is not proved. Nevertheless, Rogler and Hollingshead have demonstrated that the possibility that stress plays an important role in the genesis of schizophrenia is to be taken very seriously indeed. Certainly this study makes it imperative that we investigate the relationship of class to stress to schizophrenia far more intensively.

At the same time, we should investigate some closely related possibilities that have not to my knowledge been studied empirically. Not only stress, but also reward and opportunity, are differentially distributed among the social classes. The more fortunately situated not only are less beaten about, but may be better able to withstand the stresses they do encounter because they have many more rewarding experiences to give them strength. And many more alternative courses of action are open to them when they run into trouble. Might this offer be an added clue to the effects of class for schizophrenia?

More generally, what is there about the conditions of life of the lowest social strata that might make it more difficult for their members to cope with stress? One can think of intriguing possibilities. Their occupational conditions and their limited education gear their thinking processes to the concrete and the habitual; their inexperience in dealing with the abstract may ill-equip them to cope with ambiguity, uncertainty, and unpredictability; their mental processes are apt to be too gross and rigid when flexibility and subtlety are most required. Or, a related hypothesis, the lower- and working-class valuation of conformity to external authority, and disvaluation of self-direction, might cripple a man faced with the necessity of suddenly having to rely on himself in an uncertain situation where others cannot be relied on for guidance.

These hypotheses, unfortunately, have not been investigated; perhaps it is time that they were. The one hypothesis that has been studied, and that one only partially, is that lower- and working-class patterns of parent-child relationships somehow do not adequately prepare children for dealing with the hazards of life. Now we enter what is perhaps the most complicated area of research we have touched on so far, and certainly the least adequately studied field of all.

There has been a huge volume of research literature about family relationships and schizophrenia (79), most of it inadequately designed. One has to dismiss the majority of studies because of one or another incapacitating deficiency. In many, the patients selected for study were a group from which you could not possibly generalize to schizophrenics at large. Either the samples were comprised of chronic patients, where one would expect the longest and most difficult onset of illness with the greatest strain in family relationships, or the samples were peculiarly selected, not to test a hypothesis, but to load the dice in favor of a hypothesis. In other studies, there have been inadequate control groups or no control group at all. One of the most serious defects of method has been the comparison of patterns of family relationship of lower- and working-class patients to middle- and upper-middle-class normal controls—which completely confounds the complex picture we wish to disentangle. In still other studies, even where the methods of sample and control-selection have been adequate, the method of data-collection has seriously biased the results. This is true, for example, in those studies that have placed patients and their families in stressful situations bound to exaggerate any flaws in their interpersonal processes, especially for people of lesser education and verbal skill who would be least equipped to deal with the new and perplexing situation in which they found themselves (80).

Still, some recent studies have suggested respects in which the family relationships of schizophrenics seem unusual, and unusual in theoretically interesting ways—that is, in ways that might be important in the dynamics of schizophrenic personality development. Work by

Bateson and Jackson on communication processes in families of schizophrenics (81) and that by Wynne and his associates on cognitive and emotional processes in such families (82), for example, are altogether intriguing.

But—and here I must once again bring social class into the picture—there has not been a single well-controlled study that demonstrates any substantial difference between the family relationships of schizophrenics and those of normal persons from lower- and working-class backgrounds. Now, it may be that the well-controlled studies simply have not dealt with the particular variables that do differentiate the families of schizophrenics from those of normal lower- and working-class families. The two studies that best control for social class—Clausen's and my study in Hagerstown, Maryland (83) and Rogler and Hollingshead's in San Juan (84)—deal with but a few aspects of family relationship, notably not including the very processes that recent clinical studies have emphasized as perhaps the most important of all. It may be that investigations yet to come will show clear and convincing evidence that some important aspects of family relationships are definitely different for schizophrenia-producing families and normal families of this social background.

If they do not, that still does not mean that family relationships are not important for schizophrenia, or that it is not through the family that social class exerts one of its principal effects. Another way of putting the same facts is to say that there is increasing evidence of remarkable parallels between the dynamics of families that produce schizophrenia and family dynamics in the lower classes generally (85). This may indicate that the family patterns of the lower classes are in some way broadly conducive to schizophrenic personality development.

Clearly these patterns do not provide a sufficient explanation of schizophrenia. We still need a missing X, or set of X's, to tell us the necessary and sufficient conditions for schizophrenia to occur. Perhaps that X is some other aspect of family relationships. Perhaps lower-class patterns of family relationships are conducive to schizophrenia for persons genetically predisposed, but not for others. Or perhaps they are generally conducive to schizophrenia, but schizophrenia will not actually occur unless the individual is subjected to certain types or amounts of stress. We do not know. But these speculative considerations do suggest that it may be about time to bring all these variables

—social class, early family relationships, genetics, stress—into the same investigations, so that we can examine their interactive effects. Meantime, I must sadly conclude that we have not yet unravelled the relationship of social class and schizophrenia, nor learned what it might tell us about the etiology of the disorder.

VI. Conclusion

Perhaps, after so broad a sweep, an overall assessment is in order. There is a truly remarkable volume of research literature demonstrating an especially high rate of schizophrenia (variously indexed) in the lowest social class or classes (variously indexed) of moderately large to large cities throughout much of the Western world. It is not altogether clear what is the direction of causality in this relationship— whether the conditions of life of the lowest social classes are conducive to the development of schizophrenia, or schizophrenia leads to a decline in social class position—but present evidence would make it seem probable that some substantial part of the phenomenon results from lower class conditions of life being conducive to schizophrenia. It is not even certain that the indices of schizophrenia used in these studies can be relied on, although there is some minor comfort in that studies using several different indices all point to the same conclusion. Perhaps it is only an act of faith that permits me to conclude that the relationship of class to schizophrenia is probably real, an act of faith only barely disguised by calling it a working hypothesis.

This working hypothesis must be weighed against a number of alternative interpretations of the data. Many of them are plausible, several are supported by attractive nuggets of data, but none is more compelling than the most obvious interpretation of all: that social class seems to matter for schizophrenia because, in fact, it does.

When one goes on to see what this might imply for the etiology of schizophrenia, one finds many more intriguing possibilities than rigorous studies. There is some evidence that the greater stress suffered by lower-class people is relevant, and perhaps that lower- and working-class patterns of family relationships are broadly conducive to schizophrenia—although the latter is more a surmise than a conclusion.

Finally, it is clear that we must bring genetic predisposition and class, with all its attendant experiences, into the same investigations. That, however, is not the only sort of investigation that calls for attention. We have reviewed a large number of hypotheses, several major conflicts of interpretation, and many leads and hunches that all cry out to be investigated. The most hopeful sign in this confusing area is that several of the recent studies have gone far beyond seeing whether the usual stereotyped set of demographic characteristics correlate with rates of schizophrenia, to explore some of these very exciting issues.

References and Notes

1. The *raison d'etre* of this review, aside from its being momentarily current, is in its effort to organize the evidence around certain central issues and to make use of all studies relevant to those issues. There are no definitive studies in this field, but most of them contribute something to our knowledge when placed in perspective of all the others. For an alternative approach, deliberately limited to those few studies that meet the reviewers' standards of adequacy, see Mishler, Elliot G., and Norman A. Scotch, "Sociocultural factors in the epidemiology of schizophrenia: a review," *Psychiatry,* 26 (1963), 315–351. Dunham has recently argued for a more radical alternative; he disputes the legitimacy of using epidemiological data to make the types of social psychological inference I attempt here and insists that epidemiological studies are relevant only to the study of how social systems function. This seems to me to be altogether arbitrary. But see Dunham, H. Warren, *Community and Schizophrenia: An Epidemiological Analysis,* Detroit: Wayne State University Press, 1965, and "Epidemiology of psychiatric disorders as a contribution to medical ecology," *Arch. of Gen. Psychiat,.* 14 (1966), 1–19. Some other useful reviews and discussions of issues in this field are: Dunham, H. Warren, "Current status of ecological research in mental disorder," *Social Forces,* 25 (1947), 321–326; Felix, R. H., and R. V. Bowers, "Mental hygiene and socioenvironmental factors," *Milbank Mem. Fund Quart.,* 26 (1948), 125–147; Dunham, H. Warren, "Social psychiatry," *Amer. Soc. Rev.,* 13 (1948), 183–197; Clausen, John A., *Sociology and the Field of Mental Health,* New York: Russell Sage Foundation, 1956; Clausen, John A., "The ecology of mental illness," *Symposium on Social and Preventive Psychiatry,* Washington, D. C.: Walter Reed Army Medical Center, 1957, 97–108; Clausen, John A., "The sociology of mental illness," in Robert K. Merton et al., eds., *Sociology Today, Problems, and Prospects,* New York: *Basic Books,* 1959; Hollingshead, August B., "Some issues in the epidemiology of schizophrenia," *Amer. Soc. Rev.,* 26 (1961), 5–13; Dunham, H. Warren, "Some persistent problems in the epidemiology of mental disorders," *Amer. J. Psychiat.,* 109 (1963), 567–575; and Sanua, Victor D., "The etiology and epidemiology of mental illness and problems of methodology: with special emphasis on schizophrenia," *Ment. Hyg.,* 47 (1963), 607–621. The present review leans heavily on my earlier paper, "On the social epidemiology of schizophrenia," *Acta Soc.,* 9 (1966), 209–221, but is more complete in its coverage and represents—for all its similarities to the earlier paper—a thorough reassessment of the field.

2. Williams, Robin M., Jr. *American Society: A Sociological Interpretation.* New York: Knopf, 1951, 89.

3. Lin Tsung-yi. "A study of the incidence of mental disorder in Chinese and other cultures," *Psychiatry,* 16 (1953), 313–336.

4. This study is reported in three volumes: Leighton, Alexander H., *My Name is Legion: Foundations for a Theory of Man in Relation to Culture,* New York: Basic Books, 1959; Hughes, Charles C. with Marc-Adelard Tremblay, Robert N. Rapoport, and Alexander H. Leighton, *People of Cove and Woodlot: Communities from the Viewpoint of Social Psychiatry,* New York: Basic Books, 1960; Leighton, Dorothea C. with John S. Harding, David B. Macklin, Allister M. MacMillan, and Alexander H. Leighton, *The Character of Danger: Psychiatric Symptoms in Selected Communities,* New York: Basic Books, 1963.

5. Leighton, Alexander H., T. Adeoye Lambo, Charles C. Hughes, Dorothea C. Leighton, Jane M. Murphy, David B. Macklin, *Psychiatric Disorder Among the Yoruba,* Ithaca, N. Y.: Cornell University Press, 1963; and "Psychiatric disorder in West Africa," *Amer. J. Psychiat.,* 120 (1963), 521–525.

6. Eaton, Joseph W., in collaboration with Robert J. Weil, *Culture and Mental Disorders: A Comparative Study of the Hutterites and Other Populations,* Glencoe, Ill.: Free Press, 1955. This volume includes a valuable comparison of rates of psychosis in a variety of different cultures, from an arctic fishing village in Norway to Baltimore, Maryland, to Thuringia to Formosa to Williamson County, Tennessee. It must be noted that although Eaton and Weil find the rate of functional psychosis among the Hutterites to be roughly comparable to that for other societies, they find the rate of schizophrenia to be low (and that for manic-depressive psychosis to be correspondingly high). There is, however, reason to doubt the validity of their differential diagnosis of schizophrenia and manic-depressive psychosis.

7. Goldhamer, Herbert, and Andrew W. Marshall. *Psychosis and Civilization.* Glencoe, Ill.: Free Press, 1953.

8. For further documentation of this point, see also Mishler and Scotch, *op. cit.;* Dunham, *Community and Schizophrenia, loc. cit.;* Demerath, N. J., "Schizophrenia among primitives," in Arnold M. Rose, ed., *Mental Health and Mental Disorder,* New York: Norton, 1955.

9. Some of the principal recent studies that bear on this point are: Rosenthal, David, "Problems of sampling and diagnosis in the major twin studies of schizophrenia," *J. Psychiat. Res.,* 1 (1962), 116–134; Tienari, Pekka, "Psychiatric illnesses in identical twins," *Acta Psychiat. Scand.,* 39, Sup. 171 (1963); and Kringlen, Einar, "Discordance with respect to schizophrenia in monozygotic twins: some genetic aspects," *J. Nerv. Ment. Dis.,* 138 (1964), 26–31; *Schizophrenia in Male Monozygotic Twins,* Oslo: Universitetsforlaget, 1964; and "Schizophrenia in twins: an epidemiological-clinical study," *Psychiatry,* 29 (1966), 172–184.

10. Kety, Seymour S. "Recent biochemical theories of schizophrenia," in Don D. Jackson, ed., *The Etiology of Schizophrenia.* New York: Basic Books, 1960.

11. Faris, Robert E. L., and H. Warren Dunham. *Mental Disorders in Urban Areas: An Ecological Study of Schizophrenia and Other Psychoses.* Chicago: University of Chicago Press, 1939.

12. Clark, Robert E., "The relationship of schizophrenia to occupational income and occupational prestige," *Amer. Soc. Rev.,* 13 (1948), 325–330; and

"Psychoses, income, and occupational prestige," *Amer. J. Sociol.*, 54 (1949), 433–440.

13. The pattern is most marked for paranoid schizophrenia, least so for catatonic, which tends to concentrate in the foreign-born slum communities (Faris and Dunham, *op. cit.*, 82–108). Unfortunately, subsequent studies in smaller cities dealt with too few cases to examine the distribution of separable types of schizophrenia as carefully as did Faris and Dunham.

14. There are some especially difficult problems in interpreting the ecological findings, which I shall not discuss here because most of the later and crucial evidence comes from other modes of research. The problems inherent in interpreting ecological studies are discussed in Robinson, W. S., "Ecological correlations and the behavior of individuals," *Amer. Soc. Rev.*, 15 (1950), 351–357 and in Clausen, John A., and Melvin L. Kohn, "The ecological approach in social psychiatry," *Amer. J. Sociol.*, 60 (1954), 140–151.

15. Faris and Dunham, *op. cit.*, 143–150.

16. Schroeder, Clarence W. "Mental disorders in cities," *Amer. J. Sociol.*, 48 (1942), 40–48.

17. *Ibid.*

18. Dee, William L. J., "An ecological study of mental disorders in metropolitan St. Louis," unpublished master's thesis, Washington University, 1939; Schroeder, *op. cit.*; Queen, Stuart A., "The ecological study of mental disorders," *Amer. Soc. Rev.*, 5 (1940), 201–209.

19. Schroeder, *op. cit.*

20. *Ibid.*

21. Gerard, Donald L., and Lester G. Houston. "Family setting and the social ecology of schizophrenia," *Psychiat. Quart.*, 27 (1953), 90–101.

22. Gardner, Elmer A., and Haroutin M. Babigian. "A longitudinal comparison of psychiatric service to selected socioeconomic areas of Monroe County, New York," *Amer. J. Orthopsychiat.*, 36 (1966), 818–828.

23. Klee, Gerald D., with Evelyn Spiro, Antia K. Bahn, and Kurt Gorwitz, "An ecological analysis of diagnosed mental illness in Baltimore," in Russell R. Monroe et al., eds., *Psychiatric Epidemiology and Mental Health Planning,* Psychiatric Research Report No. 22, the American Psychiatric Association, April, 1967.

24. Sundby, Per, and Per Nyhus. "Major and minor psychiatric disorders in males in Oslo: an epidemiological study," *Acta Psychiat. Scand.*, 39 (1963), 519–547.

25. Hare, E. H. "Mental illness and social conditions in Bristol," *J. Ment. Science,* 102 (1956), 349–357.

26. Hollingshead, August B., and Frederick C. Redlich. *Social Class and Mental Illness.* New York: Wiley, 1957.

27. Srole, Leo, with Thomas S. Langner, Stanley T. Michael, Marvin K. Opler, and Thomas A. C. Rennie. *Mental Health in the Metropolis: the Midtown Manhattan Study,* vol. 1. New York: McGraw-Hill, 1962.

28. See, for example, Locke, Ben Z., with Morton Kramer, Charles E. Timberlake, Benjamin Pasamanick, and Donald Smeltzer, "Problems of interpretation of patterns of first admissions to Ohio State public mental hospitals for

patients with schizophrenic reactions," in Benjamin Pasamanick and Peter H. Knapp, eds., *Social Aspects of Psychiatry*, the American Psychiatric Association, Psychiatric Research Reports No. 10, 1958; Frumkin, Robert M., "Occupation and major mental disorders," in Arnold M. Rose, ed., *Mental Health and Mental Disorders*, New York: Norton, 1955; Dunham, *Community and Schizophrenia, loc. cit.;* Lemkau, Paul, with Christopher Tietze and Marcia Cooper, "Mental hygiene problems in an urban district: second paper," *Ment. Hyg.*, 26 (1942), 1–20; Fuson, William M., "Research note: occupations of functional psychotics," *Amer. J. Sociol.*, 48 (1943), 612–613; Turner, R. J., and Morton O. Wagonfeld, "Occupational mobility and schizophrenia, an assessment of the social causation and social selection hypotheses, *Amer. Soc. Rev.*, 32 (1967), 104–113. Relevant, too, are some early studies whose full significance was not appreciated until later. See, for example, William J. Nolan, "Occupation and dementia praecox," *New York State Hospitals Quart.*, 3 (1917), 127–154; Ødegaard, Ørnulv, "Emigration and insanity: a study of mental disease among the Norwegian-born population of Minnesota," *Acta Psychiat. Neurol.*, Sup. 4 (1932), 182–184; Green, Howard W., *Persons Admitted to the Cleveland State Hospital, 1928–1937*, Cleveland Health Council, 1939. One puzzling partial exception comes from Jaco's study of Texas. He finds the highest incidence of schizophrenia among the unemployed, but otherwise a strange, perhaps curvilinear relationship of occupational status to incidence. Perhaps it is only that so many of his patients were classified as unemployed (rather than according to their pre-illness occupational status) that the overall picture is distorted. See Jaco, E. Gartley, "Incidence of psychoses in Texas," *Texas State J. Med.*, 53 (1957), 1–6, and *The Social Epidemiology of Mental Disorders*, New York: Russell Sage Foundation, 1960.

29. Svalastoga, Kaare. *Social Differentiation*. New York: David McKay, 1965, 100–101.

30. Leighton et al., *The Character of Danger, loc cit.*, 279–294.

31. Ødegaard, Ørnulv, "The incidence of psychoses in various occupations," *International J. Soc. Psychiat.*, 2 (1956), 85–104; "Psychiatric epidemiology," *Proc. Royal Society Med.*, 55 (1962), 831–837; and "Occupational incidence of mental disease in single women," *Living Conditions and Health*, 1 (1957), 169–180.

32. As reported in Morris, J. N., "Health and social class," *The Lancet*, 7, (February, 1959), 303–305.

33. Stein, Lilli. " 'Social class' gradient in schizophrenia," *Brit. J. Prev. Soc. Med.*, 11 (1957), 181–195.

34. Lin, *op. cit.*, and Lin Tsung-yi. "Mental disorders in Taiwan, fifteen years later: a preliminary report," paper presented to the Conference on Mental Health in Asia and the Pacific, Honolulu, March, 1966.

35. Steinbäck, Asser, and K. A. Achté. "Hospital first admissions and social class," *Acta Psychiat. Scand.*, 42 (1966), 113–124.

36. Clausen, John A., and Melvin L. Kohn, "Relation of schizophrenia to the social structure of a small city," in Benjamin Pasamanick, ed., *Epidemiology of Mental Disorder*, Washington, D. C.: American Association for the Advancement of Science, 1959. In that paper, the data on occupational rates were incompletely reported. Although we divided the population into four occupational classes, based on United States Census categories, we presented

496

the actual rates for only the highest and lowest classes, leading some readers to conclude, erroneously, that we had divided the population into only two occupational classes. In fact, the average annual rates of first hospital admission for schizophrenia, per 100,000 population aged 15–64, were:

(a) professional, technical, managerial, officials, and proprietors:	21.3
(b) clerical and sales personnel:	23.8
(c) craftsmen, foremen, and kindred workers:	10.7
(d) operatives, service workers, and laborers:	21.7

Our measures of occupational mobility, to be discussed later, were based on movement among the same four categories.

37.   Sundby and Nyhus, *op. cit.*

38.   Hollingshead and Redlich, *Social Class and Mental Illness, loc. cit.*, 236.

39.   Leighton, D. C., with J. S. Harding, D. B. Macklin, C. C. Hughes, and A. H. Leighton, "Psychiatric findings of the Stirling County study," *Amer. J. Psychiat.*, 119 (1963), 1021–1026; and Leighton et al., *The Character of Danger, loc. cit.*, 308–321.

40.   Buck, Carol, with J. M. Wanklin and G. E. Hobbs. "An analysis of regional differences in mental illness," *J. Nerv. Ment. Dis.*, 122 (1955), 73–79.

41.   Hagnell, Olle. *A Prospective Study of the Incidence of Mental Disorder.* Stockholm: Svenska Bokförlaget, 1966.

42.   Ødegaard, Ø., "Emigration and insanity," *loc. cit.*; "Psychiatric epidemiology," *loc. cit.;* "Occupational incidence of mental disease in single women," *loc. cit.*

43.   Dunham, *Community and Schizophrenia, loc. cit.*

44.   Evidence that schizophrenics have been downwardly mobile in *occupational* status has been presented in Schwartz, Morris S., "The economic and spatial mobility of paranoid schizophrenics and manic-depressives," unpublished master's thesis, University of Chicago, 1946; Lystad, Mary H., "Social mobility among selected groups of schizophrenic patients," *Amer. Soc. Rev.*, 22 (1957), 288–292; Turner and Wagonfeld, *op. cit.* In addition, there has been some debatable evidence that the ecological concentration of schizophrenia has resulted from the migration of unattached men into the high-rate areas of the city. See Gerard, Donald L., and Lester G. Houston, "Family setting and the social ecology of schizophrenia," *loc. cit.;* Hare, E. H., "Family setting and the urban distribution of schizophrenia," *J. Ment. Science*, 102 (1956), 753–760; Dunham, *Community and Schizophrenia, loc. cit.* (Dunham's data, however, show that when rates are properly computed, rate differentials between high- and low-rate areas of Detroit are just as great for the stable population as for in-migrants.)

45.   Evidence that schizophrenics have not been downwardly mobile in occupational status is presented in Hollingshead, August B., and Frederick C. Redlich, "Social stratification and schizophrenia," *Amer. Soc. Rev.*, 19 (1954), 302–306, and *Social Class and Mental Illness, loc. cit.*, 244–248; Clausen and Kohn, "Relation of schizophrenia to the social structure of a small city," *loc. cit.;* and Dunham, *Community and Schizophrenia, loc. cit.;* and "Social class and schizophrenia," *Amer. J. Orthopsychiat.*, 34 (1964), 634–642. Evidence that the ecological concentration of schizophrenia has not resulted from in-migration or

downward drift is presented in Lapouse, Rema, with Mary A. Monk and Milton Terris, "The drift hypothesis and socioeconomic differentials in schizophrenia," *Amer. J. Public Health,* 46 (1956), 978–986; Hollingshead and Redlich, "Social stratification and schizophrenia," *loc. cit.;* and, as noted in the preceding note, Dunham, *op. cit.*

46. Srole et al., *Mental Health in the Metropolis, loc. cit.,* 212–222.

47. Goldberg, E. M., and S. L. Morrison. "Schizophrenia and social class," *Brit. J. Psychiat.,* 109 (1963), 785–802.

48. Dunham, "Social class and schizophrenia," *loc. cit.;* and Dunham, H. Warren, Patricia Phillips, and Barbara Srinivasan, "A research note on diagnosed mental illness and social class," *Amer. Soc. Rev.,* 31 (1966), 223–227. See also James W. Rinehart's "Communication," *Amer. Soc. Rec.,* 31 (1966), 545–546.

49. Turner and Wagonfeld, *op. cit.*

50. Ødegaard, Ørnulv, "Emigration and mental health," *Ment. Hyg.,* 20 (1936), 546–553. See also Astrup, Christian, and Ørnulv Ødegaard, "Internal migration and disease in Norway," *Psychiat. Quart., Sup.* 34 (1960), 116–130.

51. See Tietze, Christopher, with Paul Lemkau and Marcia Cooper, "Personality disorder and spatial mobility," *Amer. J. Sociol.,* 48 (1942), 29–39; Leacock, Eleanor, "Three social variables and the occurrence of mental disorder," in Alexander H. Leighton, John A. Clausen, and Robert N. Wilson, eds., *Explorations in Social Psychiatry,* New York: Basic Books, 1957; Mishler and Scotch, *op. cit.*

52. Kleiner, Robert J., and Seymour Parker, "Goal striving, social status, and mental disorder: a research review," *Amer. Soc. Rev.,* 28 (1963), 189–203. See also Myers, Jerome K., and Bertram H. Roberts, *Family and Class Dynamics in Mental Illness,* New York: Wiley, 1959; and Parker, Seymour, and Robert J. Kleiner, *Mental Illness in the Urban Negro Community,* New York: Free Press, 1966.

53. See, for example, Kaplan, Bert, with Robert B. Reed and Wyman Richardson, "A comparison of the incidence of hospitalized and nonhospitalized cases of psychosis in two communities," *Amer. Soc. Rev.,* 21 (1956), 472–479; see also all of the major community studies of mental illness.

54. Hollingshead and Redlich, *Social Class and Mental Illness, loc. cit.*

55. Jaco, *The Social Epidemiology of Mental Disorders, loc. cit.*

56. Srole et al., *Mental Health in the Metropolis, loc. cit.,* 240–251.

57. Essen-Möller, E., "Individual traits and morbidity in a Swedish rural population," *Acta Psychiat. Neurol. Scand., Sup.* 100 (1956), 1–160; Essen-Möller, Erik, "A current field study in the mental disorders in Sweden," in Paul H. Hoch and Joseph Zubin, eds., *Comparative Epidemiology of the Mental Disorders,* New York: Grune and Stratton, 1961; Hagnell, *op. cit.*

58. Srole et al., *Mental Health in the Metropolis, loc. cit.*

59. Leighton et al., *The Character of Danger, loc. cit.*

60. See Dohrenwend, Bruce P., and Barbara Snell Dohrenwend, "The problem of validity in field studies of psychological disorder," *J. Abnormal Psychol.,* (1965), 52–69.

61. Leighton et al., "Psychiatric findings of the Stirling County study," *loc. cit.*, 1026.

62. Srole et al., *Mental Health in the Metropolis, loc. cit.*, 138.

63. Star, Shipley. "The screening of psychoneurotics in the army," in S. A. Stouffer, with L. Guttman, E. A. Suchman, P. F. Lazarsfeld, Shirley A. Star, and J. A. Clausen, eds., *Measurement and Prediction.* Princeton, N. J.: Princeton University Press, 1950.

64. See John A. Clausen's incisive analysis, "Values, norms, and the health called 'mental': purposes and feasibility of assessment," paper presented to the Symposium on Definition and Measurement of Mental Health, Washington, D. C., 16 (May, 1966), mimeographed.

65. See Kramer, Morton. "A discussion of the concepts of incidence and prevalence as related to epidemiologic studies of mental disorders," *Amer. J. Public Health,* 47 (1957), 826–840.

66. Hollingshead and Redlich, *Social Class and Mental Illness, loc. cit.*

67. Jaco, E. Gartly. "The social isolation hypothesis and schizophrenia," *Amer. Soc. Rev.,* 19 (1954), 567–577.

68. Hare, "Mental illness and social conditions in Bristol," *loc. cit.*

69. Kohn, Melvin L., and John A. Clausen, "Social isolation and schizophrenia," *Am. Soc. Rev.,* 20 (1955), 265–273; see also Clausen and Kohn, "The ecological approach in social psychiatry," *loc. cit.*

70. Leighton, Dorothea C. et al., *The Character of Danger, loc. cit.;* "Psychiatric findings of the Stirling County study," *loc. cit.*

71. Schwartz, David T., and Norbett L. Mintz, "Ecology and psychosis among Italians in 27 Boston communities," *Social Problems,* 10 (1963), 371–374; see also their more extended discussion in "Urban ecology and psychosis: community factors in the incidence of schizophrenia and manic-depression among Italians in Greater Boston," 1963, mimeographed.

72. Wechsler, Henry, and Thomas F. Pugh. "Fit of individual and community characteristics and rates of psychiatric hospitalization," paper presented to the Sixth World Congress of Sociology, Evian, September, 1966.

73. Ødegaard, "The incidence of psychosis in various occupations," *loc. cit.*

74. Kleiner and Parker, *op. cit.*; Myers and Roberts, *op. cit.*

75. Dohrenwend, Barbara Snell, and Bruce P. Dohrenwend. "Class and Race as status-related sources of stress," in Sol Levine and Norman A. Scotch, eds., *Social Stress.* Chicago: Aldine, 1970.

76. Langner, Thomas S., and Stanley T. Michael. *Life Stress and Mental Health.* New York: Free Press of Glencoe, 1963.

77. The latter finding is in part an artifact of the peculiar indices used in this study, and reflects differences not in the incidence of illness but in type and severity of illness in different social classes at various levels of stress. At higher stress levels, lower-class people tend to develop incapacitating psychoses and middle-class people less incapacitating neuroses.

78. Rogler, Lloyd H., and August B. Hollingshead. *Trapped: Families and Schizophrenia.* New York: Wiley, 1965.

79. See the references in Kohn, Melvin L., and John A. Clausen, "Parental authority behavior and schizophrenia," *Amer. J. Orthopsychiat.*, 26 (1956), 297–313, in John A. Clausen and Melvin L. Kohn, "Social relations and schizophrenia: a research report and a perspective," in Don D. Jackson, ed., *The Etiology of Schizophrenia,* New York: Basic Books, 1960; and Sanua, Victor D., "Sociocultural factors in families of schizophrenics: a review of the literature," *Psychiatry,* 24 (1961), 246–265.

80. For a more complete discussion, see Clausen and Kohn, "Social relations and schizophrenia," *loc. cit.,* 309–316.

81. Bateson, Gregory, with Don Jackson, Jay Haley, and John Weakland, "Toward a theory of schizophrenia," *Behav. Science,* 1 (1956), 251–264. See also Mishler, Elliot G., and Nancy E. Waxler, "Family interaction processes and schizophrenia: a review of current theories," *Merrill-Palmer Quart. Behav. Development,* 11 (1965), 269–315.

82. Wynne, Lyman C., with Irving M. Ryckoff, Juliana Day, and Stanley I. Hirsch, "Pseudo-mutuality in the family relations of schizophrenics," *Psychiatry,* 22 (1958), 205–220; and Ryckoff, Irving, with Juliana Day and Lyman C. Wynne, "Maintenance of stereotyped roles in the families of schizophrenics, *AMA Arch. Psychiat.,* 1 (1959), 93–98. See also Mishler and Waxler, *op. cit.*

83. Kohn and Clausen, "Parental authority behavior and schizophrenia," *loc. cit.*

84. Rogler and Hollingshead, *op. cit.*

85. Kohn, Melvin L., "Social class and parent-child relationships: an interpretation," *Amer. J. Sociol.,* 68 (1963), 471–480; Pearlin, Leonard I., and Melvin L. Kohn, "Social class, occupation, and parental values: a cross-national study," *Amer. Soc. Rev.,* 31 (1966), 466–479.

Index

Index